American Chameleon

American Chameleon
Individualism in Trans-National Context

edited by RICHARD O. CURRY and
LAWRENCE B. GOODHEART

THE KENT STATE UNIVERSITY PRESS
Kent, Ohio, and London, England

© 1991 by THE KENT STATE UNIVERSITY PRESS, Kent, Ohio 44242
All rights reserved
Library of Congress Catalog Card Number 91-7150
ISBN 0-87338-443-1
ISBN 0-87338-448-2 (pbk.)
Manufactured in the United States of America

Library of Congress Cataloging-in-Publication Data

American chameleon : individualism in trans-national context / edited
   by Richard O. Curry and Lawrence B. Goodheart.
      p. cm.
    Includes bibliographical references (p.) and index.
    ISBN 0-87338-443-1 (cloth) ∞ —ISBN 0-87338-448-2 (pbk.) ∞
    1. Individualism.   2. Social values.   3. United States—Social
conditions—19th century.   4. United States—Politics and
government—19th century.   I. Curry, Richard Orr.   II. Goodheart,
Lawrence B., 1944–
HM136.A57   1991
302.5′4—dc20   91–7150

British Library Cataloging-in-Publication data are available.

To
John H. Jensen
and
Robert W. Lougee

Contents

Acknowledgments

S CHOLARLY collaboration, especially over a long period of time, is a difficult "art form" at best—one that requires a combination of qualities. In addition to having compatible interests and mutual respect, successful collaboration also requires enthusiasm, commitment, persistence, and, at times, forbearance. There are, no doubt, other factors as well. But for whatever combination of reasons, both personal and scholarly in nature, Lawrence B. Goodheart and I have managed to collaborate successfully on several projects for nearly fifteen years—most of which have had a bearing, directly or indirectly, on aspects of the history of American individualism.

In editing *American Chameleon,* Goodheart and I owe our greatest debts of gratitude to our fellow contributors: Yehoshua Arieli, Robert Calhoon, James Henretta, Linda Kerber, Loren Schweninger, Robert Shalhope, and Karl Valois. Along the way, Goodheart and I have accumulated a number of other personal and intellectual IOUs that require acknowledgment. For example, earlier versions of our essays on abolitionism and the National Liberal League published here were presented as papers at the meetings of the New England Historical Association in 1987, the Organization of American Historians in 1988, and the thirteenth biennial meeting of ANZASA (Australia–New Zealand-American Studies Association), held at the University of Newcastle, New South Wales, in August 1988. We are indebted to Lawrence J. Friedman, Edward Pessen, James Schleifer, and Gerald Sorin for their comments at the OAH and NEHA meetings, which helped sharpen various aspects of our papers. Gregory Bowen, a doctoral candidate at Flinders University in Adelaide, deserves special mention for arranging our session at the ANZASA conference.

We also want to express our appreciation to Jerrold Atlas and Joe Dorinson of Long Island University who, as chairpersons of the 1986 meeting of the International Psychohistorical Association, extended an invitation to present our jointly authored paper on psychohistorical approaches to abolitionism at the IPA meeting in New York. In addition, we are indebted to Bruce Daniels, former editor of the *Canadian Review of American Studies;* to Ralph Gray, editor of the *Journal of the Early Republic;* to John Hubbell, editor of *Civil War History* and director of the Kent State University Press; and to Murray Rothbard, editor of the *Journal of Libertarian Studies* for publishing other jointly authored pieces, most of which are related, directly or indirectly, to our essays published here.

In addition, we want to thank Robert Calhoon for sharing his insights on aspects of twentieth-century American individualism, and our colleague at the University of Connecticut, Vincent A. Carrafiello, for reading chapters one and two with his usual flair, critical acumen, and aplomb. Paul Manning, an undergraduate at the University of Connecticut, proved virtually indefatigable in tracking down scores of bibliographical references and in photocopying the manuscript and numerous other essays needed for reference. His efforts lightened our burdens considerably. Moreover, the University of Connecticut chapter of the American Association of University Professors deserves thanks for providing funds for typing portions of the manuscript.

I also want to express my own sense of appreciation to Ronald Formisano and to John Hench, Director of Research and Publications at the American Antiquarian Society, for inviting me to present two earlier papers on aspects of nineteenth-century individualism at the AAS Seminar on American Social and Political History, 1750–1850. Special thanks also go to Joseph Peden of Baruch College, CUNY, for extending invitations to participate in two conferences on American individualism sponsored by the Liberty Fund. The first was held at the Rye Hilton in New York in 1981. The second, which was devoted to the concept of individualism in Jacksonian America, took place in 1985 at Half Moon Bay, California, an idyllic setting. It was at this conference that I first had the opportunity to exchange views with scholars such as Robert Remini, Robert Shalhope, and James Schleifer.

I owe a special debt of gratitude to my colleague, Robert Lougee, for taking the time and effort to explain and explore some of the "vagaries" involved in attempting to understand German conceptions of individualism—especially the transformation of the Romantic concept of individuality into a theory of organic community which, in Germany, was still called individualism. John Jensen of the University of Waikato in Hamilton, New Zealand, deserves special mention for calling my attention to the work of Elie Kedourie and other writers on German nationalism, which helped to clarify the anti-Enlightenment basis and, indeed, the revolutionary implications of Immanuel Kant's thought. In addition to providing intellectual stimulation, Jensen and his spouse, Frannie, made my wife Patti and me part of their extended family during our sojourn as Fulbrighters in New Zealand in 1981. Goodheart and I also appreciated the warmth and hospitality extended by the Jensens to us during our visit to the Antipodes in 1988.

In addition to authoring our own essays in this book, Goodheart and I also collaborated in writing the first and final chapters. Although I wrote most of chapter 1, "Individualism in Trans-National Context," Goodheart wrote the concluding section, which deals with the British experience. Conversely, Goodheart wrote most of the last chapter, "A Confusion of Voices: The Crisis of Individualism in Twentieth-Century America." My primary contribution to this essay is the concluding sections, which analyze some of the contradictions of the Reagan-Bush era.

Finally, I want to thank Karl Valois, friend, doctoral candidate at the University of Connecticut, and occasional golfing companion with an unbelievable handicap, for writing most of the section on the transformation of American politics in the late eighteenth and early nineteenth centuries in our essay, "The Emergence of an Individualistic Ethos in American Society." The responsibility for writing the rest of the essay, for good or for ill, belongs to me.

Richard O. Curry

Individualism in Trans-National Context

Richard O. Curry and
Lawrence B. Goodheart

T HE concept of individualism in the United States, with its multiplicity of meanings, usages, and contradictions, constitutes the central focus of this book. The eleven essays published here concentrate primarily on the nineteenth century, the golden age of individualistic thought and expression in American society. As the British observer Lord Bryce commented in 1888: "Individualism, the love of enterprize, and the pride in personal freedom have been deemed by Americans not only their choicest, but peculiar and exclusive possession."[1] Bryce's formulation is far from comprehensive, but he is correct in concluding that individualism (or more precisely, what has been called individualism) has had a more pervasive influence and, indeed, a more positive connotation in the United States than elsewhere in Western culture.

Individualistic values and attitudes may well reflect reality or idealized social aspiration or perception—depending on time, place, and circumstance. But in a pluralistic society such as the United States, appeals to liberty, democracy, or laissez-faire principles may also reflect manipulative rhetoric that attempts to obscure the hegemonic goals of individuals or groups. Moreover, individualistic rhetoric has often served to conceal or minimize the limits that factors such as class, gender, and race have placed on personal and group development. But such caveats serve primarily to underscore the fact that an individualistic ethos, which began to emerge in American society during the late eighteenth century, became a dominant

Curry wrote most of this chapter. Goodheart authored the concluding section that deals with the concept of individualism in Victorian Britain.

force—a fundamental organizing principle in explaining the ways that Americans have celebrated, justified, rationalized (and in some instances attacked) their social, political, and economic institutions along with their values, perceptions, and beliefs.

This collection of essays does not attempt to provide an exhaustive analysis of what nineteenth-century American individualism means. It does, however, provide conceptual rigor and specificity to important aspects of individualistic thought and expression from several angles of vision—for example: literature, politics, philosophy, jurisprudence, laissez-faire economics, social reform movements, religion, the concepts of progress and perfectibility, the aspirations of African-Americans, and the role of women in American society. The concept of individualism is indeed difficult and challenging, but it is not an amorphous one, impossible to characterize or define in precise terms. It is, rather, a chameleonlike concept—one that encompasses or affects diverse aspects of American life in fundamentally different ways.

Individualistic thought and expression in nineteenth-century America were pervasive, but the frequent disparity between rhetoric and reality can hardly be ignored. In the twentieth century, the problem has become even more acute. Industrialization, urbanization, an increasing maldistribution of wealth, the persistence of racial and ethnic antagonisms, and the growth of a bureaucratic state obsessed with "national security" have combined to produce social, political, and economic disjunctions whereby the term "individualism" as a viable intellectual construct or explanatory principle becomes increasingly problematic. Even so, the concept of individualism as a historical phenomenon in America, and indeed in Western culture, is fundamental. Thus the purpose of our last chapter, "The Crisis of Individualism in Twentieth-Century America," is not to attempt a systematic analysis of the twentieth-century experience, a massive undertaking that requires comprehensive analysis elsewhere. Our objective, rather, is to provide a counterpoint for attempting to understand not only the complexities and contradictions inherent in the concept of individualism but also the past, present, and future of American society itself.

Types of Individualism

Our first task, therefore, is to define the concept of individualism, with its "multiplicity of meanings, usages, and contradictions." The most systematic approach to the subject is provided by the work of the English philosopher Steven Lukes. In a provocative essay, "Types of Individualism," Lukes identifies eleven major "components," "elements," or "unit-ideas," which taken together provide the most comprehensive analysis yet produced by any scholar. Lukes qualifies his analysis, however, with the caveat that none of the categories used in his work "are either mutually exclusive or jointly exhaustive."[2]

Clearly, most of the ideas associated with American individualism are of European origin. Thus, our argument about "American exceptionalism" refers not to the origins of individualistic thought and expression in America but, rather, to its pervasiveness and widespread acceptance in nineteenth-century American society, in contrast to its pejorative connotations, especially in France, and its transformation in Germany from a romantic concept that stressed individuality to a theory of organic community.* The differences that characterize American and European perspectives require detailed analysis. Our first objective, however, is to define in precise terms what individualism means. The examples cited provide clarity and specificity, but they are not intended to be comprehensive, nor are they drawn entirely from Lukes's work.

1. The first component part of individualism is the idea of *the supreme and intrinsic value of the human being.* This idea found expression in the Bible, especially in the New Testament, and was reaffirmed during the Reformation by Martin Luther's and John Calvin's "preoccupation with the individual's salvation" and the "sectarian principle that all men are alike children of God, each with his own unique purpose." This notion, in different form, also characterized the writings of Renaissance humanists, Jean-Jacques Rousseau, and Jeremy Bentham, and appeared most impressively and systematically in the work of Immanuel Kant, who asserted that "man, and in general every rational being, exists as an end in himself, not merely as a means."[3]

2. The second element is the notion of individual *self-development.* The idea of self-cultivation is present, for example, in the Italian Renaissance and in the writings of nineteenth-century German romantics. Wilhelm von Humboldt, for instance, argued that "the true end of Man was the highest and most harmonious development of his powers to be a complete and constant whole."[4] This view is also part of the English liberal tradition, most

---

*The concept of "American exceptionalism" is so closely associated by most historians with Louis Hartz's narrow and oversimplified thesis in his *The Liberal Tradition in America: An Interpretation of American Political Thought since the Revolution* (N.Y.: Harcourt, Brace, 1955) that one hesitates to use it for fear of being misunderstood. As James Henretta observes, Hartz places so much emphasis on the lack of a feudal tradition and the importance of Lockean liberal individualism in America that he fails to understand that "early American society was profoundly conservative, even profoundly 'European' in character." See Henretta's essay, "The Slow Triumph of Liberal Individualism: Law and Politics in New York, 1780–1860" in this book.

notably in John Stuart Mill's *On Liberty* (1859); and it is a crucial element in the ethical aspects of Karl Marx's thought. Under communism, Marx wrote in *The German Ideology*, the individual would cultivate "his gifts in all directions."[5] It has also been attractive to artists and poets since Lord Byron and Johann von Goethe, to whom it appealed as a guiding ideal.

3. The third element of individualism is the idea of *self-direction* or *autonomy*. From this perspective, individuals, regardless of the normative standards or social pressures to which they are exposed, have the right to reject authority and develop their own values or ethical principles. This idea was articulated by Aristotle and was reflected in Saint Thomas Aquinas's view that individuals need not obey a superior if conscience dictated otherwise. It is also present in Martin Luther's argument that each person has the right "to judge what is right or wrong in the faith."[6] The most systematic expositions of this idea are found in Baruch Spinoza's *Ethics* (1677) and, above all, in Kant's work. "To the ideal of freedom," Kant wrote, "there is inseparably attached the concept of *autonomy*."[7] Henry David Thoreau's declaration that "I am a majority of one" not only illustrates the point nicely but provides an archetype of American assertiveness.[8]

4. The fourth component of individualism is the concept of *privacy*. According to this view, individuals have a "private existence within a public world, an area within which the individual is" or ought to be free from outside interference.[9] This idea is essentially a modern one, not being present in the ideas of thinkers in medieval Europe or the ancient world. Sir Isaiah Berlin termed the right to privacy "negative liberty." "Every plea for civil liberties," he wrote, "every protest against authority, or the mass hypnosis of custom or organized propaganda, springs from this individualistic, and much disputed, conception of man."[10] It is also present, with different emphases, in the writings of John Locke, Edmund Burke, Thomas Paine, Thomas Jefferson, and Lord Acton. It is found, above all, in the work of Benjamin Constant and John Stuart Mill. Mill, in his treatise, *On Liberty* (1859), wrote that the "only part of the conduct of anyone, for which he is amenable to society, is that which concerns others. In the part that merely concerns himself, his independence is, of right, absolute. Over himself, his own body and mind, the individual is sovereign."[11]

5. The fifth constituent part of individualism is a doctrine referred to as *methodological individualism*. This view asserts, as Karl Popper phrased it, that "all social phenomena, and especially the functioning of all social institutions, should always be understood as resulting from the decisions, actions, attitudes, etc., of human individuals, and . . . we should never be satisfied by an explanation in terms of so-called 'collectives.' "[12] This idea was first stated with precision by Thomas Hobbes and was clearly articulated by Enlightenment thinkers, although wide divergences existed regard-

ing the nature of individual characteristics. Whether men were egoistic or cooperative, or were driven by "needs," "instincts," "faculties," or "drives" were questions of debate or emphasis. More recently, thinkers such as Vilfredo Pareto and Sigmund Freud appealed to psychological variables without reference to social factors. Other theorists such as Jean-Gabriel de Tarde or George Homans have emphasized the existence of " 'elementary' forms of social behavior, but with minimal social reference." In sum, methodological individualism takes the position, in John Stuart Mill's words, that the "laws of the phenomena of society are, and can be, nothing but the actions and passions of human beings," namely, "the laws of individual human nature."[13]

6. Another element of individualism, closely connected to the precepts of methodological individualism, is *epistemological individualism,* which is based on the Enlightenment assumption that knowledge of the external world is derived solely from subjective experience. Epistemological individualism, however, is also characterized by "a psychological atomism" that attempts to explain "wholes," including political and social structures, by breaking them down into their simplest forms or ideas.[14]

7. The idea of the *abstract individual* is still another component closely related to, but somewhat different from the premises of methodological individualism. The major difference, obviously, is that abstract individualism refers not to specific persons in a particular historical context but to the idea of "man in general" or to "man in the state of nature."[15] All philosophers, from Hobbes to Kant, who used natural law or social contract theory in their formulations, argued that "a previous sovereignty of the individual was the ultimate and only source of group authority."[16] In sum, they used the idea of "previous sovereignty" (e.g., man in the state of nature) to buttress their arguments that "the community was only an aggregate—a mere union— whether close or loose of the will and powers of individual persons."[17] Moreover, all such theorists agreed that "all forms of common life were the creation of individuals" and could only be regarded as a *"means to achieve individual objects."*[18]

Finally, the abstract concept of "man in general" is found in the thoughts of the classical economists and the early utilitarians. In practice, if not in theory, Lukes observes that the abstract individual always turns out on analysis to be "socially and historically specific." "Human nature," he concludes, "always in reality belongs to a particular kind of social man."[19] In short, the critics of methodological individualism (of which the idea of the abstract individual is a variant) maintain that individual persons do not create but are conditioned by social institutions created "collectively." All efforts to place individual thoughts and actions outside a historical or social context become, therefore, little more than a theoretical construct—an attempt, in F. H. Bradley's words, "to isolate what cannot be isolated."[20] These conflicting views recur in "many different guises," however, and major proponents continue to occupy polar positions.[21]

8. The concept of *political individualism* is another unit-idea. All political relations involve transactions between authority and individuals whose autonomy is, in some ways, limited by law or other sanctions. But the concept of political individualism minimizes the role of authority—limiting its power to achieve fundamental individual objectives such as life, liberty, and property. Insofar as individual purposes are abstracted from a social context, as is the case in social contract theory, political individualism becomes an application of the idea of the abstract individual. Some early social contract theorists even argued that the idea of the sovereignty of the people exists in all forms of government. "The *people* rules in all governments," Hobbes argued. "For even in *monarchies* the *people* command."[22] As Hegel correctly observed, Hobbes, unlike earlier thinkers, "sought to derive the bond which holds that state together, that which gives the state its power, from principles which lie within us, which we recognize as our own."[23] In the eighteenth century, political individualism, with its emphasis on contract and consent, became commonplace.

Historically, the concept of political individualism occasionally has been perverted by "totalitarian democrats," who, by claiming that they had a superior understanding of men's "real" purposes, used that "understanding" to justify tyranny.[24] The ideas of popular sovereignty and social contract, however, have had their greatest influence on that type of political liberalism that attempts to limit the power and authority of the state in personal, social, intellectual, and economic spheres. Nowhere, of course, has the influence of political individualism been greater than in the United States.

9. Another element, closely associated in some ways with political individualism, is the concept of *economic individualism*. In its simplest form, it stresses the idea of economic liberty and thus denigrates any form of regulation, whether by church or state. Not until the mid-eighteenth century did a coherent and systematic theory of economic individualism emerge. It is contained in the work of Adam Smith in Britain, and in the writings of Marquis d'Argenson, the physiocrats, and A. R. J. Turgot in France. As a result, economic individualism became a normative doctrine that emphasized the sanctity of private property, a free and thus competitive market, and freedom of production, contract, and exchange. In sum, by stressing the unfettered self-interest of individuals, economic individualism creates a self-adjusting system that not only provides maximum satisfaction for individuals but, in consequence, also leads to social progress.

Since the nineteenth century, however, some (but by no means all) economists have "sought to distinguish theory from doctrine and did not necessarily wish to make reality conform to the model."[25] "Only those who do," Lukes observes, can now "be counted as adherents of economic individualism."[26] The writings of Friedrich A. Hayek, founder of the Austrian school of economics, provide its most systematic defense—arguing that the preservation of "spontaneous formations," especially an "effectively competitive market," is indispensable for the preservation "of a free civilization." In contemporary society, the debate continues over what the best political means are for making capitalism work effectively. One extreme is exemplified by the doctrinal laissez-faire positions taken by Ludwig von Mises. But most twentieth-century economists who reject Marxist economic analysis have advocated various types of "selective interventionism." Even so, the theoretical differences separating the views of John Maynard Keynes from those of Milton Friedman, for example, or, indeed, the economic policies pursued by presidents Franklin D. Roosevelt and Ronald Reagan, reflect social, political, and ethical positions that are fundamentally incompatible—and are not simply differences over means to achieve similar ends.

10. The next component, *religious individualism,* is closely related to the ideas of autonomy and privacy. It rejects the idea that individuals need intermediaries to communicate with God. Accordingly, individuals have the right, and sometimes the duty, to establish their own personal relationship to the Deity. Furthermore, the dictates of conscience, often referred to as the right of private judgment, sometimes necessitates the rejection of established authority—regardless of the consequences. Religious individualism also refers to the idea of spiritual equality and spiritual self-scrutiny. The former was emphasized by the early church, and the latter found "supreme expression" in the writings of Saint Augustine. The Reformation, however, with its emphasis upon the idea of the priesthood of all believers and the doctrine of the "inner light," perpetuated its influence in the modern world. But spiritual self-scrutiny and the internalization of conscience is associated far more closely, if not exclusively, with religious groups or denominations having a Calvinist heritage. As Max Weber observed, the Calvinist's intercourse with his God was carried on in "deep spiritual isolation." Weber emphasized that the doctrine of predestination led to a "feeling of unprecedented loneliness" for the "single individual" because it eliminated the achievement of salvation through the church and the sacraments (which was in Lutheranism by no means developed to its final conclusion). These aspects of the Calvinist heritage, Weber concluded, "forms one of the roots of that disillusioned and pessimistically inclined individualism which can even today be identified in the national characters and institutions of the peoples with a Puritan past."[27]

However valid Weber's interpretation may be as regards Europe or even some aspects of twentieth-century American thought, the rejection of predestination in nineteenth-century America and its replacement by the doctrines of free will and universal atonement gave rise to visions of human perfection. In short, the decline of Puritanism in nineteenth-century America became a liberating force that emphazied optimism, not pessimism, and a fiercely assertive and perfectionist individualism shared by many religious leaders and groups such as William Ellery Channing and the younger and more radical generation of Unitarians, Ralph Waldo Emerson and the transcendentalists, and the Garrisonian abolitionists. The beliefs of these individuals and groups differed in important respects, but the views expressed by the Garrisonian nonresistant, Bronson Alcott, underscores the highly individualistic and liberating aspects of Puritan declension. "What guide have I but my conscience?" Alcott wrote in 1838.

> Church and State are responsible to me; not I to them. They cease to deserve our veneration from the moment they violate our consciences. We protest against them. I believe that this is what is now going on. . . . I look upon the Non-Resistance Society as an assertion of the right to self-government. Why would I employ a church to write my creed or a state to govern me? Why not write my own creed? Why not govern myself?[28]

11. *Ethical individualism,* the last constituent element, is clearly associated with the ideas of autonomy and religious individualism. According to this concept, the individual is the final arbiter of moral values and behavior. Ethical individualism applies not only to religious concerns but to secular values as well; it carries the idea of autonomy to its logical and extreme conclusion. Lukes maintains that the issues involved are "latent in the thought of Kant and Hume, but both avoided its implication, the former by postulating an impersonal moral law, the latter by appealing to the moral uniformity of mankind."[29] Lukes's conclusions on Kant, however, clash head on with the views of Elie Kedourie.[30]

Kedourie argues that Kant's search for an adequate philosophic basis for human freedom led him to separate conceptions of morality from conceptions of knowledge of the external world. Kant, Kedourie observes, rejected Enlightenment theories of knowledge, which emphasized that at birth the mind was a clean slate—that all human knowledge depended upon our senses, which alone enable us to perceive the external world. According to Kant, sensations simply deal with the subjective experiences of individuals. Therefore, the senses provided no scientific basis for understanding reality. At best, they deal in probabilities, at worst in delusion. How then could Enlightenment philosophers talk with any degree of certainty about the existence of a rationally ordered universe based on natural laws—including the inalienable rights of individuals? The trouble with Enlightenment thought, Kant reasoned, was the attempt to prove the existence of the laws of morality as if they stemmed from the principles of physics. Such efforts led only to dogmatism or skepticism.[31]

By separating conceptions of morality from theories of knowledge, Kant was able to argue that morality was a quality that existed only within ourselves and had nothing to do with obedience to external authority. "Nothing," Kant wrote in the *Groundwork of the Metaphysics of Morals* (1785), "can possibly be conceived in the world, or even out of it, which can be called good without qualification, except a Good Will."[32] Kant referred to this inward law of morality derived from a "Good Will" as "the categorical imperative." This alone is what permits man to be free in the "transcendental sense." If a person's will is free, being subjected to imprisonment or political tyranny cannot deprive a person of his freedom if he is acting in accordance with the inward laws of morality. In fact, only when individuals are moved by the categorical imperative (or inward law) can we talk about good and evil, morality, and justice.

Kant, in his preface to the *Critique of Practical Reason* (1781), "denied that he was proposing a new principle of morality." Rather, he stated, he was offering "only a new formula."[33] Kedourie argues, however, that Kant's "new formula" was, in fact, revolutionary in its implications. The Good Will, the Free Will, is the Autonomous Will. It is a sweeping claim, annihilatory in nature. As an intellectual revolutionary, few could compare with Kant. In his thought, the individual became the center—indeed, the sovereignty in the universe.[34]

If Kant refused to recognize the revolutionary implications of his thinking, some of his disciples, especially Friedrich von Schlegel, did not. Every good man, Schlegel asserted, "ceaselessly becomes more and more God. To become God, to be Man, to cultivate oneself, are expressions which all have the same meaning."[35]

The extent to which Kant's thought influenced the thinking of nineteenth-century Americans—most notably, William Ellery Channing and the radical Unitarians as well as Ralph Waldo Emerson and other transcendentalists—is a matter of debate. It is an unresolved but intriguing problem that requires additional and extensive analysis.[36]

The dilemmas of ethical individualism became most apparent (indeed acute) in the twentieth century, especially in the writings of Friedrich Nietzche and Max Weber. Weber argued that individuals confronted with disjunction (i.e., conflicting moral principles) "must decide which is God for him and which is the devil." Moreover, as Lukes observes, "Most species of existentialism, emotivism, and prescriptivism—all three denying objective moral principles—are forms of ethical individualism."[37] The early writings of Jean-Paul Sartre—e.g., *L'existentialisme est un humanisme* (1948)—and the work of the Oxford philosopher R. M. Hare—for instance, *The Language of Morals* (1951)—provide the most coherent modern expressions of the concept.

Individualism in Trans-National Context

The constituent elements or unit-ideas contained in the concept of individualism have been challenged from a variety of perspectives. Critics of epistemological and methodological individualism, for example, argue that human beings simply do not live in psychological, social, or historical vacuums. Proponents of individualistic theories, by denying the existence of a public world and the importance of collective or, perhaps, shared experience, overlook, denigrate, or deny the historical development or evolution of social, political, religious, and economic institutions—institutions that, over time, establish normative standards that must be judged, measured or evaluated. Furthermore, critics of ethical individualism stress the importance of objective moral standards rather than the validity of "inward laws" such as Kant's "categorical imperative" or the Protestant doctrine of "private judgment."

Our purpose here, however, is not to analyze or evaluate the numerous philosophical, epistemological, or sociological objections to the various types of individualism. It is, rather, to place the usages, definitions, and, at times, contradictory meanings of individualism in a trans-national framework during the nineteenth century.

In France, the concept of individualism has ordinarily had negative connotations—being repudiated as the "disease of the Western world," as Auguste Comte phrased it,[38] or else a transitional state of historical development which, in Saint-Simonian parlance, would be eventually harnessed and its best elements incorporated in a utopian socialist society. In Germany, by contrast, the romantic conception of individuality, which had positive connotations, would eventually be transformed into a theory of organic community that the Germans called individualism. It was, however, a construct in which individuals could find identity only in the "whole" or "group"— e.g., the nation or the *Volk*. In Victorian Britain, thinkers rarely used the term "individualism" per se. But most of the unit-ideas now associated with the concept—for instance, personal liberty, economic individualism, and social contract theory—had a greater influence there than in any other western nation with the exception of the United States. American ideas and attitudes stemmed, in part, from their British heritage. As we shall see, individualism in Britain was, however, constrained in ways that were not characteristic of the American experience.

Many of the key elements or component ideas of what we now call individualism found expression, as noted earlier, during the Renaissance, the Reformation, and the eighteenth-century Enlightenment. Still others existed in the ancient world or in medieval society. But the word "individualism" was not coined until the early nineteenth century. Its earliest known usage occurred in 1820 when Joseph de Maistre, the French theocrat, excoriated the Enlightenment as "this deep and frightening division of minds, the infinite fragmentation of all doctrines, political protestantism carried to the most absolute individualism."[39] De Maistre, Félicité Robert de Lamennais, and Joseph de Bonald, champions of the ancien regime, abhorred the Enlightenment's emphasis on reason, individual rights, natural law, and, indeed, its repudiation of revealed religion. By proclaiming the heretical doctrine of the absolute sovereignty of the individual, Lamennais declared, the philosophers paved the way for "an irremediable anarchy" that "overturns the very bases of human society."[40] In sum, French theocrats believed that men by nature were evil. Unless their base passions were controlled by authoritarian elites who had established a clear-cut hierarchy of authority, social dissolution was inevitable.

The Saint-Simonians, however, were the first social group in France to use the term *individualisme* systematically. They shared with the counter-revolutionaries the idea that the Enlightenment, with its glorification of the individual, would bring about the atomization of society. Unlike the theocrats, who wanted to restore the ancien régime, the Saint-Simonians were forward-looking and believed that the Industrial Revolution threatened to bring about social and economic chaos in its wake. As utopian socialists, the Saint-Simonians were opposed to what they termed the "constitution of property" based on the "privileges of birth." Equally important, the Saint-Simonians viewed history in cyclical terms, characterized by "critical" and "organic" periods. Theirs, they believed, was a "critical" era, ushered in by the Protestant Reformation, and they used the concept of individualism to characterize what they believed was the penultimate stage of civilization—a period of disharmony and disorder that eventually would be overcome by an era of "order, religion, association and devotion."[41]

Other French socialists, including Louis Blanc, likewise were not critical of individualism for its emphasis on Enlightenment political ideals stressing the natural, inalienable rights of man. Blanc, like the Saint-Simonians, was bitterly opposed to laissez-faire economics, which brought about the brutalization of the proletariat in the name of competitive, impersonal market forces.

Blanc, the disciples of Charles Fourier, and, later in the century, Jean Jaurès, saw no fundamental conflict between individualism and socialism. Jaurès maintained that socialism was the logical end of individualism, a view shared by Émile Durkheim, who believed that a type of centralized socialism would serve to complete, extend, and organize individualism. Stated another way, individualism, in its anarchic form, was a source of social atomization and chaos; but its emphasis on freedom, autonomy, and the dignity of the individual were positive ideals that could be preserved by the creation of an organic, cooperative, and organized social system.[42]

Another French variation that attributed negative social and political characteristics to the concept of individualism was most clearly articulated by the liberal French aristocrat, Alexis de Tocqueville. *Individualisme,* Tocqueville wrote, is a modern and potentially dangerous concept that weakens traditional social bonds. Tocqueville believed individualism is "of democratic origin and threatens to grow insofar as conditions get more equal." Democracy, Tocqueville stated, not only "makes men forget their ancestors" but also "clouds their view of their descendants and isolates them from their contemporaries. Each man is forever thrown back on himself alone and there is a danger that he may be shut up in the solitude of his own heart."[43]

What Tocqueville feared, therefore, was that individuals in a democracy would withdraw from active participation in society. By ignoring society at large, by retreating into a close-knit circle of family and friends, they would become isolated, apathetic, and indifferent. This could lead not only to alienation and unbridled egoism but to the centralization of political power in the hands of the state—a trend that, left unchecked, would subvert liberty. The solution to this calamity, Tocqueville believed, was the development of an active participation in spontaneous, local intermediary groups by large numbers of individuals. According to Tocqueville, the United States, with its tradition of free institutions and active involvement by its citizenry in voluntary societies and politics, thus managed to avoid the evils of individualism.

In sum, in French thought *individualisme* has almost always been linked to the possibility of social dissolution, although wide divergences in conception exist (depending upon time and historical circumstance) regarding its historical origins, and how and why individualism was considered a dread social disease that threatened the social order with dissolution.

The most characteristic German conception of individualism was propounded by late-eighteenth- and early nineteenth-century romantics, whose outlook can be best described as a *Weltanschauung* (world view) that rejected the rationalist premises of Enlightenment thought.

In brief, Enlightenment rationalism emphasized the use of reason and an empirical approach to discover and verify the existence of immutable universal laws that would liberate the human race from vice, superstition, and authoritarianism. Enlightenment thinkers also believed that human nature was more or less the same, regardless of time, place, and circumstance. It followed, therefore, that men, like atoms, would always respond alike to universal laws or forces. Historical development thus played no role in social contract theory; if men possessed rights, they were not unique. Men were, rather, like peas in a pod.

The early German romantics used the term "individuality" rather than "individualism" in attacking Enlightenment ideas. By the 1840s, however, individualism was commonly used to define traits referred to as individuality in the writings of earlier romantics such as Friedrich von Schlegel and Friedrich Schleiermacher.[44]

In the place of abstract doctrines such as natural rights, uniformity, and reason, German romantics emphasized antirationalist factors—e.g., subjectivity, originality, multiformity, diversity, and uniqueness. In addition, they stressed the importance of emotion, intuition, experience, and irrationality (the unconscious) in understanding the meaning of life, the nature of society, and the significance of history. By recognizing the importance of history, the German romantics thus emphasized the idea that societies were organic—characterized, that is, by change, growth, evolution, and decline. Such a view not only precluded the existence of universal standards of judgment, as Enlightenment thinkers would have it, but emphasized the idea that history was the result of spiritual rather than material forces.[45]

The early romantics also emphasized the necessity for solitude and introspection so that people of genius might experience self-realization uncorrupted by undesirable social influences. Later romantic thinkers, however, rejected this concept, concluding that too much emphasis on solitude and introspection would lead to isolation, alienation, and social irresponsibility. Such fears were exemplified by the egoism of Max Stirner and other "Young Hegelians" who preached "a form of anarchism and nihilism unparalleled in its extremism by any other European country at that time."[46] As Stirner phrased it:

I, the egoist, have not at heart the welfare of this "human society." I sacrifice nothing to it. I only utilize it: but to be able to utilize it completely I must transform it rather into my property and my creature—i.e., I must annihilate it and form in its place the Union of Egoists.[47]

Such unbridled individualism, however, was not dominant in German thought. By far the most important, pervasive, and long-lived conception of German individualism was developed by the later romantics, who fused the idea of individuality with the idea of organicism.

If the romantics valued the individual and his right to freedom and self-development, they also stressed the importance of the group, which they "considered a living organism whose laws of organization placed the constituent individuals in a relation of mutual dependence."[48] This conception of the one and the many "is distinctive and, for the Western mind, remarkable."[49] The "Western mind" tends to place the group and the individual in opposition—assuming that one of the two must have primacy. Thus, romantic individualism, in contrast to the atomistic individualism so characteristic of Enlightenment thought, did not stress the subordination of the individual to the group but rather the coordination of the two.

Historian Robert W. Lougee expresses these ideas in cogent terms:

> The same age which displayed such striking individualism, reacted against the isolation of the individual. From the mid-1790s romantic writers more and more stress the role of the individual as a vital part of a larger organic whole. This stress did not aim at subordinating the individual to the group but rather at coordinating him with it. Still less did it aim at eliciting likeness of contribution or equality of treatment. Rather the group was thought strong according to the uniqueness and diversity of its elements. The assumption was that the individual by being true to himself would best represent and contribute to the character of the whole.[50]

German romantics thus ascribed individualism not only to persons but to suprapersonal forces—e.g., the *Volk,* religions, or nations. A person could achieve individuality or self-expression only within the group or whole.

The idea of organic community, or social organicism, which has been referred to as "political biology," did not originate in Germany. It occurs, for example, in the reflections of Jean-Jacques Rousseau and Edmund Burke, but clearly, it has had its most radical expression in Germany. Moreover, the idea of organicism has been a dynamic one, providing extremely fertile soil for the growth and development of diverse political and social theories—whether democratic, socialist, or anarchist. In short, organicism has conjured up what Franklin L. Baumer refers to as "rapturous futurism"—a myriad of utopian dreams tied to no particular political viewpoint.[51]

In addition, the romantic idea of organic individualism and nationalism are inextricably intertwined. It must be emphasized that German Pietism, which emerged during the last quarter of the seventeenth century, was one of the great wellsprings of cultural nationalism in Germany.[52] Cultural nationalism, of course, developed long before political unity. Pietism not only emphasized the importance of emotion and feeling in bringing about individual salvation, but it also minimized class distinctions, which helped to make national identity or *Gemeinschaft* (community of feeling) possible. It must be remembered that romantic nationalism in early nineteenth-century Germany did not connote superiority or inferiority. It referred only to difference. As Johann Gottlieb Fichte explained:

> Only in so far as each one of these nations, left to itself, develops and takes shape in accordance with its own peculiarities, and in so far as each individual in each of these nations also develops and takes shape with this common peculiarity as well as his own individual peculiarity, is the phenomenon of divinity reflected the way it should be.[53]

If the seeds of organicism in German thought antedated the French Revolution, it cannot be too strongly emphasized that the chaos engendered by the Revolution and by Napoleonic domination "intensified the anti-Enlightenment basis of German political thought."[54]

Prussia, with its strong monarchy, centralized bureaucracy, and its socially and politically dominant aristocracy, ultimately paved the way for political unification in Germany. The Hohenzollern monarchy, after Napoleonic victories at Jena and Auerstädt, began to initiate a "revolution from above." That is to say, Prussian bureaucrats, partially out of fear of Enlightenment ideals, began to initiate a series of economic, political, and social reforms designed to link the populace to the monarchy. As Georg Iggers has phrased it, the Prussian bureaucracy believed that the creation of a strong, efficient and modernized monarchy could provide "the conditions under which personal liberty, juridical security, and a degree of popular participation in public affairs would be balanced with respect for traditional organs of authority."[55]

The radically equalitarian demands of the French Revolution, and its challenge to all established political and historical traditions, led to a systematic effort to establish political as well as cultural unity in Germany. Thus, on a practical level, German theories of individualism—which attributed individuality not only to persons but to suprapersonal forces such as the *Volk* and the state—partially reflected the attempts of Prussian intellectuals and bureaucrats to create broad middle- and lower-class support for the Hohenzollern monarchy in its efforts to achieve national unity and to ward off French domination. In time, this led to what Iggers has termed the "Bismarckian synthesis," in which Germany achieved not only national unity but a sense of social and political integration in which the perennial problem of the "one and the many" was resolved in a manner that was distinctively German—a formulation that lasted well into the twentieth century.[56]

In Victorian Britain, the concept of individualism was linked to liberalism, the ideology of an ascendant middle class that legitimated its rise to power during the Industrial Revolution. Yet the political emergence of individualism, part of a long-standing social and economic tradition unique to England, took concrete form during an intellectually fertile period marked by the turmoil of the English Civil War in the seventeenth century. After 1642, Oliver Cromwell's revolutionary challenge to the Stuart monarchy of Charles I provided the opening for some of his Puritan supporters to propose an innovative democratic constitution. Influenced by their experience in their self-directed congregations, these radicals wanted protection of individual rights and universal male suffrage guaranteed by the state.[57]

Not only were the Puritans' democratic ideas too advanced for the social structures of the day, but they engendered a political backlash. Thomas

Hobbes's *Leviathan* (1651) is notable for using individualistic premises to justify not democracy but authoritarianism. Writing in the midst of civil war, he concluded that human nature is degenerate, a relentless quest for power that led to a "war of all against all." Life without government was, in his damning words, "solitary, poor, nasty, brutish, and short."[58] In order to find social harmony, man must relinquish his freedom to a sovereign, the Leviathan, who through supreme power maintains political stability. Hobbes's secular argument might justify Stuartian absolutism or Cromwellian dictatorship. Nonetheless, he rested state power on the basis of the individual willingly empowering the Leviathan.

With the advent of the Glorious Revolution in 1688, John Locke reappropriated individualism for a limited monarchy. He refuted Hobbes's authoritarian version of the social contract while attacking the divine right theory of monarchy. For Locke, individuals in the state of nature were free and equal, possessing natural rights to life, liberty, and property. According to his labor theory of value, a natural right to property occurred when an individual gave economic value to raw materials through the incorporation of his labor. Because of the potential danger existing in the ungoverned state of nature, Locke posited that individuals created government "for their comfortable, safe, and peaceable living amongst another, in a secure enjoyment of their properties, and a greater security against any that are not of it."[59] In establishing the state through a social contract, Locke made the legitimacy of government dependent upon the consent of the governed. If the established authorities did not secure the people's natural rights, they might ultimately revolt and establish another government.

Locke's famous *Two Treatises on Government* (1690) legitimated Parliament's power to unseat James II and to enthrone William and Mary. In addition, he provided the rising middle class with a timely argument that rested the moral basis of society on the political obligation to protect the private appropriation of wealth. At the heart of Locke's theory of capitalist accumulation is what political scientist C. B. MacPherson calls "possessive individualism." The "possessive quality," he explains, "is found in its conception of the individual as essentially the proprietor of his own person or capacities, owing nothing to society for them."[60]

The conservative aspect of Locke's formulation is that it excluded from political participation the bulk of the laboring classes, dependent people who possessed no property, the sine qua non for suffrage and office holding. Lockean individualism further delegitimated the socially radical demands of economically dispossessed groups for the redistribution of wealth. The revolutionary aspect of "possessive individualism" for the seventeenth century was, nevertheless, that it subverted the feudal privileges of the upper classes that did not coincide with his labor theory of value. In linking political society with the safeguarding of bourgeois market relations, Locke significantly broadened the definition of freedom for his day, at least for the middle class.

Well into the next century, University of Glasgow professor Adam Smith extended Locke's conceptions. He developed the assumptions of Francis Hutcheson, Adam Ferguson, Thomas Reid, and others known as the Scottish moral philosophers into a grand synthesis. He and his countrymen revised the Enlightenment belief that reason alone was a sure guide to the good society. In *The Theory of Moral Sentiments* (1759), Smith argued that an instinctual sympathy with the welfare of others provided an emotional bond uniting humanity, an attractive idea that gained wide currency in America, notably with Thomas Jefferson.

Smith added in *The Wealth of Nations* (1776) that the desire for material improvement was an innate characteristic that did not produce an inevitable conflict between the individual's pursuit of self-interest and the natural rights of others. He argued that the individual "by pursuing his own interest . . . frequently promotes that of society more effectually than when he really intends to promote it."[61] He sought to liberate the entrepreneurial spirit from the mercantile and monopolistic manipulation of a privileged few who secured self-serving trade legislation and economic subsidies that kept their grasping fingers in the public till. Smith foresaw that the benevolent "invisible hand" of the marketplace would limit greed, social disorder, and maldistribution of wealth as it opened opportunity to men of merit from the middle and lower classes. For Smith, what later became known as laissez-faire economics would not collapse into a Hobbesian war of rapacious individuals because of the restraining influence of the inbred moral sentiment linking humanity. Smith's vision, as historian Robert Shalhope points out in an essay in this collection, was that of a moral economy—an economic means to a moral end.

The universal moral sentiments and economic laws that Smith thought would lead to a naturally harmonious society in which all classes prospered degenerated into derivative theories that rationalized the exploitation of the industrial and agricultural proletariat during the nineteenth century. Instead of human progress, the Manchester school of economics held that poverty was inevitable, earning economics the grim title of the "dismal science." For Thomas Malthus, man's unrelenting sexual desire would lead to a population increase that would outstrip the pace at which food could be produced. War, famine, plague, and widespread misery were the predictions of his gloomy demographic study. The economic implications of Malthus's arguments were clearly seen by his friend, David Ricardo, in what became known as the "iron law of wages." The inevitable destitution of the working classes was correlated to an excessive labor supply that depressed wages below a subsistence level. To raise wages and improve the standard of living contradicted the ruthless logic of the marketplace in which labor was regarded as another commodity for sale. Not only would productive investment capital be diverted, profits lowered, and the national economy depressed, but with better living conditions the working class would breed even more children, again glutting the market and depressing wages. The laissez-faire philosophy of economic individualism postulated that governmental social reform was futile because it opposed fundamental biological and economic laws.

At the start of the nineteenth century, the intellectual aggressiveness of middle-class liberalism in Britain was manifested not only in classical economics but also in the individualistic philosophy of utilitarianism. Unlike Locke and other Enlightenment thinkers who predicated the moral purpose of society on protecting universal natural rights, Jeremy Bentham and his disciple James Mill argued from the practical point of view of utility or usefulness—i.e., what worked best for most people. Bentham held that man functioned according to a pleasure principle—namely, to avoid pain and to pursue pleasure. The freedom to pursue personal happiness would lead in the aggregate to the "greatest happiness for the greatest number." The political system that best achieved this goal was representative democracy, in which it was implicitly assumed that the lower classes would defer to the leadership of their social betters. Unlike the organic harmony of individual interests that Adam Smith said existed in a free market with a minimal governmental role, Bentham saw that in the political realm, legislative action was necessary to create an affinity between divergent individual interests and the society as a whole.

The effort to reconcile individual freedom with social harmony led Bentham to abandon laissez-faire ideals in the areas of education, child labor, health, and aid to the poor. The argument for state intervention among utilitarians was carried furthest by John Stuart Mill, who in the revision of the dogmatic theories of Bentham and his own father, established a foundation for a new style of liberalism after the mid-nineteenth century. He declared in *On Liberty* (1859) that the principle of "utility" authorized "the subjection of individual spontaneity to external control, only in respect to those actions of each, which concern the interest of other people." Despite his fundamental belief that "the individual is sovereign," he was highly critical of economic injustice, social inequities, and sexual discrimination, a compassionate outlook that set him apart from a largely complacent British middle class.[62] Mill's argument for the expanded role of the government foreshadowed the welfare state, which became an emerging political reality after the turn of the twentieth century in Britain.

Why, unlike the Americans, did the Europeans not embrace individualism so enthusiastically during the nineteenth century? England, most of all, had a long tradition of individualistic thought and expression—a legacy that significantly influenced American conceptions. In England, the word "individualism" was little used and then had a restricted application. Men of means, breeding, and intellectual substance—the Thomas Carlyles, the William Wordsworths, the John Stuart Mills, the Matthew Arnolds—had the wherewithal to be independent, to be individuals. In America, these men believed, a provincial middle class had corrupted the individualistic tradition in their unchecked materialistic pursuits. "We regard it as one of the greatest advantages of this country over America," Mill pronounced, "that it possesses both these classes [the leisured and learned], and we believe that the interests of the time to come are greatly dependent upon preserving them."[63] Dependency, if not outright subservience, was the expected lot of the English ironmonger, the Welsh miner, the Scottish mill worker, and the Irish peat digger. The persistence and pervasiveness of class barriers (whether between nobility and commoner or, with the onset of the Industrial Revolution, between bourgeoisie and proletariat) limited the widespread use of the term "individualism" in a positive sense in England and even more so on the Continent.

The Emergence of an
Individualistic Ethos in
American Society

Richard O. Curry and
Karl E. Valois

I N the half-century after the American Revolution, American society underwent radical change—major transformations in the political, economic, and religious fields that created a social order which, in comparative terms, was the most liberal and individualistic the world had ever known. The American political system, which was based upon Enlightenment and Lockean principles and, indeed, the civil and religious traditions of the colonies themselves, not only reflected hostility to the creation of a highly centralized government but, in the Declaration of Independence and the Bill of Rights, stressed the "natural rights" of individuals—equality before the law, freedom of expression, trial by jury, habeas corpus, freedom from unreasonable searches and seizures, religious toleration, and the right of revolution against tyrannical governments. Today, of course, most Americans tend to take such principles for granted; but in the late eighteenth century, "self-evident truths" and "unalienable rights" were considered to be not only radical but patently nonsensical throughout most of the Western world.

Many of the basic assumptions of liberalism or political individualism had been expressed by John Locke in *A Second Treatise on Government* (1690). Locke asserted that human beings in the natural state were "free, equal, and independent." This state of *perfect freedom*, however, had been

Curry wrote approximately three-fourths of this chapter. Valois authored most of the section dealing with political conflicts and transformations during the early national period. Lawrence B. Goodheart provided quotations from the work of Bernard Bailyn, Gordon Wood, Thomas Jefferson, Thomas Paine, and James Madison cited in the early part of the chapter.

limited by the formation of governments that would preserve "Lives, Liberties and Estates, which I call by the general name—Property."[1] But government power was limited, being based on the consent of the governed, who agreed to obey only "so far as the preservation of himself and the rest of society required." There was a catch, however, in Locke's formulations. Locke emphasized that his use of the term "Property" referred to "Property which men have in their Persons as well as Goods." To Locke, "a man's labour is so unquestionably his own property that he may freely sell it for wages." "The labour thus sold," therefore, "becomes the property of the buyer, who is then entitled to appropriate the produce of that labour." In practice, as well as theory, Lockean rights belonged almost exclusively to men of substance—the aristocracy, the landed gentry, and the rising middle class.[2] As C. B. MacPherson observes:

> Locke was indeed at the fountain-head of English liberalism. The greatness of seventeenth-century liberalism was its assertion of the free rational individual as the criterion of the good society; its tragedy was that this very assertion was necessarily a denial of individualism to half the nation.[3]

In the United States, however, Lockean principles were extended far beyond anything that Locke and his contemporaries could have imagined. In fact, as Bernard Bailyn observed, a number of the political and social aspirations of the European Enlightenment already had been fulfilled in America during the colonial era. When confronted by the imperial crisis of the 1760s and 1770s, Americans at last began to systematize a political philosophy. Many of the key concepts that became enshrined—of the necessity of written constitutions, of natural rights superceding the law, of representative assemblies as servants of the people, and of political sovereignty as being divisible—were reflections of actual conditions in the colonies. Indeed, what imbued the Revolution with a "peculiar force" and marked it a "transforming event," proclaimed Bailyn, was the "radical idealization and conceptualization of the previous century and a half of American experience."[4]

However idealistic and sanguine the Spirit of '76 may have been, it still required a little more than a decade for the Americans to complete their revolutionary political philosophy. Although the long road to Philadelphia and the adoption of the Constitution was paved with tribulation, debate, and compromise, the journey ultimately led them to forge, in Gordon S. Wood's apt phrase, an "American science of politics."[5] In heralding the superiority of individual citizens to their government, the Founding Fathers articulated a central body of beliefs: that supreme sovereignty was vested in, and derived from, the people only; that written constitutions were charters of power granted by the people and were unalterable by government; that the separation of powers served not to represent different social constituencies but to check and balance the various branches of government; that all parts of the government and all public officials were agents of the people; that political power, emanating from the sovereignty of the people, could be partitioned among various levels of government; that freedom entailed not only the privilege of citizens to participate in government but the safeguarding of individual rights from all government encroachments; and that republics could be founded on self-interest because the multiplicity of interests would assuredly preclude anyone from achieving domination. In short, a remarkable revolution in the history of politics had transpired—"the rulers had become the ruled and the ruled the rulers."[6]

As a result, Americans had founded their Republic on individuals, whom they believed could govern themselves through a harmony of mutual self-interest. "Man was destined for society," Jefferson observed."He was endowed with a sense of right and wrong merely relative to this."[7] The presupposition of a "moral instinct," an idea borrowed from the Scottish moralists, meant that not only were "all men created equal" but, as Thomas Paine concluded, the "public good . . . is the good of every individual collected."[8] The concept of innate sociability freed individuals from the coercive power of church and state, so Jefferson and Paine believed, while it maintained a balance between liberty and social responsibility.

Not all republicans shared Jefferson's and Paine's belief in a natural order that emanated from each person, a perception that, in time, came to constitute a dominant and distinctive strain in American individualism. John Adams feared the passions of democracy as well as the arrogance of aristocracy. Rather than assume a natural harmony of the one and the many, he argued that only a mixed polity that incorporated each class in a specific branch of government—the natural aristocracy of "the rich, the well-born, and the able" in the upper house and the people in the lower house—could contain the antagonism that grew from their divergent interests and abilities.[9]

Similarly, James Madison recognized that "the most common and durable source of factions has been the various and unequal distribution of property."[10] His solution, which triumphed in the Constitution, was to frustrate the formation of powerful interest groups through the function and structure of government. Checks and balances, the separation of powers, and the large size of the Republic would make it difficult for factions "to act in unison with each other."[11] Yet, as Wood pointed out, the creators of the American Republic had by 1787 rejected the classical politics of John Adams for a romantic vision in which the preservation of liberty depended finally on "the concern each individual would have in his own self-interest and personal freedom."[12]

The importance of Enlightenment ideals, especially those of Locke and the Scottish moralists, in explaining the foundations of American political thought cannot be exaggerated. However, another source of American republicanism derived from the religious and civil traditions of the Puritans and their descendants. For example, New Englanders developed covenants, compacts, and/or written constitutions early on, as exemplified by the Mayflower Compact and the Fundamental Orders of Connecticut. Such documents anticipated what later became Christian republicanism. By the late eighteenth century, New England Congregationalists understandably believed that natural reason and morality were insufficient safeguards to maintain social order and morality. They emphasized the natural depravity of human beings and insisted that civil government be riveted to the worship of God. The Massachusetts Constitution of 1780 summarized the attitudes of this version of Christian republicanism succinctly:

> As the happiness of the people, and the good order and preservation of civil government, essentially depend upon piety, religion, and morality; . . . therefore . . . the people of this Commonwealth have a right to invest their legislature with power . . . to make suitable provision . . . for the institution of the public worship of God, and for the support of public protestant teachers of piety, religion and morality.[13]

Such views were soon reflected in the attacks of the Federalist party upon Jeffersonian democracy—emphasizing as they did the corruption and perversity of the "natural man." The rise of political parties in America had been an unforeseen development. It was no accident that all references to political parties were omitted in the constitution of 1787. As Richard Hofstadter explained, "factions," the eighteenth-century term for political organizations, had long been regarded as invidious aggregations designed to procure selfish ends at the expense of the community. Though viewed as necessary evils in a free state, they were, in the opinion of James Madison, the greatest danger to law, order, and the preservation of liberty.[14] Nevertheless, when virulent disputes arose in the 1790s over the nature of man and the security and future of the Republic, the revolutionary generation created the first party system.

Analysis of the first party system involving the Federalists and the Jeffersonian Republicans is fraught with difficulties. For years, scholars have debated whether a "modern" party system did exist and, if it did, when it was in operation. To complicate matters further, recent revisionist studies of each party's ideology have challenged and, at points, overturned the conventional wisdom.[15] Finally, the fact that the Jeffersonian Republicans, once in power after 1800, appropriated some of the key elements of their adversaries' program serves even more to blur distinctions. Clearly, no simple dichotomy encompassing party membership, regional support, and political philosophy can be made. Still, in broad terms, it is possible to distinguish the salient features of the two groups and to gain an understanding of the two very different Americas each envisioned.

Led by Alexander Hamilton, the Federalists favored a strong national government with highly centralized authority. Employing a loose construction of the Constitution and lodging political power in the hands of an elite ruling class would, they believed, produce a government that was energetic, stable, and effective. Because they placed little faith in the common man and even less in the notion that American society could be held together by virtue, they were determined to halt the egalitarianism that had been unleashed after the Revolution and to enlist the support of the wealthy. Viewing the United States as a homogeneous, socially cohesive nation-state, and sensing their loss of political influence, they vehemently opposed westward expansion. Instead, they looked eastward to Great Britain for friendship and forward to the day when America would become an international power. Economically, their conception of the national interest entailed the fostering of complex commercial development and manufacturing. Like the Jeffersonian Republicans, the Federalists garnered support from each section of the country and from all social and economic classes. Their chief strength, however, came from the Congregational churches in New England and the Episcopalians in the Middle Atlantic states and the South, and from the well-to-do in the Northeast and the commercial ports of the South.[16]

Gathering under the leadership of Jefferson and Madison, the Republicans preferred a "wise and frugal" government that was far more modest in scope and that would not encroach upon the rights of states or individuals. To prevent tyranny and to implement a philosophy of "that government is best which governs least," they at first advocated a strict construction of the Constitution. Entrusting the good intentions of ordinary citizens, they felt that the masses, if properly educated, could fully participate in a democratic republic. These same sympathies and their ardent defense of democracy also permitted Jeffersonians to defend, though somewhat waveringly, the revolutionary upheavals in France and to favor a foreign policy of Franco-American friendship. Because Jefferson and his disciples believed that the ideal republic consisted of sturdy citizen-farmers, they enthusiastically endorsed westward migration. Yet they did not condemn all commercial activity, and opposed only extensive industrialization. They merely insisted that America's future lay not in a highly urbanized, commercial, and industrial economy but, rather, in the conservation of a rural society dominated by small property owners engaged primarily in agricultural pursuits. Appealing to a variety of social classes in all regions of the nation, they were especially popular with farmers in the West and small landowners and the rural gentry in the South. In the Northeast, the groups that rallied behind their banner included religious outsiders (Catholics, Baptists, Methodists, deists, atheists) and enterprising, upwardly mobile businessmen and politicians who sought to challenge entrenched leaders.[17]

Although the Federalists and Jeffersonian Republicans never evolved into political parties in a modern sense, they did organize newspapers, societies, and clubs to sway voters and to win elections. In a highly charged political atmosphere, each party accused the other of constituting an illegitimate faction bent on destroying the solid achievements of the Revolution. To the Jeffersonians, the Federalists were Anglophiles, aristocrats, monarchists, and mischievous scoundrels plotting to subvert the Bill of Rights and the Republic; to the Federalists, the Jeffersonians were atheists, fanatics, traitors, Jacobins, and social levelers hostile to property and social order. Although these indictments were groundless, they did resurrect a sinister and recurring theme in American history—the fear of conspiracy.[18]

Interestingly, in the Federalist assault upon the Jeffersonians, republican principles were disassociated from the philosophy of natural rights and reinterpreted to highlight the religious conservatism of Federalist conceptions of government and society. Such concerns were reflected not only in the established state churches of Connecticut, Massachusetts, New Hampshire, and Vermont but in conspiracy theories of history—most notably the myth of the Bavarian *Illuminati* "in which religion was to be overthrown by atheism and materialism, and with it all existing institutions and natural governments, so that democratic Jacobism, leveling, and lawlessness should prevail."[19]

By the 1820s, however, this particular version of religious conservatism (if not conspiracy theory) was becoming increasingly anachronistic. With the expansion of the frontier, the advance of political democracy, the decline of deference, the emergence of increasingly egalitarian attitudes and mores, and the growth of religious pluralism, the laws supporting established state churches in Connecticut, Massachusetts, and New Hampshire were repealed between 1818 and 1833. To be sure, religion would continue to play a major role in American society; but churches, by necessity, now began to maximize the use of moral suasion based on voluntarism in their efforts to blend religious principles with political democracy and an equalitarian ideology.[20]

Accompanying these changes was yet another major event in American political culture: the transformation of attitudes and beliefs that occurred between the War of Independence and the Age of Jackson. It has also been a perplexing development for scholars to comprehend. Essentially, the problem has centered around the existence, the comparative strength, and the evolutionary course of two distinctive modes of thought in the early national period: "civic humanism" or "classical republicanism," and "modern liberalism."

As delineated by Caroline Robbins, Bernard Bailyn, Gordon S. Wood, J. G. A. Pocock, and Lance Banning, the republican heritage was an extraordinary collection of ideas that exerted a powerful influence upon the revolutionary generation. In brief, it constituted an ethical, idealistic, even utopian vision of American society that required from the people and its leaders a complete subordination of their self-interest to the commonwealth. Among the numerous values it embraced were liberty, equality, social solidarity, virtue, simplicity, temperance, and frugality.[21] Recently, however, another group of historians (including Joyce Appleby and John P. Diggins) have argued that a countervailing tradition of liberalism animated the American populace. In this contrasting scheme, the public welfare was best advanced by the people pursuing their own self-interest. The proper role of government, it was believed, was to protect individual rights and to give free vent to a capitalistic, bourgeois set of values. In this interpretive framework, America had almost always been modern, with its inhabitants busily immersed in a quest for private fortune.[22]

At present, there appears to be a consensus that both traditions were in force during the early Republic, that neither won ideological hegemony during the 1780s and 1790s, but that, in some fashion, modern liberalism came to achieve ascendancy by the Jacksonian era.[23] Indeed, in 1987, John Murrin deemed this "Great Transition" to be "the most important controversy taking shape in recent years about early American history."[24] Although no wholly persuasive work has yet surfaced to clarify the issues, it may well be that rapid economic and social change—more intensive than previously assumed—holds the interpretive key. Accordingly, Wood has issued the call for a massive reconceptualization of the entire early national period.[25] In the meantime, the definitive treatment of liberalizing change awaits its author.

Less controversy has surrounded the movement that during these years truly began to revolutionize American life—the onward march of political democracy. Foremost among the many changes was the swift extension of the suffrage. As Chilton Williamson and J. R. Pole have written, a variety of factors combined to broaden the American electorate: the natural rights philosophy and the heritage of the Revolution, the substitution of tax payments or militia service (on the frontier) for property qualifications, the desire of political parties to recruit new supporters, and the increasing economic and social mobility that threatened established elites in the East and precluded the entrenchment of privileged classes in the West. As a result, by 1825 prohibitive restrictions on suffrage remained only in Rhode Island, Virginia, Mississippi, and Louisiana. With a steady and unyielding pace, the United States was moving inexorably in the direction of white male suffrage.[26]

A number of significant reforms accompanied the expansion of voting rights in the trend toward a more democratic political order. Several states abolished "stand up" voting in favor of written ballots in an effort to safeguard the privacy and autonomy of the voter. Many others increased the number of offices that were elective rather than appointive, and more governors and judges were being elected not by the legislatures but by the voters themselves. At the same time, property qualifications for office holding were ending, and legislatures were reapportioning their states to redress the lack of political power in underrepresented areas. By 1836, all but South Carolina had transferred the election of presidential electors from the legislatures to the voters. In the selection of presidential candidates, the secret caucus system of congressional party leaders was replaced after 1824 by nominations from state legislatures and, in 1832, by national nominating conventions.[27]

Still, some scholars (notably Edward Pessen) have questioned the magnitude of these democratic reforms and the very idea that the age was one of egalitarianism or of the common man.[28] Certainly, most candidates for public office continued to be culled from the wealthier classes, and party potentates did retain a firm grasp over nominations and legislation. In the main, however, there can be little doubt that the tremors occasioned by these political changes were placing the United States on the path toward a more equalitarian and participatory democracy.

Further evidence of this dramatic shift was the decline of deference. Since the founding of the colonies, generations of Americans had adhered to a system of deferential politics whereby only a select minority were considered worthy to wield the reins of power. In this classical model, it was expected that gentlemen of wealth, education, and virtue—motivated by obligation and duty—would serve in government office to promote the public good. Forming, in Jefferson's phrase, a "natural aristocracy," they would govern in the interests of the entire society, guided by the highest ideals of honor, integrity, and probity. They would never commit the ignominy of seeking office; rather, the office would seek them.

Originally weakened by the egalitarian thrust of the American Revolution, the long-standing deferential system came under heavy attack throughout the early national period. As David Hackett Fischer has shown, even some Federalists were reduced to politicking to secure office.[29] In effect, what had occurred was the supplanting of an older world by a more modern one in which politicians, backed by political parties, now competed for votes among an ever-expanding electorate. Unfortunately, it is impossible to measure precisely the decline of deference, and different historians have pronounced its death to have taken place at various points between the Revolution and the Civil War.[30] Yet, in a blistering commentary in 1823, *Niles Weekly Register* was already labeling the new breed of political candidates as "persons who have little, if any, regard for the welfare of the republic unless immediately connected with . . . their own private pursuits."[31] Although the editors were undoubtedly engaging in hyperbole, their cynical assessment of public officials did reflect both the popular perception and the degree to which politics in America had become modern.

Interwoven with the democratic reforms and the new political realities were significant developments in the realm of economics. By the time the nation reached the Age of Jackson, advancing political democracy also exhibited an economic dimension in its hostility to monopoly and special privilege of any kind in the passage of general incorporation laws, in the destruction of the Second Bank of the United States, and in the Charles River Bridge case.

Ideals of limited government, which translated in the United States into laissez-faire liberalism, obviously had important implications for economic as well as political and religious life; but economic development was also transformed by other major factors and developments, including territorial expansion, the transportation and industrial revolutions, immigration, and urbanization. As a result of the Revolution, the United States expanded to the Mississippi. Then, in 1803, the acquisition of the Louisiana Purchase created what Jefferson called his "empire of liberty." In Jeffersonian parlance, the yeoman farmer was the backbone of a free society, and Louisiana conjured up visions of independent, self-sufficient individuals dependent on no one for their sustenance. In fact, however, most farmers lived lives of rude plenty if the elements cooperated on a subsistence level. Cooperative ideals as reflected in mutual self-help (barn and house raisings, for example) and hierarchal notions based on status, family, community, church, and deference reflected the realities of rural life and limited economic horizons. As late as 1820, only 20 percent of all farm goods were sold in nonfarm markets because only those farmers who lived near urban areas or within a few miles of river transportation could engage in commercial agriculture.[32] With the passage of time, older values were challenged and eventually undermined by the emergence of a market economy in which the construction of canals, turnpikes, and railroads and the improvements in river transportation were permitted by the invention of the steamboat. The market economy, national and international in scope, encouraged specialization in the production of wheat, corn, flour, and other products and replaced the ideal of cooperative self-sufficiency, with an economic system that emphasized not only specialization but the spirit of acquisitiveness and economies of scale that led to competition, risk taking, technological advances, and increasing social atomization characteristic of modern capitalism. If a market economy increased wealth or the prospects of increased wealth, it proved liberating for those who succeeded; but the blessing of possessive or acquisitive individualism based upon market realities and considerations eluded the vast majority of adult white males.

The Industrial Revolution produced the same kind of inequities and inequalities. Factory owners and upwardly mobile skilled craftsmen, some of whom were incipient entrepreneurs, reaped great wealth and social standing as a result of successful competition based, in part, on the exploitation of wage earners whose bargaining power in the marketplace consigned them to not only increased regimentation and impersonality in the work place but subsistence wages.[33]

Older ideals died hard, but die they did. As Sean Wilentz points out in his study of New York artisans, the "middling" republican politics of the mechanics—with their distrust of the power and culture of New York's nabobs and their lack of sympathy for the dependent poor—call to mind what C. B. MacPherson has described as the more radical variants of bourgeois "possessive individualism." Yet, the mechanics, "with their artisan republicanism," represented far more than individuals whose values contained the "germ of bourgeois propriety." As Wilentz phrased it:

> Artisan independence conjured up, not a vision of ceaseless, self-interested industry, but a moral order in which all craftsmen would eventually become self-governing, independent, competent masters. . . . Men's energies would be devoted, not to personal ambition or profit alone, but to the commonwealth; in the workshop, mutual obligation and respect . . . would prevail. . . . This fusion of independent liberties and personal sovereignty with social and corporate responsibilities—very akin to what others have called "collective individualism," the core of early American political thought—remained in uneasy and increasingly contradictory relation to the bourgeois tendencies of artisan thinking and to the inescapable fact that with the expansion of the craft economy and the transformation of labor relations, some craftsmen would never escape dependence on their masters and on the wage.[34]

Artisan ideals of cooperative or collective individualism were doomed by the entrepreneurial spirit in which competition, large-scale production, impersonality, social atomization, and above all, profits and increasing wealth for the few gained ascendancy. By the 1850s, half of the adult white males in American society were without property. A wealthy elite, a mere 5 percent of the population, owned 60 percent of all property. In between the wealthy elite and dependent poor was a rising middle class—farmers, merchants, professionals, and artisans, who managed to maintain their independence and who were involved in the market economy. This rising and increasingly self-conscious middle class comprised one-third of the population and controlled most of the businesses, churches, newspapers, and professions.[35]

Laissez-faire liberalism produced more losers than winners in the economic sphere. The right to compete on an equal basis with one's fellows for advancement that, in theory, was based on the work of the "invisible hand" in the marketplace inevitably produced insecurity, uncertainty, anxiety, and in many instances, alienation—and this among the rising middle class as well as wage laborers and subsistence farmers, who lived on the margins of society. As Tocqueville observed, men, in an equalitarian society, must ever strive for superiority and thus can never achieve "an equal and tranquil existence."[36] In short, the uncertain joys of an individualistic ethos, which has had such a profound influence on the way Americans have defined themselves and their society, was limited primarily to white, middle-class males.

The underclass, however, was not confined solely to white males who failed to achieve upward social mobility, but it included women, blacks, and Indians, who were perceived as being biologically inferior and not entitled, therefore, to equality in any form. A sharp distinction was made between what were perceived as "natural" inequalities and "unnatural" inequalities resulting from special privilege.[37]

In time, reform movements would challenge social stereotypes based on race or gender, and attempts would be made to bring these groups into the American mainstream. These reform impulses would stem, in part, from religious concerns as well as changing social realities and ideological commitments; but the major, if not exclusive, concern of evangelical Protestants in the decades during and after the 1820s was to come to grips with the massive political, social, and economic changes that were rapidly transforming American society. As the theologian Phillip Schaff phrased it: The "great work and the divine mission of Protestantism [is] to place each individual soul in immediate union with Christ and His Word; to complete in each one the work of redemption, to build in each a temple of God, a spiritual church; and to unfold and sanctify all the energies of the individual."[38]

Protestant ministers thus stressed the idea that sin stemmed mostly from selfishness and that all human beings by their own volition could achieve salvation. Shortly after the War of 1812, Protestant churches also began organizing interdenominational societies designed to save American society from sin and usher in the millennium. Phrased in more practical terms, the primary, if not the exclusive, objective was to establish and maintain social control in American society by organizing missionary societies, tract societies, Bible societies, Sunday school unions, the temperance movement, the Magdalen Society for "females who had departed from the paths of virtue," academies and colleges in the West, and, indeed, to wage crusades to unmask and repudiate the perceived sophistries both of Unitarianism and Roman Catholicism. Lyman Beecher, the Protestant evangelist, not only edited *The Spirit of the Pilgrims,* an important anti-Unitarian journal published in Boston, but wrote the influential *A Plea for the West,* which was, in part, an anti-Catholic tract. Moreover, Beecher's support for the establishment of public schools was not based primarily upon a desire to combat ignorance in a democratic society, but a desire to teach the children of Roman Catholic immigrants the differences between liberty and license.[39]

Predictably, the rising middle class were pillars of the church as well as the community because evangelical Protestantism represented, in part, a marriage between moralism and materialism. As Emerson phrased it: "A dollar is not value, but representative of values and, at last, of moral values."[40] Because American society placed fewer legal and social barriers to the individual's pursuit of economic self-interest than did European society, the relative absence of external controls bred intense anxieties and insecurities. Thus, one of the objectives of evangelical religion and laissez-faire individualism was to persuade individuals to internalize values and attitudes that legitimized the emerging new social order by guaranteeing social stability itself. Thus, success or failure was determined by an invisible hand that rewarded virtue and self-restraint and punished those who were deficient in moral character. The self-made man was industrious, prudent, and in control of himself, whereas the unsuccessful were often viewed as indulgent idlers who were slaves to their passions. The self-reliant individual who pursued his own self-interest was ordinarily a successful person who had proved his own self-worth in the marketplace and, indeed, in the race of life itself.

If evangelical Protestantism was compatible with the emergence of a market economy and the rise of industrial capitalism, it would be a mistake to dismiss Evangelicalism as merely a conscious or even subconscious rationalization of self-interested acquisitiveness or as an instrument to maintain social order in an expanding and often unruly democracy. Evangelical Protestantism, after all, also produced a radical strain—a strain that not only condemned the institution of slavery but produced a radical individualist critique of American society and institutional arrangements. In the abolitionist equation, slavery was a sin because it denied slaves free moral agency. As the constitution of the Lane Seminary Anti-Slavery Society phrased it, God created the black man as "a moral agent, the keeper of his own happiness, the executive of his own powers, the accountable arbiter of his own choice." Slavery not only stifled "the moral affections" and repressed "the innate longings of the spirit," but it "paralyze[d] conscience," turned "hope to despair," and "kill[ed] the soul."[41]

The Garrisonian or "ultra" wing of the abolitionist movement, however, went beyond condemning slavery and provided a ringing indictment of all human government. If God was sovereign, they reasoned, then all government that was not based on divine law (which would result in the establishment of God's kingdom on earth) was corrupt. The Garrisonians opposed not government itself but human pretensions to govern. This doctrine of no human government the Garrisonians called "nonresistance." In sum, the Garrisonians believed in the possibility of human perfection and condemned all coercive relationships (e.g., war, slavery, taxation) that were not based on divine authority. Moreover, the Garrisonians championed the rights of women, which, along with nonresistance, the idea of human perfectibility, pacifism, and other doctrines, triggered bitter controversy that tore the American Anti-Slavery Society apart.[42] As the non-Garrisonian abolitionist Elizur Wright, Jr. phrased it: "It is downright nonsense to suppose that the Anti-Slavery cause can be carried forward with forty incongruous things tacked on it."[43] And he frankly told Garrison that his "notions of government and religious perfection" were "absurd" and credible only to a "diseased" mind.[44] It was complete folly, Wright argued, to revile human government instead of working for equality before the law for blacks, and it was utter stupidity to rile needlessly the orthodox clergy on "theoretic theology" instead of struggling against the churches' anti-abolitionism. If Garrison could not desist from promulgating nonresistance in the *Liberator*, Wright demanded that he plainly state that he had "left the old track" and had "started on a new one—or, rather, two or three new ones at once."[45] Wright warned that nonresistant anarchism would produce "an Anti-Slavery sect" that would obfuscate the goal of emancipation and provoke and abolitionist schism. In contradistinction to nonresistance, Wright emphasized enlightened voting, just laws, and good government in order to hold in check man's sinful propensities. For Wright, man was imperfectible, but civil government could be just; for Garrison, man was perfectible, but only divine government could be just.[46]

There was, however, far more ambiguity in radical abolitionist thought than either the Garrisonians or their critics fully recognized at the time. If the theoretical consequences of nonresistant thought were clear enough, its practical applications were problematic. It was clear that a nonresistant should not vote or hold office. But should one refuse to testify in court, to pay taxes, or to use banks chartered by civil government? Garrison even believed that a man, when called to militia duty, should refrain from engaging in civil disobedience. Garrison paid a fine for refusing to serve, believing that the state bore the responsibility for what it did with the money. As historian Lewis Perry observes: "Nonresistance, quite simply, did not offer a practical understanding of the evils of government, of anarchistic alternatives to existing arrangements, or of the duties of nonresistants in the present dispensation. What really mattered to the nonresistant was the declaration that the only proper government was divine." Phrased another way, the Garrisonian nonresistants attempted the almost impossible task of fusing "the quietistic attitude of nonviolence with the revolutionary purpose of millennial perfectionism."[47] As a result, nonresistance declined in importance because the Garrisonians would not allow their commitment to the abolition of slavery to be circumvented by their quest for personal liberation from sin.

The existence of ambiguity, ambivalence, or contradiction in Garrisonian thought is further illuminated in their attitudes toward the use of violence in attacking slavery. Early on, the Garrisonians were committed to pacifism; but by the 1850s, increasing numbers of abolitionists, including the Garrisonians, began to advocate righteous violence. But there was also an important ideological component in abolitionist thought, an intellectual loophole permitting nonresistants who had not themselves abandoned the principles of nonviolence to acquiesce in or condone violence on the part of others, e.g., John Brown. This, of course, was the nonresistants' emphasis upon the idea of private judgment or individual accountability to God.[48] As Bronson Alcott wrote in 1839:

What guide have I but my conscience: Church and State are responsible to me; not I to them. They cease to deserve our veneration from the moment they violate our consciences. We then protest against them. I believe that this is what is now going on. . . . I look upon the Non-Resistance Society as an assertion of the right to self-government. Why should I employ a church to write my creed or a state to govern me? Why not write my own creed? Why not govern myself?[49]

In the end, however, attempts to apply the principles of nonresistance failed to survive the political turmoil of the 1850s, the secession crisis, and the Civil War. The vast majority of Garrisonian abolitionists would not permit their nonresistance principles to take precedence over their commitment to the cause of the slave. Their slogan, "No Union With Slaveholders," was not simply a device to exonerate themselves from personal complicity with sin, but a political tactic to counter Southern threats of secession. In the final analysis, many abolitionists were also committed nationalists, believers in an American nation endowed with a unique mission in the world. In historian Peter Walker's words, "The political Union was an arena in which a providential moral drama was being enacted." And without a Union, this "morality play was impossible."[50] Garrisonian ideology was characterized by ambiguity, ambivalence, and contradiction; it was not surprising that in the late nineteenth century, as pacifist Leo Tolstoy learned to his sorrow, the Garrisonian version of Christian anarchism withered and died.[51]

Nevertheless, if the religious strain of libertarian individualism had expired by the end of the nineteenth century, it was replaced by secularized versions—doctrines of free thought, free love, and individualist anarchism. Indeed, two longtime abolitionists, Elizur Wright and Parker Pillsbury, held offices in the National Liberal League, the leading free-thought organization of the 1870s, which shows a strong linkage between prewar and postwar concerns with personal freedom and civil rights.[52] In some ways, Benjamin R. Tucker, the late-nineteenth-century American anarchist and editor of *Liberty*, reflected a greater affinity for Garrisonian doctrines of nonresistance than any other nineteenth-century thinker. Tucker believed that "every man [was] his own church," that "every man [was] his own nation," and he called for the abolition of all involuntary institutions; but in addition to elements of radical Protestantism, Tucker also incorporated elements of Jeffersonian democracy, Emersonian individualism, and the ideas of Herbert Spencer insofar as they lent themselves to laissez-faire liberalism. Until his death in 1939, Tucker called for the destruction of all monopolies—and he viewed the state as the worst form of monopoly because the state created or sheltered the worst forms of political, social, and economic privilege. Tucker's sympathies were always with the "little entrepreneur, whether small farmer, artisan, or businessman." But Tucker's vision of "a classless society of equal opportunity" was nostalgic—a yearning for the verities of a golden day that had long since passed, if it had ever existed.[53]

The Garrisonian's nonresistant anarchism was not the only variant of individualistic thought containing a perfectionist strain during the antebellum period. The evangelist Charles Grandison Finney also believed in the potential of human beings to achieve perfection, but his was a gradualist approach that avoided confronting the vital social issues of the day—especially slavery. Finney argued that instead of attacking social evils, Christians ought to concentrate on the task of perfecting human nature itself. In time, social problems would automatically cease to exist as increasing numbers of regenerate Christians, living lives of perfect purity, would eventually usher in the millennium. The Garrisonians rightly dismissed Finney's gradualist approach to achieving perfection as little more than a rationalization designed to preserve the status quo—a smokescreen that, in theory, envisioned spiritual progress but, in fact, did nothing to alter or resolve the burning social questions of the day.[54]

In sharp contrast to the nonresistant anarchism of the Garrisonians and the gradualist Christian perfectionism of Charles Grandison Finney, there emerged during the 1830s still another variant of perfectionist individualism—a perfectionist strain that rejected the doctrines of orthodox Christianity. This major variant emerged out of Unitarianism, especially from the ideas of the younger generation of liberal Unitarians, whose views were most clearly articulated by William Ellery Channing. Channing, in turn, had a major influence on the thinking of Emerson and other major figures associated with New England transcendentalism.

Unitarianism appealed, of course, to the wealthy and erudite social and cultural elite in the coastal cities of Massachusetts, especially Boston. If Unitarianism rejected most of the doctrines of orthodox Protestantism, and stressed the importance of reason, it also rejected the Enlightenment view that human beings, through the use of reason and empirical research alone, could discover universal laws and immutable principles. Unitarians developed an evolutionary (or historical), not a static, view of human and social development whereby they stressed the importance of reason, free will, discipline, and arduous study as aids to improve the mental and moral capacities and, indeed, the spiritual development of human beings. Even so, the older generation of Unitarians did not totally reject the historical doctrines of Christianity—including emphasis on the Scriptures as one source of divine truth. The Unitarian minister James Freeman emphasized the redeeming power of the life and teachings of Jesus, which, in his view, exemplified God's love. Men achieved everlasting life "not by believing in a mediator . . . but by keeping the commandments." Christianity, Freeman continued, "has raised the character of human nature higher than it ever was before; it has refined and ennobled men, and made them kings and priests unto God."[55] Equally important, traditional Unitarians, with their emphasis on reason and the acquisition of knowledge, paid little attention to the "inner light," which played a central role in the thought of the younger and more liberal generation of Unitarians led by William Ellery Channing. As Octavius Brooks Frothingham phrased it, the more traditional Unitarians of New England were "good scholars, careful reasoners, clear and exact thinkers, accomplished men of letters, humane in sentiment, sincere in moral intentions, [and] belonged . . . to the class which looked without for knowledge, rather than within for inspirations."[56] In short, Channing and the younger generation of Unitarians moved much farther afield from the traditional and historical doctrines of Christianity than their predecessors. Channing believed that the spark of divinity existed in every human being and that each individual had not only the capacity for spiritual growth but the ability to achieve perfection. Rejecting all dogma, Channing was striving to create the "universal church of all good and holy men" in which man, not Divine Providence, was the center of the universe:

> The dignity of a human being . . . consists, first, in that spiritual principle, called sometimes the Reason, sometimes the Conscience, which rising above what is

local and temporary, discerns immutable truth and everlasting right. . . . This principle is a rare Divinity in man. . . . He is the free being; created to decide his own destiny; connected intimately with nature, but not enslaved to it; connected still more strongly with God, yet not even enslaved to the Divinity.[57]

In abstract religious and philosophical terms, the revolutionary implications of Channing's ideas are clear enough; but individuals are also social beings, and Channing rejected not only submission to God but to society. "Society," he declared,

is chiefly important as it ministers to, and calls forth, intellectual and moral energy and freedom. Its action on the individual is beneficial in proportion as it awakens in him a power to act on himself, and to control or withstand the social influences to which he is first subjected. . . . Inward creative energy is the highest good which accrues to us from our social principles and connections. . . . Our social nature and connections are means. Inward power is the end; a power which is to triumph over and control the influence of society.[58]

Stated in slightly different terms, all political institutions should be judged by their ability to encourage the self-expression and self-determination of individuals. To the extent that they discouraged or denied these ends, "a people may have the name but want the substance and spirit of freedom."[59]

Far more influential, but philosophically less radical than Channing was Ralph Waldo Emerson, who resigned his position as a Unitarian minister in Boston at age twenty-nine to become a lecturer and writer. Emerson's major concern, as he phrased it, was "the infinitude of the private man." Emerson acknowledged his debt to Channing, whom he referred to as "our bishop," and, up to a point, there are major intellectual affinities in the outlook of both men. Like Channing, Emerson believed that the spark of divinity existed in every person, and that all human beings had the potential to achieve perfection—not by rational but by intuitive means, by flashes of inspiration and creativity that came from communion with "God," the "Universal spirit," or the "Oversoul." "A man contains all that is needful to his government within himself," Emerson wrote. "He is made a law unto himself," and whatever good or evil that befalls him "must be from himself." The major purpose of life "seems to be to acquaint a man with himself," and the "highest revelation" that a man can receive "is that God is in every man."[60]

Emerson's writings, in fact, are filled with arguments for self-trust and the need to reject all authority except the heart's. Emerson even admitted, at one point, that his writings "easily incurred the charge of antinomianism" as a result of his claim that "he who has the Law-giver, may with safety not only neglect, but even contravene every written commandment."[61]

In light of such statements, it is easy to understand why Cornelius Felton, a Harvard professor who reviewed *Emerson's Essays, First Series* in 1841, concluded that self-reliance, "if acted upon, would overturn society, and resolve the world into chaos."[62] Moreover, as Amy Lang observes, Felton's estimate of the "subversive potential" in Emerson's thought has been shared by a long line of scholars who argue that Emerson "brought to full consciousness . . . the antinomianism latent in the thought of his Puritan forebears."[63]

By the 1980s, however, a new generation of Emerson scholars began to challenge the idea that Emerson was either an antinomian or the leading proponent of radical individualism during the antebellum era. Lang, for example, argues that Emerson clearly recognized the radical tendencies in his own thought and deliberately transformed its potential for antinomianism into a "conservative idealism" that had a wide appeal among nineteenth-century Americans. Emerson's problem, Lang contends, was "to refine his theory of individualism to allow self-reliance, to encourage faith in human intuition and in the divinity of man, without thereby justifying lawlessness."[64] If this is true, how then did Emerson bring about a "conflation of individual and shared interests" that posited the existence of shared values and a sense of community dominated by a Universal Being?

First, Emerson looked to nature and found a "radical correspondence" in all things. There is "no fact in nature," Emerson declared, "which does not carry the whole sense of nature." In short, Emerson posited the existence of universal laws. Because there "is only one truth, all men move in the same direction, albeit by different paths." The "more exclusively idiosyncratic a man is," Emerson asserted, the more general, infinite, and representative he is. In Emersonian parlance, representative man, the true exemplar of individualism, is not an "individual, but a universal man." Therefore, "when a man says I think, I hope, I find,—he might properly say, the human race thinks, hopes, finds."[65]

How then does an individual become a representative man? By reflection, by looking inward, by engaging in what Emerson calls "self-trust," individuals will "receive truth from God without any medium." But truth will come "only to he who feels that he is nothing." At that moment, "all mean egotism vanishes. I become a transparent eyeball; I am nothing; I see all; the currents of the Universal Being circulate through me; I am part and particle of God." As Lang phrases it: "Ultimately, the transcendent self . . . is no self at all, but God."[66]

Emerson's version of self-reliance, self-trust, or individualism thus eliminated the dangers of, or even the possibility of, a "subversive assertion of self." Equally important, Emerson argued not only that a "higher law than that of our will regulates events" but that being in harmony with God and the universe required "a passive acceptance of the world and its conditions."[67] The elimination of evil, famine, war, and pestilence cannot be accomplished by human intervention. If evil exists, it is only because men have not yet reached a state of perfection that would automatically eliminate evil or disharmony from the universe. The "infinite potential" of men is infinite only in some men. Disharmony, therefore, is caused by "secondary men," who have the potential to achieve perfection, but who refuse to discover the Divinity that exists in every man. Thus, evil is transitory, and as individuals move inexorably toward a state of perfection, evil will automatically disappear. As Emerson exhorted his readers:

> Build, therefore, your own world. As fast as you conform your life to the pure idea in your mind, that will unfold its great proportions. A correspondent revolution in things will attend the influx of the spirit. So fast will disagreeable appearance, swine, spiders, snakes, pests, mad-houses, prisons, enemies, vanish. . . . The advancing spirit . . . shall draw beautiful faces, and warm hearts, and wise discourse, and heroic acts around its way, until evil is seen no more.[68]

Emerson was not so much a systematic thinker as he was a prophet—a romantic whose views, far from reflecting social reality, envisioned a utopian future once mankind had achieved perfection. If he was not blind to the realities of social injustice, his views provided no practical alternatives to an acceptance of the status quo. "The basis of political economy," Emerson said, "is noninterference."

> The only safe rule is found in the self-adjusting meter of demand and supply. Do not legislate. . . . Give no bounties, make equal laws, secure life and property, and you need not give alms. Open the door of opportunity to talent and virtue and they will not be in bad hands. In a free and just commonwealth, property rushes from the idle and the imbecile to the industrious, brave and persevering.[69]

At times, therefore, Emerson appeared to be perpetuating the myth of the self-made man. Channing, whose ideas played a formative, if not ultimately decisive, role in shaping Emerson's thought, was a far more perceptive social critic. "A society," Channing wrote:

> is improved in proportion as individuals judge for themselves, and from their own experiences and feeling, and not according to general opinion. . . . A Society is well organized, whose government recognizes the claims and rights of all . . . and aims to direct the pursuits of *each to the general good* . . . Liberty is the great social good,—exemption from unjust restraints,—freedom to act, to exert powers of usefulness. Does a government advance this simply by establishing

equal *laws?* The very protection of property may crush a large mass of the community, may give the rich a monopoly in land, may take from the poor all means of action. Liberty is a blessing only by setting man's powers at large, exciting, quickening them. A poor man, in the present state of society, may be a slave, by his entire dependence.[70]

It was Emerson, however, whose ideas more accurately reflected nineteenth-century American attitudes; fairly or not, when Spencerian and Darwinian ideas became influential later on, Emerson's idealism was ignored or forgotten, and his views on individualism were increasingly identified with laissez-faire principles.

If Emerson was not an uncompromising individualist, his friend and neighbor, Henry David Thoreau, most surely was. Thoreau, unlike Emerson, was not preoccupied with metaphysical abstractions that attempted to explain the nature of the cosmos, or with containing the "subversive potential" inherent in aspects of his own thought. Thoreau, rather, was a social critic who transformed the concept of self-reliance into a form of transcendental anarchism that resulted in a total rejection of organized society. Society, with its institutional demands and social arrangements, Thoreau concluded, led most men to "lead lives of quiet desperation."[71] The two years Thoreau spent living in a hut on Walden Pond, far from being a hermitlike existence characterized by alienation, was, in his view, a voyage of self-discovery based on reflection, solitude, and communion with nature. "It is very evident," Thoreau wrote,

what mean and sneaking lives many of you live . . . lying, flattering, voting, contracting yourselves into a nutshell of civility, or dilating into an atmosphere of thin and vaporous generosity, that you may persuade your neighbor to let you make his shoes, or his hat, or his coat, or his carriage, or import his groceries for him. A stereotyped but unconscious despair is concealed under what are called the games and amusements of mankind. There is no play in them, for this comes after work.[72]

Thoreau rejected organized associations of any kind. He attacked not only the idea of majority rule which, he stated, "cannot be based on justice," but the idea of government itself. "I heartily accept the motto," Thoreau declared,

"That government is best which governs least"; and I should like to see it acted upon more radically and systematically. Carried out, it finally amounts to this— which I also believe—'That government is best which governs not at all,' and when men are prepared for it, that will be the kind of government they will have."[73]

Thoreau, whose writings on civil disobedience, had an international impact—especially in the twentieth century—spent a day in jail in 1846 rather than pay a poll tax to support a government that recognized slavery. In the final analysis, Thoreau, who believed that questions of conscience transformed every individual into a "majority of one," was far closer in outlook to William Ellery Channing, who rejected submission to both God and society, than he was to Emerson. "If a man does not keep pace with his companions," he wrote, "perhaps it is because he hears a different drummer."[74]

American literature reached its most profound insights into the human condition in the novels of Nathaniel Hawthorne and Herman Melville. Injecting an element of tragedy in their writings, they rejected Emerson's cosmic optimism, Thoreau's version of radical individualism, and Channing's belief that man, not Divine Providence, was the center of the universe.

Melville, who had been a sailor, used the sea as a background for much of his work. In his novel *White Jacket* (1850), he exposed the brutality of life aboard American warships; and in *Omoo* (1847) and *Typee* (1846), he wrote about his life among cannibals in the South Pacific. But it was in *Moby Dick* (1851) that Melville created the greatest romantic hero in American fiction, Captain Ahab.

In one sense, Ahab's obsessive search for the great white whale symbolizes man's unsuccessful attempt to cope with the problem of evil in the universe. In another, Captain Ahab's fate at the hands of Moby Dick, whom he called "thou all-destroying but unconquering whale,"[75] can be viewed as an example of individualism gone mad. Ahab's self-reliance is transformed into monomania, the end result of which is not only the destruction of nearly everyone around him but spiritual anguish for Ahab. "This lovely light," Ahab says, "it lights not me. All loveliness is anguish to me, since I can ne'er enjoy. Gifted with high perception, I lack the low enjoying power; damned, most subtly and malignantly."[76] Little wonder then that Melville wrote to a friend in 1849: "I do not oscillate in Emerson's rainbow, but prefer to hang my self in mine own halter."[77] "To one who has weathered Cape Horn," he wrote in the margins of one of Emerson's essays, "what stuff all this is."[78] Emerson's "astounding errors and illusions," he concluded, "spring from a self-conceit so intensely intellectual and calm that at first one hesitates to call it by its right name."[79] Hawthorne said of Melville on one occasion: "He can neither believe, nor be comfortable in his unbelief."[80] Moreover, Hawthorne stated that Melville wrote him that he had "pretty much made up his mind to be annihilated," but "he does not seem to rest in that anticipation."[81]

Up to a point, major affinities exist in the work of Hawthorne and Melville. Hawthorne, like Melville, rejected Emerson's optimistic world of self-reliant individualism in which direct communication with God would lead to social harmony and human perfection. Melville liked what he called the "blackness" in Hawthorne's work, which emphasized the existence of sin and the permanence of evil in the universe.[82]

Hawthorne's novels, on one level, deal with persons caught in a struggle between individual values and the demands of society, a struggle which the individual generally loses. More importantly, Hawthorne's characters are alienated individuals who reject society's standards, but because they are fallible individuals prone to sin—especially the unpardonable sin of pride (or intellectual arrogance)—are destroyed or undone by their guilt or monomania. Dr. Rappacini, for example, employs science in an effort to make his daughter a superior being, but in the end he poisons her. In the *Scarlet Letter*, Arthur Dimmesdale's adultery with Hester Prynne goes undiscovered. Although Dimmesdale continues to serve as a minister and spiritual leader, his guilt, which he could not admit, led to spiritual estrangement and the ultimate disintegration of his personality. Hester's real sin was not adultery but pride—her refusal to bow to community standards. Hawthorne thus deals with the consequences of sin within the structure of society, and perhaps more importantly, within the conscience of the individual. Hawthorne was above all a moralist who argued that the subversive assertion of self leads only to spiritual anguish, alienation, and tragedy. Even so, Hawthorne's pessimism, unlike Melville's, was tempered by hope. Love and the "sanctity of the heart" were redeeming qualities which, Hawthorne contended, would "purify that inward sphere and the many shapes of evil that haunt the outward, and which now seem almost our only realities," [will] turn to "shadowy phantoms" and "vanish of their own accord."[83]

Hawthorne's social views, however, were far more conventional. Individuals, he said, were responsible for making their own way in the world. "The fault of a failure is attributable," he wrote, "in a great degree at least—to the man who fails. . . . Nobody has a right to live in the world unless he be strong and able, and applies his ability to good purpose."[84] Hawthorne, furthermore, was suspicious of reformers who attacked social ills. He shared Thoreau's hostility to all forms of association and agreed with Emerson that slavery would be destroyed—not by human effort, but by Divine Providence, in due time, and by means that could not then be predicted.

James Fenimore Cooper, like most other nineteenth-century writers, also tried to come to terms with the emergence of an individualistic ethos in American society. In *Home as Found*, Cooper deplored the leveling tendencies of democracy and criticized the crass materialism of self-made men. He disliked their acquisitive spirit and their relentless pursuit of self-interest, wealth, and status. In this novel, the central character, Aristobolous Bragg, was described as

a compound of shrewdness, impudence, common sense, pretension, humility, cleverness, vulgarity, kind-heartedness, duplicity, selfishness, law-honesty, moral-fraud, and mother wit, mixed up with a smattering of learning and much penetration in practical things.[85]

The Effinghams, by contrast, were idealized as members of the landed gentry, whose gentility and refinement made them natural leaders of society, and whose traditional role was gradually being usurped by acquisitive newcomers such as Bragg.

Cooper's reputation, however, was based primarily on his Leatherstocking tales, published between 1823 and 1841. In Leatherstocking, also known as Natty Bumppo, Hawkeye, and Deerslayer, Cooper created a romantic, mythical frontier hero who, on the surface, personified the triumph of self-reliant individualism over the encroachments of civilization and the demands of organized society. Although Cooper attributes the quality of "natural goodness" to Natty Bumppo, closer examination reveals a darker side to his character. In *The Deerslayer*, the last of the Leatherstocking novels, Natty rejected the love of Judith Hutter because "such love in and of itself would contaminate his freedom and independence."[86] Thus, Bumppo was a solitary individual (or, to use Georg Lukács's phrase, a "solitary, asocial" person) who could not relate to other human beings.[87] As a result, his individuality and freedom became perverted. Deerslayer, whom D. H. Lawrence referred to as a "saint with a gun,"[88] must kill in order to survive in the wilderness. Cooper's interpretation of the frontier experience, therefore, can be read not primarily in terms of innocence, natural goodness, and self-reliance, but isolation, alienation, and disintegration. Cooper's work invites comparison not to the cosmic optimism inherent in Emerson's work but to the darker vision found in the novels of Herman Melville and Nathaniel Hawthorne.

Up to this point, we have viewed the emergence of an individualistic ethos in American society from a variety of perspectives: the widespread acceptance of Enlightenment ideas, the advance of political democracy, the emergence of a market economy, the rise of a middle class, hostility to monopoly and special privilege, and equality of opportunity, which rewarded virtue and punished those who failed to prove their self-worth by achieving upward social mobility in a free society. As religion became increasingly democratized as the nineteenth century progressed, individuals no longer were viewed as sinners in the hands of an angry God, but as free moral agents responsible for achieving their own salvation. The decline of Hell, in fact, led not only to the democratization in religion, but, in some instances, to perfectionist visions that emerged from evangelical Protestantism, radical Unitarianism, and transcendentalism.

Perfectionism had radical implications, as evidenced by the beliefs of John Humphrey Noyes, William Ellery Channing, and the Garrisonian, or "ultra," wing of the abolitionist movement; it also had conservative overtones that justified the status quo, as exemplified by the thoughts of Charles Grandison Finney, Ralph Waldo Emerson, and, later on in the century, John Fiske and other Darwinian optimists. Even so, the celebration of individualism during the first six decades of the nineteenth century was hardly a universal phenomenon in American society. In our efforts to comprehend nineteenth-century American society, politics, and culture we can neither exaggerate its importance nor forget that its applicability had limits.

The ideals of equal opportunity and upward social mobility hardly applied to the great mass of wage earners and small farmers who lived on the subsistence level or at its edge. The fact that in 1850, 60 percent of the wealth was owned by 5 percent of the population illustrates the fact that in terms of social reality, if not aspiration, the American dream of self-reliant individualism applied not to the many but to the few. And even among those who succeeded, the uncertain movement of the invisible hand in the marketplace led inevitably to widespread anxiety and insecurity. Among the have-nots, aspiration, more often than not, was replaced by alienation. The novels of Melville and Hawthorne, the Leatherstocking tales of Cooper, and even the tales of horror and the macabre penned by Edgar Allan Poe not only called into question the cosmic optimism of Emerson and Walt Whitman (who once remarked that Emerson "brought me to a boil")[89] but anticipated the pessimistic vision of society and human nature that emerged as the dominant, if not universal, world view of writers and intellectuals in the late nineteenth century and throughout the twentieth century.

The fact remains, however, that no matter how we limit or qualify the importance or reality of an individualistic ethos in mid-nineteenth-century American society, individualism was the dominant ideology, containing elements of not only myth or aspiration, but reality. In short, perceptions of reality, accurate or not, if widely accepted and acted upon, are critically important parts of the historical landscape. Political, social, religious, and economic variants of individualism were inextricably related not only to each other but to the growth and development of a nationalist ideology in the North. The South, of course, rejected that ideology. In fact, proslavery apologists, in defending the South's peculiar institution, began to attack the concept of a free society itself. This, in turn, not only intensified sectional conflict during the 1840s and 1850s but helped pave the way, during a long and bloody civil war, for the crystallization and triumph of the political, economic, social, and religious principles on which the ideology of American individualism was based.[90]

Religion and Individualism in Early America

Robert M. Calhoon

INDIVIDUALISM—the personal and civic celebration of the potentiality, creativity, and psychic wholeness of the autonomous self—was a human invention and the product of historical experience. While the history of American individualism at full flood in the middle of the nineteenth century can be written from sources that are unambiguously individualist, the long transition from the seventeenth to the early nineteenth centuries, during which individualism crystallized and emerged from older notions of hierarchy and the subjection of the self to the demands of the existing order, must be documented from sources that are, at best, mixtures of individualism and social constraint. Protestant Christianity in early America provides a long stream of examples of individuals discovering and affirming, in fear and trembling, their personal selves within a culture skeptical of individual self-worth.

The transition from a preindividualist culture to an individualist ethos has been, and remains, a matter of controversy among at least three contending interpretations. The oldest—dating to conservative French theorists of the early nineteenth century and enjoying something of a revival in the writings of Allan Bloom and the Chicago school of political philosophy—regards individualism as a pathology of modern society.[1] The dominant interpretation among historians today considers individualism as a contest with, and in the American context a victory over, older traditions of communalism and hierarchy.[2] A third view treats individualism and social discipline as constant ingredients within American culture from the early seventeenth century through the present, attributing the impetus and the content of individualism to the very constraints that have bound individuals to society as well as those idiosyncratic qualities that set particular persons apart from the demands and expectations of others. "Industry and frugality have usually been thought of as aspects of a supposed American individualism," J. E. Crowley writes in his study of the work ethic in early America, "but in the colonial period they were thought of *simultaneously as social duties and as means for the preservation of autonomy.*" For this paradoxical reason, Crowley contends that individualism and social constraint have had a "dialectical" relationship of persistent interconnection throughout the whole of early American history rather than the "isomorphic" relationship usually assigned by historians who saw the latter inexorably giving way to the former.[3] In contrast with the widespread view that the colonial experience represented a largely successful movement toward "total self-realization," Jack P. Greene counters that "the mood of optimism and rhetoric of success [was] counter-balanced by, and existed in an uneasy state of tension with, a deep and probably growing sense of failure" to develop "any explicit or new sense of 'American' identity."[4] In Crowley's and Greene's view, individualism was the unexpected result of converging personal desires and societal needs.

None of these three interpretations—pathological abnormality, victory over communalism and hierarchy, or persistent tension between self and society—is devoid of usefulness or mutually exclusive. Employed in the study of American religious history, each has a high degree of utility. The view of individualism as a form of social deviance helps account for the millennial radicalism of the transcendentalists and the counterculture idealism of the 1960s—both of which considered the unfettered individual as a being at one with the cosmos. The emergence of the individual from the womb of the community coincided with the revivalism in which churches derived their vitality from reaching outward to sinners rather than repairing inward to nurture tradition. But the dialectical tension between unique persons and authentic collectivities—in which shared values nourished and sustained existential integrity—most fully illuminates American religious experience, with its theological inheritance of law and grace, its intense sharing of salvation and restless yearning to embrace unsaved multitudes.

When Christians consider with equal seriousness both personal consciousness and cosmic creation, they flirt with the heresy known as Pelagianism—the teaching that all of the knowledge and moral will necessary to make people good resides in their souls. Though repudiated and discredited by Pelagius's rival and contemporary, Saint Augustine, Pelagianism—like all the great heresies of the early church—remained influential and periodically emerged as a visible religious belief whenever Christians exhorted each other in God's name to strenuous moral effort and whenever the idiosyncratic qualities of human beings became regarded as having eternal significance.[5]

American individualism is a Pelagian concept. America was an environment where Pelagian desires and expectations coexisted fruitfully with traditional theological orthodoxy. The point of contact between Pelagian self-confidence and historic creeds was a kind of religious synapse—like a juncture in the nervous system—where highly charged stimuli generated by experience elicited a response from an existing structure of human energy and spirituality. By drawing on older concepts of human nature but interpreting them in radically new ways, religious individualism arose from the synapse connecting older and newer kinds of human learning and interaction. Religious discourse, with its capacity to articulate new meanings and reflect the structure of both tradition and experience, therefore provides concrete evidence of the birth of individualism.

Puritans deeply distrusted the individual, but because they devoted such effort and ingenuity to the task of lodging individuals securely within the community and the fellowship of the saints, they powerfully illuminated the tension between self and society during the seventeenth century. The earliest and most dramatic instance of American individualism dwelling in the vortex of the community was the case of Anne Hutchinson in the Massachusetts Bay Colony in 1636–38. Charged with "troubl[ing] the peace of this commonwealth" by "promoting and divulging the opinions that are the cause of this trouble," Mrs. Hutchinson faced banishment for spreading the doctrine that the strictures of moral law did not apply to those in a state of grace and that the preaching of morality to the Boston Puritans was heretical. In an experience of self-discovery—like that of nineteenth-century romantic individualist—she felt led by God, "after solemn humiliation and pondering on the thing," to know the truth, in this case, that ministers who preached both grace and obedience to God were

> the antichrist. . . . Since that time, I confess, I have been more choice, and he hath let me distinguish between the voice of my beloved and the voice of Moses, the voice of John the Baptist and the voice of antichrist. . . . Now if you condemn me for speaking what in my conscience I know to be truth, I must commit myself to the Lord.

Asked "How did you know it was the spirit [of God]?" she countered, "How did Abraham know it was God that bid him offer his son?" Deputy Governor Thomas Dudley interjected that Abraham heard "by an immediate voice."

> [Mrs. Hutchinson:] So to me by an immediate revelation.
> [Dudley:] How? An immediate revelation[?]
> [Mrs. Hutchinson:] By the voice of his own spirit to my soul.[6]

It was a spectacular exchange. The voice of God had directed her to Scriptures about both grace and evil. In an intriguing phrase, she said that God had made her "more choice," perhaps freer to make choices and to think for herself, but also literally more choice, more lovely in His sight, more deeply touched with the sublime. That kind of delicious freedom and heightened consciousness became a hallmark of strenuous individualism in the nineteenth century and made the term "antinomian" a synonym for radical personal ethicism.[7]

Instead of being regarded as the first American individualist, Anne Hutchinson should be viewed more as a participant in the controversy in the early Massachusetts Bay Colony over how ministers should characterize morality, piety, and spiritual inquiry. If they held that "works" were irrelevant in the life of a Calvinist church, they forfeited much of their own rule as interpreters of Scripture. But if they made adherence to their sermons and respect for their theological knowledge the exclusive core of Puritanism, they stifled the mystical ingredient in Puritanism and neglected the participation of the saints in the life of the covenant. Therefore, most Boston Puritan clergymen sought to reconcile these two positions by making good works a means of readying prospective saints for their encounter with the spirit of God. For Anne Hutchinson and her adversaries, Puritanism acknowledged the tension between personal faith and submission to the teachings of Christianity and stabilized it by making sainthood an identity that freed the believer from claims of corrupt human authority. Her role in the antinomian debate was to insist that works were not a part of that identity, that they prepared people for nothing at all and that God spoke directly to the unready in messages of unmistakable clarity.

It is plausible to argue that her rebellion was an early instance of individualism because she championed feminine equality in the face of overbearing male chauvinism. But it was not primarily her gender or her solitary audacity that made the antinomian movement a searing emotional and cultural wound in early Massachusetts—though her feminism and her personal courage magnified her impact. At the core of antinomianism were two conditions, one intellectual and the other social. First, non-Separatist Puritanism hinged on paradoxes of being in, but not of, the world. None of these paradoxes was more delicate than that between theology and mysticism as opposite poles of Puritan spirituality. By boldly making the mystical element of God's voice superior to all other modes of revelation, she caused her clerical adversaries to repair defensively to the larger and more complex structure of Puritan theology. Secondly, she mounted this challenge from within a fragile and vulnerable community that absorbed and utilized every bit of leadership and personal magnetism available to it, though at the cost of terrifying assaults on constituted authority. By granting women a more prominent role in the church, Carol F. Karlsen argues, Puritans opened the door, if only a crack, to equating femininity with the work of the Devil: "Anne Hutchinson's interpretation of Puritan doctrine allowed women a vastly enlarged sphere of religious activity. . . . The special vindictiveness with which she was treated stemmed from her appropriation—as a woman—of a central spiritual role in the community."[8]

The love of paradox built into American non-Separatist Puritanism, as well as the demands for simple consistency by champions of particular Puritan beliefs, created not only painful controversy; this configuration of paradoxical versus single-minded belief prompted individuals in both camps to articulate inner feelings and to vindicate the integrity of their own faiths:

> When I was on my bed in Monday morning the Lord let me see I was nothing else but a mass of sin and that all I did was very vile [Thomas Shepard recalled]. . . . The Lord suddenly appeared and let me see there was a strength in him to succor me, wisdom to guide, mercy in him to pity, spirit to quicken, Christ to satisfy, and so I saw all my good was there, as all evil was in myself . . . and so I become his, for him to take care for me and love me, and I to pitch my thought and heart on him.[9]

This passage moved with stunning directness from a sense of nothingness to one of wholeness and of great intellectual and emotional capacity. The writer did not celebrate his own autonomy, for he felt none, but his words did preserve the situation in which the self came to terms with itself.

Similarly, even the radical Puritan mystic Samuel Gorton found in his own spirituality a stable definition of who he was and the reason he had to reject orthodox Puritan teachings about when the incarnation of God in Christ began and how it continued. He held that Christ had been incarnated into Adam and into every subsequent believer. "Like many seventeenth century mystics," Philip F. Gura writes, Gorton

> argued for an essential divinity in all human beings, a divinity that was defined for him by the miracle of Christ's presence and that excluded any arbitrary distinctions . . . between saints and sinners. . . . If men understood the true meaning of God in Christ, they would discover the inherent divinity of all mankind, . . . "the eternal nearness of the divine spirit to the sinner and the saint."[10]

Radical, unorthodox spirituality, like orthodox Puritanism, induced a highly focused and potentially liberating sense of self. Puritans were not individualists, but in their appreciation of the problem of the self, they recognized earlier than any other group in colonial America the struggle of the self for autonomy.

Cotton Mather, the Puritan intellectual of the late seventeenth and early eighteenth centuries who sought to interpret and revitalize all that New England Congregationalists had done with their tradition, knew that personal self-consciousness was a natural by-product of Puritan spirituality as well as a source of moral vulnerability. In his biographical sketch of John Winthrop, founder of the Massachusetts Bay Colony, Mather sought to discern how a sovereign deity could bring to fruition personal piety and moral autonomy without unleashing the willfulness and selfishness of individual sinners. Mather called Winthrop "the American Nehemiah" and placed a strange twist on the adjective "American." Nehemiah's example as an Old Testament ruler was not one which Winthrop followed so much as one which Winthrop validated, made more vibrant and famous in the seventeenth century. Only Cotton Mather would have had the gall to congratulate an Old Testament figure for prefiguring the excellence of the founder of the Massachusetts Bay Colony. "The eschatological focus" in Mather's view of sacred history, Sacvan Bercovitch explains, "shifted from memory to anticipation, [as] the correspondence between the believer and the Bible narrative took on a radically changed significance. The *process* now, not the fact of fulfillment, demanded elucidation. The source of personal identity was not the Jesus of the gospels but the ongoing works of Christ leading towards the Messiah of the apocalypse"—the climax of history for which Mather wanted Puritan New England to prepare.[11]

Mather's grotesque centering of Christianity in a historical process that the early Puritan brought close to fulfillment was just the sort of bizarre, highly charged imaginative act needed to place the Puritan self to the forefront of American thinking in the early eighteenth century. In his description of Winthrop's son and namesake, Mather emphasized that John Winthrop, Jr.'s piety and public duty were etched in his individual character:

> He was a studious, humble patient, reserved, and mortified person, and one in whom the love of God was fervent, the love of man sincere: and he had herewithal a certain extension of soul which disposed him to generous behavior toward those who, by learning, dignity, and breeding, deserve respect, though of a perswasion and profession in religion different from his own.[12]

In resisting the temptations of fame, applause, and self-assertion, the younger Winthrop came to discover within himself personal qualities—"a certain extension of soul"—also present in other pious individuals and forming what Mitchell Robert Breitwieser calls "an underlying commonality" within a "divided, litigious" society.[13]

From the end of the second generation of settlement in every British American colony until the onset of the prerevolutionary controversy, the colonists' struggle for a sense of identity consisted of their efforts to deal with their own provincialism—their dependence on, yet remoteness from, cultural moorings in the British Isles. Two powerful evidences of that struggle and those difficulties were the forms of collective behavior known as revivalism and gentility. The outburst of religious experience known as the Great Awakening and the development of a code of behavior among better-educated and wealthier planters had much in common. Both were collective responses to cultural isolation and psychic apprehensions; as such, both patterns of behavior made individuals acutely conscious of their personal qualities and human vulnerability—their individuality.

If Cotton Mather had taken the single step of defining the individual in New England as Puritan character writ large in the lives of particular persons, Jonathan Edwards took the much larger step of defining the individual as the human vessel into which flowed the "divine influx or indwelling of the Holy Spirit."[14] Edwards's greatness as theologian and philosopher lay not in being a solitary intellectual giant who understood and accepted the terror of living in an impersonal universe (as depicted in 1949 in Perry Miller's biography) but in appreciating and radically extending the orthodox Christian and Calvinist view that, while the human *will* gave people relatively little perspective on their place in the universe, the *affections* could— once awakened—transform a person's sense of being and of possessing moral choice. Edwards accomplished this feat by borrowing selectively from John Locke examples of sensory religious learning and then denying Locke's larger claim that all learning is sensory, even religious inspiration.[15] By arguing that the majesty, wrath, and love of God can be transmitted through sensory data but are by no means limited to that medium, Edwards sought to account for the "influx" of the Spirit into the human psyche: "The Spirit of God . . . may indeed act upon the mind of a natural man, but he acts on the life of a saint [that is, one whose affections have been awakened by conversion] as an indwelling, vital principle." Edwards contended that "the mind" of an individual, once awakened to the operation of "holiness" in the universe, "becomes susceptable of the due force of rational arguments" so that a new spiritual sense expels those "prejudices that are in the heart against the truth of divine things."[16]

Seeking to encapsulate the spiritual needs of all humankind within a system of precise theological and spacious philosophical suppositions, Edwards emphasized the autonomy and the irresistibility of the Holy Spirit as a "sense" moving directly into the "frame," "habits," "inclinations," and "propensities" of individuals—giving them personal citizenship in the spiritual universe.[17] Evangelical revivalism fostered individualism to the precise extent that it created this new vocabulary describing the spiritual human qualities that conversion and ecstasy redeemed and were, therefore, unique and precious in the eyes of the Savior.

If Puritanism and revivalism in New England produced the most penetrating insights into the nature of the self, the Chesapeake planters of colonial Virginia also struggled to convert the personal qualities of individuals into stable, dependable social material. In contrast with Puritans who made a high degree of tolerance for dissonance between the world and the spirit into a kind of moral psychological armor, Chesapeake Anglicans found that a low tolerance for such disturbing ambiguity was a useful early warning that hierarchy and order were under attack. Averse to manifestations of individualism, the Chesapeake gentry prescribed how greater and lesser planters, yeoman farmers, slaves, and free blacks ought to behave. Whether conforming to those standards or reacting against them, colonial Virginians became increasingly conscious of their own desires, needs, aspirations, and capabilities in ways which constantly disturbed the collective tranquility of planter society.

Virginia was a stratified society of aristocratic gentry, lesser planters, and indentured servants. Each group had come to the region out of stark economic and social necessity, the aristocracy to reap enough wealth from growing tobacco to return to England in style and rescue distressed aristocratic families, planters in search of a better economic foothold, and servants to escape the swift death of the executioner or the lingering death of imprisonment and poverty. The passage of time during the seventeenth century did little to soften the antagonisms these groups felt for one another. When a planter named Bartholomew Owens of Surrey County called his social superior, militia captain George Jordan, "a Raskell and Rogue and short Arsed Raskell" and threatened to "kick that short arse," he ran grave risk of prosecution and a heavy fine. But he also articulated who he believed himself to be in the only terms available. Likewise when William Spring replied to a summons that he meet a creditor, Colonel Thomas Swaim, he offered this assessment of his own character and of his adversary's motives:

> "I will meete him at Court, and shall not be afraid to speake to him for he but a man . . . and soe I will tell the Court before his face. . . . " Spring furder said (his Anger flameing) [the court bailiff recorded] that he, the said Spring, knew "what the Colonel aimed at; it is my Cattle (said he) to be bound over."[18]

The Anglican church in Virginia may not have enjoyed the intellectual preeminence of the Congregational churches in New England, but Anglicanism voiced, clarified, and sharpened the insights into human nature and behavior available to the planter elite. Like Puritans, Anglicans preached that the willful human psyche wreaked havoc on society at large, and in a circular fashion, they went on to suggest that individuals, scarred by their own misdeeds, could innoculate themselves against symptoms of their own depravity:

> The life of every sincere Christian is a warfare against a great number of enemies, some of them very potent and others very politick [explained Thomas Cradock of Maryland]. Virtue is a rich prey rescued narrowly out of the fire with the purchase of labor and sweat of care and vigilance. We are too liable to loose [lose] it by our own sloth and treachery. . . . Our own inclinations are the seeds of most vices and lay the first stone of hell within us.[19]

The popular English behavior manuals, widely read by the gentry, *Advice to a Son: Precepts of Lord Burghley, Sir Walter Raleigh, and Francis Osborne* and Henry Peacham's *The Compleat Gentleman,* advocated a set of values thoroughly imbued with Anglican notions of decorum. According to one historian, the behavior manuals set forth an elaborate program for individuals seeking civilized autonomy:

> (1) intense piety; (2) emphasis on material success; (3) desire to acquire a landed estate and establish a family; (4) devotion to hard work; (5) distaste for form without substance; (6) respect for learning, albeit learning that resulted in profit as well as pleasure; (7) pragmatic conception of history and the arts; (8) distrust of human nature; (9) balance and moderation as a means to curb the "rank and unruly passions" of men; (10) respect for law; (11) the quest for honor and dignity.[20]

Only through this kind of socialization and calculation, guided by "God almighty . . . to prepare myself for his service and for eternall beatitude hereafter," did William Fitzhugh believe he could safely indulge his ambition and appetites. "Better never be born, than ill bred," he cautioned himself.[21]

Avoiding being "ill bred"—being a refined, self-sufficient, morally accountable gentleman—was a muted but authentic individualism of personal volition held in tension by inhibitions against self-assertion. By the middle of the eighteenth century, that blend of inhibitions and autonomy fused into the concept of the "gentleman." "The quality which most nearly epitomized what was needed to make a gentleman," Rhys Isaac explains,

> was "liberality," . . . freedom from material necessity, . . . from . . . servile subjection, . . . from sordid subordination of . . . honor and dignity to calculations of interest, . . . freedom to elevate the mind by application to the authoritative books that contained the . . . "liberal arts." . . . In the eighteenth century world a man had to be either a master or a servant. . . . The means that secured independence to the gentleman fixed the dependence of other upon him.[22]

Anglicanism taught that this hierarchy was prescribed by God, that independence was a gift of the Creator, and that power held over social inferiors was a moral trusteeship.

Evangelical preachers who ministered to poorer whites and to blacks on the fringes of plantation society rejected this entire notion that God was implicated in the social hierarchies of this world. By positing a direct relationship between God and each recipient of Christian grace, Evangelicals created a powerful spiritual individualism; yet, respectful as they were of the sinful nature of individuals, they sought to encapsulate the heightened self-consciousness of individuals within a community of believers that constrained individualism even more thoroughly than the social inhibitions of the aristocracy. Evangelicals constructed their new religious world out of experiences and qualities of their individual selves.

Evangelicals placed themselves at the synapse between Pelagian creativity and pious submission to orthodoxy. They believed that their own identification with, and sharing of, the emotional upheaval of other converts instilled into themselves a keener appreciation of theological orthodoxy; and conversely, they drew from their participation in the common life of the Spirit a confidence in their own ability to remake the social world in ways which were redemptive for themselves and others. "For about a year and a half past I have had more success with the poor Negroes," wrote Samuel Davies in Virginia in 1757. "I have baptized in all 150 adults and at the last sacramental occasion I had the honor (for so I esteem it) of sitting down at the table of the Lord with about 60 of them." The key to this success had been Davies's surprising ability at teaching slaves to read. "Multitudes of them are eager to learn to read, . . . some from a pious thirst after Christian knowledge, some from curiosity, and some from ambition." This division of the first black Christian community in Virginia into the pious, the curious, and the ambitious surveyed and identified the conditions of the human psyche in need of, and prepared for, internalization of the message of salvation.

Slaves brought to Davies's services presuppositions he had never before encountered. They exhibited "high notions of the efficacy of baptism" so that as soon as they realized what it meant to be in "a state of heathenism" they desired baptism as an immediate purifying act of cleansing without grasping "the necessity of proper preparative qualifications for it." This restless, questing state of mind fascinated and perplexed Davies. "Many of them only seem to have a desire to be," he groped for words, "they know not what." He tried to penetrate this murky insight and found an ominous implication. Some slaves considered baptism a lighthearted communal rite; others saw it as a means to "be put upon an equality with their masters." "Many" confessed such a motivation to Davies so that "I am obliged to

exclude them from that ordinance." Davies's discomfiture at black spontaneity and presumption and his refusal to baptize the irrepressible sounds
very much like an exercise in social control—an early instance of the conservative white mission to the slaves, which taught respect for the authority
of the master and divine sanction of master-slave relationships. There is certainly a tincture of paternalism in Davies's strictures about black misunder-
standing of the sacrament.[23]

For several reasons, however, it is a mistake to depict Davies and other
Evangelicals in the colonial South as being either fearful white males trying
to exert social control on restive racial and social underlings or as unwitting
subversives undercutting the status quo by affirming black spiritual autonomy. First, as Mechal Sobel argues in a major new study of transracial cultural interaction, Davies was as much controlled by the reactions of his
black parishioners as they were by his ministerial authority. Sobel has found
scores of examples of this kind in which blacks assumed and maintained in
dealings with whites, including masters, an authoritative stance as interpreters of death and dying, of spirituality, and of the meaning of suffering.[24]

Second, Evangelicals who encountered slaves in the eighteenth century
condemned recognized evils emanating from slavery, but they did not anticipate, as would later abolitionists, that the issue of slavery itself was the
supreme moral problem. Their fixation with the spiritual consciousness—
what they would call the spiritual "condition"—of masters and slaves, and
the bondage of both types of individuals to sin, dominated their experience.
Proslavery Christianity in the 1850s would spin this concern into a cliché
and timeserving rationalization, but in the 1750s, the distinction between
personal liberty and spiritual freedom was an authentic judgment on slavery.
George Whitefield's famous South Carolina converts, Hugh and Jonathan
Bryan, talked in 1741 to their own slaves about the imminence of God's
judgment and discovered to their amazement that blacks knew a great deal
more about this subject. Hugh Bryan accordingly broadcast the news that a
second coming or some other divine assault on white privilege and ease,
such as a slave uprising, might well be imminent in South Carolina. Chas-
tened by the vitriolic reaction of their contemporaries to this warning, the
Bryans apologized and retreated to their plantation where over the next decade they built a community in which both races appeared to share equally
in dignity, rewards, and responsibility. Freeing his slaves did not occur to
Hugh Bryan, and yet his treatment of them as religious and social equals—
albeit done quietly so not as to upset neighboring plantations—was thoroughly libertarian.[25]

The modern concept of social control did not occur to such eighteenth-
century Anglo-Americans, finally, because—as Gordon S. Wood argues—
they lived in a culture that did not conceive of society as an entity

consisting of interests, linkages, institutions, and norms. They knew only of the personal moral qualities of individuals or of broad categories like the virtuous many, the powerful few, the deluded crowd, those with the Spirit, or those without it. They could thus recognize personal duplicity or straightforwardness, secretive plotting or public civic responsibility, malignity or social integrity. "Cause and effect," in such a world, Wood writes, "were so intimately related that they necessarily shared the same moral qualities."[26] To understand social control—in any conscious way to contribute toward or to undermine it—required assumptions that premodern people would not have understood. Individuals as discrete psychological entities did not yet exist. Experiencing conversion and witnessing it in others did, however, loosen the bond between cause and effect and complicated the moral qualities of actions like preaching and hearing the Christian message.

Davies's solution to the personal autonomy and resourcefulness of slave converts was to make "their temper and conduct, rather than their speculative notions, the standard of my judgment concerning them. . . . A number of them . . . I have not the least doubt are genuine children of Abraham by faith; some of them seem to have made a greater progress in experimental religion than many sincere Christians of a fairer complexion."[27] Davies's term "experimental religion" went to the heart of the meaning of Evangelicalism as proclamation of the central and paramount role of the individual in the drama of salvation. The experiment was the hearing of the message of salvation by individuals, their personal application of that message to their flawed lives, and the opening of the emotional windows of each private personality to the inward flow of assurance and grace.

Try as he might in his sermon on *The Duty of Christians to Propagate their Religion among the Heathen* (1758) to return to a conventional paternalistic view of slavery, Davies could not escape the haunting images of the personal uniqueness of slaves in penetance and conversion. When they first "see their sins" and "their hearts are broken with penetential sorrows," a miracle occurs within their character; "their lives" stood as convincing evidence that conversion truly transformed the convert.[28] Appreciation of the depth and authenticity of black discipleship and frank criticism of planter indifference to the slaves' human condition represented a presumptuous reconsideration of the location of moral authority. "Mr. Davies hath much reproached Virginia," complained one planter. "And [he] informs the Negroes that they are [numerically] stronger than the whites." Davies had said nothing of the kind, nor had he "sent" the published sermon "among our Negroes." But his celebration of black Evangelicalism and his blunt words to slave owners about "your stupid carelessness about religion" struck a nerve.[29] Even in the hand of cautious Presbyterians like Davies, Evangelicalism had a subversive underside. His outrage at planter indifference to their slaves' spiritual needs moved Davies from conventional views about obedience to masters to a more ambivalent sensitivity about his responsibilities in a biracial society:

> It was a time of unusual anxiety to me [he said after one service]; I hardly ever felt so much of a pastoral heart, I mean affection and concern for my flock, and yet I had not a proportionate liberty to vent it. However, I hope it was a refreshing time to some hungry souls. I had the pleasure of seeing the table of the Lord adorned with about 44 black faces. . . . In the land of their slavery, they have been brought into the glorious liberty of the sons of God. But alas! notwithstanding these promising appearances, an incorrigible stupidity generally prevails thro' this guilty land.[30]

As his perception of Virginia as a "guilty land" crystallized, Davies came to see himself and his contemporaries of both races as moral individuals—their individuality forged in the ordeal of a society that sanctioned both slavery and Christianity.

As a Pelagian popularization of Protestant Christianity, Evangelicalism blurred technical issues of redemption and grace while exciting people to think about abstract questions of good and evil, human destiny, and the nature of the Deity. Thus Evangelicalism made Christianity accessible to individuals and invented new forms of religious communication that focused on individual behavior, thought, and cultural preference. George Whitefield's enormous contribution to this process was a new form of preaching that confronted sinners, slave owners among them, with a searing candor they had never before encountered: "Your dogs are caressed and fondled at your tables, but your slaves, who are frequently stiled dogs or beasts, have not equal privileges."[31] As James D. Essig observes, Whitefield's "abrasive criticism of the slaveowning class" undercut, more than the great itinerant realized, his tolerance toward slavery as an institution.[32] The Anglican commissary in South Carolina, Alexander Garden, saw at once this tendency in Whitefield's rhetoric. The very idea of linking divine wrath to a particular social arrangement, Garden fumed, smacked of blasphemy. "What is it you had in mind to inform them [i.e., the slave owners]? . . . You THINK God has a quarrell with them. Had God sent you, charged with this special *Message*, you might well say that you must inform them of it; but as 'tis only a matter of your *thoughts*, the necessity of it does not so well appear." The issue here was more than a forensic point turning on Whitefield's moral authority.

Whitefield's Calvinist sense that sin was collective as well as individual revealed to Garden how radical and irresponsible the itinerant was, and Whitefield's pleas for evangelization of the slaves further exposed to

Garden a dangerous presumption. Of course, the commissary admitted to Whitefield, Christianity could benefit the slaves by making them meek and tractable. But, Garden astutely noted, Whitefield inserted into that plea phrases that were deeply troubling and—though this was not Garden's concern—surprisingly Arminian: "Christianizing" blacks; "mak[ing them] *thorough Christians*"; and "*the gospel* [to slaves] *preached with power.*" For Garden, these words implied that human beings could appropriate for themselves the "power" to convert, to indict the sinful, to forgive, to proclaim salvation—all functions that only the Holy Spirit could perform. "Men may teach true *Christianity,* but no man can make a true *Christian.*"[33] That was precisely what Whitefield believed men, invoking the power of the Spirit and the love of Christ, could do, what revivalism was all about.

Davies's and Whitefield's Anglican critics realized that Evangelicalism had charged old concepts of the self with new energy and direction. The fiesty Anglican itinerant on the South Carolina frontier, Charles Woodmason, showed discernment as well as contempt when he complained of backcountry Baptist services: "Another vile matter . . . is what they call their *experiences*. It seems that before a person can be dipp'd, he must give an account of his secret calls, conviction, conversion, repentance, & c & c."[34] Those stages were exactly the ones Evangelicals considered necessary for coming to terms with God. An account of the conversion of Richard Furman, in the very part of South Carolina visited by Woodmason, had the same structure:

> The justice, spirituality, universal extent & application of the divine law were displayed to his view, with his inability as a sinner to fulfill its requisitions or make satisfaction for its violation. The inevitable ruin involved in this condition filled him with apprehension of instant destruction, & he regarded the lightning as the messinger of vengeance. Penetrated with these feelings he was prepared for a discovery of the free grace & mercy of God in the gospel, & was led by the spirit of truth to embrace the righteousness & salvation of the redeemer.[35]

The operative verbs were "displayed," "filled," "penetrated," and "embraced." The system of Christian theology was *displayed* to him; its implications *filled* his consciousness; its essentials then *penetrated* his personality; he was thereby enabled to *embrace* salvation—ecstatic with the redeemer. Woodmason's four stages of evangelical experiences dovetailed with Furman's levels of spiritual perception: secret calls displayed, conviction filled, conversion penetrated, and repentance embraced.

In place of external decorum and respect for one's superiors, Evangelicals built a new set of restraints on human emotionality and spontaneity, not an external system of social control but checkpoints at each stage of the conversion and sanctification process that involved individuals in conversation with fellow converts. This new structure of discipline gave individuals perspective on the myriad of feelings that washed across their consciousness, and it allowed each individual to plunge into the sublime knowing that each kind of ecstasy was but one level of an orderly, intelligible spiritual universe. "Can I feel my soul in sacred raptures, burning with love of God and of Christ, and [have] all my best passions alive?" asked Josiah Smith, Whitefield's chief defender in Charlestown, rhetorically. "Can I feel the secret pleasure in the word, ordinances, and communion of God? Can I taste all the powers of the world to come? Can I groan under the burthen of my corruptions or exult in the liberty of spirit?" Smith, like other Evangelicals, could ask these questions because he had experienced secret raptures and groaning mortification, which were the poles of evangelical individualism.[36]

Benjamin Franklin, who depicted himself in his autobiography as the inventor and embodiment of secular individualism in America, knew and liked George Whitefield and admired the Evangelist's ability to affect the personal consciousness of thousands of individual listeners to his open-air sermons in Philadelphia and Boston in the late 1730s. Franklin carefully distanced himself from Whitefield's views on conversion and human guilt, and deliberately embraced the deistic, Enlightenment view that God was a benevolent yet detached architect of the universe.[37] Franklin's own success as printer, inventor, politician, and philosopher convinced him that a kind of principled opportunism—in which egocentric individuals employed rational methods to secure public approval and personal advancement—was in itself a learning experience that civilized those who internalized it and that inculcated virtue into the community. The stronger and more potent one's individualism, Franklin concluded, the more fully personal desires and ambitions had to be enfolded in and contained within what one critic calls Franklin's "strategy of humility":

> Would you win the hearts of others, you must not seem to vie with but admire them; give them every opportunity of displaying their own qualifications, and when you have indulged their vanity they will praise you too in turn and prefer you above others in order to secure to themselves the pleasure your commendation gives.[38]

All the while, however, Franklin's skeptical habits of mind, his despair at human folly and viciousness, and his periodic fascination with religious ideas undercut his optimism and his advocacy of reason and moderation as keys to the happiness of individuals. This darker side of Franklin enhanced

his stature as a prophetic figure in American culture. His optimism anticipated an individualism of self-reliance and personal advancement; his
flirtation with despair prefigured the anguished individualism of pessimistic
romanticism.[39] Where he joined the two perspectives, especially in his spec-
ulations about religion and about moral philosophy, he produced a view of
truth and morality in individuals that J. A. Leo Lemay calls "almost Melvil-
lean in its grasp of different orders and structures of reality."[40]

Franklin's troubled spiritual speculation was not conventional religious
belief, but it was a psychological anchor for his rationalism and optimism
and one of the connecting links between his individualism and conformity to
the expectations of others. In 1728, he composed for his own use a worship
service that departed sharply from the mechanistic and predictable treatment
of man in the cosmos that had informed his *Dissertation on Liberty and
Necessity, Pleasure and Pain* (1725). "When I stretch my imagination thro'
and beyond our system of planets," his liturgy reflected, "then this little
ball on which we move seems even in my narrow imagination to be almost
nothing and myself less than nothing and of no sort of consequences." Elizabeth E. Dunn argues that here Franklin's religious sense of himself as a
created being took on a new form in which "Franklin now saw in the design
of the universe not deterministic purposefulness initiated by an omniscient
God but a vast and intricate network whose ultimate purposes remained obscure and unknown."[41] Later in his service, Franklin included a passage
from Joseph Addison's *Cato: A Tragedy* in which Cato, on the verge of
suicide, despaired of finding either meaning or virtue amid the "shadows,
clouds, and darkness" of the world. Franklin's remedy for such psychic
rootlessness was to speculate that an inscrutable deity must have created
subordinate gods, one for each solar system, which humans could aspire to
comprehend and to whom they could pray. The whole idea, Dunn suggests,
may have been Franklinesque irony and comedy employed "to undercut the
most widely accepted beliefs, values, and institutions of his day,"[42] but this
unusual religious notion expressed the inadequacy of all remedies against
despair as well as it mocked all traditional Christian orthodoxy. Anger, and
an angry wit, as well as skepticism lurked just out of sight in Franklin's
adept, opportunistic individualism.

In calmer moments, Franklin considered how individuals could teach
themselves how to live moral lives in a baffling universe. Drawing from
his extensive reading in British associationalist ethics, especially George
Turnbull's *The Principles of Moral Philosophy* (1740), Franklin concluded
that neither benevolent nor vicious qualities were innately human but were
acquired by gradual practice, "reiterating small acts" of kindness or generosity until they became ingrained into one's character or allowing repeated
actions of aggression toward others to grow into a "habit of viciousness."

"If Franklin was original in his ethical program," Norman Fiering concludes, "it was in his [unorthodox] proposal to break down the virtues into relatively small units of behavior"[43] in order to simplify the task of habituating himself to their practice. For example:

1. TEMPERANCE.
Eat not to Dulness. Drink not to Elevation.
2. SILENCE.
Speak not but what may benefit others or your self.
Avoiding trifling Conversation. . . .
6. INDUSTRY.
Lose no time. Be always employ'd in something useful.
Cut off all unnecessary Actions. . . .
11. TRANQUILITY.
Be not disturbed at Trifles, or at Accidents common
or unavoidable. . . .
13. HUMILITY.
Imitate Jesus and Socrates.[44]

Franklin's enumerated list of virtues drew on familiar sources in Western culture; his accompanying instructions for inculcating those virtues were designed to convert the common guidance of the culture into personal moral experience. Franklin here came closer than any American before Emerson to defining individualism and affirming its reality.

The Revolution and creation of the Republic tightened further the tension between the collective identity of the American people and the sense of personal autonomy that citizenship in a republic imparted to individuals. Republicanism both instilled a sense of civic comradeship and assigned to individuals critical roles in either purifying or corrupting the defense of liberty. Historians continue to puzzle over the paradox. Some argue that republicanism, with its roots in Roman and Renaissance ideas, fostered the communal side of revolutionary ideology, and so-called liberalism—ideas from Calvinist and Lockean sources on the sinfulness of each individual and the possibility of a social covenant among sinful individuals—upheld the individualist values of the Revolution. Such a distinction characterizes republicanism as overtly pessimistic in its belief that liberty and virtue were always in danger of extinction, but as subtly optimistic in believing that fraternal action could rescue those values in the eleventh hour. By the same reasoning, liberalism was overtly optimistic in conceiving of the compact as giving individuals a sense of security and subtly pessimistic in viewing all individuals and institutions as inherently flawed.[45]

Recognizing that republicanism and liberalism both existed and interacted in the Revolution, historians now increasingly ask how this interaction occurred and what consequences it produced. Republicanism and liberalism appealed to both religious Evangelicals and religious rationalists. Benjamin Rush and Thomas Jefferson respectively exemplified the evangelical and rationalist blending of these ideologies, and both men did so in order to enhance the social autonomy and political responsibility of the individual. For both men, the critical test of a free society was its ability to perpetuate its values through the education of individuals.

Rush believed that evangelical Christianity was a natural reinforcement of republicanism and the only means of containing "the irregular and compulsive impulses of the human heart" that weaned individuals away from devotion to the common weal. The cause of liberty could have lasting meaning, he warned, only if it was a prelude to "the *salvation of all mankind.*"

> Republican forms of government are the best repositories of the Gospel: I therefore suppose they are intended as preludes to a glorious manifestation of its power and influence upon the hearts of men. The language of these free and equal governments seems to be like that of John the Baptist of old, "Prepare ye the way of the Lord—make his paths strait."

If Christian discipleship was, in Rush's thinking, an antidote to the individualism of egocentric desires flying off in all directions, then infusing civic virtue with the "power" of "the gospel" would, he predicted, create a disciplined, sustainable experiment in republican government. Personal service to the community—especially moral leadership inspired by worship—would fill individuals with premonitions of immortality and assure them of fame beyond the grave. Rush told Elhanan Winchester, author of a funeral sermon about John Wesley and a volume on prophesy that Rush admired,

> How delightful to a good man should be the thoughts of surviving himself. Your works however much neglected or opposed now will be precious to those generations which are to follow us. . . . The persons who are to exist a hundred years hence are as much our fellow creatures as . . . are our contemporaries. It only requires more grace to love them than the persons whom we see . . . every day; but in proportion as we attain to this supreme act of love, we approach nearer the source of all love.

Individualism in a republic was for Rush that kind of ardent service of fellow souls yet unborn.[46]

Christianity in a republic appealed to Rush, not only as a way of fixing ambition on the spiritual well-being of others but also as the only reliable way of deepening personal consciousness and effecting a reformation of the deepest roots of behavior. By fusing republican notions about equality and virtue to Christian habits of introspection and humility, Rush developed a theory about education and discipline. "Solitude," he insisted, was the only appropriate form of discipline in a republic:

> Too much cannot be said in favor of SOLITUDE as a means of reformation, which should be the *only* end of *all* punishment. Men are wicked only from not *thinking*. O! that they would *consider,* is the language of inspiration. A wheelbarrow, a whipping post, nay even a gibbet, are all light punishments compared with letting a man's conscience loose upon him in solitude. Company, conversation, and even business are the opiates of the Spirit of God in the human heart. For this reason, a bad man should be left for some time without anything to employ his hands in his confinement. Every *thought* should recoil wholly upon *himself.*[47]

The process by which solitude turned an individual "wholly upon himself" was for Rush the essence of pious individualism.

Solitude was a shimmering republican concept—the inverse of civic virtue, it was the state of moral withdrawal from civic life for the refurbishing of personal virtue. Evangelical conversion and discipleship, with its stress on living in but not of the world, heightened the potency of solitude and weakened the authority of learned ministers and systems of theology. After hearing a Calvinist sermon on predestination, Samuel Crane in New York in 1812 returned to the privacy of his home and "meditating on what he had heard . . . became so vexed with himself on account of his dullness of apprehension that he suddenly stopped and commenced pounding his head with his fist for he really thought his stupidity must be owing to his having an uncommonly thick skull." Only after being converted by a Methodist itinerant, Tobias Spicer, did he hear "for the first time a doctrine I could understand, . . . a system that seemed to harmonize with itself, with the Scriptures, with common sense, and with experience."[48]

Rush's piety disturbed Thomas Jefferson and tested their quarter-century political and intellectual friendship. Urging Jefferson in 1800 to read William Paley's *Evidences of Christianity* and to commit to paper his personal religious creed, Rush reiterated his old conviction that "I have always considered Christianity as the *strong ground* of republicanism. . . . It is only necessary for republicanism to ally itself to the Christian religion to overturn all the corrupted political and religious institutions in the world."[49] Jefferson parried that "I have a view of the subject which ought to displease neither the rational Christian or Deist." Jefferson went on to complain bitterly to Rush that Federalist partisans had so slandered him for his alleged lack of religious orthodoxy that no amount of calm explanation of his religious views could win a fair hearing. In the midst of this uncharacteristically passionate letter on the subject of religion, Jefferson blurted out the now-immortal declaration that "I have sworn upon the altar of god eternal hostility against every form of tyranny over the mind of man." That Enlightenment credo encapsulated Jefferson's sense of belonging to the human race and having some responsibility for the liberty of others ("eternal hostility") and consciousness of his unique experience as one who had personally "sworn eternal hostility upon the altar." Like Puritans sharing the covenant, Anglicans prizing propriety, Evangelicals experiencing ecstasy, Franklin and his protégés seizing the main chance, republicans defending liberty, Jefferson's religion and his individualism existed within—and acquired concrete definition from—powerful communal, consensual bonds linking him to others.

Even the philosophical, rationalist Jefferson found religion an indispensable vehicle for thinking about individuals. Although most Americans did not embrace deism, Jefferson's deistically oriented individualism had a powerful impact on nineteenth-century American culture—an impact equal to Franklin's, which it complemented, and to Emerson's, of which it was a precursor.[50] Jefferson's fame, eloquence, and towering political stature help account for the popularity of his view that the pursuit of happiness, the love of liberty, and the harmony between nature and human personality were what made life at once delicious and painfully euphoric for individuals. But even more important than the play of his mind on the potential and sensibility of the individual was his conviction that individualism was a religious concept, inseparable from "nature and nature's God." "Fix reason firmly in her seat and call to her tribunal every fact, every opinion," Jefferson advised his nephew, Peter Carr. "Question with boldness even the existence of a god; because, if there be one, he must more approve the homage of reason than that of blindfolded fear."[51] That admonition explained how the energies of rational, moral individuals should enter the life of the nation and bring those people into harmony with the cosmos.

Jefferson's public career was filled with projects to make that kind of intellectual candor and honesty attractive and feasible to other citizens: his proposals for a public school system in Virginia, his condemnation in *Notes on Virginia* of the morally debasing effects of slavery on whites, his design for the University of Virginia, and his hope that western land would become the setting for an agrarian democracy of yeoman farmers. One such project, in which he invested great expectation, was the encouragement he extended to Joseph Priestley—the radical English scientist, religious Unitarian, and emigrant to America—to write and publish a demythologized version of Christianity along the lines of Priestley's pamphlet, *Socrates and Jesus*

Compared (1803). As encouragement, he composed the outline of his own beliefs, which Rush had requested of him in 1800. The closing lines of that outline, "Syllabus of an Estimate of the merit of the doctrines of Jesus, compared with those of others," firmly lodged the individual in the company of all humanity and with equal emphasis identified the element of divinity within each individual:

> He [Jesus] taught emphatically the doctrine of a future state . . . as an important incentive supplementary to the other motives to moral conduct. . . . He pushed his scrutinies into the heart of man; erected his tribunal in the region of his thoughts, and purified the waters at the fountain head.[52]

As Jefferson contemplated the autonomous individual, he made the individual named Jesus a link between Enlightenment rationalism and romantic naturalism. The ethical "tribunal" over which God presided was situated in the "thoughts" of men, and the pure water of moral truth flowed from the Creator into the civic life of the human mind.

From the Puritans and Virginia cavaliers of the early seventeenth century to the revivalists and rationalists of the early nineteenth century, Americans employed religious teachings as a way of searching for, defining, and domesticating the elusive energy within individuals. The inability of any particular Protestant church or denomination to impose itself on American society produced the pluralism and pervasive Protestantism of the new nation. That pluralistic, moralist climate, in turn, allowed any single belief shared across the spectrum of American religious experience to assume special potency and influence. The free choice and moral responsibility of individuals, which emerged in the early nineteenth century, was an idea that skeptical rationalists and devout revivalists alike could affirm. Steven Watts correctly identified this discovery:

> The notion of "moral free-agency" defined both the thrust and the difficulty . . . of culture and character in early nineteenth-century America. In an atmosphere conducive to ambition and pursuit of the main chance, the individual was taking shape as the conceptual building-block of society. . . . The solitary citizen, many Americans became convinced, had to take responsibility for his own actions and destiny.[53]

That assignment of responsibility and redefinition of consciousness was a fateful point in American history. It came at a time when theology, in decline since Edwards's death, was being replaced by practical, adaptable civic-religious disciplines such as secularized Calvinism and Scottish moral philosophy.[54] Moreover, the advent of nineteenth-century American individualism built on two centuries of experimentation with safe, permissible, salutary forms of ego penetration into the collective life of the community—much of it sanctioned by churches or justified by appeal to religious beliefs. Patricia U. Bonomi calls this process "latitudinarian"—the smoothing off of troublesome theological distinctions and the positioning of churches to become during the nineteenth century both advocates of reform and proponents of business enterprise.[55] Latitudinarian religion triumphed in America because it sustained traditional beliefs without restricting the voluntarist and individualist desires of Americans of European descent.

Individualism in
the Early Republic

Robert E. Shalhope

THE images or perceptions of the individual and individualism that prevailed in late-eighteenth-century America emerged from a dialectical tension between competing views of social and political authority. These conflicting world views—one hierarchical and the other localistic— pitted gentlemen anxious to Anglicize American society against ordinary, obscure people devoted to a far more egalitarian localism.[1] Genteel attitudes rested upon a belief in a hierarchically structured, deferential society wedded to the ideal of organic unity under the guidance of gentlemen; more common folk displayed a stubborn allegiance to parochial community values that bred an increasingly suspicious attitude toward any attempt by a sophisticated elite to forge a centralized hierarchy oblivious of local needs and threatening to local customs.

The struggle between hierarchy, a familiar ideology with a rich European heritage, and localism, a much more visceral, inchoate response to rapidly changing new-world conditions, pervaded American society throughout the latter half of the eighteenth century. During the decade of the 1760s, it lay behind conflicts as diverse as the Regulation movements in the Carolinas, growing unrest in northeastern cities, the Baptist revolt against the Virginia squirearchy, tensions between Separatist and orthodox Congregationalists throughout New England, land riots along the Hudson River, and the Green Mountain Boys' defiance of New York authorities on the New Hampshire grants. Later it spawned conflicting expectations of the Revolution in the minds of gentle and simple folk, led to disagreements between "cosmopolitans" and "localists" within newly established state legislatures, and exacerbated the stress between Federalists and Anti-federalists over the

Constitution.[2] The conflict became most clearly manifest, however, during the 1790s, in the struggle between Federalists and Jeffersonian Republicans over what form of government and type of society should emerge within the new republic. It was this contest that gave birth to the image of democratic individualism so familiar to nineteenth- and twentieth-century Americans.

Federalism and Republicanism—ideological persuasions that emerged from preexisting cultural tensions—existed as modes of thought long before they became modes of politics. The political issues of the 1790s provoked the public expression of deeply ingrained cultural beliefs; they forced to the surface opposing conceptions of society that had long remained unexamined. Throughout it all, each party to the conflict continued to view itself as the true champion of American republicanism—the cultural system believed to be so vital to the continued existence of the new nation.[3]

For its part, Federalism rested upon a social ideal that stressed stability, harmony, tradition, dependence, and the common good.[4] It appealed to those accustomed to deferential behavior as well as to those seeking reassurance in a changing world. More than anything else, a mental association with established authority and an identity with customary ways of life and traditional behavior attracted individuals to Federalism. Whether economically dependent upon an established member of the community, psychologically wedded to a deferential society, or a member of the elite themselves, those who became Federalists identified with a hierarchical social and political order. They esteemed their "betters" and felt obliged to guide and direct those inferior to themselves. Such individuals and groups found a stable, structured society to be a source of real security and psychological comfort in a rapidly changing, chaotic world.

Adherents of Federalism articulated the social attitudes of men imbued with the hierarchical attitudes of an earlier era. George Cabot, perhaps the wealthiest man in New England, spoke in terms of society as a "well regulated family"—an organic whole whose harmony resulted from "each one learning his proper place and keeping to it." For Cabot there was no such thing as equality of condition. The "better sort," ruled rather than governed in a political system held together by a deferential spirit that imbued the "multitude" from birth to "submit to the subordination necessary in the free'est state" and accustomed the "natural rulers of society" to expect such behavior.[5] A prominent import merchant, Stephen Higginson, declared: "The people must be *taught* to confide in and reverence their rulers."[6] Jonathan Jackson, a leading import merchant and banker, concurred. In his mind the education of youth was terribly important. Young people must be taught "their just rights, at the same time they are taught proper subordination." Therefore, the militia took on great significance for Jackson precisely because it could instill these lessons in adults. Indeed, it inculcated the most important principle to be learned by individuals: "that discipline of the mind—*subordination*—for who can govern properly in any department that has not learned to obey?"[7] Nathaniel Chipman, chief justice of the Vermont Supreme Court, declared: "The greater part of his [man's] rights are not exclusively, and independently, in himself. They arise in society and are relative to it. . . . The rights of all have a reciprocal relation to the rights of each, and can never be rightly apprehended distinct from that relation."[8] Wedded to a conservatism, elitism, and a belief in the organic nature of society, Federalists remained very much aware of inequalities in society and preached subordination. They thought first of society, then of the individual, and intended to maintain a governing elite supported with the votes of the people by strengthening traditional habits of deference through family, church, and government. They believed, above all else, in *"a speaking* aristocracy *in the face of a silent* democracy."[9]

From a Federalist perspective, though, something deeply disturbing was at work within American society. As a result of the economic and social changes wrought by the Revolution and the corrupting influence of the French Revolution, older standards of behavior were coming under attack and new ones arising in their stead. Instead of accepting their status in life, all sorts of men now believed that wealth and privilege could be theirs. Those previously content with a simple existence of limited means had become caught up in a frenzied lust for material wealth and political prominence. Individuals who had always sought only the good feelings and quiet respect of their neighbors now clamorously appealed for the votes of the mob. Worse yet, these degenerates had banded together to form a political party—the very bane of a republican government's existence—that aimed at nothing less than the total transformation of society. Courting all men regardless of their status or worth, this new party intended to create the new man who would demand equality—social, political, and economic—with even the most genteel.

To men socialized into communal, traditional, and deferential politics, the Republican party appeared to be the means by which individuals detached from or alienated by society advanced their selfish interests at the expense of the whole community. The party, led by new men rather than by the natural leaders of society, would place men of obscure origins in power by bypassing the established hierarchical structure. The Republican party was becoming the primary vehicle for entrepreneurship in and through politics. It stimulated the egalitarian beliefs and expectations of men who might otherwise never have dreamed of holding political office. Thus, it created the very men to whom it appealed for support and became the means by which these men advanced in society.

Such behavior outraged the Federalist elite. By pitting man against man and man against the community, Republican actions were eroding the corporate nature of society. Quick to recognize the affinity between economic individualism and democracy, Federalists thus saw in the Republican movement a demand for a society based upon equality rather than subordination. All individuals, not just those of rank, family, and office would be free to compete for wealth, success, power, and esteem. Such unrestrained competition not only threatened the social harmony of a republican commonwealth, but set into motion a dangerous proclivity on the part of Americans to disdain rank, status, and order—the very foundations of a true republic.

From a Federalist viewpoint, then, Republicans, totally devoid of private virtue and public spirit, masked their socially disruptive, self-seeking actions behind a rhetoric of public service and the general interest. They flattered the public and gained positions not by serving the commonwealth but by boldly advancing their own selfish interests. Indignant Federalists viewed such men as "creatures who, under pretense of serving the people, are in fact serving themselves."[10] While Federalists manfully attempted to safeguard principle, integrity, and traditional institutions, Republicans sought only "to obtain office, and change the customs and habits of the country." Republicans could only be considered "the enemies of order who are seeking their own emolument in the confusion of innovation & misrule"; they were "modern Reformers" who irresponsibly endangered long-cherished foundations of harmony and good order.[11] In their scramble for personal advantage, Republicans proposed ludicrously impractical measures that would prove dangerously unsound if ever put into actual practice. "Never," Noah Webster warned his countrymen in a Fourth of July oration, " . . . let us exchange our civil and religious institutions for the wild theories of crazy projectors; or the sober, industrious moral habits of our country, for experiments in atheism and lawless democracy. *Experience* is a safe pilot; but experiment is a dangerous ocean, full of rocks and shoals."[12] Taking the term from Jonathan Swift, Federalists considered Republicans "Laputans" — men who walked about with their heads in the clouds and by their abstract impracticability threatened the destruction of a harmonious, stable, and ordered republic.

In the eyes of Federalists, the worst trait of Republicans was their unscrupulous search for popular favor. Rather than depending upon their own inner resources and drawing their rewards from private satisfaction, Republicans lusted after public approval. Lacking the values that might serve as a compass in changing times, such men altered their course according to the superficial opinions of the day, patterning their lives according to fashionable current tastes in a futile effort to gain status and recognition. What troubled Federalists was the knowledge that Republican efforts were futile only if judged by traditional criteria that recognized true merit working within customary hierarchical channels. The problem for Federalists was that such traditional standards seemed themselves to be passing out of existence. In the place of esteemed political figures who had risen slowly to positions of honor after years of dedicated public service, "mushroom politicians" sprang up overnight. They bypassed the traditional hierarchy and curried favor with the people. An angry Federalist warned of the dangers of "the novel doctrine of new-fashioned republicans, that the hasty opinions of the populace are infallible" and, even worse, *"that character should be tried at the bar of public opinion."* In exasperation he bemoaned: "What senseless jargon! The decision would frequently be against the truly meritorious, and in favor of the most worthless."[13]

For most Federalists, the Republican party represented the culmination of troubling tendencies that had been at work within their society since the time of the Revolution. Throughout the 1780s and 1790s, Federalists became increasingly disillusioned. The Revolution, which was supposed to usher in a stable, virtuous republican society under the leadership of a natural elite, had instead loosed all manner of ambitious individuals who, espousing egalitarian and democratic principles, tore at the organic fabric of the community. Instead of an ordered, Augustan society, America seemed to be in danger of becoming a scrambling, commercial society dominated entirely by the pecuniary needs and desires of ordinary citizens rather than the austere and rational guidance of its natural aristocrats. No longer were Americans knit together by simple virtue; a process described by John Adams as "disaggregation" was taking place.[14] A variety of antagonistic interests emerged in the place of a simple, unified, homogeneous, virtuous people.

The problem facing the Federalists consequently became how to maintain order and stability in a society rapidly splintering into competing interests. Most supported the creation of strong institutions of social control in which power and liberty would be mutually dependent, and where true freedom could exist only within clearly circumscribed limits. Jonathan Jackson exclaimed that in "simple democracies" there was "no regularity; no one knows his place, or how to keep it." "Governments, in which the principles of all are combined, and which are properly limited by sufficient checks, are those only which can promise us permanency, at the same time they can afford us any real freedom."[15] In an oration presented to the Massachusetts Society of Cincinnati, a Federalist speaker definitively stated that "a relaxation in the reins of government is as productive of anarchy and confusion as the despotick law of an eastern monarch is of tyranny and oppression."[16] Chief Justice John Jay articulated such Federalist beliefs in his first charge to grand juries (1790), observing that "nothing but a strong government of laws, irresistibly bearing down arbitrary power and licentiousness can defend it [United States] against those two formidable enemies." In an earlier letter (1788) to George Washington, Jay had been even more frank. "Experience has taught us, that men will not adopt, and carry into execution, measures best calculated for their own good, without the intervention of coercive power."[17]

Energetic government became the means whereby Federalists intended to preserve order and stability within the new Republic. Dogmatically adhering to their vision of an ordered, hierarchical, Augustan society, Federalists abandoned their reliance upon the virtue of the people and the natural tendency toward subordination that emanated from that virtue; in its stead they placed their reliance upon a powerful central government under their own direction. From a Federalist perspective, the Constitution created a government based upon a filtration of talent intended to ensure that the wise and the good would rule. It meant to put better men in office and to enable them to exercise mature and independent political judgement. Federalists thereby supported Alexander Hamilton's fiscal policies in order to recreate the traditional lines of dependency that had begun to fragment and were so desperately needed to knit the society together. Under the leadership of the secretary of the treasury, they intended to move America ahead into a more complex stage of social development—to emulate the eighteenth-century English model where the nation's economic development was directed from the center through governmental fiscal and banking policies. Thus, Federalists envisioned a centrally organized, economically activist government overseeing a social order characterized by deference and established authority. The newly created national government provided a powerful vehicle for promoting the cosmopolitan urge to extend the sway of hierarchy over the entire nation.

The Federalist actions of the 1790s had an unsettling effect upon those Americans bred upon an egalitarian localism. Such people, accustomed to viewing the world about them in terms of a country perspective, had an innate suspicion of distant governments and the men who wielded power within them. And yet localism itself was undergoing a fundamental and crucial transformation. By the 1790s, the forces of change spawned by the Revolution had begun to affect great portions of the American population previously isolated from the mainstream. As commerce and the market economy—with their self-interestedness, individualism, and urge for profit making—penetrated interior areas, localism's stress upon communal egalitarianism gradually became transmuted into an emphasis upon individual success and popular control of government. The old communal distrust of higher authority, the fear that these authorities would erode local customs and doom provincial life-styles to extinction gradually gave way to a personal distrust of all social distinctions and elites that would impede the ordinary individual's personal quest for profit and status. Throughout the postrevolutionary period, many Americans slowly, hesitantly, perhaps unconsciously, worked toward the creation of an ideology that would afford legitimacy to these feelings. This impulse found its strongest voice, its clearest articulation, in the political opposition to the Federalists in the last decade of the eighteenth century.

Like so many Americans, those who became Republicans inherited the same revolutionary ideology as their countrymen. They, too, integrated a strong belief in John Locke's insistence upon the protection of property and the good of the people as the only legitimate end of government with a libertarian fear of power and the enslavement of the people at the hands of corrupt officeholders. Along with these ideas, however, Republicans emphasized a peculiar perspective that coursed through the essays and books of a number of English writers—most particularly James Burgh, John Cartwright, Richard Price, and Joseph Priestley.[18] Embedded within the Lockean and libertarian language that characterized the writings of these men was a cluster of ideas that carried particular meaning for those people who were becoming restive with social distinctions and elites. These authors believed that mankind was capable of unbounded improvement. Such improvement would come about, however, only in the least constraining civil, political, and religious environment. Progress resulted not from the benevolent paternalism of an elite, they contended, but from the individual efforts of free and equal individuals. Such beliefs hinged upon the related ideas that all men were by nature created free and equal and that whatever distinctions arose in society should result from talent, intelligence, hard work, and merit, not from wealth, status, or birth. Thus, when Cartwright thundered out in "Take Your Choice" (1776) that "all are by nature free; all are by nature equal: freedom implies choice; equality excludes degrees in freedom," he meant the same as James Burgh when the latter exclaimed: "All honours and powers ought to be personal only, and to be given to no individual, but such as upon scrutiny, were found to be men of such distinguished merit, as to deserve to be raised to distinguished places, though sprung of mean portents."[19] From such a perspective monarchy, aristocracy, and other civil or religious establishments thwarted the natural proclivity of men of talent and ability to prosper and to change society for the better. A natural civil society rewarded talent and merit; artificial manipulations of the political economy by government created privileged elites and spawned corruption and degeneracy.

Given this heritage, Hamiltonian fiscal measures created a restlessness among many Americans, a restlessness stemming from grave apprehensions about the effect such governmental actions would have upon the future development of the young Republic. These doubts prompted a searching critique of the role of government in the political economy of the nation and searing indictments from individuals representing a wide variety of local perspectives. In the process of castigating their Federalist opponents, these men groped toward the articulation of a new political persuasion that would at last translate the realities of the American environment into a dynamic social and political ideology.

From the time debates first began in Congress over Hamilton's financial program until the election of Thomas Jefferson to the presidency in 1800, individuals from all regions of the nation and from a wide diversity of callings attacked Federalists and their policies in the most vitriolic manner. In his "Letters Addressed to the Yeomanry of the United States" (1791), George Logan, wealthy Pennsylvania landowner and physician, wondered how long Americans would suffer themselves "to be duped by the low cunning and artifice of half-informed Lawyers and mercenary Merchants" who passed laws that sacrificed the productive members of society to "indolent characters desirous of lucrative government offices supported by the labor of their fellow men."[20] John Taylor of Caroline, senator from Virginia, declared Hamilton's National Bank to be the "master key of that system that governs the [Federalist] administration."[21] The pernicious secretary of the treasury, "by administering gilded pills to influential characters," stimulated "exorbitant wealth, to provide an aristocracy as the harbinger of monarchy."[22] In Taylor's opinion, "the *natural interest* . . . ought exclusively to legislate" within a truly republican society.[23] This was not the case under the Federalists. By means of their program, "Government, though designed to produce national happiness, will be converted by a paper junto simply into a scheme of finance. Instead of dispensing *public welfare,* it will become a credit shop only, to dispense *unequal wealth.*"[24]

Taylor's charge that the Federalists perverted the natural republican order within America by means of self-serving legislation received ample support. In a pamphlet entitled "A Review of the Revenue System adopted by the First Congress under the Federal Constitution" (1794), William Findley, Republican congressman from western Pennsylvania, saw a "systematic plan for subverting the principles of government" that was creating "an aristocracy formerly unknown in the United States." He wondered if "changing the state of society by a rapid increase of wealth in the hands of a few individuals, to the impoverishing of others, by the artificial aid of the law; the instituting a bank, with an enormous paper capital, and connecting it in such a manner with the government as to be a center of influential, ministerial, and speculating influence; and to promote this influence, filling both Houses of Congress with bank directors or stockholders, [was] a national blessing?" All Findley could see was the creation of a "consolidated government" that would create a wealthy aristocracy.[25]

In the pages of his newspaper, *The Farmer's Letter,* and his magazine, *The Scourge of Aristocracy,* William Lyon kept up a constant attack upon

Federalists and their policies. Lyon had arrived in America from Ireland as an indentured servant, fought with Ethan Allen's Green Mountain Boys, and risen to become a Republican congressman from Vermont. In his mind, Federalists constituted "a set of gentry who are interested in keeping the government at a distance and out of the sight of the people who support it."[26] By means of a "phalanx of falsehood and corruption" they intended to foster an "aristocratic junto" that tried to "screw the hard earnings out of the poor people's pockets for the purpose of enabling the government to pay enormous salaries" and to "vie with European Courts in frivolous gaudy appearances."[27]

Republican leaders in urban areas hammered at these same themes. George Warner, a sailmaker in New York City, declared in a Fourth of July oration (1797) that all citizens must acquaint themselves with political affairs and keep a vigilant eye on their leaders. He spoke particularly to "tradesmen, mechanics, and the industrious classes of society" who for too long had considered "themselves of TOO LITTLE CONSEQUENCE to the body politic." Far too often, voters had been attracted to men of wealth. Instead, citizens needed to turn to "men of TALENTS and VIRTUE whatever their situation in life may be." If this were not done and the present administration was not altered, "the dividing line between the *rich* and the *poor* will be distinctly marked, and the *latter* will be found in a state of vassalage and dependence on the former."[28]

When Federalists mocked the sort of ideas expressed by Warner, Republican leaders responded with sharp newspaper essays tauntingly signed "one of the swinish multitude" or "only a mechanic and one of the rabble," berating Federalists as men who "despise mechanics because they have not snored through four years at Princeton."[29] The most adept of the urban Republican authors, Benjamin Austin, articulated the egalitarian distrust of elites forming within the cities in a series of essays published under the title *Constitutional Republicanism in Opposition to Fallacious Federalism* (1803). In these essays, Austin declared that governments were "organized for the happiness of the whole people; no exclusive privileges are the birthright of particular individuals." Unfortunately, under the Federalists—a " '*self-created*' body of dictators"—the bulk of the Americans constituting "the industrious part of the people" had fallen prey to an "aristocratical junto" and were forced to support "in idleness a set of stock jobbers."[30]

The Republican cause in America gained two articulate spokesmen when the English radicals Thomas Cooper and Dr. Joseph Priestley settled in Northumberland, Pennsylvania in 1794. Cooper's essays, *Political Arithmetic* (1798) and *Political Essays* (1800) and Priestley's *Letters to the Inhabitants of Northumberland* (1799) became Republican campaign literature in the election of 1800. Both men spoke out in the strongest terms in favor of social, political, and economic freedom. Legislation that artificially altered the wealth of the nation in favor of a privileged few subverted republicanism and smacked of old-world decadence and corruption.

The most violent attacks upon Federalism appeared in the pages of Republican newspapers and periodicals that flourished throughout the 1790s. From the time that Madison and Jefferson established Philip Freneau as the editor of the anti-administration *National Gazette* in 1791, a burgeoning number of Republican editors bluntly attacked Federalist men and measures in direct language aimed at an ever-increasing political constituency.[31] Indeed, one editor promised his readers to review the history of the United States in such a way as to reveal the "origins, progress and alarming influence of that system in iniquity, robbery, bribery, and oppression, hypocrisy and injustice, which may be traced from the attempt of Alexander Hamilton to palm off upon the [Constitutional] Convention a monarchical constitution, through the corrupted mazes of funding and banking, stock-jobbing, and speculating systems, down to the alien and sedition laws, standing army and navy of the present day." Another exhorted his fellow Americans to "keep up the cry against Judges, Lawyers, Generals, Colonels, and all other designing men, and the day will be our own." A fellow editor saw American society divided into those who worked and those who "live on the stock of the community, already produced, not by *their labor,* but obtained by their *art* and *cunning.*" These were "for the most part merchants, speculators, priests, lawyers and men employed in the various departments of government."

How effective this Republican rhetoric was in influencing the broader populace is difficult to determine. That its primary themes permeated the thoughts of one untutored Massachusetts farmer, William Manning, is clear. In 1798, Manning addressed a lengthy essay, "The Key to Libberty," to "all the Republicans, Farmers, Mecanicks, and Labourers in America" under the signature of a "Labourer."[32] Claiming to be a "Constant Reader" of newspapers, Manning, in his own simple, straightforward manner, articulated his perception of the condition of the Republic. For him, good government meant the protection of life, liberty, and property—a society in which "the poor man's shilling aught to be as much the care of government as the rich man's pound. A free government was one "in which all the laws are made judged & executed according to the will & interest of a majority of the hole peopel and not by the craft cunning & arts of the few." The failure of free states in the past had always resulted "from the unreasonable demands & desires of the few," who could not "bare to be on a leavel with their fellow creatures, or submit to the determinations of a Lejeslature whare (as they call it) the Swinish Multitude are fairly represented, but sicken at the eydea, & are ever hankerig & striving after Monerca or Aristocracy whare the people have nothing to do in maters of government but to seport the few in luxury & idleness."

The assault upon Federalism thus joined such men as John Taylor of Caroline, the Southern slaveholding planter; Matthew Lyon, the aggressive man on the make on the Vermont frontier; William Findley, the self-made political leader from western Pennsylvania; Benjamin Austin, the urban agitator; the radical British émigrés, Joseph Priestley and Thomas Cooper; and the simple Massachusetts farmer, William Manning. It produced no quintessential Republican. Rather, a variety of elements throughout the nation joined to form Republican coalitions against Federalism: agrarian and urban entrepreneurs resentful of the power and prestige of urban merchants who controlled the Atlantic trade; ambitious, unconnected individuals no longer willing to defer to entrenched elites; radical republicans innately suspicious of centralized government; old republicans fearful lest widespread commercial development diminish American virtue; groups caught up in the egalitarianism spawned by the revolutionary attack on the corporatism of the old order; and independent producers frustrated with the elite control and social restraints characteristic of an ordered, paternalistic hierarchy. Republicans thus reflected the essentially fragmented and localistic nature of American society; for, although the Revolution had created a single political nation, it certainly had not created a unified national community. Rather, regional or local pockets of culture prevailed and various groups and individuals found in Republicanism a means to promote their ends or assuage their anxieties.

But if Republicanism incorporated a diverse constituency, its adherents spoke an incredibly uniform language. Whether urban radicals or southern gentry, they employed similar ideas, principles, and even rhetoric. This resulted from the fact that their Republicanism drew upon several traditional modes of thought and incorporated ideas long familiar to Americans. Lockean liberalism and classical republicanism provided the essential underpinning for this political persuasion. For Republicans, though, Locke's concept of individual liberty promoted an affective individualism—a concern for one's fellow man and the larger community—rather than the possessive individualism associated with philosophers like Thomas Hobbes.[33] Republicans thus emphasized the individual, but not as a figure freed from social restraints and set against other individuals and the community.

Such a perception of the individual blended nicely with the new party's belief in the classical republican tenets of virtue and citizenship. In order to protect an always fragile civic virtue, classical republicanism called for vigilant, well-informed, independent citizens to guard against corruption in government—particularly in the executive branch—and to maintain private virtue. Individuals found meaning and identity in their lives through service that promoted the common good. Such republicanism, of course, saw a constant struggle by advocates of liberty to fend off the forces of power—standing armies, unnecessary and unfair taxes, ministerial influence, special privilege, and corrupt elites. Republicanism instilled a fear of centralization, and centralization came to stand for the corruption of a natural society by an avaricious set of government officials intent upon creating an aristocracy.

The strain of thought that fused the traditions of liberalism and republicanism into a well-integrated cultural system sprang from the Scottish Enlightenment. The Scottish philosophers Francis Hutcheson, Adam Ferguson, Thomas Reid, Dugald Stewart, and, to a lesser extent, David Hume, for all their disagreements, remained firmly committed to a belief in the individual's responsibility to the larger community. These Scots employed a great variety of local and cultural forms of association in their search for a means to foster virtuous community life. By far, however, the most influential and far-reaching effort focused on economic associations and came from the fertile mind of Hutcheson's pupil, Adam Smith. In *The Wealth of Nations* (1776), Smith elucidated a mysterious force—an "invisible hand"—working within a free market economy that could transmute the actions of the least virtuous individual into socially beneficial behavior.[34] Smith sought to establish the viability of a free market economy not to promote the unrestrained pursuit of personal wealth but to encourage a peaceful, prosperous, and just world. Artificial barriers that restrained freedom for most people and created poverty for many would give way to market mechanisms that fostered general prosperity. Working within the tradition of natural law refined by his teacher Hutcheson from the ideas of Grotius and Pufendorf and the tradition of political economy articulated by late-seventeenth-century British critics of mercantilism, Smith envisioned his market mechanism as an economic means to a moral end. Thus, for him, a free market economy did not constitute an end in itself. He fully expected such an economy to encourage the magnanimous regard or sympathy that men naturally felt for one another that he first posited in *The Theory of Moral Sentiments* (1759).

In *The Theory of Moral Sentiments,* Smith had developed the fundamental concepts that underlay the central message of *The Wealth of Nations.* The earlier book revealed his conviction that eighteenth-century Enlightenment philosophers had promoted false hopes regarding the nature of man's mental capacities. They made a serious mistake, he felt, in offering systems of thought based on a belief in the infinite capacity of man's power of reason; reason and the scientific method simply could not determine the causes of all behavior. Consequently, Smith felt it necessary to elucidate as clearly as possible the true nature of man. For him, man was, above all else, a passionate creature motivated principally by an inner drive for self-preservation. Individuals also possessed an innate sympathy for others— an instinctive, irrational desire to share their pain and to feel genuine concern for their welfare. Passion, therefore, and not reason, created all that was beneficial in society. The good of society resulted not from rational instruction and guidance at the hands of an educated and responsible elite, but instead from arranging public policy in such a way as to release every man's true psychological nature, to free his instinctual drives so that they might develop in socially useful directions. No group of men, no matter how broad-minded or intelligent, was capable of directing all the affairs of a nation. The task was simply too overwhelming. For this reason, government in the hands of an elite, no matter how responsible or benevolent, created chaos and stultified national economies. Societies should, therefore, be based on the "rights" of men, not their "duties"; they must be structured around justice—the protection of individual rights, not benevolence—a comprehension of the duties owed to others.

Such philosophic breadth underlay *The Wealth of Nations* and contributed to its popularity. The sharply critical tone with which Smith presented his message, however, and the conclusions he drew from his philosophic stance accounted for the book's incredible appeal and broad impact. In a brilliant synthesis of economic ideas that were everywhere in the air by the middle of the eighteenth century, Smith provided penetrating observations on the vast transformations sweeping across the economic and social life of mid-eighteenth-century England. These changes had resulted in great fortunes for some and grinding poverty for many others. *The Wealth of Nations* offered a trenchant critique of the system that resulted in such maldistribution of wealth and such terrible social disorder.

In Smith's mind, British devotion to mercantilism stifled economic growth and created terrible inequities. It was all boldly justified as being a "benevolent" system in which an aristocratic few, in their infinite wisdom and disinterestedness, knew best how to direct the government so as to produce a vibrant and prosperous economy and society. In the ostensible interests of producing a greater Britain, those in power created navigation laws, privileged monopolies, bounties, tariffs, and a great variety of excise laws. From Smith's perspective this whole panoply of commercial regulations resulted entirely from the greed and monopolizing impulses of British merchants and manufacturers. Under the guise of promoting national strength and prosperity these groups had gained vast governmental subsidies for commerce and industry. The entire system, therefore, was not only ridiculous and corrupt but counterproductive. Trade should be allowed to follow its natural course, not be artificially diverted for the benefit of a few. Only when Britain removed all her commercial restrictions and stultifying mercantile shackles would true prosperity be possible.

A belief that legislators must know their own limitations also formed a basic element in Smith's critique. Governments must base their decisions on natural facts and thus enable a "system of natural liberty" (Smith never employed the terms "capitalism" or "laissez-faire") to emerge. Any economic system based on natural facts must, above all, take into consideration man's passion for self-preservation. If a national leadership was incapable of creating vast nationwide economic programs, individuals in their own more limited environments would always know what policies best suited their interests. A prosperous, productive society could not result from the government's trying to teach people virtue; it could, however, come from each citizen's desires, if these desires could be freed to take whatever direction that individual felt necessary.

To achieve a free and open society would require a profound change in the social order. Instead of benevolent rule by a "disinterested" elite of wealth, status, and education, government would pass into the hands of a natural aristocracy of men who would inevitably emerge from the middle and lower orders once all artificial social and economic restrictions had been removed. Through talent and ability these men would rise to positions of leadership. They would be peculiarly suited to govern not because of any natural virtues, but because of their ambition, their will to succeed, and their dogged determination to hang onto whatever they had gained. Each man's drive for achievement served as a counterweight to every other man's and resulted in a balance that prevented anarchy or tyranny. For Smith, no distinct interest or particular order in society manifested an inherent capability to govern. Instead, those participating in government would be a heterogeneous mix of individuals who had naturally risen above the others. Thus, *The Wealth of Nations* comprised a clarion call for a pluralistic and entrepreneurial society and state.

Smith's book had an enormous impact upon Republicans. It provided them with a blueprint, a grand design, for bringing about wealth and prosperity for their entire society. Not only that, it supplied them with distinct policy stances regarding banking, tariffs, bounties, taxes, and a whole range of commercial problems. *The Wealth of Nations* also confirmed the Republican perception of Federalists as the enemies of a natural society. More important, however, Adam Smith allowed Republicans to speak and to write with a confidence and optimism grounded in what they considered to be irrefutable authority. If certain fundamental requirements were only fulfilled, America would be placed on the road to inevitable progress and abundance for all. In this single book, Smith articulated inchoate beliefs that had permeated American society for decades. Republican pamphleteers had long employed ideas drawn from Locke and the Commonwealthmen, but Smith harmonized these into a coherent social philosophy. But most of all, his ideas integrated the egalitarian and communal impulses of American localism just as they were breaking apart. Citizens could now be devoted to the community through their own individual efforts. In many ways, then, individualism was becoming the apotheosis of localism.[35]

The Republican persuasion that evolved in the last decade of the eighteenth century emphasized individual rights and popular sovereignty. Adherents of this political ideology assumed, though, that the Revolution secured individual autonomy rather than individual freedom: Republicans stressed the combination of independence and moral responsibility—affective individualism—so prominent in the thoughts of John Locke, James Burgh, and Adam Smith. At the same time, they assumed that the Revolution would guarantee the sovereignty of the people, to establish for all time that the ultimate decision-making process in government could safely rest with the people. In their minds, the Federalists stood as an obstacle to the full realization of these goals. Rather than their society being characterized by an open-endedness, where autonomous individuals remained free to change their society for the better, it seemed to be developing in a closed, elitist manner under Federalist control. Consequently, Republicans felt they must effect two integrally related revolutions: one economic and one political—both premised upon the idea of equality.[36] The first could be accomplished only by expanding commercial opportunities for a larger number of people in such a way as to promote greater prosperity and equality of opportunity. The other demanded the destruction of an elitist, deferential politics in favor of one that fostered the active participation of all men. Within its broadest parameters, then, the Republican persuasion held out the promise to Americans of autonomy as both economic and political individuals.

Unlike many previous political theorists, the Republicans assumed that social hierarchies rested upon economic realities and an unthinking deference to tradition. Consequently, they worked to create a revolutionary theory of government integrating a program of economic development with a social policy for nation building.[37] Believing that hard-working, self-sufficient farmers represented the natural economy of America, Republicans made the commercial prosperity of ordinary farmers the primary economic base for a democratic, progressive America. In their minds, agricultural prosperity would release a human potential long held in check by poverty and ignorance. This belief underlay the Republican conception of a democratic republic: a fusion of economic freedom and political democracy. Such a perception rested upon a faith in the innate capabilities of man, an optimistic hope for a new political and social order in America, and a readiness to submit to the natural forces within society.

Although most political leaders realized the tremendous economic potential in America, the critical and divisive issue of the late eighteenth century became how and in support of which values this potential could best be realized. Federalists and Republicans both agreed on the need for an effective, unified national government, but they violently disagreed over whether that government should become highly centralized through the manipulation, by a few citizens, of public credit and public funds, or should be open and responsive to the individual needs of ordinary men.

For their part, Republicans considered republics superior to all other forms of rule precisely because they prevented governments from restraining the free acquisition of wealth. In a republic all men should enjoy an equal opportunity to acquire a comfortable livelihood. This would be the case, however, only if government did not acquire significant powers over the economic behavior of its citizens. Here many Republicans voiced the classical libertarian fear that increasing governmental power inevitably meant encroachments upon the realm of liberty. The more powerful the government, the stronger the exploiters and the weaker the producers. The best hope for a republic remained the constant free access of its citizens to both their government and the means of getting a living. Consequently, Republicans firmly believed that republican government endured only so long as opportunities for the acquisition of property remained available to an ever-increasing population. By "property" they most always meant land. Widespread landholding and the predominance of farming in the economy was essential to Republicanism; these created precisely the sort of individual industriousness that spawned the virtue upon which all republican states depended.

The worldwide demand for grain that emerged in the early national period provided a practical material base upon which to build this vision of America. Rising prices held out the promise of a flourishing trade in American foodstuffs that could easily be produced on family farms. Rather than stagnating in subsistence farming, the independent husbandman could partake in a rapidly spreading economic abundance. Indeed, the prosperity of the ordinary farmer could now become the basis for a democratic, progressive America. Free land, free trade, and scientific advances in agricultural methods meant progress and prosperity open to all rather than just a privileged few.

Thus, Republicans intended at all times to promote the free competition of individual citizens in an open, competitive marketplace. Their hope that ordinary men might free themselves from economic and political subservience to their social superiors rested upon the bright promise of commercial agriculture. Republicans united the husbandman and commercial prosperity to form a radically new moral theory of government and society. Dissolving society into its individual human elements, they invested each person with a basically economic nature and an innate capacity for autonomy. The purpose of government in such a society was no longer to raise power to balance power but instead to liberate man's self-actualizing capabilities.

The Republican perception of government and society that evolved throughout the decade of the 1790s inevitably brought its advocates into conflict with Federalists—eighteenth-century-minded men who clung to a traditional belief in hierarchy. For their part, Republicans believed that self-interest provided every man with the capability of making rational decisions regarding his own personal needs. As a result, self-interest, as viewed by the Republicans, became a powerful leveling force; it placed all men—ordinary as well as genteel—upon the same level of autonomy and competency. In this regard, the emergence of Democratic Republican societies in the early 1790s particularly offended the genteel. One indignant Federalist complained to Alexander Hamilton in 1793 that "banditti-like" people were organizing into societies to oppose Federalist policies. Another characterized a local society as comprised of "butchers, tinkers, broken hucksters, and trans-Atlantic traitors." Convinced that these societies harbored "the lowest orders of mechanics, laborers and draymen," Federalists took great offense at the presumption of such people to declare it "the unalienable right of free and independent people to assemble together in a peaceable manner to discuss with firmness and freedom all subjects of public concern, and to publish their sentiments to their fellow citizens, when the same shall tend to the public good." Worse still, these societies seemed to think that all people, no matter what their station in life, should "freely discuss and publish as we do or as they might choose, that the views of each might be made manifest and bear the proper weight with an enlightened and orderly people." Such groups even had the nerve to declare that they preferred such self-created societies "because in them every grade and capacity can furnish something to the general stock of improvement, and because they tend to fraternity, consistence, and due order."[38] The activities of these societies, however, paled in comparison to the Republican newspapers that sprang up like mushrooms to spew their venom at will upon genteel individuals of character and status.

Federalist gentlemen could accept vituperative attacks upon themselves from men of their own social status; this had been an integral part of Anglo-American political life for over a century.[39] To endure such vitriol from social inferiors and to have such open criticism and abuse spread throughout the lowest orders of society, however, created terrible indignation and alarm. In the hands of ordinary individuals—Republican editors and members of Democratic Republican societies—such abusive language could seriously damage the public character of governmental leaders and undermine the entire political order. Convinced of the malicious and traitorous intent of Republican editors, Federalists enacted the Sedition Law (1798) to enable the government to stifle these dangerous elements within American society.

The passage of the Sedition Law inaugurated a controversy between Republicans and Federalists that went to the heart of their cultural conflict. Federalists clung doggedly to the traditional perception of the universal and constant nature of truth. Truth could always be determined by well-educated, rational men. Republicans argued that a great variety of opinions regarding both the principles of government and elected officials circulated at any given point in time, and their truth or falsity could not be definitively determined by any judge or jury, regardless of how reasonable and intelligent they might be. Thomas Jefferson declared that all opinions, no matter whether true or false, malicious or benevolent, should be allowed to "stand undisturbed as monuments of the safety with which error of opinion may be tolerated where reason is left free to combat it."[40] Madison echoed these sentiments when he observed that "some degree of abuse is inseparable from the proper use of every thing"; consequently, it was "better to leave a few of its noxious branches, to their luxuriant growth, than by pruning them away, to injure the vigor of those yielding the proper fruits."[41] Such sentiments left Federalists incredulous. The notion that all free individuals should be allowed to express their opinions, no matter how scandalous or abusive, was beyond their ken. Republicans, who had come to the conclusion that a gentlemanly elite no longer had an exclusive right to voice political attitudes, not only believed that true and false statements should be tolerated equally, but that all members of society should be free to articulate them. Instinctively, Republican theorists viewed public opinion in the same manner as the free-market economy: just as an invisible hand led a great variety of competitors in the marketplace to promote an end that was not part of the conscious intent of any of those involved, so too might the efforts of a great variety of individual minds—intellectual competitors in a free market—create an end result that was not the conscious creation of any single group or individual, but sprang spontaneously from the collective efforts of all men.

By 1800, then, the cultural forces of the previous decades became clearly delineated: Federalists staunchly defended the traditional past and Republicans championed an optimistic, open-ended future.[42] Federalists, in spite of all their promotion of overseas commerce and a national banking structure, remained doggedly skeptical of the emergence of a liberal society, with its emphasis upon self-restrained ambition. Instead, they adhered desperately to a paternalistic world of hierarchy and social order that prompted them to view the emergence of the self-made man with a mixture of fear and disdain. Their encouragement of commercial growth, too, remained entrenched within traditional economic channels. Although playing a major role in the expansion of the Atlantic trade that took place in the 1790s, they remained inclined to justify their efforts in the customary and limited terms of mercantilism: expanding profits among established merchants would revitalize and thereby perpetuate the existing social structure, strengthening the republic's chances for survival. Their progressive economic programs were meant, in short, to reinforce a conservative social world.

In opposition to Federalism, the followers of Thomas Jefferson called upon the egalitarian spirit of revolutionary republicanism to protect American society from dangers they perceived in Federalist control of government: the corruption of American society emanating from detestable old-world "court" politics, the social inequities resulting from a mercantilist political economy, and the artificial and unfair restraints imposed upon ordinary men by an elitist, paternalistic society. Republicans held out the promise of a dynamic republic of independent producers, a nation in which hard-working individuals—farmers, artisans, mechanics, and entrepreneurs—would be able to attain economic independence and thereby strengthen their capacity to fulfill their role of virtuous political citizens. They offered the vision of a virtuous republic in which a limited government would respect the political integrity and influence of independent citizens, where social freedom would allow autonomous individuals the free exercise of their talents, and where a political economy based on increasing production and territorial expansion would reward the industry and energy of the independent producer. Against the paternalistic and centralized power represented by the Federalists, the Republicans pitted their image of individual opportunity and social mobility. By so doing they endowed their political economy of self-interest with the same moral force that they bestowed upon a social order comprised of autonomous individuals. Their vision, grounded in the optimistic hope that the seemingly limitless resources of their young nation could support the prosperity of all citizens, promised an equal commitment to material and moral progress under a government where the ultimate authority for all decision making rested with the sovereign people. Thus, with the victory of Thomas Jefferson in 1800, Republicans committed the nation to support individual autonomy and popular sovereignty. In this dual commitment lay the roots of modern American democracy.

What kind of society would emerge from the democratic roots formed in the late eighteenth century was difficult for anyone to envision in 1800. Even by that time the republican perception of autonomy and the liberal one of self interest had become so inextricably intertwined that few Republicans had any clear comprehension of the entrepreneurial and capitalistic nature of the social forces shaping their lives. Under the pressure of rapidly changing socioeconomic conditions, the independent republican producer—integrally related to the welfare of the larger community—gradually underwent a subtle transmutation into the ambitious self-made man set against his neighbors and his community alike. Ironically, republican traditions formed a fertile seedbed within which the liberal commitments to possessive individualism, a competitive ethos, and economically self-interested politics flourished. By incorporating as its own the dynamic spirit of a market society and translating it into a political agenda, Republicanism had unself-consciously developed a temper and a momentum that would carry it far beyond its original goals.

Indeed, by 1800 personal independence no longer constituted a means by which to ensure virtue; it had itself become the epitome of virtue. The process by which this took place was invariably complex, quite often confused, and more often than not gave rise to unforeseen consequences. Its ultimate outcome resulted, nonetheless, in profound changes in American culture in the nineteenth century. Republicanism spawned a social, political, and cultural persuasion that quite unintentionally, but nevertheless quite certainly, created the framework within which the nineteenth-century liberal commitments to interest group politics, materialistic and utilitarian strivings, and unrestrained individualism emerged. Simultaneously, however, Republicanism also fostered a rhetoric of selfless virtue—of honest independence devoted to the communal welfare—that obscured the direction in which American society was moving. By promoting the desire for unrestrained enterprise indirectly through an appeal to popular virtue, Republicanism helped produce a nation of capitalists blind to the spirit and original purpose of their enterprise. The Republican movement enabled Americans to continue to define their goal as the pursuit of traditional virtue while actually devoting themselves to the selfish pursuit of material wealth. Irresponsible individualism and erosive factionalism eclipsed the original commitment to the common good. Still, the free-enterpriser, who by the 1850s would even include publicly chartered business corporations, fell heir to the Republican belief that an independent freehold attached a man's interests to the good of the commonwealth. Entrepreneurial fortunes became an investment in the general welfare and the entrepreneur himself, freed by the American belief in virtuous independence, could proceed unencumbered by self-doubts in his attempt to gain dominion over a society of like-minded individuals who could only applaud his success as their own.[43]

The Republican triumph in 1800 rested upon a belief attributed to Thomas Jefferson that "the public good is best promoted by the exertion of each individual seeking his *own good* in his own way."[44] Their victory initiated a brief period—a "Jeffersonian moment"[45]—that witnessed the virtues of republicanism and eighteenth-century liberalism integrated into a cohesive political philosophy offering the bright promise of equal social and economic advancement for all individuals in a land of abundance. That the moment was brief stands less as a critique of those people who combined to bring Jefferson to the presidency than it stands as a comment on the forces that impelled them: forces over which they had little control and, perhaps, even less understanding. Just at the time when an ideology finally emerged that translated the realities of the American environment into a coherent social philosophy, those very realities carried American society far beyond the original goals of the Jeffersonian movement as they transmuted the civic-minded republican citizen of the eighteenth century into the aggressive, self-centered, democratic individual of the nineteenth century.

The Slow Triumph of Liberal Individualism: Law and Politics in New York, 1780–1860

James A. Henretta

I N 1955, Louis Hartz published *The Liberal Tradition in America: An Interpretation of American Political Thought Since the Revolution*. Almost immediately the book became a classic, read avidly by historians and political scientists and assigned in undergraduate classes and graduate seminars. It is not hard to understand why. The *Liberal Tradition* was elegantly written, filled with brilliant phrases that proclaimed Hartz's argument: "European liberalism, because it was cursed with feudalism, was forced to create the mentality of socialism, and thus was twice cursed. American liberalism, freed of the one was freed of the other, and hence was twice blessed." Or again: In America, "Locke's basic social norm, the concept of the free individual in a state of nature [liberated] . . . from the myriad associations of class, church, guild, and place . . . [began] to look like a sober description of fact."[1]

The powerful argument of *The Liberal Tradition* proceeded, in part, from its narrow perspective. Hartz took two assumptions—the lack of a feudal tradition and the preeminence of Lockean liberal individualism—and used them to explain the entire course of American history. The book's subtitle was misleadingly modest: *The Liberal Tradition* was not merely an interpretation of political thought, because its argument presupposed a society of liberal individualists. Nor did it apply only to the postrevolutionary period because the thesis hinged on the absence of feudal practices or of strong communal, religious, or group ties during the long colonial period.

Few books can claim such elegance, power, and scope—or such an important impact within the academy. In this regard, *The Liberal Tradition* anticipated Stanley Elkins's *Slavery: A Study in American Institutional and*

Intellectual Life (1959), a book which greatly resembled it in method and interpretation. Both Hartz and Elkins mostly eschewed archival sources, empirical data, and the inductive method. Rather, they began with various theoretical or historical assumptions, deduced broad hypotheses about American society and culture from them, and used evidence drawn primarily from secondary sources to substantiate their interpretations. Both historians were also "exceptionalists." They posited the "unique" character of the civilization of the United States and ascribed this exceptionalism, in Elkins's words, to the absence of "customary feudal immunities," "prior institutional restraints," and an "unmitigated capitalism." According to Hartz, these circumstances produced a white society composed of self-willed and dynamic individuals; according to Elkins, they yielded an exploitative slave system that left blacks in precisely the opposite condition of "utter dependence and childlike attachment." Thus, a uniquely oppressive system of slavery appeared in the United States as the mirror image of a uniquely individualistic form of liberalism.[2]

The interpretations advanced in *The Liberal Tradition* and in *Slavery* have not stood the test of time. Studies of slavery by Kenneth Stampp, Eugene Genovese, Herbert Gutman, and other scholars have repudiated Elkins's assumptions and conclusions. They have also provided a richly nuanced picture of African-American life and of the complex relations between white masters and black slaves. Subsequent scholarship has also undermined Hartz's assumptions and many of his specific arguments. More importantly, it has suggested an alternative "republican" synthesis of the American historical experience. To reassess *The Liberal Tradition* is therefore to trace the progress of our understanding of the social and intellectual world of the pre-Civil War period (to which Hartz devoted two-thirds of his book) and to achieve a more complex understanding of American individualism.

Hartz began his book with a quotation from Tocqueville, the intellectual hero of the "consensus" historians of the 1950s: "The great advantage of the Americans is, that they have arrived at a state of democracy without having to endure a democratic revolution; and they are born equal, instead of becoming so." Building on this statement, "surely one of his most fundamental insights into American life," Hartz advanced his theory of American exceptionalism. "Where did the liberal heritage of the Americans come from in the first place?" he asked rhetorically. "Didn't they have to create it?" "These questions drive us back to the ultimate nature of the American experience," he replied.

The men of the seventeenth century who fled to America from Europe . . . were revolutionaries with a difference . . . for it is one thing to stay at home and fight the "canon and feudal law," and it is another to leave it far behind.

By fleeing to America, Hartz argued, the early settlers opted out of the "social diversity and social conflict" of Europe and its "basic feudal oppressions." In their place, the colonists found an "abundance of land" that pushed forward "the distinctive element in American civilization: its social freedom, its social equality."[3]

We now know that Hartz's picture of colonial America was deeply flawed. Early American society was profoundly conservative, even profoundly European, in character. Seventeenth-century migrants to Massachusetts re-created the diverse traditional worlds of their English villages, transplanting place names, local laws, patriarchal family patterns, and Calvinistic theology. In the Chesapeake colonies, ambitious sons of English gentry and merchant families used their land claims and capital resources to re-create an aristocratic social order. Initially the tobacco lords arrogantly ruled over thousands of penniless white indentured servants. Subsequently they instituted an even more oppressive system of racial slavery. Few historians would now argue that America in 1700 was, in any fundamental sense, a liberal society. Nor would they accept Hartz's claim that the implicit recognition of slavery by the United States Constitution of 1787 was a "historic anomaly, contradicting the larger liberal tradition in which it had been created." The rise of freedom for ordinary whites in the Chesapeake region, as Edmund Morgan has demonstrated, was the result of the enslavement of blacks.[4]

Recent scholarship likewise casts doubts on Hartz's picture of eighteenth-century Europe as a bulwark of traditional feudalism. Research on the ancien regime in France paints a confused picture of bourgeois entrepreneurs with aristocratic pretentions struggling for power against titled families managing capitalist estates. In England, Whig aristocrats likewise pushed forward capitalist agriculture, commerce, and manufacturing. Indeed, upper-class agricultural "improvers" enclosed vast tracts of northern England and Scotland between 1745 and 1775, setting in motion a major migration to British North America.[5]

The mainland colonies shared this evolution toward economic complexity and a blurring of traditional social categories. The slave-owning planters of the Chesapeake and the Carolinas were active participants in the new system of transatlantic commercial capitalism, buying African slaves and selling rice, tobacco, and wheat. Simultaneously, they eagerly emulated the artistocratic manners of the English gentry. Similar contradictions extended throughout the social order. Beginning in the 1740s, rapid population growth and the booming grain trade brought a dramatic increase in American land values. Rising land prices stimulated capitalistic land-speculation schemes along the trans-Applachian frontier and, in New York and the southern colonies, a "feudal revival" based on land grants made to English aristocrats in the seventeenth century. In the Hudson River valley, the number of tenants on manorial estates rose dramatically. Many tenant farmers prospered (as did tenant middlemen on capitalistic estates in England), even as they held land-use rights that were essentially feudal in character. Hartz's rigid dichotomy between Europe and America will not hold. Feudal practices and cultural values coexisted uneasily with capitalistic ones throughout the Atlantic world during the eighteenth century.[6]

Only the resolution of these contradictory tendencies was different. Monarchical and aristocratic forces in the British North American colonies were less pervasive and powerful than they were in Europe. Consequently, Americans had a broader range of historical options. "We have it in our power to begin the world over again," proclaimed Thomas Paine. And so they did. The American patriot revolutionaries created a republican political and legal order, a result that took another half century in western Europe.

Hartz correctly discerned the *relative* weakness of the ancien régime in America, but called it by the wrong name. Not "liberalism" but "republicanism" best describes the political and social ethos of early America. The system of representative government that had evolved by the late colonial period rested firmly on two principles. The first was the "virtue" of the people, their capacity to prefer the common good to self-interest. The second was the "independence" of politically active citizens, their ability to resist social or economic coercion. These principles granted political rights only to propertied men who could be expected to be virtuous—established planters, freehold farmers, and master craftsmen. Conversely, they denied full citizenship to most dependent males—farm tenants and laborers, urban journeymen and apprentices, slaves, dependent sons—and to all women. As Joyce Appleby has recently pointed out, this classical republican tradition contained "an assertion of human inequality presumed to be rooted in nature and therefore unavoidable in social practice." "As free men," the poet Euripedes had written of his fellow citizens in the ancient Greek republics, "we live off slaves."[7]

The American Revolution did not completely repudiate this postulate of inequality. Backcountry farmers and aspiring artisans won the vote and greater representation in the halls of government, while gradual-emancipation laws slowly ended slavery in the northern states. However, wealthy merchants, rentier landlords, and slaveholding gentry—now allied with ambitious entrepreneurs—remained dominant in the new American state and national governments. They ruled in the name of the people, but remained committed to traditional principles of hierarchy and authority. Hartz and Tocqueville to the contrary, governments founded on popular sovereignty constituted a "genuine revolutionary tradition," but their significance was ambiguous. In Januslike fashion, they faced both toward aristocracy and toward democracy, toward the American past and the American future.

Hartz failed to appreciate the strength of the aristocratic aspects of postrevolutionary American republicanism. He seized upon General Erastus Root's statement in the New York Constitutional Convention of 1821 that "we are all of the same estate—all commoners." Seizing on this correct but misleading Tocquevillian premise, Hartz was outraged by the "massive empirical blindness" of Federalists such as New York chancellor James Kent. "Instead of wooing [the common man, the American democratic] giant," the Federalists and their Whig successors "chose, quite without any weapons, to fight him." "The suicidal grandeur of Fisher Ames," and Kent and Thurlow Weed and Daniel Webster, he concluded, "is tinged with a type of stupidity which makes admiration difficult. . . . Their crime was not villainy but stupidity."[8]

The failure of perception, of course, was Hartz's. Federalists and their Jeffersonian opponents still lived in a world that, in social composition and political ideology, was more republican than liberal. As Appleby has suggested, three partly contradictory, partly complementary definitions of liberty struggled for intellectual supremacy in the late-eighteenth-century world. The first was a "classical republican definition of liberty" that "pertained to the public realm" and involved a claim "to share in the power of the state." Following Greek and Roman models, many of the American Founding Fathers conceived of "political freedom . . . as an end in itself." "Liberty in the historic rights tradition" influenced other American leaders. This second conception of freedom was more "negative, private, and limited." It derived from the constitutional "rights of Englishmen," and was often rooted in a "legal title to a piece of property" or to a legal "privilege" that would be upheld by the common law court system. Hartz's Lockean liberal concept formed a distinct third definition of liberty. Founded in "the law of nature," it lacked an institutional presence in the public realm. Its advocates taught (as Locke himself put it) that because mankind are "equal and independent, no one ought to harm another in his life, health, liberty, or possessions."[9]

These three secular definitions of liberty—republican, legal, and liberal—coexisted uneasily with an increasingly strong evangelical religious prescription. This religious definition of liberty began from the premise of divine power rather than from faith in human ability or popular sovereignty. It demanded that men and women make an overriding commitment to God, "whom to serve is perfect freedom."[10]

Repudiating Hartz, Appleby denies the importance of Lockean liberalism in colonial and revolutionary America. She maintains that the "modern . . .

liberal definition of liberty" emerged prominently only in the 1790s as part of the struggle between Federalists and Republicans. In her view, Jefferson's emergent Democratic Republican party embraced Lockean liberalism to counter the hierarchical ideology of the Federalists. Jeffersonians attacked classical republican notions of deference and balanced government as "an elitist rhetoric." It was not "an American conception," thought one Jeffersonian, because it "favored too much the poignant principles of aristocracy." In reply, Federalists sharply challenged the Lockean apotheosis of self-interest and the "free and independent" man. They heaped scorn on the assumption that a liberated individual "will voluntarily submit to the restraints which the good of the community requires of him." This rhetorical conflict between Federalists and Jeffersonians, between republican "virtue" and liberal "self-interest," becomes the central hinge of Appleby's interpretation of the political struggles of the 1790s."[11]

Various scholars have challenged Appleby's liberal interpretation of the Jeffersonians and have pointed to their strong neoclassical republican values. More fruitfully, James Kloppenberg has argued that most American thinkers subordinated Lockean self-interest to communitarian values stemming from the natural law tradition, Scottish common sense philosophy, or their own religious world view. The result, in each case, enhanced what Kloppenberg calls the "virtues" of liberalism, such as Locke's "strictures against extravagant accumulation" or Adam Smith's benevolent assumption that the "market mechanism . . . would serve as a means to a moral end." Kloppenberg's interpretation contrasts Lockean virtuous self-interest from both the "hardheaded, nonreligious skepticism" of Thomas Hobbes and the mid-nineteenth-century doctrine of possessive laissez-faire individualism. And it points directly to the reception of Locke by American politicians and thinkers in 1800. Introduced into a world dominated by republican and religious discourse, Lockean principles yielded a belief in "autonomy rather than freedom," a Kantian notion of individual self-government "inseparable from the nuances of restraint, law, and moral responsibility."[12]

This transitory intellectual synthesis between republican virtue and liberal self-interest is apparent only in retrospect. The men and women of the time felt confused, torn between traditional hierarchical, communitarian values and new democratic, individualistic principles. "Had Tocqueville visited the United States a generation earlier," Appleby points out,

> he would have witnessed the process through which the new nation shed it borrowed European ethos. In the 1790s the aristocratic model of society was isolated and attacked. Those who experienced it as a set of discordant values faced those who knew it as a reality and an ideal.[13]

In fact, the *ideological* conflict of the 1790s was only the preliminary skirmish between republicanism and liberalism. Lockean principles now informed the thought of some prominent intellectuals and political leaders. But historical change has many dimensions, and liberal ideas still lacked a firm institutional base in the social structure, political system, and legal order of the new American Republic. Even Hartz conceded as much. Despite his emphasis on America's historic "liberal unity," he had to admit that conservative leaders gave up "the false aristocratic frustrations of the past" only in the 1840s. Only then did the appeal of Jacksonian democracy and the logic of institutional transformation encourage them to articulate a "philosophy of democratic capitalism."[14] Only then did the era of liberal individualism really begin.

The transition from republicanism to liberalism took place partly in the legal arena. Patriot revolutionaries wrote inherited notions of liberty into the new state constitutions. The New York Constitution of 1777 was primarily a republican document. Conceiving of property ownership as a civic right, it limited voting privileges for assembly elections to adult men possessing a freehold of twenty pounds, and for senate and gubernatorial contests to freeholders with estates of 100 pounds. The constitution also reflected the "historic rights" tradition. Constitutional provisions that persons could not "be deprived of life, liberty, or property, without due process of law" rested on legal precedents stretching back to the Magna Charta. Moreover, the New York Constitution explicitly recognized the legal validity of English common law doctrines. These legal rules extended deep into the structure of the society, guaranteeing (among many other things) "the liberty of secure possession" of property. Even without Lockean liberalism, property rights were secure in the new American states.

Indeed, Lockean principles of individual rights contradicted existing precepts of American property law. Most property in early America consisted of land and buildings ("real" rather than "personal" property). Individual men owned most of this real property, but legal rules pertaining to families limited their right to sell it. Paradoxically, these limits on men's economic individualism stemmed from their dominant position within the family. The definition of marriage under English common law placed power primarily in the hands of men. In Blackstone's famous definition: "The very being or legal existence of the woman . . . during marriage is incorporated and consolidated into that of the husband." This legal condition of coverture imposed serious procedural and substantive disabilities on married women. It limited their right to own property, to sue, or to make contracts and wills.[15]

Coverture also limited men's economic freedom by giving their wives the right to dower. At his death, a man had to set aside a certain proportion of the family's real property (usually one-third) for the use of his widow during her lifetime or until remarriage. If he failed to do so, his widow could seek a writ of dower, a court order forcing the executor of the estate to surrender her portion. To protect the widow's dower, the common law prohibited a husband from selling or mortgaging any of the family's land without his wife's express consent. Property alienated by a husband without such consent lacked a clear title; his widow could sue the present owner for her dower. And the court would usually award her a life interest in the estate as though the conveyance had never taken place.[16]

Like quitrents and primogeniture and entailments, right of dower was a feudal principle. It was one of the legal rules that ascribed social status to women, regardless of their personal achievement. In fact, it circumscribed their ability to act in the world by limiting their contractual freedom as individuals. Thus, a widow ordinarily had to preserve her dowered lands intact for transmission to her husband's children; her rights were not those of ownership but those of use. The rights of the family—as a legal entity persisting across the generations—were superior to those of the individuals who composed it.

Unlike many other feudal practices, dower was as pervasive in colonial America as it was in England. It affected every family that owned real property, and had far-reaching economic implications for substantial landowners. "The claim of the wife to her dower at common law diffusing itself so extensively," Blackstone noted with regard to England, "it became a great clog to alienations, and was otherwise inconvenient to families."[17] In response, English aristocratic families used various legal devices, such as trusts, to permit them to buy and sell lands at will.

Dower endured, nonetheless, in England and in British North America. Indeed, it was probably more important in the colonies, because of broader ownership of real property. However, some colonial jurisdictions limited the scope of dower rights. During the seventeenth century, Puritan legislators in Connecticut and Massachusetts eliminated the traditional common-law rule requiring a wife's signature on a land deed. Moreover, a widow in Connecticut had rights only to the lands owned by her husband at the time of his death, not those he had possessed at any time during their marriage. These Puritan legal innovations eroded the economic position of widows and encouraged a patriarchal social order in New England. In Pennsylvania, new rules favored creditors at the expense of widows. Under English common law, a deceased man's personal possessions could be seized to pay his debts but not his real property. The Pennsylvania General Assembly, however, allowed creditors to seek repayment from the entire estate—thus diminishing the size of the widow's dower.[18]

These incursions on dower were limited to areas controlled by Puritans and Quakers, radical dissenters in law as in religion. New York and all of the southern colonies continued the traditional common-law preference for widows over creditors. They also protected security-conscious wives over ambitious (or spendthrift) husbands, usually by requiring a judge or government official to determine a wife's consent to a land transaction. Thus, in 1771, the New York legislature enacted a stricter conveyancing law, requiring the private examination of wives in all future land transactions.

Following the Revolution, the New York legislature abolished various feudal restraints on land ownership. It directed, for example, that the land office grant all newly patented land in "fee simple," without quitrents or any legal encumberances on its sale. Yet neither the legislature nor the courts repudiated dower or curtesy (a legal rule which gave a widower a life estate in any real property owned separately by his wife). Indeed, the New York Supreme Court ruled in 1799 that the forfeiture, for treason, of a Tory husband's estate, "did not forfeit the wife's right of dower." It passed with the land, becoming the responsibility of the subsequent owner. Chancellor James Kent of New York reaffirmed this traditional common-law rule in *Humphrey v. Phinney* (1807), awarding a widow dower in land sold by the husband without her consent. "The tenant in dower," Justice Brackenridge of the Pennsylvania Supreme Court remarked a few years later, "is so much favored, as that it is the common byword in the law, that the law favors three things, life, liberty, and dower."[19]

This use of Lockean language in relation to a feudal principle is more than ironic. It underlines the indeterminacy of American legal doctrines and political values in the early nineteenth century. Kent was a staunch Federalist, committed to social hierarchy and traditional authority. Because of his classical republican values, the chancellor strongly opposed the extension of suffrage to all adult male taxpayers in the Constitutional Convention of 1821; he favored the representation of property and not of individuals. However, Kent condemned entails and other legal devices that allowed fathers to devise large estates to a single heir. Indeed, he defended the general American trend toward fee-simple land ownership in expansive, almost liberal, terms. "Entailments are recommended in monarchical governments, as a protection to the power and influence of the landed aristocracy," he observed in his *Commentaries on American Law* (1827–30),

> but such a policy has no application to republican establishments, where wealth does not form a permanent distinction, and under which every individual of every family has his equal rights, and is equally invited, by the genius of the institutions, to depend upon his own merits and exertions.[20]

Kent's politics and jurisprudence thus revealed a tension between liberalism and republicanism, between the rights of the individual and those of the social body. This ambivalence reflected a larger debate in legal doctrine and practice. As Morton J. Horwitz and William E. Nelson have argued, judges (and juries) in the late eighteenth century often interpreted private contracts

according to community standards of a "just" bargain. Subsequently, lawyers and judges turned away from this equitable (or classical republican)
notion of contract. In its place, they devised a (liberal) "will theory" that
exhalted the primacy of private bargains.[21]

Two decisions by the New York Court of Errors during the 1820s overturned Kent's traditional reading of contract principles and signified the triumph of the emergent will theory. Like the British House of Lords, the
Court of Errors was a quasi-political judicial institution. Its membership
consisted not only of the chancellor and the judges of the New York Supreme Court but also the lieutenant governor of the state and the thirty-two
members of the elected senate. Judges and legally trained senators dominated the deliberations of the court. However, they frequently had to con-
strue legal precedents in creative ways to win the support of a majority of
their elected colleagues, who were motivated by more immediate political
concerns.

The court's propensity to make "new" law that reflected emergent social
and economic forces accounted for its reversal of two of Kent's decisions.
The first involved the property rights of married women. Like other judges
in courts of equity (which were not bound by common law), Kent upheld
passive trusts. This legal device allowed a bride to assign her estate to a
male trustee, thus removing it from her husband's control. He also validated
antenuptial agreements without a trust, which permitted married women to
control their own property. In these cases, the chancellor's respect for property rights outweighed his support for the customary legal privileges of husbands. In *Methodist Episcopal Church v. Jacques* (1815), however, Kent
gave a narrow reading to the contractual rights of married women. Before
her marriage to Richard Jacques, Mary Alexander had used a trust deed to
set up a separate estate. Kent ruled that this deed prevented her from dis-
posing of her estate in a second trust deed written during her marriage. In
overturning Kent's decision in 1820, the court of errors ruled that Mrs.
Jacques could dispose of her property in any manner not explicitly prohibited by the original agreement. The court ignored her subordinate status as a
femme couverte while exhalting her capacities and intentions as a free contractual individual.[22]

The famous case of *Seymour v. Delancy* affirmed even more clearly the
triumph of a liberal will theory of contract. In 1822, Kent refused to uphold
a private contract exchanging two farms for two town lots. "The village lots
were not worth half the value of the country farms," he wrote in his decision, and such a "hard bargain" was not "fair and just." Two years later,
the court of errors reversed Kent's decision. "Purchases are constantly
made upon speculation," it pointed out, and "the value of real estates is
fluctuating." Therefore, courts should intervene only when there was "fla-

grant and palpable'' fraud; in other instances, judicial tribunals should re-spect the bargains freely made by contracting individuals.[23]

The will theory of contract, and the support for women's separate estates by courts of equity, undermined the common-law fiction of martial unity. Indeed, these legal doctrines facilitated passage of the Married Women's Property Act in New York in 1848. Members of the emergent women's movement pushed this legislation forward, as did businessmen who wished to protect their wives' property from creditors. In conjunction with subse-quent legislation, the property act enabled every married woman to own real and personal property ''to her sole and separate use,'' and ''to convey and devise real and personal property . . . as if she were unmarried.''[24] These laws gave a liberal Lockean definition to the property rights of mar-ried women. In this particular legal sphere at least, they had rights as indi-viduals equal to those of men.

Simultaneously, tenant farmers used armed violence and political pres-sure to overthrow the feudal land system of the Hudson River valley. The New York Constitution of 1777 had affirmed the ''historic rights'' tradition of liberty by granting legal immunity to existing land titles and franchises. Exploiting this constitutional provision, a new generation of republican aristocrats refused to sell farmsteads to their tenants. Continuing the tradi-tional leasehold system, landlords imposed restrictive legal covenants on their tenants, requiring them to pay a heavy fine (usually one-quarter of the sale price) if they transferred their lease through sale or inheritance. Democratic-minded legislatures had tried to abolish these ''feudal tenures'' during the 1780s, only to see them upheld in the courts. In the best common-law tradition, the courts enforced leases executed prior to the ab-olition of feudal tenures and upheld covenants on previously granted Hudson River valley lands.

The traditional landlord-tenant system likewise survived the constitu-tional convention of 1821. The new constitution eliminated the freehold property requirement for voting but retained the constitutional immunity of existing landed estates. Significant change in land law came only in the Constitutional Convention of 1846. A majority of the members expressed a general commitment to ''equal rights'' and liberal economic principles. The new constitution explicitly restricted agricultural leases to twelve years and voided ''all fines, quarter sales or other like restraints upon alienation re-served in any grant of land.'' Judicial decisions also reflected the impact of new economic principles. In *De Peyster v. Michael* (1858), the New York Court of Appeals innovatively employed English common law doctrines to prevent landlords from subverting the new constitutional provisions. It ruled that landlords could not convey land while reserving rent and requiring pay-ment of a quarter of the sale price on subsequent resale. Such a provision, the court intoned in somber legal language, was "void as repugnant to the estate granted and an illegal restraint upon alienation." But the court also held, in *Van Rensseler v. Hays* (1859), that an owner could sell land while reserving an annual rent in perpetuity. Such a conveyance, the court argued, did not drastically impair the purchaser's ability to resell the land. Hence, it was compatible with the ancient English statute of *quia emptores* (1290), which still governed the transfer of property in New York. The historic rights tradition of liberty remained strong, perpetuating feudalistic notions of land ownership well into the nineteenth century. In the last analysis, liberal ideology and legal doctrines were no more important in overturning the traditional leasehold system than the threat of continued rural violence.[25]

Nonetheless, the constitution of 1846 and the Married Women's Property Act of 1848 affirmed the emergence of a liberal and individualistic legal order. At the same time, they placed its advent in the 1840s, not the 1790s. It had taken a full half-century of social change and political conflict to dislodge republican cultural values and to embody Lockean liberal principles in the legal institutions of New York.

The emergence of liberal individualism occurred alongside, and in part because of, the growth of an activist "party state." The simultaneous expansion in America of individual freedom and state power confounded many European observers. In Tocqueville's eyes, American governments worked like an "invisible machine." They were not controlled by a heredity ruler, a legally privileged aristocracy, or an exclusive governing class—in each case "a power which, though it is in degree foreign to the social body, directs it." Rather, "in the United States, society governs itself for itself." As Tocqueville explained:

> The nation participates in the making of its laws by the choice of its legislators, and in the execution of them by the choice of the executive government; it may also be said to govern itself, so feeble and so restricted is the share left to the administrators.[26]

Hegel likewise questioned whether American governments were a "Real State" because they lacked a distinct class of bureaucrats, formal corporate bodies, or a sense of collective purpose that transcended the interests of individuals. Looking across the Atlantic, the great German philosopher saw "private interest devoting itself to that of the community only for its own advantage."[27]

Karl Marx came closest to an understanding of governmental power in the United States. Americans lived in a particularly democratic polity, he argued, which allowed self-interested individuals and social groups to enact their programs into law. At that point, the legal system imposed their values or interests upon the rest of the community. Thus, the "real" or "material" American state did not consist of a traditional ruling class but of the laws governing property and other social relationships. In this respect, Marx thought, "the entire content of the law and the state is, with small modification, the same in North America as in Prussia."[28]

Just as Marx perceived the significance of legal rules in nineteenth-century America, so Tocqueville understood the crucial importance of political parties in making them. The two notions were related. In one sense, parties were an instrumental institution. By representing the will of public leaders, ethnocultural voters, or ordinary citizens, they translated the abstract ideology of popular sovereignty into concrete legislative programs. In another sense, parties were a coercive force. Using their legislative majorities, they elevated the policies or values of particular regions or special interest groups into public policy. As delegate Lemuel Stetson cautioned the New York Constitutional Convention of 1846, "The legislature represented an aggregation of localities, and not the whole people themselves."[29]

In terms of Tocqueville's analysis, American political parties served the same function as an established aristocracy or ruling elite in a traditional regime. They stood apart from the society, acting as the instrument of particular individuals and interests. This relationship between parties and power emerged with clarity during the Civil War. In 1862, a Republican Party Convention in Oneida County, New York, told President Abraham Lincoln that "he has no army, he has no navy, no resources of any kind except what the people give him." But the president had no cause for worry, the convention declared, because

the Republican Organization, in all its principles, in all its practices, and by all its members, is committed to the preservation of the Union and the overthrow of the Rebellion. It is the power of the State and the power of the Nation.[30]

Political parties enhanced the authority of the state in more mundane ways as well. Beginning in the 1790s, but particularly after 1815, New York's Jeffersonian Republican party created an identity of interest among hundreds of quasi-professional politicians in scores of towns and counties. Under the leadership of Martin Van Buren, the party served as both a conduit for public opinion and as an arm of the state—explaining and justifying legislative enactments and ensuring their implementation on the local level. As Hendrik Hartog has demonstrated, the Corporation of the City of New York relied increasingly on the positivist authority of the state government. After 1800, the corporation did not employ the ample powers granted by its charter of 1730 to impose taxes or fire restrictions. Nor did it continue to use its extensive property holdings to ensure orderly urban growth. Rather, the corporation regulated the affairs of the city by soliciting appropriate legislation from the popularly elected state government.[31]

Party organizations also served as a quasi-public bureaucracy. A political state, John R. Commons once remarked, consists of "officials in action." American state governments had small paid bureaucracies throughout the nineteenth century; yet the patronage of political parties extended the reach of the state far into the society. The New York Constitution of 1777 created a Council of Appointment composed of the governor and four state senators. The council appointed thousands of local officials, most of whom were nominated by regional party leaders or organizations. The constitution of 1821 eliminated the council but gave the governor extensive patronage powers, including the right to appoint hundreds of justices of the peace. This centralized patronage network rewarded local party notables with positions of significant status and power.

Equally important, these appointments enhanced the authority of the judicial system, the second major institution of governmental power in the American states. Justices of the peace made up the lowest level of the court system. Most justices were longtime residents of their towns, and they were paid by user fees, not state salaries. Nonetheless, they were quasi bureaucrats. Appointed by elected state or county officials, justices kept the peace in their communities by enforcing the criminal laws of the state and by adjudicating minor civil disputes. The state paid judges and officials in higher courts or authorized them to extract fees-for-service from the citizenry. Privately paid lawyers likewise served, in a sense, as functionaries of the state-mandated legislative and judicial systems. To defend their interests in court, citizens were well advised to purchase the services of lawyers who possessed a thorough knowledge of the coercive rules of statute and common law. Taken together, the members of the judiciary and legal profession constituted the American equivalent of the European bureaucratic order. By implementing legislative statutes and common-law rules, they provided a measure of direction to social and economic change.

At times, the bureaucratic aspects of the American legislative-judicial system emerged prominently into view. In 1813, for example, the state legislature mandated a quasi-judicial process for laying out new streets in New York City. The city government had to seek approval from the New York Supreme Court, which appointed "commissioners of estimate and assessment" to supervise the "taking" of private land. Sitting as an administrative tribunal, the court then confirmed (or rejected) the assessor's findings. It awarded compensation to the owners of seized land and defrayed the cost by taxing nearby property, which (theoretically, at least) had increased in value because of the new street. Many landowners objected bitterly to this "betterment" system. It forced an individual "to become a capitalist for the public," one property owner complained, imposing "a tyranny, with respect to the rights of property . . . no monarch in Europe would dare to exercise."[32] Would Hegel have viewed this complaint with amusement? Or would he have taken it as evidence of a "Real State" in America?

There is no doubt, in any event, that the postrevolutionary courts were more powerful than their colonial predecessors. Eighteenth-century American judicial systems lacked a strong hierarchial structure. At the lowest level, juries had discretionary power. In many instances, they decided not merely the facts of the case but also which law to apply. Their freedom stemmed in part from judicial practice. When a bank of judges heard a case, they frequently delivered mutually contradictory seriatim opinions. Appellate courts abetted this confusion of power and legal doctrine. They frequently held new trials on appealed cases rather than simply reviewing legal issues raised in subordinate jurisdictions. By the first decades of the nineteenth century, however, judges exerted firmer control over juries, declaring their decisions "contrary to the law," appellate courts coerced local tribunals through reversals, and printed decisions (as well as treatises such as Kent's *Commentaries on American Law*) encouraged common judicial standards and a more uniform legal mentality.[33]

The centralization of authority both expanded and curtailed the freedom of individuals. Before 1776, as John Reid has argued, most Americans lived within a "Whig" (or classical republican) system of legal and political power. The polity was characterized by local legal autonomy and the deference accorded to men of "substance." This system enhanced the authority of resident notables and propertied jurymen at the expense of royal governors, judges appointed by the Crown, and the majority of the local populace.[34] The new party state had a different locus of power. By expanding the suffrage to all white adult males and competing for their votes, parties destroyed the traditional deferential regime. Centralized party patronage undermined the local authority of established gentry and merchants; they now served as justices of the peace at the will of party politicians in Albany. The world of power was more open to rising men of talent, particularly those who pursued legal careers.

The changing membership of the New York constitutional conventions of 1777, 1821, and 1846 graphically reveals this transition from a classical republican to a liberal political world. Most members of the "Convention of the People" who wrote the constitution of 1777 were in fact "men of affairs"—merchants, lawyers, and wealthy rural landlords. Their political outlook was shaped less by their specific occupations than by their social position as men of property and their knowledge of the classic works of political theory. "He was sick of politics and power," delegate

Robert R. Livingston confessed to a friend, and would willingly trade "one scene of Shakespeare for a 1000 Harringtons, Lockes, Sidneys and Adams to boot."[35]

Men of affairs still predominated numerically in the convention of 1821. The published debates listed sixty-eight of the 126 members (54 percent) as "farmers." Some of these gentlemen farmers and landed oligarchs, such as John Duer and General Jacob Van Rensselear, took a prominent part in the debates. Yet no fewer than thirty-seven men of the law sat in the convention. These lawyers and judges—Van Buren and Kent, among others—dominated the debates. Nonetheless, their rhetoric did not reflect a narrow craft outlook. For the most part, they spoke neither as legal technicians nor as practical politicians, but as broadly educated men with coherent political philosophies.

By 1846, lawyers and farmers sat in the convention in equal numbers, each with forty-two members. More significantly, a distinction between ignorant "lay members" and skilled lawyer-politicians divided the delegates into two self-conscious groups. "Certain gentlemen," complained Isaac Burr, a sixty-five-year-old surveyor from Delaware County,

> thought that no proposition, no matter how trivial it might be, could be understood by the lay members, unless three or four speeches were made on each side. . . . He believed that himself and others, though they were but farmers, could read these reports and understand them . . . and so could their constituents.[36]

Whatever the capacities of the lay members, lawyer-politicians dominated the convention. The new constitution reflected their expertise. It was a long and detailed document, alive to the nuances of legislative power and legal doctrines.

The content of legislation changed as dramatically as the composition of the political leadership. Beginning in the 1790s, the state government stimulated economic development through the award of corporate charters. This system of "state mercantilism" entered a new phase after 1815. The legislature granted charters to dozens of banks and set up commissions to finance an ever-growing canal system. These initiatives encouraged economic growth—and intense political battles for preferential charters and subsidies. By the early 1820s, opposition politicians attacked Van Buren and his associates in the Albany Regency as a "cabal," a "Royal Cabinet," which had "conspired against the people's rights." "The present controversy," the new People's party argued in the election of 1824, "is the PEOPLE against a purse proud overbearing ARISTOCRACY." "The political organization which controls this state," an opposition newspaper charged (with considerable accuracy) in 1831, is combined with a moneyed aristocracy existing in the city of Albany, which owns the Mechanics' and Farmer's bank. . . . Their identity of interest with the canal commissioners, the canal board, with the comptroller, and with a majority of the bank commissioners, enables them to exercise a most dangerous influence over all the moneyed institutions in the state.

"This identity of interests," the *Albany Evening Journal* concluded, "causes a combination of political influence, which bids defiance to all legislative control."[37]

Delegates to the Constitutional Convention of 1821 had recognized that political parties enacted private legislation at the expense of the public. "In a free representative government," complained Judge Jonas Platt, "there is a strong and natural tendency to *excessive* legislation." To inhibit the passage of special-interest legislation, the delegates strengthened the separation of powers among the various branches of government. The new constitution required a two-thirds vote by both houses of the legislature to override the governor's veto. This Federalist-inspired mechanism failed to address the fundamental issue. As Philip R. Livingston warned his fellow delegates, "your governor . . . comes in by a party" and would not ordinarily veto a bill enacted by his political allies.[38]

The concentration of power in an activist party state was papable and threatening. To combat it, the Anti-Masonry party of the 1830s moved beyond the rhetoric of the 1790s—the worlds of Federalist political theory and Jeffersonian republican thought. It was futile to rely on either the "virtue" of rulers or internal "checks and balances," the Newburgh Antimasonic Convention argued in October 1830. Rather, "the ballot boxes afford a remedy peculiarly adapted to the removal of all evils which may be beyond the reach of the judicial, executive, or legislative departments of government." "The PEOPLE are sovereign," the *New York Whig* thundered a few years later, taking up the assault on the entrenched political party led by Martin Van Buren.[39]

Popular sovereignty was not a new concept in the 1830s. For half a century it had served as the ideological justification for American republicanism. But "real" popular sovereignty—manifest in a genuinely competitive, mass-based political system—was something new. Indeed, it was at once the product of a generation of party building and a peculiarly liberal and democratic solution to concentration of party power. Like other liberal measures, such as equal property rights for married women and a fee-simple land system, the new political system achieved legal form only in the late 1840s. Article VII of the constitution of 1846 instituted a popular referendum to control state spending and thereby to restrain the special economic interests represented by political parties.

The new constitutional provision was the handiwork of Michael Hoffman, a radical Jacksonian Democrat. A lawyer-politician from Herkimer County, Hoffman served first as a United States congressman during the 1820s and 1830s. He then emerged as an important New York politician and an astute critic of legislative power within the state constitutional system. "The constitutions of every State in the Union," Hoffman pointed out,

> have given the legislative power in the mass—in general terms—and then sought to restrain it . . . by express limitations. [Hence,] there is no law over the Legislature but the Constitution itself.

A better "mode of proceeding," Hoffman maintained, would be to specify directly "what the powers of the legislature should be." "All powers not granted to the legislature" in the constitution, he continued, would remain "the residuary, reserved powers of the people, not to be exercised unless they make an express grant of them."[40]

Article VII implemented Hoffman's strategy of using popular sovereignty to restrain party politicians from dispensing governmental subsidies to special interests. It prohibited the state from extending its financial credit to assist private individuals and corporations. In addition, it limited the state debt to $1 million, except as funded by taxes approved by a popular referendum. Moreover, Article XIII specified that in 1866, and at least every twenty years thereafter, "the question, 'shall there be a Convention to revise the Constitution, and amend the same?' shall be decided by the electors." The popular will had become a constituent and continuing feature of the constitutional system. This new mechanism—pitting the people en masse against the self-interests of parties and private interests—was fundamentally different from the restraints on the power proposed by Federalists and Jeffersonians.

The character of public life and of private existence in New York had been transformed between 1776 and 1846. Hierarchy and authority had given way to a democratic outlook and a philosophy of "equal rights." Yet the emergence of the liberal party state and self-interested (rather than "virtuous") Lockean individualism was not an unmixed blessing, as the radical Jacksonian architects of the constitution of 1846 knew well. To counter the power of political parties and an interest group, pork-barrel system of legislative government, they devised the popular referendum. And to ensure that the constitution would be enforced, they insisted on the popular election of judges. The people would be the final arbiter of all things. Hoffman assumed that state legislators and party politicians would not be virtuous but selfish, acting to benefit themselves, their localities, or their corporate friends. But self-interest would also motivate individual voters, who would use their new powers to ensure fiscal conservatism and responsible government.

Yet the character of Lockean individualism in America was deeply influenced by the other traditions of Anglo-American liberty inherited from the eighteenth century. The "historic rights" embedded in the English common law and the New York Constitution of 1777 had preserved feudalistic values and privileges into the 1840s. Equally significant, it instilled an abiding respect for orderly legal procedures among democratically inclined lawyer-politicians. "Let reverence for the laws, be breathed by every American mother, . . . be taught in schools, seminaries, and in colleges . . . ," Abraham Lincoln told the young men of Springfield, Illinois, in 1838. "Let it become the *political religion* of the nation."[41]

Evangelical Protestant definitions of liberty likewise shaped public values and private behavior. Intense revivals swept across New York during the 1820s, impressing Christian values on thousands of men and women. The theology of Charles Grandison Finney stressed the ability of believers to choose salvation through an act of will, and thus had a strong individualistic (and contractual) cast. Yet strong church organizations and communal identity were equally important results of the Second Great Awakening. In religion as in politics, the growth of organized power accompanied and complicated the emergence of individual rights. People were not simply "more free" in 1846 than they had been in 1776. Rather, they pursued their personal goals within a more diverse (and therefore less directive) system of institutional and cultural restraints.

The classical republican tradition lived on as well. Its emphasis on virtue and independence had been replaced, in the world of civic discourse, by a liberal morality of "equal rights, equal laws, and equal privileges." Nonetheless, the classical republican emphasis on the glory of public achievement shaped the character of political life well into the nineteenth century. "We are not only lawyers, but citizens and men," Simon Greenleaf announced in his inaugural lecture as Royall Professor at the Harvard Law School in 1834,

> [and] our clients are not always the best judges of their own interests. . . . It is for us to advise to that course, which will best conduce to their permanent benefit, not merely as solitary individuals, but as men connected with society by enduring ties.[42]

Lawyer-aristocrats such as Greenleaf (and Kent or Webster) could not claim a monopoly on public spirit, for the goals of Jacksonian lawyer-politicians such as Michael Hoffman were no less lofty. Indeed, the enduring achievement of the architects of the New York Constitution of 1846 (and similar documents in other states) was to reconcile the liberal individualistic order of popular sovereignty, equal rights, and self-interested political parties with the traditional quest for the public good.

The hand of the past was not dead but living. The colonial heritage of radical Protestantism communitarianism, classical republican virtue, and the common rights of Englishmen shaped the character of Lockean liberal individualism in America. "Individualism," as Tocqueville defined it,

> disposes each member of the community to sever himself from the mass of his fellows and to draw apart with his family and friends, so that after he has thus formed a little circle of his own, he willingly leaves society at large to itself.

But the great political theorist discovered this state of affairs not in America, but in nineteenth-century France. His fellow Frenchmen, Tocqueville wrote bitterly in *The Old Regime and the French Revolution,* "being no longer attached to each other by any tie of caste, class, association, or family, are . . . too given to thinking of themselves alone and to retreating into a narrow individualism where all public virtue is stifled." Conversely, in the United States, he found that the "continual exercise of the right of association has been introduced into civil life," resulting in a plethora of activist voluntary organizations. Tocqueville likewise took issue with Hegel's claim that Americans' pursuit of their private advantage was antithetical to the welfare of the community. "The principle of self-interest rightly-understood," he explained, prompts Americans "to assist one another and inclines them willingly to sacrifice a portion of their time and property to the welfare of the state."[43]

Taken together, the cultural precepts of enlightened self-interest and voluntary association created a vital public culture in the United States. Rightly understood, Tocqueville emerges not as the chronicler of American possessive individualism but of its public virtue. And, rightly understood, antebellum American individualism stands forth as a complicated phenomenon. It was the product of a social heritage that had feudal as well as capitalist elements and complex and contradictory definitions of "liberty." Most important of all, it reflected new definitions of state power and individual rights created by the party state and the legal system of the nineteenth century.

The Right to Self-Government: Anti-Institutionalism and Individualism in Abolitionist Thought

Richard O. Curry

ARLY nineteenth-century American society was characterized by major upheavals and transformations—e.g., westward expansion, the development of a market economy, the transportation and industrial revolutions, the advance of political democracy, the separation of church and state, and the development of an individualistic ethos that stressed personal liberty, equality before the law, and equality of opportunity which, most Americans believed, would result in upward social mobility for those who believed in frugality, sobriety, and the work ethic.

Protestant leaders viewed such fundamental changes in the American social, political, and economic landscape with foreboding and alarm. If their view of a Christian republic was to triumph over secular forces that threatened to produce societal disintegration, Protestant leaders had to devise strategies to persuade sinners to voluntarily accept Jesus Christ as Lord and Savior. Churches, as a result of the separation of church and state, could no longer compel allegiance. Moral suasion thus became the major weapon in their arsenal.

Fortunately, for Protestant ministers, the Calvinist idea of predestination or election had been in decline since the mid-eighteenth century. By the 1820s, which witnessed the beginnings of the Second Great Awakening, evangelical ministers began to stress the idea of universal salvation, and some, such as Charles Grandison Finney, began to talk in terms of human perfectibility, which would usher in the millennium. Although a few individuals took the idea of perfection to extremes—e.g., John Humphrey Noyes—most Protestant thinkers emphasized the potential for perfection, not its reality.

Stated somewhat differently, the emergence of an individualistic ethos in American society necessitated appeals by evangelical ministers to an individual's sense of guilt, inadequacy, and need to experience communion with others. Only by their personal decision to accept salvation and thereby help create God's kingdom on Earth could isolated and alienated individuals hope to find meaning in their otherwise drab, dreary, and meaningless lives. In sum, if the evangelists' appeals were pitched, by necessity, to the achievement of personal salvation, their primary objective was to achieve social cohesion. In the evangelical formula, repentant sinners would no longer be isolated monads condemned to perdition but members of the community of Christian believers whose collective efforts would revolutionize the world. Protestant energies, therefore, were channeled into religious revivalism, the establishment of tract societies, Bible societies, Sunday school unions, temperance societies, and antivice crusades—all of which were designed to contain and ultimately control secular forces which, in their view, threatened the existence of Christian virtue itself.

Yet, if social control represented the major thrust behind evangelical thought and activity during the antebellum years, they were not totally successful in diverting individualistic impulses into conservative channels. For example, the modern abolitionist movement also emerged out of this cauldron of social ferment. The vast majority of early abolitionists were also evangelical Protestants—an outspoken and influential minority who utilized individualistic concepts to denounce the South's peculiar institution in thunderous, vituperative terms. Abolitionist rhetoric called down upon their heads mobs in the North and threats of reprisal in the South, and, ultimately, secession if slavery was not granted absolute security by the North. Abolitionists, however, were not only courageous but unrelenting in condemning slavery as sin and calling for the elevation of black people to an intellectual, moral, and political equality with whites.

Some anti-abolitionist evangelicals became members of the American Colonization Society rejecting the idea that liberated slaves could be assimilated into American society. Other conservative evangelical leaders—e.g., Charles G. Finney—found slavery abhorrent, but argued that its abolition should await the achievement of human perfectibility, thus avoiding the inevitable conflicts that would destroy Protestant unity and threaten the destruction of the republic itself.[1]

Abolitionists rejected such "anti-Christian" rationalizations and launched a sustained assault upon the "man stealers." In essence, the "sin of slavery" was not simply the brutalization and exploitation of one human being by another. It also stemmed from the fact that enslavement prevented black people from being "free moral agents." As the constitution of the Lane Seminary Anti-Slavery Society phrased it, God created the black man as "a moral agent, the keeper of his own happiness, the accountable arbiter of his own choice." Slavery "stiffle[d] the moral affections, repress[ed] the innate longings of the spirit, paralyze[d] conscience, turn[ed] hope to despair and kill[ed] the soul." But if most early immediate abolitionists advocated the use of moral suasion to bring about the repentance of slaveholders, they nevertheless warned that if slaveholders did not take heed by voluntarily emancipating their slaves, an angry God would visit his wrath on a sinful nation—the end result of which would be violence, bloodshed, and civil war. As the constitution of the Lane Seminary Anti-Slavery Society warned, slavery "aroused feelings of desperation and revenge, provoke[d] insurrection and periled public safety." It "fomented division and alienation in our public councils and put in jeopardy the existence of the union," and it paralyzed "all missionary effort" and "expose[d] the nation to the awful judgment of God."[2]

From the outset, there was a degree of ambiguity or ambivalence in the commitment of many abolitionists to nonviolence. Even so, it is clear that the principles of nonviolence were still the dominant abolitionist credo in the 1830s and early 1840s. But between the Mexican War of 1846–48 and the secession of the South in the winter of 1860–61, pacifism declined in importance, and the call for a holy war against slavery increased in some abolitionist circles. One of our major tasks here, therefore, is to explain in comprehensive terms why nonviolent principles gradually lost ground to the idea of waging a jihad against sin.[3]

Before attempting that, however, the nature of the abolitionist commitment to moral suasion and pacifism, particularly that of the Garrisonian or "ultra" wing of the abolitionist movement, needs to be examined. The Garrisonians, unlike other abolitionists after 1837, not only attacked the institution of slavery but challenged the legitimacy of all human institutions, including civil government. In order to understand what is known as Garrisonian nonresistance, we must analyze the implications of the work of historian Lewis Perry. His book, *Radical Abolitionism: Anarchy and the Kingdom of God in Antislavery Thought,* and his recent biography of the Garrisonian abolitionist Henry Clarke Wright provide the most detailed, perceptive, and complex analysis of Garrisonian thought yet to reach print. Perry does not believe that

there was an anarchistic wing—that is, a few identifiable anarchists—in the antislavery movement. I would argue that certain of the most basic ideas honored throughout abolitionism turned out in experience to have anarchistic implications. Besides attacking violence, institutional religion, and human government, they occasionally tried to establish new, noncoercive styles in human relationships. This quest led them to departures in religion, community life, marriage, spiritualism, and even political parties. But the quest was so varied and inconsistent that it would be difficult to define an anarchistic wing of abolitionism. We are on safer ground, I think, in taking note of the importance of the problem of authority in antislavery ideology and then in recognizing a wide range of attempted solutions to that problem in the lives of abolitionists.[4]

First of all, what does Perry mean by anarchy? It is, as he admits, a highly ambiguous term, one that ordinarily has been vilified as a philosophy of disorder leading to violence, pandemonium, and license. But as perceived by Pierre-Joseph Proudhon, the French social thinker, by Tolstoy, and, indeed, by some American antislavery radicals, anarchy was the secret of order, not chaos. Proudhon, a contemporary of American abolitionists, did not influence them in any way. By comparing Proudhon's ideas with those of American nonresistance, however, one discovers many valid parallels. Proudhon's thought contained three basic premises: (1) the assumption that the coerciveness and violence of government indicates that it is evil, (2) the existence of an antipathy toward law, and (3) the belief that government is unnecessary to produce a harmonious and just society. While there is no necessity to apply the phrase "unequivocal anarchism" in a Proudhonian sense to Garrisonian nonresistance, definite affinities in outlook do exist. As Perry phrases it: "Some abolitionists had come to believe that the Biblical injunctions against violence meant that Christians had to renounce all manifestations of force, including human government; this is the belief we call nonresistance."[5]

Although such a view contains anarchistic overtones, Garrisonian nonresistants resented the charges of "no-governmentism" attributed to them, and "insisted that they were striving for, and placing themselves under, the only true and effective government, the government of God. They maintained that they opposed not government but human pretensions to govern. By becoming regenerate, man would become free of ordinary shackles and restraints, and would develop noncoercive, spontaneous, voluntary relationships that would not only lead to harmony but usher in the millennium, the kingdom of God on Earth. "With their minds set on the government of God," Perry concludes, "it was possible for abolitionists to seek an end to slavery, to call for governments of perfect moral purity or to say . . . that human government was no more necessary than sin."[6]

There is, however, still another aspect on nonresistant anarchism that needs to be stressed—the potential for internalized "social control." Henry Clarke Wright, the chief theoretician of nonresistance, argued that if one is committed to God, and therefore free of corrupt human institutions, controls are internalized. As Wright said, "The action of each human body must be controlled by a *power within it*—or by a power without it—by an Interior or by an Exterior power.'' The potential for individual self-control was not appreciated by contemporary opponents who viewed the extreme libertarianism of nonresistance as dangerously disruptive to social stability because of its strong indictment of institutions such as civil government. Although Wright was a "belligerent nonresistant, a combative, divisive figure," he also urged "mankind to be calm and harmonious." In Wright's view, nonresistance was more than a pacifist doctrine. He was self-conscious enough to realize that "it was a form of restraint as well as a form of expression: it represented his own victory over murderous feelings," which empowered him through professions of pacifism and love "to show the blood on his brother's hand and prove his own innocence." In contrast to some anarchists and pacifists, Wright did not view human nature as benign. As Wright explained, "Combativeness and destructiveness are essential parts of our nature, that our guilt lies not in the possession, but in the abuse of these propensities; and they are to be regulated and not destroyed." The key was not to seek out individuals for "vengeance," but rather principles and institutions that were corrupt.[7]

Perry analyzes a variety of manifestations of anarchism or anarchistic tendencies within the American antislavery movement: come-outers, the Hopedale Community, the New England Non-Resistance Society, no-organizationists, libertarian deists, political secessionists, and others. These groups frequently differed greatly in theory and practice—oftentimes in ways that qualified their anarchism; but they all shared the belief that "force violated the scheme of law that God had laid out for the world." Of all the groups, "the nonresistants probably gave this conviction its sharpest statement."[8]

Yet even in the ranks of the New England Non-Resistance Society, a wide range of opinion existed; and, more importantly, their convictions often reflected ambiguity, contradiction, or paradox. As Perry states it, "The theoretical consequences of the government of God were clear enough, but the practical applications were problematical." It was clear that a nonresistant should not vote or hold office. But should one refuse to testify in court, to pay taxes, to use banks chartered by civil government? Garrison did not even believe that a man, when called to militia duty, had to engage in civil disobedience: Garrison paid a fine for refusing to serve but believed the state bore the responsibility with what it did with the money. In brief, Perry writes: "Nonresistance, quite simply, did not offer a comprehensive practical understanding of the evils of government, of anarchistic alternatives to the existing arrangements, or of the duties of nonresistants in the present dispensation. What really mattered to the nonresistant was the declaration that the only proper government was divine."[9]

Furthermore, even though nonresistants were not supposed to vote, they "were seldom indifferent to the results of elections, as might have been expected of a movement which held even republican government to be a usurpation of God's throne." On one occasion, in the same issue of *The Liberator*, Garrison not only urged antislavery men to vote against proslavery candidates for Congress, but "ridiculed a vote for either presidential candidate." At times, Garrisonian nonresistance sounded "more like an instrument of political influence than a declaration of independence from government." Perry observes that the source of confusion as regards politics stemmed in part from the uncertainty of the Garrisonians as to whether nonresistance "was merely one among many other secular reforms or the most fundamental and divine of all reforms." Phrased another way, the Garrisonian nonresistants attempted the almost impossible task of fusing "the quietistic attitude of nonviolence with the revolutionary purpose of millennial perfectionism." As a result, nonresistance declined in importance as the Garrisonians would not allow their commitment to the abolition of slavery to be circumvented by their quest for personal liberation from sin.[10]

If there were from the outset contradictions, ambiguities, and ambivalence in nonresistant abolitionist thought toward violence, it is necessary, nevertheless, to explain more precisely why it was not until the period between the Mexican War and John Brown's raid on Harpers Ferry in 1859 that abolitionist acquiescence in or militant advocacy of "righteous violence" became dominant, if not universal.

In part, abolitionist receptivity to violent means can be explained by a "stimulus-response" reaction to the growing sectional crisis over slavery and slavery expansion.[11] Numerous abolitionists, although condemning the Mexican War, expressed the hope that the American army would be repelled with heavy losses by Santa Anna and his legions. The strengthened Fugitive Slave Law of 1850 also escalated demands for physical opposition. As the Garrisonian Samuel J. May exhorted: "If you are fully persuaded that it would be right for you to maim or kill the kidnapper who had laid hands upon your wife, son or daughter, or should be attempting to drag yourself away to be enslaved, I see not how you can excuse yourself from helping by the same degree of violence, to rescue the fugitive slave from the like outrage."[12] And Frederick Douglass, who had earlier broken with the Garrisonian circle and abandoned pacifist principles, stated in 1852, that "the only way to make the Fugitive Slave Law a dead letter [is] to make a half dozen or more dead kidnappers."[13] Moreover, when guerrilla warfare broke out in "Bleeding Kansas" in the mid-1850s, nonresistant Charles Stearns wrote to Garrison that if nonresistance is not a safe principle it is not a true one."[14] Garrison staunchly responded that Stearns had been frightened out of his commitment to pacifism. But the close colleague of Garrison, Wendell Phillips—revealing the conflict that had developed between his "head" and his "heart" (that is, his emotions and his intellect)—agreed with

Stearns. "I believe in moral suasion," Phillips said. "I believe the age of bullets is over. I believe the age of ideas is come. . . . Yet, let me say in passing, that I think you can make a better use of iron than forging it into chains. If you must have metal, put it into Sharp's rifles."[15]

It was John Brown's raid, however, that produced the greatest reaction, the largest number of defections from pacifism. Lydia Maria Child declared: "All I know, or care to know, is that his example stirred me up to consecrate myself with renewed earnestness to the righteous cause for which he had died so bravely."[16] And Henry Clarke Wright, undoubtedly the most brilliant nonresistant theorist, recanted in 1859 when he proclaimed that "resistance to slaveholders and slavehunters is obedience to God, and a sacred Duty to man" and that "it is the right and duty of the North . . . to instigate the slaves to insurrection."[17]

Although the stimulus-response phenomenon goes far toward explaining the abandonment of nonviolence among an increasing number of abolitionists, there had to be, as previously noted, ambivalent feelings toward violence in the first place. But there was also an important ideological component in abolitionist thought, an intellectual loophole that permitted nonresistants who had not themselves abandoned the principles of nonviolence to acquiesce in or condone violence on the part of others. This, of course, was the nonresistant's emphasis upon the idea of private judgment or individual accountability to God. In essence, Garrisonian emphasis upon the uncontested sovereignty of God meant that the individual must follow his own best light. An explicit statement of this doctrine was made by Bronson Alcott in 1838 when he said:

What guide have I but my conscience: Church and State are responsible to *me;* not I to them. They cease to deserve our veneration from the moment they violate our consciences. We then protest against them. I believe that this is what is now going on. . . . I look upon the Non-Resistance Society as an assertion of the right to self-government. Why should I employ a church to write my creed or a state to govern me? Why not write my own creed? Why not govern myself?[18]

In other words, nonresistants emphasized the contrast between their ideal of noncoercion in all human affairs with the violent reality of American society. This distinction allowed them to condemn violence in the abstract while spurring those who in good conscience advocated violence on behalf of the just end of the abolition of slavery. As William Lloyd Garrison put it, "We are taking the American people on their own ground and judging them by their own standard."[19] The right of private judgment thus allowed nonresistants a brilliant, if not very logically consistent, agitational tactic: on one hand, they condemned violence, but on the other hand, they supported its use against slavery. As Garrison argued to the unconvinced pacifist Adin Ballou during the Civil War: "Although nonresistance holds human life in all cases inviolable, yet it is perfectly consistent for those professing it to petition, advise and strenuously urge a prowar government to abolish slavery solely by the war-power."[20]

In addition, there are other factors that help to explain the repudiation of pacifism by an increasing number of nonresistant abolitionists. The use of moral suasion in the 1830s and early 1840s (which was accompanied by millennial expectations of creating God's kingdom here on Earth) simply had not worked. In the minds of abolitionists, the "slave power" was not in decline, but advancing aggressively on all fronts. Nor had they succeeded in influencing most of the nation's churches and benevolent societies to adopt an antislavery stance. Lack of apparent success caused not only feelings of failure but of powerlessness among abolitionists, which historian Lawrence J. Friedman has called a sense of "fragmented personal selfhood."[21] Resorting to violence, therefore, transformed their original missionary impulse based on moral suasion into a crusade for righteous violence, a Manichean quest to destroy evil. As Friedman put it in referring to the Unitarian minister William Furness, "Whereas unmodified moral suasion doctrines had faltered and had left him with a deep sense of personal inadequacy, the violent means of devout warriors promised to secure God's kingdom on earth."[22]

The outbreak of war itself convinced still other nonresistants to abandon their pacifist principles. When confronted by charges that the Civil War was not a war to free the slaves, abolitionists expressed their hope and belief that in time the war could be transformed into a righteous crusade to destroy evil. In the spirit of "The Battle Hymn of the Republic," Garrisonian Lydia Maria Child was "convinced that this is the great battle of Armageddon between the Angels of Freedom and the Demons of Despotism."[23] Abolitionists saw the war as heavenly retribution on a sinful people. To regain divine favor, Americans would have to undergo a bloody expiation, and, if they proved worthy, the could remake the nation into a model Christian republic that would be an example to the world. Nonresistants viewed slavery as the example par excellence of sinful coercion, and by the advent of the Civil War it became clear that most desired slavery's extinction even at the cost of a national bloodletting. The nonresistant Stephen Foster had pointed out earlier the direction that much abolitionist sentiment would follow when he militantly commented on the Fugitive Slave Law that he would "rather a hundred lives should be sacrificed than that one fugitive should be carried back to bondage."[24]

In conclusion, it must be said that if the concept of righteous violence became the dominant view of nonresistants, a minority still clung tenaciously to their original pacifist beliefs. Adin Ballou, the founder of the nonresistant Hopedale Community, was perhaps the most prominent individual. In response to Henry Ward Beecher's charge that nonresistants were cowards, Ballou asked if it was not "absurd twaddle" for Christians to argue that it was moral to kill their enemies if it was done "in pure love, with holy affection, for the sake of justice?"[25] The most significant group of nonresistants who conscientiously objected to the war were young, second generation Garrisonians, including Ezra Heywood, Francis and Wendell Phillips Garrison, Alfred Love, John Wesley Pratt, and Moncure Conway. With quintessential nonresistant logic, Heywood declared that the draft law must be disobeyed because it was "plainly in conflict with divine law."[26] Although William Lloyd Garrison supported the war effort and conscription, he argued that nonvoting conscientious objectors, whether church members or not, should be exempted from military service. It is true that Garrison respected his son George's decision to enlist in the army, but his ideological sympathy was clearly with his sons Francis and Wendell Phillips, who were conscientious objectors.[27]

The case of Moncure Conway, scion of a Virginia slaveholding family, is instructive because it illustrates that William Lloyd Garrison, Wendell Phillips, and most other nonresistants valued their commitment to the Union war effort before their peace principles. When on a mission to England to stir up British abolitionist sentiment in favor of the Union cause, Conway startled his compatriots with his proposal to the Confederate commissioner, James M. Mason, that if the South would emancipate its slaves, the "abolitionists and antislavery leaders of the Northern States shall immediately oppose the further prosecution of the war on the part of the United States government, and, since, they hold the balance of power, will certainly cause the war to cease by the immediate withdrawal of every kind of support from it and with its seccession a restoration of peace and the independence of the South."[28] Conway need not have bothered, as his view raised a furor in both American government and abolitionist circles. In a somewhat exaggerated statement, Wendell Phillips remarked: "Moncure Conway does not represent one single-man on this side of the Atlantic."[29]

What Conway had not understood was that the Garrisonian slogan of the 1850s, "No Union with Slaveholders," was not simply a device by which to exonerate themselves from personal complicity with sin but a political tactic to counter Southern threats of secession. For, in the final analysis, many abolitionists were also committed nationalists, believers in an American nation endowed with a unique mission in the world. As historian Peter Walker phrases it: "The political Union was an arena in which a providential moral drama was being enacted."[30] And without union this "morality play was impossible." Little wonder then that the experiment in attempting to apply the principles of nonresistance failed to survive, that pacifist Leo Tolstoy in the late nineteenth century learned to his sorrow that the American version of Christian anarchism had withered and died.[31]

If the Garrisonian strain of Christian anarchism failed to survive, however, the highly individualistic approach of most abolitionists to social change dominated their thinking during the Reconstruction era. In short, intellectual continuity, not radical change, characterizes the social attitudes of the vast majority of abolitionists in both the antebellum and postwar eras. This essay attempts to provide a much-needed corrective to conclusions by historians who attempt to apply the Civil War as "intellectual watershed" thesis to American abolitionism.

George M. Fredrickson, for example, argues that "the triumph of Unionism and nationalism during the Civil War led to assumptions which obviated the anti-institutional philosophy that had been the basis of [antebellum] abolitionism." Fredrickson shows beyond reasonable doubt that nine Northern intellectuals (some of whom were not abolitionists) developed greater regard for nationalistic and imperialistic ideals during the war, and admired the order and stability inherent in the idea of a positive state. Fredrickson also argues that the emergence of Social Darwinism provided "scientific" reasons why Reconstruction was an uncompleted social revolution. Fearing that he has claimed too much, Fredrickson later qualifies his thesis by stating: "If the set of attitudes summed up in the phrase 'Social Darwinism' did not really rule the architects of Reconstruction, it was nevertheless *in the air* [emphasis added], and some applied it explicitly to Reconstruction and the Negro." Clearly, such conclusions are imprecise and problematic at best.[32]

In a related approach, historians John G. Sproat and James M. McPherson argue that some abolitionists recognized the need for national planning by calling for a program of economic reconstruction. According to Sproat, the findings of the American Freedmen's Inquiry Commission, composed of Robert Dale Owen, James McKaye, and Samuel Gridley Howe, showed real insight by recognizing that "the freedmen must receive land if they ever are to achieve economic independence." Sproat shows beyond question that McKaye held such views; Howe and Owen, however, did not. Similar criticism must also be made of McPherson's analysis of the confiscation issue. McPherson succeeds in demonstrating that a few abolitionists did, on occasion, consider the possibility of confiscation as a way "to provide the freedmen with education, land and economic independence." Contradictory evidence, however, cited in McPherson's work and elsewhere clearly demonstrates that most abolitionists never considered national planning in any form and that most of those who did—Phillips, Higginson, Edmund Quincy, and Samuel J. May—occupied contradictory positions early on and ultimately rejected such formulations altogether.[33]

The views expressed by Willie Lee Rose are more ambivalent than those of other historians. Rose, who has written an influential study of the Port

Royal experiment, argues that while anti-institutionalism remained a potent
force during Reconstruction, she does not, in the final analysis, attach overriding importance to its strength and influence. By 1860, Rose argues, abolitionism "had become a much broader stream . . . than could be contained
in the old channel cut by those earliest pioneers in the cause of the slave."
Among the "younger recruits to the Freedmen's aid movement in the anti-
institutional attitudes of the veterans of the 1830s are hardly discernible."[34]

Rose cites the Port Royal experiment as one example of successful planning, but in so doing fails to emphasize that even among the abolitionists
working at Port Royal many were more concerned with "the purification of
the soul" than with providing the education and training required to transform freedmen into independent farmers. Rose also raises more questions
than she resolves when she contends that freedmen's aid work was "safely
institutionalized" after the war by the American Missionary Association
and other church-related groups. Her conclusion that these groups founded
numerous colleges and normal schools that made important contributions
"to the steady increase in able leadership for Southern Negroes" does not
come to terms with the fact that widespread Northern interest in freedmen's
aid "flared spectacularly for only a few short years" after the war.[35]

Christian benevolence, as dispensed by the AMA, was based primarily
upon evangelical assumptions that social change begins with the moral reform of individuals. Church-related freedmen's aid societies did not take
into consideration the long-range socioeconomic needs of the freedmen. The
existence of voluntary associations concerned primarily with improving or
preserving the moral standards of freedmen demonstrates continuity, not
radical departures in abolitionist thought. Rose's argument that freedmen's
aid work was "safely institutionalized" after the war is, on the surface, a
plausible one. But it fails to deal with the aims, objectives, and perceptions
of the reformers themselves.[36]

Intellectual continuity—not radical departures in thought patterns—characterizes the thinking of the vast majority of abolitionists during the Reconstruction era. Their approach to social change was highly individualistic;
that is, most abolitionists tended to think in atomistic terms—the belief that
social change begins with the moral reform of individuals. The idea of social progress, or of social engineering and planning, were alien concepts to
most nineteenth-century Americans, including abolitionists, workingmen's
associations, intellectuals, and others. As William Lloyd Garrison pointed
out, moral reform and social change were not matters of "laws to be
passed, but of error to be rooted out and repentance to be exacted."[37]

"I ask nothing more for the Negro," Wendell Phillips declared in 1865,
"than I ask for the Irishman or German who comes to our shores. I thank
the benevolent men who are laboring at Port Royal—all right!—but the
blacks do not need them. They are not objects of charity. They only ask this

nation 'Take your yokes off our necks.' They will accomplish books, and education, and work."[38] Samuel Gridley Howe stated: "The white man has tried taking care of the Negro, by slavery, by apprenticeship, by colonization, and has failed disastrously in all; now let Negro try to take care of himself."[39]

Howe, when writing a Massachusetts congressman about the establishment of a freedmen's bureau in 1864, expressed his views even more candidly: "whatever plan is adopted," he wrote, it "should be founded upon the principle that the Negro, once emancipated, is as free as a white man; free to go or to come; free to accept or reject employment; free to work or to starve." What was desirable was "some general system for putting Negroes upon their own legs, and defending them against those who will strive to put them down and keep them down."[40]

Even Frederick Douglass, in replying to the question of what should be done with the Negroes, stated: "Our answer is, to do nothing with them; mind your own business, and let them mind theirs. . . . They have been undone by your doings, and all they now ask and really have need of at your hands, is just to let them alone."[41]

On other occasions, both Douglass and Phillips referred to freedmen's aid as "an old clothes movement." "Alms giving to the Negro is very well," Phillips declared, "highly honorable to the newly-converted givers, very useful to the Negro and may be necessary for a little while. . . . But I protest against its continuance for any length of time. I am still an abolitionist, still believe in the Negro's ability to take care of himself, and do not intend to insult him by holding him up before the country as a chronic pauper. Let us . . . stand claiming for the Negro Justice, not privileges, *Rights,* not alms."[42]

Such views exist in abundance—standing in stark contrast to the idea that during Reconstruction the "genuine radicalism" of the antebellum period had been turned into "an obvious anachronism," or that a significant number of abolitionists were prototypes of twentieth-century social reformers who recognized the need for social planning by the federal government. Thus the failure of the nation to engage in social planning during Reconstruction cannot be comprehended without understanding the elemental fact that twentieth-century theories of social change were alien to most nineteenth-century Americans, including the abolitionists. One must also conclude, without challenging the idea that most abolitionists were dedicated equalitarians, that their conception, in practice if not in theory, was that of equality before the law—nothing more. Many Garrisonians, as noted earlier, found it extremely difficult to embrace political activism (which reflected a modest institutionalization of their ideological commitments after years of dedication to the idea that moral reform and social change were not matters "of laws to be passed or steps to be taken, but of error to be rooted out and repentance to be exacted"),[43] and it was precisely this issue, political activism versus moral suasion, that served as a prime motivating force behind the abolitionist schism of 1865.

After the ratification of the Fifteenth Amendment in 1869, the American Anti-Slavery Society disbanded. Most abolitionists committed themselves to a myriad of other reforms which led, for example, to the creation of the NAACP, the establishment of the National Liberal League (a forerunner to the ACLU), and to participation in antivice crusades. Such departures are complex phenomena requiring a systematic analysis that this essay does not encompass.

The decision, however, of Wendell Phillips, Lydia Maria Child, Abbey Kelly Foster, Henry Clarke Wright, John Greenleaf Whittier, and other abolitionists to become labor reformers provides a strikingly important illustration supporting the idea of continuity in abolitionist thought during the antebellum and postwar periods.[44]

Jonathan Glickstein's closely argued essay, "Poverty is Not Slavery: American Abolitionists and the Competitive Labor Market," provides a perceptive analysis of antebellum abolitionists' commitment to possessive individualism.[45] As Glickstein observes, abolitionists failed to associate "individualism and self-interest with conditions of injustice and exploitation in free-labor market societies." Why? Essentially because abolitionists, like other Americans, looked upon competition with "pre-industrial expectations." That is, they believed that the United States provided upward social mobility in which healthy competition allowed individuals to control their own destiny. As Wendell Phillips declared in 1847, the failure of workingmen to succeed in life (including their ability to leave their wage earning status behind them) was impeded only by their failure to acquire "economy, self-denial, temperance, education, and moral and religious character."[46]

In twentieth-century terms, such a vision of society seems romantic at best. As Glickstein observes, abolitionist emphasis on individual mobility, rather than the improvement of the working class as a whole, proved that they did not have "a truly industrial mentality"—that is, a mentality that sought accommodation "with hardening class divisions under industrial capitalism." Stated another way, they did not understand the potential for exploitation that industrial capitalism could and would, in time, produce on a large scale.

Did Wendell Phillips and other former abolitionists who championed the cause of labor undergo a radical transformation in their attitudes toward relations between capital and labor? The answer is a resounding no.[47] True, Phillips did call for the passage of an eight-hour work law; but, in essence, Phillips's solutions to labor's plight reflect as much of a "pre-industrial" mentality in the 1860s and 1870s as they did in the 1840s and 1850s. To wit: Phillips opposed strikes, advocated temperance, and relied on the power of the ballot to correct social evils. "There should be no capitalist of laborer as such," Phillips declared in 1865, "for each individual can be and must be made to combine both in his own person." Classes, he said on another occasion, "must be made to blend like the colors on a dove's neck."[48] What does this tell us about not only abolitionist thought but the mentality of working men that Phillips was accepted as a labor leader?

Social historians such as Paul Boyer and Allan Dawley avoid this question by arguing that postwar crusades such as temperance, public education, and workingman's politics were little more than a reflection of attempts by urban elites to undermine or destroy the cultural autonomy of working-class people.[49] Historian Herbert G. Gutman, however, who draws heavily upon the conceptual formulations of British historians E. P. Thompson, Asa Briggs, and Eric Hobsbawm, provides a frame of reference that historians of postwar reform movements ignore at their peril."[50]

In order to understand how people respond to industrial change, Asa Briggs writes, "it is necessary to examine fully what kind of people they were at the beginning of the process, to take account of continuities and traditions as well as new ways of thinking and feeling."[51] Applied to the United States, Gutman writes:

> Protestantism in its many and even contradictory forms, but particularly the Christian perfectionism of pre–Civil War and evangelical reform movements, lingered on among many discontented postbellum workers. It was no different in the United States than in Great Britain where labor and religious historians have documented the close relationship between Protestant Nonconformity, especially Methodism, and labor reform. None of this should surprise students of social movements. The bulk of industrial workers in all countries, Eric Hobsbawm notes, 'began . . . as first generation immigrants; they looked backward as much as forwards.' The non-industrial world had no pattern of life suited to the 'new age' and so men and women 'drew on the only spiritual resources at their disposal, preindustrial custom and religion.'[52]

The implications of these insights for the history of postwar labor movements, religion, reform movements in general, and the study of abolitionist ideology during the Reconstruction era in particular ought to be apparent. In fact, it suggests, in combination with other studies, the pervasiveness of an individualistic ethos in nineteenth-century American society—the existence of shared values that helps not only to explain the lack of class consciousness, in relative terms, but the pursuit of nonrevolutionary solutions to wrenching dislocations caused by rapid and unprecedented change in the American social and economic landscape.[53]

From Assertiveness to Individualism: The Difficult Path from Slavery to Freedom

Loren Schweninger

F OR many years, David Imes, a farmer in Juniata County, Pennsylvania, had heard stories about the famous black abolitionist Frederick Douglass, but it was not until a neighbor loaned him a copy of *My Bondage and My Freedom* that he discovered how similar their lives had been: they had both begun life as slaves in Maryland, they both claimed white ancestry, and they had both left the South to become extremely successful in their chosen fields of endeavor. Imes was so struck with these similarities that he wrote Douglass a long letter, detailing how his grandfather had been a white Maryland slave owner named William Imes, his grandmother a plantation slave, and how his father had remained in bondage for nearly fifty years before securing his freedom and moving to Pennsylvania, where young Imes had grown to manhood. During the 1840s and 1850s, Imes had purchased several tracts of land, and eventually he had acquired a substantial estate. His neighbors—black and white—considered him one of the best farmers in the region. Indeed, he would have been ashamed to have written "such a letter to a stranger" were he not convinced that Douglass knew as well as anyone how difficult it was "to accumulate where there is nothing to begin with and when everything was as dark as night in behalf of the coulerd race." But with hard work, Imes concluded, "it indeed is remarcable what one man [can] do."[1]

The ascent of David Imes, like that of Frederick Douglass, was truly remarkable, but his letter reveals an important paradox in the attitudes and values of blacks who had moved from slavery to freedom: he spoke as "a stranger" about what one individual could accomplish; yet, he also wrote "in behalf of the coulerd race." This essay seeks to explore the contradictory and complex nature of black cultural values by examining how such self-assertion was a necessary precondition for an eventual emergence of individualism. Assertiveness involved the paradoxical venturing into "white culture," and either achieving a measure of social competence and personal vindication there, or, as was often the case, being frustrated by the prevailing racism and inequality. To understand this process, the pages that follow will examine the values of blacks in West Africa, how these attitudes changed in the New World, how they evolved among slaves in the antebellum South, and how they changed even more during the first generation of freedom following the Civil War. It should be noted at the outset that the antebellum groups to be examined—runaway slaves, "quasi-free" bondspeople, slave entrepreneurs, and blacks who purchased their freedom or attempted to do so—represented a relatively small portion of the total slave population in the South, but their assertiveness revealed an inchoate individualism.[2]

Africans who arrived in the New World began their journey somewhere in the vast region stretching from the Senegal River, west and south along the great savannah and rain forests, to the mouth of the Congo River and beyond, a region of enormous ethnic and cultural diversity, inhabited by the Fulani, Mandinka, Wolof, Ashanti, Fanti, Hausa, Ibo, Yoruba, Bakongo, Nsundi, and numerous other peoples. Despite their many differences, a common thread bound these peoples together: they were inextricably bound to their villages and to their communities. From birth, through puberty, marriage, maturity, and old age, individuals passed through various rites binding them to others in their communities. Even in death they entered the spiritual world of "the living dead," created by the collective memory of the living. This corporate existence, the "seamless web" holding people together, dominated every aspect of life among blacks in their native land— social, economic, political, religious; it was, as historian Nathan Huggins has said, "a common imperative pulling all together to an insistent command that was above and beyond the individual self, the family, or the clan."[3]

Kidnapped or captured in war, herded in coffles to the coast, branded and incarcerated in the holds of slave ships bound for the New World, enslaved Africans suffered physical and mental anguish of indescribable dimensions. Those who survived the squalor and disease of the middle passage, the trauma of the "seasoning process," the grinding toil in the cane, tobacco, rice, and cotton fields, discovered that the old bonds, hardened through generations of village and communal life, began to weaken. However much they yearned to return to the slow, tranquil life of the village, or dreamed of returning to their families or friends, with each passing year, as they learned a new language and new way of life, the spiritual oneness of the village seemed more remote, less vivid to the memory.[4]

This was true everywhere in the Americas, from South and Central America, to the Caribbean and Gulf region of the United States, to British mainland North America. In some regions the process of cultural change took longer than in others, and in some sections of the same region there were differences among various groups of slaves, but the New World environment created new exigencies, the necessity of adapting to new conditions. Even on the largest plantations, including those with sizable numbers of African-born slaves, such as the sugar plantations in St. Domingue, Jamaica, Cuba, and Brazil, blacks began to accept new values and attitudes more compatible with their new condition. "Torn from societies that had not yet entered into the capitalistic world, and thrust into settings that were profoundly capitalistic in character on the one hand, yet rooted in the need for unfree labor on the other," anthropologist Sidney Mintz writes concerning the Caribbean islands, "the slaves saw liquid capital not only as a means to secure freedom," but as a means of creating a new identity, one less dependent on the communal values of the past and more dependent on "something even their masters would have to respect." Everywhere slavery took root in the Americas, blacks gradually began to look upon themselves differently than had their African ancestors.[5]

This was especially true in the Southern colonies of British mainland North America. During the seventeenth and eighteenth centuries, as the institution of slavery took hold and expanded, there was also a process of cultural change among blacks. As historian Ira Berlin pointed out, this varied according to time, place, condition of labor, and the number of blacks arriving directly from Africa. During the early years, with a majority of the slaves arriving in the colonies from the West Indies—Barbados, Jamaica, and Antigua—where they had already adjusted to the New World environment, and with both masters and slaves facing the same harsh frontier conditions, blacks were allowed a good deal of autonomy; thus, the "acculturation process," as some scholars have called it, occurred relatively rapidly. During the eighteenth century, as planters turned to the production of staple crops in the Southern colonies, and began importing large numbers of blacks directly from the Guinea coast, the acculturation process slowed, and in some areas, such as the Sea Islands of South Carolina and Georgia, blacks remained "physically separated and psychologically estranged from the Anglo-American world and culturally close to Africa." But even in the low country slaves found themselves becoming "New Negroes"—comprehending and speaking English, rejecting certain African customs and ways, and accepting some of the values and attitudes of their captors.[6] Even those who yearned to return to their old habits found their world view, rooted in the past, being changed and transformed.[7]

Perhaps no individual's life reflected this transformation better than that of Georgia slave Andrew Bryan, who had gained his freedom and founded the first black Baptist church in America. In 1800, in a letter to a high church official in London (probably written by a sympathetic white), Bryan not only told about his life in the New World but revealed his cultural values and attitudes, values which were markedly different from those of his forebears in West Africa. "With much pleasure, I inform you, dear sir, that I enjoy good health, and am strong in body, tho 63 years old, and am blessed with a pious wife, whose freedom I have obtained, and an only daughter and child, who is married to a free man, tho' she, and consequently, under our laws, her seven children, five sons and two daughters, are slaves." By kind Providence, he was well provided with "worldly comforts," owning a house and lot and several rental properties in Savannah, a fifty-six-acre farm in the country, four mules, and eight slaves, "for whose education and happiness, I am enabled, thro' mercy to provide." Each Sabbath he preached to three different congregations totalling seven hundred souls at his Second Baptist Church, frequently baptizing ten to thirty converts at a time.[8] Bryan's missive not only exposed his ambiguous feelings toward material success and religious salvation, but revealed a world view quite different from his African ancestors: life as a journey of personal experiences and Christian spirituality.

By the early nineteenth century, with the outlawing of the African slave trade to the United States, the vast majority of blacks in the South were native born. Lacking the renewal of cultural forms so essential to maintaining a continuity with Africa, the old values and customs were transformed even more than they had been previously. In other ways, too, conditions in the South lent themselves to these cultural changes. Compared with the huge estates in the Caribbean and elsewhere, Southern slaves worked on comparatively small units (usually smaller than fifty slaves), lived on the same estates as their masters (absentee landlords were extremely rare), and came in daily contact with white overseers. In addition, they were encouraged to embrace Christianity, with its doctrines of individual redemption and individual regeneration.[9]

Although historians and other scholars have often emphasized the "communal" and "community" aspects of slavery in the nineteenth-century South, how slaves—through an emotional religion, folk songs, and folk tales, dances, superstitions, language, extended kinship networks, different customs—created a unique African-American culture, slavery was a diverse and multisided institution.[10] It developed differently in different sections of the South, in rural and urban areas, in black belt and up-country, in the lower South (stretching from South Carolina to Texas) and the upper South (stretching from Virginia to Tennessee). Within each of these areas there were contrasts between slaves who worked on large plantations and slaves who worked on smaller plantations and farms, slaves who had acquired skills as artisans and slaves who labored as field hands, slaves who worked under the task system (being assigned a task each day and having the left-over time to themselves), the gang system, or a combination of both and slaves who were hired out, who hired their own time, or who achieved what contemporaries called "virtual freedom," living apart from their masters and earning their own living. Under each of these circumstances, black as-sertiveness took different forms and confronted varying degrees of white oppression.[11]

The most extreme type of assertiveness was to challenge the system openly. Unlike the Caribbean and South America, where there were numer-ous large-scale slave revolts, overt resistance in the United States came pri-marily in two forms—individual acts of violence and running away. Typical of the first was an incident involving the Tennessee slave Jacob, who was described as "about thirty years old, six feet or upwards high, of rather bright complexion, weighs about 160 or 170 pounds, has a rather down look." On August 17, 1840, the same day as a great Whig political conven-tion in Nashville, Jacob refused to go to the fields, and when confronted by the plantation overseer and by his master, Robert Bradford, an "old and respected farmer," he drew a knife, and in an attempt to kill the overseer, he accidentally slit Bradford's throat. "Everybody was going to town to drink hard cider, wear a coontail in his Hat, and Yell for Tippicanoe and Tyler too," a former Tennessee slave said, recalling the incident, "and likely Jake wanted a holliday."[12]

A close study of runaways in Virginia points to the same type of individ-ual resistance. Earlier, "outlandish" slaves, those recently arrived from Af-rica, typically ran away in groups and attempted to establish villages on the frontier, but by the late eighteenth and early nineteenth centuries, blacks virtually always ran away alone and tried to pass as free persons of color in the most settled areas of the state. Moreover, in Virginia and other sections of the South, the most skilled slaves ran off in numbers greater than any other group. "RAN away from the Subscriber, living in Baltimore," a typ-ical notice read, "a brownish yellow Man, named Jacob Cockkey . . . a blacksmith by trade, and can do very good work if he will keep himself from gambling, to which he is much adicted [sic]." This not only posed a dilemma for slave owners who sought to create a more efficient labor force by teaching their blacks necessary skills, but revealed the disintegration of the "seamless web."[13]

Most of those who resisted bondage in such a manner were quickly ap-prehended and punished. But there were other more subtle ways to avoid the harsher aspects of slavery. Success would depend on a shrewd understanding of Southern society, an intuitive sense for anticipating danger, and the abil-ity to earn a livelihood. It would also sometimes depend on the aid and protection of whites. Whatever the individual circumstances, as the doors to legal emancipation slowly closed during the antebellum decades, an increasing number of slaves, by one means or another, moved into what contemporaries called "quasi freedom"—halfway between bondage and liberty. While legally enslaved, these blacks lived independent, sometimes completely autonomous lives, securing their own employment, maintaining their own families, and moving about from place to place.[14]

Observers were constantly struck by the ubiquitous nature of this group. According to a Georgia resident, there were more "free negroes manufactured and made virtually free" in the town of Athens than there were "bona fide" free blacks in Clarke and any ten surrounding counties. A visitor to New Orleans noticed "a great many loose negroes about," slaves who hired their own time, earned their own living, and paid "wages" to their owners. Even in sparsely settled rural areas observers noted the presence of virtually free blacks. "Although they are Slaves yet they have been living to themselves for about 20 years," Samuel Rhea, a Sullivan County, Tennessee, farmer explained, describing one black family. "They have supported themselves on land of their masters and are tolerable farmers." In nearly every region of the South, observers told about nominally free slaves who went about according to their own fancy, seemingly oblivious to any law or regulation.[15]

Ironically, some slaveholders assisted these blacks in various ways and defended them as honest, reliable, and hard working. They argued that quasi-free slaves possessed skills necessary in the community and that they could be counted on as informants during periods of slave unrest. "This man has served his time in my neighbourhood, and has always maintained an excellent character," Virginia planter Samuel Anderson wrote concerning one quasi-free Negro. "He is a good workman and an honest and industrious man. I have no doubt the he can obtain the sanction of every man in the neighbourhood." Another black who had secured "the sanction" of local whites was Parlour Washington, "a good industrious mechanic in the arts & trades of tanner & currier of leather and also a good shoe, boot and harness maker." Nearly one hundred Hamilton County, Tennessee, residents explained that his services were greatly "needed and required by the Citizens of the section of the County where he now resides." Blacks with such reputations, these white defenders believed, posed no threat to the "peculiar institution."[16]

A few of the most successful free slaves actually established small businesses. Virginia's Robert Gordon sold slack from his white father's coal yards to local blacksmiths, amassing a small fortune of fifteen thousand dollars by 1846, when he purchased his freedom and moved to Ohio. South Carolina slave Thomas David owned a construction business, negotiating contracts, hiring day laborers (many of them who were also bondsmen), and supervising the erection of numerous houses as well as several larger buildings. "Those who were mechanics had extra privileges," a postwar investigator explained, "some of them hiring their own time, & working as master builders—hiring labourers & teaching them—making contracts for buildings &c." Such practices became so prevalent in some sections that white mechanics signed remonstrances to state legislatures complaining that they were being outbid on contracts by slaves, who "undertake work on their own account at sometimes less than one half the rate that a regular bred white Mechanic could afford to do it."[17] Future Alabama congressman Benjamin Turner hired his own time, purchased a livery stable, and during the Civil War managed his owner's financial affairs. "I [ran] a livery-stable in Selma, and r[a]n omnibuses, hacks, etc.," Turner testified in 1871, seeking restitution for the eight thousand dollars worth of property he had lost at the hands of Wilson's Raiders. "That was my business, and my boss [Dr. Gee] left me some business of his to look after, such as collecting money for him, and attending to his affairs as a matter of encouragement to me and to make me behave myself and not run away while the war was going on."[18]

Slave businessmen demonstrated a remarkable degree of business acumen, but even the most enterprising among them found it difficult, if not impossible, to secure their legal emancipation. With each passing decade, Southern states passed new and more restrictive laws governing the manumission of slaves. In North Carolina, a relatively liberal state in this regard, an owner was required to put up a substantial bond, file a petition with the superior court, publish the intended manumission in the *State Gazette*, notify the local probate judge, and promise that the freed slave would leave the state within ninety days. Prior to 1830, in Louisiana, owners could free only those blacks who had shown "good conduct" and were at least thirty years old; during the 1830s, the state prohibited manumission altogether. In some states it took a special act of the legislature to free a slave; and in Tennessee, prior to passage of such an act, county probate judges were instructed to appoint trustees for manumitted blacks, trustees who could hire freed slaves out "from year to year" and possessed "all the rights and privileges" of slave owners. During the 1850s, several states followed Louisiana's example by prohibiting the manumission of slaves altogether.[19]

Besides the web of legal restraints, self-hired and quasi-free blacks confronted other obstacles in their quest for freedom, including the avaricious designs of some slave masters. The literate house servant and barber James Starkey, though quasi-free and earning a good income, was required to turn over his earnings to his master. If he were allowed to work only partially for himself, he could raise his purchase price in a few years, "but as long as I have wages to pay," he lamented, "it is impossible." With the assistance of a Northern abolitionist, Starkey eventually bought his freedom, but such was not the case for bondswoman Mary Carrol, who signed an agreement in 1855 to pay for herself over a period of years. According to the agreement, she was advanced her purchase price of six hundred dollars in the form of a mortgage note, and when she had paid the principle and interest as well as any personal medical expenses and the premiums on a life insurance policy, she would be free. After four-and-a-half years, she still owed her owner nearly four hundred dollars. Still, she was probably no worse off than Fanny Smith, a Virginia slave who made a verbal agreement with her master to pay for herself and her two children over a period of ten years. Shortly before the final payment she was sold.[20]

Even under the best of circumstances, self-purchase was an enormous undertaking. During the 1820s, a young male slave could purchase himself for about three hundred and fifty dollars in Virginia, and about seven hundred dollars in Louisiana. A generation later these prices had nearly doubled. Although the earning power of hired bondsmen and women had appreciated considerably during the interim, by the 1850s even the most frugal and dedicated slave found twelve hundred dollars or fourteen hundred dollars beyond his means. Those who, through extraordinary effort, could save enough to buy themselves often faced wrenching decisions about their families. "The man himself has been actually free for some time, his master holding only a pro-forma ownership over him until recently when he has been fully emancipated," a white Virginian explained about one black who was making plans to move to the North. "He is of the very best character, honest, industrious, submissive, and much confided in and so thrifty." But after purchasing himself, his wife, and a child, he was forced to inform his other children that they would be left behind in slavery. Such decisions could cause deep remorse in subsequent years, leaving wounds that would never heal. As if sinking deeper in quicksand, the struggles of many blacks to free themselves or members of their families often ended only in desperate failure.[21]

Given the legal, economic, and racial barriers they faced, it was not surprising that so many failed. It is remarkable, however, that thousands of slaves somehow worked their way out of bondage. "He was 7 years laying up his freedom-money," an acquaintance of South Carolina slave George Moss said, "and during the whole of this time, he performed the ordinary labor of a slave for his master." Allowed to work for himself on Sundays, holidays, and in the evenings, Moss strung baskets and fashioned brooms, selling these items to whites. He used his profits to make small loans, and charged interest on this money. It took Virginia slave Godfrey Brown twenty-three years to purchase himself, his wife, and his nine children. "I have no hesitation in saying," his owner, John T. Bowdoin, said after receiving $2,375 from Brown, "that I was influenced [to free him] by the high character which he supported for honesty, industry, and inoffensive behavior." Another slave who spend nearly a lifetime freeing her family was Elizabeth Cromwell, who paid more than $3,000 for her husband and eight children.[22]

A significant percentage of blacks who acquired their freedom did so through their own efforts. According to an 1839 survey in Cincinnati, Ohio, among the 1,129 former slaves in this city, a total of 476, or 42 percent, had purchased themselves out of bondage. They paid a total of $215,522, or an average of $453 each. In addition, there was a "large number in the city who are working out their own freedom,—their free papers being retained as security." Among the 1,077 ex-slaves in Philadelphia and the surrounding area nearly a decade later, approximately 275, or 26 percent, had bought themselves, paying a total of $63,034. Similarly, a number of slaves who obtained their freedom and remained in the South had either paid their masters for their freedom papers or in various other ways worked their way out of bondage. If slaves attained their freedom in a variety of ways—manumission, running away, a special legislative act—a significant proportion somehow accumulated enough to buy themselves or their loved ones out of bondage.[23]

The vast majority of blacks in the South, of course, would remain in bondage throughout their lives. Only a few were successful runaways, attained quasi-free status, purchased themselves or members of their families, or acquired deeds of emancipation. Among those who did, however, few lacked an assertiveness that served as a precursor to individualism. Perhaps no one expressed this more clearly than Tennessee slave James Thomas, who, after securing his freedom at age twenty-three, set out on a ten-thousand-mile odyssey to the North, the West, and Central America. In 1859, at the end of his pilgrimage, he wrote his nephew about the meaning of life: "[M]elville . . . says that a man is any thing but pleasure on his way to a certain point where there is no one awaiting him. . . . Upon the whole no one cares much whether he comes or not. Now I ask you as a rational man if that would not be an ill spent life."[24]

The fear of traveling to a place where no one awaited his arrival betrayed Thomas's existential understanding of life. It can best be explained in terms of assertiveness as a cultural form of antebellum blacks living close enough to white society to break into some of its activities, an assertiveness that led to the perception of life as a journey. For David Imes, Andrew Bryan, James Thomas, and others, life's path led to painful choices between uttering words of a solitary speaker or invoking the aspirations of blacks as a collective whole. In seeking to resolve this dilemma, various groups of antebellum blacks created a type of individualism recognizable to whites but also consistent with their peculiar history of moving from slavery to freedom.

The coming of freedom during the Civil War created a new environment for Southern blacks. In various ways, the assertiveness that had evolved among some groups of slaves during the early nineteenth century now became more widespread as freedmen and freedwomen abandoned the slave quarters, journeyed to a town or city, chose new names, and refused to address whites as "marsa" or "missus." They also haggled over wages, working conditions, and set their own pace in the fields. As historian Leon Litwack observed, at the base of freedom was the determination of an individual to become his or her own master; again and again, former slaves expressed the same idea: "To belong to ourselves."[25]

It quickly became apparent, however, that belonging to oneself would not provide blacks with food, clothing, and other basic necessities. The failure of the federal government to give adequate assistance, the ironlike grip of whites on the land, and the turbulence and violence of the postwar era caused hardship and destitution in many sections of the South. Even after the entry of blacks into politics, and the passage of the Fourteenth Amendment, promising citizenship rights for ex-slaves, the economic condition for the vast majority of the nearly four million freed people changed only slightly. "I don't know as I 'spected nothin' from freedom," one Texas freedman recalled, "but they turned us out like a bunch of stray dogs, no homes, no clothin', no nothin', not 'nough food to las us one meal."[26]

Even so, belonging to oneself and being on one's own had significant implications for the cultural evolution that occurred during the first generation and a half of freedom. Although the forces pushing blacks in upon themselves (racial hostility, violence, economic oppression, repressive laws and institutions) remained powerful, as did some of the cultural values molded in bondage (folk beliefs, folk religion, kinship networks) during the decades following the Civil War, growing numbers of blacks began to embrace the type of individualism that had emerged among various groups of slaves during the antebellum period.

This transformation can be seen in the quest of former slaves and their children for economic self-sufficiency. Of course, no amount of assertiveness nor individual initiative could overcome the barriers to economic advancement in areas where whites refused to sell land to blacks, instituted the crop lien system, charged exorbitant interest rates, and mounted campaigns of violence and intimidation. As W. E. B. Du Bois noted, freedmen "in the power of unscrupulous landowners and merchants sank to a condition hardly better than slavery."[27]

Nevertheless, freedmen and freedwomen and their children slowly began to acquire land, farms, and homes. In the Deep South, where whites were most resistant, the pace was very slow. Within five years after the war, only eleven thousand blacks owned farm land, about 2 percent of the rural family heads. During the next two decades, the number rose to only seventy-four thousand, about 18 percent of the black farmers in the region. A similarly slow rise occurred among nonfarm families, mostly in towns and cities, who purchased their own homes and businesses. But in the upper South (from Maryland to Tennessee), where economic conditions were more favorable and whites less resistant, black property ownership rose more rapidly. The proportion of farm owners increased from 2 percent immediately following the war, to 33 percent in 1890, and to 44 percent in the first decade of the twentieth century. By then, in Virginia, Maryland, and Kentucky, about the same proportion of black as white farmers owned their own farms. For a people emerging from bondage, historian James McPherson writes, this "was a significant achievement."[28]

It was just this type of achievement that Frederick Douglass believed would lead to economic salvation for his race. The former runaway slave admonished his brethren to improve themselves through hard work, diligence, frugality, industry, and property accumulation. In an oft-repeated speech on "Self-Made Men," he articulated what one historian called a "heady individualism": through strength of character and indefatigable efforts, blacks could raise themselves up "by their own bootstraps." The same theme was present in the concluding chapter of his autobiography, when Douglass averred that

> neither institutions nor friends can make a race stand unless it has strength in its own legs; that there is no power in the world which can be relied upon to help the weak against the strong—the simple against the wise; that races like individuals must stand or fall on their own merits.

This connection between races and individuals was at the heart of Douglass's philosophy. Indeed, his career embodied the evolution from assertiveness to individualism. As a slave, his quest for literacy, his rebelliousness, his hiring out for wages, his attack on the "nigger breaker" Covey, and finally escape to freedom were all forms of assertiveness. As the pre-eminent postwar black leader, Douglass urged his brethren to become rugged individualists.[29]

A few months after Frederick Douglass's death in 1895, the then little-known black educator Booker T. Washington addressed the Cotton States and International Exposition in Atlanta. In a speech dubbed by his critics as the "Atlanta Compromise," Washington emphasized self-help and individual economic achievement as a means for solving the race problem. "No race can prosper till it learns that there is as much dignity in tilling a field," he proclaimed, "as in writing a poem." It would be "merest folly" for blacks to agitate for "social equality," but the two races could work together for "all things essential to mutual progress." The speech, articulating the views of many whites, catapulted Washington to national fame.[30]

Although Washington and Douglass differed in their views on civil and political equality, they agreed that racial progress would come primarily through individual effort. "The price of success means beginning at the bottom," Washington said in a typical speech; "it means struggle, it means hardship, it often means hunger, it means planning and sacrificing today that you may possess and enjoy tomorrow." He, too, admonished blacks to practice patience, perseverance, economy, thrift, and unrelenting toil. Those who did so would be rewarded; those who were impatient, wasteful, and indolent would not only fail in life but would bring disgrace to the race.[31]

Thus, by the early twentieth century, the assertiveness of the slavery era had evolved into a full-blown individualism. The myth of the self-made man was especially pernicious for blacks who lived in regions of white terror and lynchings because no amount of individual effort nor industriousness could lift the masses out of poverty and destitution. Indeed, even former slaves and their children who owned their own farms and homes were not immune to the vagaries of the marketplace or the violent repression of whites. Some of them lived barely above the subsistence level.

Yet, they had traveled a great distance from the values and attitudes of their West African ancestors. By the early twentieth century, few blacks would have recognized the "common imperative pulling all together to an insistent command that was above and beyond the individual self." The individualism that emerged, however, was complex and contradictory. Even those who espoused it in its purest form, who truly believed that individual effort would bring individual success, believed just as fervently that individualism would somehow advance the race as a whole. The evolution from slave assertiveness to race conscious individualism symbolized the unique and difficult path blacks traveled from slavery to freedom.

The Ambiguity of Individualism: The National Liberal League's Challenge to the Comstock Law

Lawrence B. Goodheart

F REE Thought, Free Speech, Free Ballot, and Free Mails Must be Secured by a Secular Republic Emancipated from Church Domination."
So resolved the delegates at the 1879 convention of the National Liberal League at Cincinnati. The league organized about a specific mandate to extend what Thomas Jefferson termed "the wall of separation" between church and state.[1] Yet the league's commitment to secularism and free thought became inextricably linked with the divisive issues of obscenity and censorship. Already contending with a Protestant antivice campaign that equated irreligion with immorality, league members quarreled over whether to endorse total repeal or partial reform of the Comstock censorship law. Unsuccessful in implementing its goals, the short-lived organization nevertheless represented the culmination of nineteenth-century anticlericalism and the growing erosion of a religiously dominated moral order. Its defense of free thought and challenge to censorship was a landmark stand on behalf of First Amendment rights. Working at cross-purposes to the league's efforts, however, was its inability to define with precision the nebulous boundaries of individual rights during the Gilded Age.

The formation of the National Liberal League in 1876 occurred during a period of fundamental social flux in America. The emergence of industrial capitalism, rapid urbanization, and technological innovation profoundly affected late-nineteenth-century culture. Gazing from his club window on the hubbub of Fifth Avenue traffic, a pensive Henry Adams captured the sense of bewildering change. Adams "felt himself in Rome, under Diocletian, witnessing the anarchy, conscious of the compulsion, eager for the solution, but unable to conceive whence the next impulse was to come or how it was

133

to act." What Adams rightly regarded as a turning point in Western civilization was accompanied by an intellectual and moral challenge to the traditional Christian order. Social theorists as diverse as Auguste Comte, Karl Marx, Herbert Spencer, and Lester Frank Ward heralded the arrival of a new secular orientation, the emergence of which Charles Darwin's publication of *The Origin of the Species* in 1859 served as a bench mark. Concluding his analogy, Adams—himself an agnostic—wrote with appropriate fin de siècle ruefulness, "The two-thousand years failure of Christianity roared upward from Broadway and no Constantine the Great was in sight."[2]

In a more modest way than the Roman emperor, Francis E. Abbot also had a vision of religious unity for a fragmented world. A Harvard graduate and Unitarian minister, he was the person most responsible for the founding of the National Liberal League. Unlike many of his contemporaries, exemplified by Bishop Wilberforce and Thomas Huxley in their celebrated 1869 debate on evolution, Abbot argued for the harmony between science and religion. "The future of theology," he believed, depended on "its coalescing with science." A "scientific theism," he thought, would strip away the superstitious hull and leave the spiritual kernel, a rational deity at home in a Darwinian world. His iconoclastic thought led inevitably to a break with Unitarianism, which he indicted as creed-bound. In 1867, he joined with other religious dissenters to found the Free Religious Association, an organization dedicated to the creation of a universal "Religion of Humanity." Although free religionists differed widely in their beliefs, they united in support of freedom of individual thought and in their rejection of Christian dogma. They concurred with Abbot's liberal sentiment, expressed in the constitution of the Free Religious Association, that "the grand end of human society is the freest, fullest, the highest development of the individual."[3]

Abbot remained a prominent figure in the Free Religious Association, but an opportunity to found his own newspaper, *The Index,* offered new possibilities. The weekly, first published on January 1, 1870, allowed Abbot to promote his own ideas about rational theism. In addition, the newspaper provided an ideological and organizational forum for what became the National Liberal League. To Abbot's credit, he translated the abstract individualism and antisectarianism of the Free Religious Association into the more concrete First Amendment issues of free speech and the separation of church and state. Complete disestablishment of religion was Abbot's response to what he regarded as the spiritual authoritarianism of Christianity and its unconstitutional alliance with the state. His own controversial dismissal in 1868 from a Dover, New Hampshire, pulpit for heterodox views— a decision sustained by the state supreme court—made him sensitive to the collusion of church and state. Moreover, an ongoing effort of Protestant fundamentalists to add a Christian amendment to the Constitution provided the occasion for secularist opposition.

The concept of a Christian amendment was a latter-day version of covenant theology. During the dark days of the winter of 1863, eleven Christian denominations convened at Xenia, Ohio, to declare that the bloody Civil War was a divine retribution on a godless nation. The official establishment of Christian nationhood was necessary to restore God's favor on his chosen people. The churchmen further argued that the government and its magistrates were responsible to the Deity, the ultimate sovereign, and subject to His moral law. In contrast, they asserted that a secular state, based solely on the will of the majority and dependent on human reason, was a blasphemous usurpation of divine governance.

Out of the Xenia convention grew the National Reform Association, with the object of Christianizing the Constitution, not unlike current fundamentalist crusades. Their proposed amendment called for the declaration that "Almightly God [is] the Author of National Existence and the source of all power and authority in Civil Government, Jesus Christ [is] the Ruler of Nations, and the Bible [is] the formation of law and supreme rule for the conduct of nations." Through allegiance to God, Christ, and the Bible, the amendment provided a sense of group unity and common purpose in the face of disturbing social trends. In addition to endorsement from various Protestant denominations, the officers of the association were nationally prominent, including William Strong, a U.S. Supreme Court justice, as president, and a number of state governors as vice-presidents. The Reverend J. P. Stevenson, editor of *The Christian Statesman,* employed his paper as the association's organ.[4]

In reaction to a concerted drive in 1872 for the Christian amendment, Abbot first published a countermanifesto in *The Index.* "The Nine Demands of Liberalism" declared that "our entire political system shall be founded and administered on a purely secular basis." Churches would lose their tax exemption; the Bible would be prohibited as a "book of religious worship" in the schools; and Sabbatarian laws would be repealed. Chaplains, religious fast days, judicial oaths, and the public subsidy of any church-related institution would also be eliminated. More abstractly, the eighth demand called for "natural morality, equal rights and impartial liberty" to replace "Christian morality." "The Nine Demands" proved to be the rallying point for secularists for the rest of the century.[5]

Abbot acted on two fronts to translate "The Nine Demands" into political action. First, he used *The Index* to publicize a petition against the Christian amendment. On January 1, 1874, Senator Charles Sumner of Massachusetts presented the 953-foot-long document with 35,180 names to the Senate. Second, during the same week, Abbot proposed a "Religious Freedom Amendment" to strengthen the protection of the Bill of Rights. The existing wording of the First Amendment that "Congress shall make no law respecting an establishment of religion or prohibiting the free exercise thereof" would be revised to include "or favoring any particular form of religion," a reference to Christianity. Abbot opposed what in the 1980s the Reagan administration has termed "accommodationism" in which the state directly supports Christian practices such as Sabbatarianism, financial aid to sectarian schools, and prayer in public schools. Instead, Abbot advocated a strict neutrality between church and state, emphasizing that "the Christian church is not a national church, and the Christian religion is not the national religion."[6]

After the publication of "The Nine Demands," some forty liberal clubs with eight hundred members sprang up in a number of northeastern and midwestern cities. The constituency for a secular movement was located in those urban centers where industrialization and access to scientific ideas had created a cosmopolitan environment that made conventional religious beliefs and practices suspect. In the fall of 1875, planning began for a national organization. Under Abbot's direction, 170 delegates gathered in a general convention at Philadelphia, which coincided with the festivities marking the national centennial on July 4, 1876. The delegates consciously linked their concern with individual freedom to the principles of the Declaration of Independence and to the legacy of Thomas Jefferson, Benjamin Franklin, Thomas Paine, and Ethan Allen, Founding Fathers who had challenged Christian orthodoxy. After several days of the conclave, the participants announced the creation of the National Liberal League on the Fourth of July.[7]

For the first time in American history, an organization for the secularization of the state existed on a national scale. The founding convention drafted a constitution, approved a score of resolutions, and elected officers. The league declared that its object was "the total separation of church and state: to the end that equal rights in religion, genuine morality in politics, and freedom, virtue, and brotherhood in all human life, may be established, protected and perpetuated." In order to achieve its goal, the league endorsed "The Nine Demands of Liberalism" and "The Religious Freedom Amendment." Unlike the Free Religious Association, it was clearly an advocacy group on behalf of state secularization. Furthermore, the league anticipated the formation of the American Civil Liberties Union by almost fifty years in its pledge to defend the legal rights of any citizen whose religious opinions were unconstitutionally suppressed. Provisions were also made for annual membership at one dollar, yearly conventions, and auxiliary societies. In recognition of his energetic leadership, the delegates chose Abbot their president and made *The Index*, which had relocated from Toledo to Boston, its official organ.[8]

The National Liberal League gathered a diverse host of individualists under the common flag of secularism. Whether theists or atheists, they rejected Christian orthodoxy, substituted reason for faith, and hailed the technological triumphs of the era as convincing evidence of humanity's liberation from centuries of superstition and backwardness. They saw themselves at a privileged moment of time. By midcentury, the mobility, market forces, and modernization of a dynamic, expansive capitalism had undercut many customary practices, including a traditional deference to creeds and clergy. "This is an age of success," Felix Adler, a president of the Free Religious Association and Jewish agnostic who founded the Ethical Culture Society, confidently told a *New York Times* reporter. Exuberant in their assessment of the potential for human development, liberals eagerly embraced individualism as an end in itself. "The platform of the coming millions is the individual," prophesied Elizur Wright, an early supporter of the league. There was little recognition of sin or of man's inherent limitations. In what amounted to romantic Darwinism, liberals assumed that the new, independent person was leading the species on an ever-upward course of progress, freedom, and enlightenment.[9]

According to a widely held convention among historians, the Civil War represented, as Eric Foner put it, "the deathknell of the antebellum tradition of radical individualism." For the National Liberal League, Foner's obituary is quite premature. Liberals accurately saw themselves as part of a continuum of radical nineteenth-century individualism. They celebrated black emancipation, bemoaned women's degradation, and identified themselves as heirs of the abolitionist movement. It was a logical step from the abolitionist argument that slaves, like all people, were autonomous moral agents with the right of self-ownership to the liberal's stress on individual rights and freedom of thought. For liberals, orthodox religion represented a spiritual tyranny akin to a slave master's physical dominance of his bondsman. The Reverend William James Potter, a major figure in the Free Religious Association, spoke of the need for "a spiritual antislavery society." Abbot significantly characterized Christianity as "an organized slavery of the mind." And America's best known agnostic, Robert G. Ingersoll pointedly asked, "Why should we take the chains from bodies and enslave minds?"[10]

A number of prominent first generation abolitionists, including William Lloyd Garrison, Wendell Phillips, Parker Pillsbury, and Elizur Wright, endorsed the league. The failure of the major religious denominations to embrace abolitionism or feminism provided the league with a ready constituency of antebellum reformers, such as Lucretia Mott, Thomas Wentworth Higgenson, Robert Dale Owen, and Samuel E. Sewall. Lucy N. Colman, a veteran abolitionist and feminist, warned, "Christianity demands entire subordination to its ethics. Until the majority of people are emancipated from authority over their minds, we are not safe." Sexual reformers Ezra H. Heywood and the father and son physicians Edward Bond Foote and Edward Bliss Foote, dissident minister Samuel P. Putnam, biographer

James Parton, lawyer Thaddeus B. Wakeman, and editor D. M. Bennett of *The Truth Seeker* also joined the league.[11]

Abbot had successfully organized the league to counter the proposed Christian amendment to the Constitution. The fundamentalist National Reform Association was never able to marshal sufficient support to alter the First Amendment restrictions on the separation of church and state. The tradition of religious freedom and sectarian rivalry frustrated the association's campaign, as did greater public attention focused on the economic turmoil, labor unrest, and political scandals of the Gilded Age. Nevertheless, Christian fundamentalists and purity crusaders achieved a striking victory with the passage of the Comstock act on March 3, 1873. On its face, the law dealt with "the suppression of trade in, and circulation of, obscene literature, and articles of immoral use." In practice, the federal government legitimated the imposition of arbitrary restrictions on First Amendment freedoms in the name of protecting the people from exposure to obscenity and in outlawing contraceptives. Both, it was believed, subverted sexual morality.[12]

Anthony Comstock, the eponymous author of the statute, was initially the agent of the Young Men's Christian Association and then in 1874 agent of its independent offshoot, the New York Society for the Suppression of Vice. A large, rotund man whose bulldog tenacity was mirrored in his muttonchop whiskers, he claimed to have destroyed more than five tons of obscene publications, 180,000 lewd photographs, and thirty thousand assorted contraceptives during only one year in the Empire State. Dissatisfied with the nominal national legislation on obscenity, his successful lobby of the Congress included a special exhibit of offensive material in the capitol office of the vice-president. With only cursory deliberation, the Congress overwhelmingly passed the legislation. Comstock's timing could not have been better. Congress was seeking to cast blame for the Credit Mobilier scandal (a flagrant example of endemic graft in the Gilded Age) and was reluctant to oppose a bill designed to restore the nation's besmirched virtue. The law made the manufacture, possession, or distribution of obscene publications, contraceptives, or abortifacients a misdemeanor with punishment not to exceed five years imprisonment at hard labor for each offense and total fines of two thousand dollars. The postal laws were amended to allow prosecution for the mailing of such material, and Comstock secured appointment as a federal postal inspector. His achievement was no less than to enforce the legislation he wrote.[13]

The Comstock Law was the first systematic effort to police the nation's morals through federal legislation. In a postwar era of ubiquitous political corruption and unsettling social change, obscenity in Victorian America was a catchall term for moral deviance. The original bill and subsequent amendment in 1876 failed, as only a few senators and congressmen tentatively acknowledged, to define obscenity with any precision, to make clear the legal ramifications, or to specify how the post office was to censor offending material. "The indignation and disgust which everyone feels in reference to the acts which are here aimed at," Senator Roscoe Conkling of New York alerted, "may possibly lead us to do something which, when we see it in print, will not be the thing we would have done if we had understood it and were more deliberate about it." Nevertheless, Conkling and his fellow senators voted unanimously for the bill, despite its readily apparent ambiguities. Although thirty-three representatives voted against the legislation, none spoke against it on the House floor. Cautious politicians did not want to be identified with opposition to an anti-obscenity statute, however loosely worded it was.[14]

The vagueness of the law gave Comstock broad enforcement power. He defined obscenity in an open-ended way that included erotic material, anatomical illustrations, sexual-reform literature, and atheistic tracts. His vigorous prosecution of religious infidels and sexual reformers raised serious questions about constitutional guarantees of freedom of speech and the press. Moreover, the post office developed an independent policy of censorship over the mail without recourse to policy decisions by the Department of Justice or the U.S. district attorney as to what materials should be confiscated and subjected to criminal charges. Comstock's enforcement of the postal laws also raised the question of legal entrapment, much as recent FBI "sting" operations have done. His modus operandi was to solicit suspected material in a "decoy" or "test" letter signed with an alias, and then to arrest the sender if he judged the mailed literature obscene.[15]

Comstock was indefatigable. He personally arrested several hundred people a year and methodically recorded in a logbook their names, offenses, dates, and judicial verdicts. In addition, he noted their religion and nationality, an indication of nativist Protestant fears about the unchurched and the increasing numbers of Catholic and Jewish immigrants. A youthful arrival from rural Connecticut to bustling New York City, Comstock was shocked at the breakdown of village morality in America's largest metropolis, especially the ready availability of "evil reading" material. The problem with a diet of such fare, whether dime novels, adventure stories, blasphemous tracts, or sexual depictions, was that it weakened self-control and stimulated lust. Unbridled desires threatened the social fabric, the former dry-goods clerk warned, corrupting the innocence of youth and the purity of womanhood, and undermining the viability of the family and the survival of government.[16]

Comstock fits the stereotype of the authoritarian personality, one which is emotionally attracted to strong external sources of regulation, especially during periods of social flux, in order to shore up a deficient sense of ego control. His motto, "Eternal vigilance is the price of moral purity," mimicked a Freudian superego at war with the libido. The danger posed by freethinkers, Comstock instructed, was that "by ridicule and laughter" they lulled "the watchman, Conscience, to sleep," and thus led others into temptation. His own relentless drive to ferret out and punish immorality in others may well have derived from a powerful imperative to suppress his own forbidden fantasies, including sexual anxieties. Speaking knowingly of the effect of pictures of naked women on young men, he warned that "cursed as thousands of the present day are with secret vices [a Victorian euphemism for masturbation], these photographs . . . fan the flames of secret desires." The socially sanctioned purity crusade also allowed Comstock to puruse the pleasures of the fleshpot. On one occasion he solicited a striptease in a brothel but arrested the women only at the conclusion of their act, billed intriguingly as the "Busy Fleas." Comstock's genius was the ability to translate his private obsession with sexuality, disorder, and infidelity into the publically condoned role of censor.[17]

Complementing the psychological motivation for order was a mandate for social control that intertwined the preservation of Protestant hegemony with the legitimation of the dominant class interests. Prominent New Yorkers controlled the boards of the YMCA and the Society for the Suppression of Vice. Comstock was literally their agent. His patrons included Morris K. Jessup, William E. Dodge, J. P. Morgan, Samuel Colgate, Killaen van Rensselaer, and Moses Beach. Ironically, these powerful men, celebrants of rugged individualism in a Spencerian world red in tooth and claw, funded the campaign to supervise other people's morals. Individualism was a social good as long as it confirmed their preeminent position as the "survival of the fittest," but an evil in the subversive form of free thought and sexual reform.

It was also an appropriate exercise in noblesse oblige and self-justification for the wealthy to subsidize a crusade on behalf of home and hearth, purity and piety. "Recent revelations have convinced us that no home, however carefully guarded, no school however select, has been safe from these corrupting influences," Clinton L. Merriam, a New York banker and spokesman for the Comstock Law in the House of Representatives warned about obscenity. The seal of the Society for the Suppression of Vice showed a smut dealer being jailed while a gentleman in top hat burned banned books. Yet these newspaper publishers, financial moguls, copper barons, and soap magnates were the very men who had profited inordinately from the Industrial Revolution that had disrupted the values of the traditional world that they now piously sought to recover. Vice and infidelity were the focuses of the well-to-do's civic engagement because their crusade ultimately reinforced their reigning-class ranking. Individual immorality, not structural inequities, was the source of social malaise according to their gospel.[18]

The encroaching secularism of late-nineteenth-century America was reflected in the influence of laymen in the purity crusade that only a half-century before would have been controlled by ministers. Capitalists joined hands with clergymen and other custodians of public morality to buttress an authoritarian value system. Fearful of the effect of a "filthy book or picture" on the younger generation, the Reverend J. M. Buckley preached that "the purity of youth is to be maintained only by repressing, under moral principal, the uprisings of passion and the play of a prurient fancy." Harriet Beecher Stowe, a member of the century's most illustrious family of clerics, editorialized in *My Wife and I,* her didactic novel, against "the permitted garbage of uncleansed literature and license." A college professor estimated that nearly 75 percent of male teenagers masturbated, spurred to that handiwork by lascivious publications. And Comstock predicted that "unless the restraining forces of religion and morality keep ahead of all other considerations, the ship of state will soon be dashed to pieces upon the boulders and quicksands of immorality."[19]

The vice crusaders were Christian soldiers marching in the army of evangelical Protestantism. Their appeal was to the social and psychological function of religion, not to doctrinal innovation, let alone complexity and nuance. After all, the muscular Christianity of revivalists Dwight L. Moody, Sam Jones, and T. Dewitt Tallmadge was as theologically simplistic as that of Billy Graham, Oral Roberts, and Jerry Falwell a century later. Clinging tenaciously to blind faith and standard shibboleths, conservative Christians were unwilling to respond to the challenge of the late nineteenth century on its own terms as their progressive brethren in the Social Gospel movement did. They aggressively defended their biblical barricades without understanding that they had been intellectually and morally outflanked.

But emotion, not reason, has remained the enduring strength of Protestant revivalism in the modern world. The fundamentalists successfully appealed to the very real fears of people whose lives had been disordered by Civil War, rapid technological change, urbanization, and fluctuating economic cycles. "That old time religion," which Moody celebrated in urban revivals, provided the continuity, certainty, and comfort for people to face the disruption, alienation, and, most alarmingly, the apparent meaninglessness of the new age. Obscenity was a conservative metaphor—just as communism, homosexuality, and abortion later would be—not only for the dissolution of the values of a largely mythic golden age but of authoritarian order itself. In their own way, the Gilded Age censors anticipated Sigmund Freud's axiom that civilization is based on the repression of sexual desires.

Immorality threatened, as Comstock ominously put it, to turn "the whole human family loose to run wild like the beasts of the forest." Obscenity was a spector haunting Victorian America.[20]

Evangelical Protestantism provided a set of assumptions that vice crusaders sought to impose on society. Original sin, it was preached, left humanity with a ready predisposition for sexual gratification. "Lust, indulged in thought or deed apart from love, is moral impurity," the Reverend J. M. Buckley catechized. "Sexual love with lust, apart from wedlock, is the spirit of adultery." (One hundred years later the "born again" Jimmy Carter confessed to the amused readers of *Playboy Magazine* that he had committed such sins in his "heart.") In an 1870 publication dedicated "To the Advocates of Christian Marriage," John Ellis warned of reformers who "sought to break down the restraints of society and secure an unrestricted range for their base desires." In the fall of 1872, the sensational Beecher-Tilden scandal (involving the accusation that America's best-known preacher had seduced his friend's wife) led to a 112-day trial and extended newspaper coverage. The feminist challenge to patriarchy also was a source of worry. Victoria Woodhull, the embodiment of the liberated woman of the era, was satirized in the writings of Harriet Beecher Stowe, caricatured by cartoonist Thomas Nast, and arrested by Comstock for her role in exposing the Reverend Henry Ward Beecher's purported adultery. In Congress, Representative Clinton L. Merriam claimed that the "victims" of obscene literature were filling "the prisons and madhouses." For the censors, obscenity eroded religious restraints, encouraged general copulation, and eliminated civilized behavior.[21]

With little faith in voluntary constraint or moral suasion, the vice crusaders opted, as most antebellum reformers had also eventually done, for legal coercion to produce desired behavior. Censorship of the mails was nationalized, a sign of the increasing role of the federal government as the institution of last resort in ordering the society, whether in Reconstruction policies, supplying troops to break strikes, or regulating the railroads. The arbitrary enforcement of the Comstock Law, however, quickly brought it into open conflict with freethinkers. "Religion and morality are," Comstock postulated, "the only safe foundations for a nation's future prosperity and security." The prima facie intent of the 1873 censorship law was to ban obscene literature and materials from the mail. But it logically followed that if religion was essential to maintaining the common good, infidel publications had to be confiscated. In a huge mound of twenty-four tons of seized material, Comstock found that the "most obscene and infamous thing" was a book parodying "The Rock of Ages" and "The Long Meter Doxology." The 1873 obscenity law was also a blasphemy statute.[22]

The Comstock Law was not on the official agenda of the National Liberal League's inaugural meeting of 1876. Stephen Pearl Andrews, an eclectic

New York City reformer, quickly raised the issue from the floor. Recent prosecution of freethinkers, including the conviction of the elder E. B. Foote for disseminating birth-control information, underscored the urgency for an effective response from the league. Delegates concurred that the postal law was being abused in order to censor free thought under the guise of protecting public morality. There was, however, a fateful impasse on what action to take. Some, notably Andrews, argued that the Comstock Law ought to be replaced entirely, but others supported the removal of what they deemed obscene material from the mail. On the last day of the convention, B. F. Underwood, a delegate from Massachusetts, proposed a compromise. He urged that the obscenity law be exactly worded so as to prevent the arrest of "honest and conscientious men" from presenting views that did not violate "the acknowledged rules of decency," a pious phrase that Underwood unhelpfully declined to define. He deplored Comstock's power to inspect the mails as a danger to civil liberties, but the resolution did not commit the league to the modification or repeal of the statute. Instead, Underwood's compromise was an ambiguous expedient that postponed the hard decision on what the league's position on the Comstock Law should be.[23]

While the league temporized, Comstock acted. His arrest of two vocal reformers, Ezra H. Heywood and D. M. Bennett, in the fall of 1877 shortly after the league's annual convention, dramatized the vulnerability of free-thinkers to prosecution under the postal laws. The activities of Heywood, a resident of Princeton, Massachusetts, exemplified the little-recognized continuity of radical individualism throughout the nineteenth century. After graduation from Brown University in 1856, he abandoned divinity studies and joined the Garrisonian abolitionists. He lectured widely on the topic "Individualism and Institutionalism" on the lyceum circuit, and remained a pacifist during the Civil War. After the war, he engaged in labor reform before joining with his wife in 1872 to edit *The Word,* the voice of the New England Free Love League, which the Heywoods organized the next year. In a consistent extension of the individualist anarchism of the antebellum Garrisonians, Heywood believed that each person was a responsible moral agent who must "seek truth" in opposition to the institutional coercion of church and state.[24]

In the language of the time, Heywood was a freethinker and freelover. His publication in 1876 of *Cupid's Yokes* (inspired in part by the experimental sexual practices at the Oneida community in upstate New York) denounced marriage as the husband's legalized "tyranny of lust" over his victimized wife. Heywood precociously called attention to the existence of what is now termed marital rape, noting the sensational case of a priapic clergyman who caused his spouse's death through repeated intercourse up to eight times a day. "Sexual organs are not less sacredly the property of individual citizens than other bodily organs. . . . Who but the individual owners can rightly determine When, Where, How, and for What purpose they shall be used?'' Heywood queried. ''It will ere long be seen,'' he predicted, anticipating the present-day argument for the noncriminalization of sexual relations between freely consenting adults, ''that a lady and a gentleman can as innocently and properly occupy one room at night as they can now dine together.'' He openly challenged the authority of church and state asking, ''Is coition pure only when sanctioned by a priest or magistrate?''[25]

''Yes!'' was Comstock's resounding retort. On November 2, 1877, he boldly arrested the author of that ''most obscene and loathsome book'' just as Heywood finished addressing 250 people at a convention of the New England Free Love League in Boston. Ten days later, he arrested D. M. Bennett, a vice-president of the National Liberal League, in the New York office of *The Truth Seeker*. Comstock charged Bennett with mailing *Cupid's Yokes* in addition to his own atheistic tract, ''An Open Letter to Jesus Christ,'' and a scientific treatise on marsupial reproduction. A convert to free thought later in life, Bennett moved his radical newspaper from rural Illinois to New York City in 1873, where he established *The Truth Seeker* as a leading antireligious organ. *The Truth Seeker* was pugnacious and muckraking, befitting its self-educated, small-town editor who lacked the Ivy League polish and erudition of Heywood and Abbot. Bennett delighted in revealing, for example, that Samuel Colgate, the soap tycoon and patron of purity, had once advertised Vaseline as a spermicide (it was not and is not). In his defense against Comstock, Bennett appealed to other liberals that the reason for his arrest was, ''I am a prominent advocate of heterodox opinions and have made myself obnoxious to the theological powers that be.''[26]

Comstock's concerted prosecution of Heywood and Bennett drew applause from the New York Society for the Suppression of Vice. ''Another class of publications issued by Freelovers and Freethinkers is in a fair way of being stamped out,'' the society reported at its January 28, 1878, meeting. ''The public generally can scarcely be aware of the extent that blasphemy and filth commingled have found vent through these varied channels.'' In response to the vice crusaders' success and the failure of the National Liberal League to take a stand, a group of concerned members of the league organized the National Defense Association in New York City on June 12. The association pledged ''to investigate all questionable cases of prosecution under what are known as the Comstock laws, State and National, and to roll back the wave of intolerance, bigotry and ignorance which threatens our cherished liberties.'' They gathered some seventy thousand signatures for repeal of the Comstock Law. On behalf of Heywood and Bennett, both of whom were eventually convicted under the Comstock Law and served prison terms, the association circulated petitions, organized rallies, and provided legal counsel.[27]

The press of events compelled the league to confront the divisive issue of censorship and obscenity at its third annual convention at Syracuse on October 26–27, 1878. Should the Comstock Law be partially reformed or totally repealed? Since the inaugural Philadelphia meeting, Abbot, who remained president, had so firmly committed himself to the reform position that in event of a majority vote for repeal he vowed not to run for re-election. At the emotionally charged gathering most delegates favored repeal. A tangle of conflicting resolutions and contentious debate led to the postponement of the explosive question until a future convention. The majority, however, dominated in another way. By a vote of seventy-six to fifty-one, they swept Abbot from office and voted in Elizur Wright, who favored repeal. Alleging bad faith on the repealers' part, Abbot angrily left the organization that he had founded and established a short-lived rival society.[28]

Despite their common commitment to individual freedom, the issue of obscenity and censorship revealed significant philosophical and tactical differences among liberals. All opposed obscenity, but none could define it. The best that E. P. Hurlbut, a former judge of the New York Supreme Court and supporter of Abbot, could offer the Syracuse conventioners was, "The instinct of every man and woman of ordinary intellect and common modesty defines the meaning of that word." This Solon's additional injunction to "reverence the family" and to "tolerate nothing which can corrupt the morals of youth" only clouded an already obscured subject. Unable to agree on what constituted obscenity, liberals split over whether the Comstock Law had any redeeming qualities.[29]

Abbot and Ingersoll, a vice-president of the league, dominated the reform position, which sought modification of the Comstock Law. Above all, both men wanted respectability for their challenge to Christianity. They believed a meaningful distinction could be made between publications that appealed to the intellect and those that pandered to the passions. They firmly supported the exclusion of obscene, but not infidel, literature from the mails. "The only objection I have to the law of 1873 is," Ingersoll wrote, "that it has been construed to include books and pamphlets written against religion of the day, although containing nothing that can be called obscene or impure." Abbot conspicuously avoided any support for the beleaguered Heywood and Bennett, mired, he believed, in the smut of *Cupid's Yokes*. In what amounted to apostasy for most liberals, Abbot declared, "Anthony Comstock has done a great deal of dirty but most necessary work." Abbot and Ingersoll wished to disassociate free thought completely from free love. As Ingersoll quipped about freelovers, "Let them spend their time examining each other's sexual organs, and in letting ours alone."[30]

D. M. Bennett, Courtland Palmer, James Parton, Thaddeus B. Wakeman, and Elizur Wright led the effort to repeal the Comstock Law. The repealers had a different vision of the league than the Abbot and Ingersoll faction. They too were concerned with challenging the Christian establishment, but postal censorship raised for them the broader question of civil liberties, not just for infidel publications but for free speech in general. This faction was active in forming the National Defense Association and subsequently extending the league's solidarity to the cause of Bennett and Heywood.

The schism in the league was dramatically played out on the floor of the 1880 convention. Thaddeus B. Wakeman, a New York lawyer and principal advocate of repeal, presented to the delegates a resolution endorsing abrogation of the Comstock Law and pledging the league to defend all who were prosecuted under it. Regarding the proposals as completely unacceptable, Ingersoll confronted Wakeman in an emotional debate:

> Ingersoll: There is not a man here who is not in favor, when these books and pictures come into control of the U.S. of burning them up when they are manifestly obscene. You don't want any grand jury there.
> Wakeman: Yes, we do.
> Ingersoll: No, we don't. When they are manifestly obscene, burn them up.

At that point in the heated exchange, a Wakeman partisan shouted from the floor, "Who is to be the judge of that?" This was the crucial question that Ingersoll, Abbot, Underwood, and Judge Hurlbut had not been able to address to the satisfaction of the repeal faction. Despite Ingersoll's effort to steer the league clear of what he called "this infernal question of obscenity," Wakeman's proposals passed. Frustrated, Ingersoll resigned as vice-president and stalked out of the convention.[31]

Wakeman carried the vote because he had developed the most thoughtful analysis of the obscenity issue for the time. He agreed with James Parton's observation, "It is not possible to put into human language a definition of the word obscene which shall let the Song of Solomon, Rabelais, Juvenal, and Tom Jones pass, and keep out works intended and calculated to corrupt." Wakeman opposed obscenity, but the Comstock Law, he emphasized, violated "the freedom of the press and speech as well as the right of property." It allowed Comstock, the agent of a private organization, to monitor the moral content of the United States mail. The 1873 law was in Wakeman's words the "reappearance of the Christian Inquisition."[32]

Wakeman also inveighed against the judicial decisions that upheld the Comstock Law. He likened the liberals' opposition to the Supreme Court's *Ex Parte Jackson* decision in 1877, which affirmed congressional power to authorize postal censorship, as akin to the Republican party's condemnation of the controversial Dred Scott ruling in 1857. Continuing the antislavery analogy, he stressed that "through all the dark night of the slave power, through all the dread necessities of the Rebellion, if the mails were ever violated, it was without the form or countenance of law,'' precedents that the Comstock statute repudiated.[33]

The other judicial anathema for liberals was the application of the Hicklin standard for obscenity. This 1867 British court precedent justified the conviction of D. M. Bennett in 1879 for having mailed *Cupid's Yokes*. Isolated passages, even selected out of context, were considered obscene if the "tendency of the matter is," as the British jurist C. J. Cockburn put it, "to deprave and corrupt the morals of those whose minds are open to such influences and into whose hands a publication of this sort may fall." If a book suggested "impure and libidinous thoughts" to anyone, it was thus obscene for all. To Wakeman's consternation, "To use it as a test of obscenity is simply monstrous, for everything could be condemned under it from the Bible down to the *N.Y. Herald.*" As the appellate judge who upheld *U.S. v. Bennett* ruled, "Freedom of the press does not include freedom to use the mails for the purpose of distributing obscene literature." Significantly, the "deprave and corrupt" formula remained the basis of obscenity law in the United States until the Supreme Court revised it in *Roth v. U.S.* (1957).[34]

Wakeman feared that federal censorship curtailed personal freedom. "If Congress can create and punish crimes without regard to the Constitution," he predicted, "it is the end of all popular liberty." Instead of the nationalization of obscenity law, he advocated its decentralization. The common law operating on the community and state level, despite "all risks and defects," was the best way, he argued, to deal with the elusive nature of obscenity. "You have long-standing and sufficient laws on the whole subject in Massachusetts," he instructed a Bay State audience; "and if Mr. Heywood had been found guilty under them, I should have left the matter to you, as her citizens." In the tradition of eighteenth-century antifederalism, Wakeman valued local decision making as the best preservative of individual liberty.[35]

Yet, Wakeman's reliance on the common law was not a panacea, as he at least tentatively recognized. William Blackstone, the eighteenth-century authority on common law, pointed out that the English legal tradition dealt with offending publications through the criminal prosecution of the literary malefactor on an individual case basis, not through a general policy of governmental censorship. The common law was attractive to many liberals because it sanctioned their demand for the elimination of governmental interference with the free circulation of the mail while it provided redress through state and local courts for the suppression of offensive material.

Wakeman's position somewhat anticipated the most recent major U.S. Supreme Court decision on obscenity, *Miller v. California* (1973). The pivotal Miller case, written by Chief Justice Warren Burger, provided in part that local community standards, not a uniform national test, were necessary to determine obscenity. But what Wakeman and Burger ignored was that the Bill of Rights was national in scope, not a local option to obey or not. They did not appreciate that a multitude of regional interpretations of what constituted free speech would vitiate the integrity of the First Amendment and create a chilling effect on the publication of unpopular opinions, such as *Cupid's Yokes*. The local Massachusetts laws that Wakeman touted probably would have led to Heywood's imprisonment as readily as did the national Comstock Law.[36]

What made Wakeman and other liberals ideologically akin to Burger and a majority of the Supreme Court in the Miller decision was their presupposition that obscenity, however defined, did not warrant First Amendment protection. Nineteenth-century liberals deplored obscenity as much as they did the Comstock Law. At its 1880 Chicago convention, the league resolved that "reasonable and effective laws" against obscenity should be carried out in the same manner as other laws. Similarly in *Roth v. U.S.* (1957), which upheld the Comstock Law, Justice William Brennan declared for the majority that obscenity was "utterly without redeeming social importance." Therefore it did not constitute speech and warrant constitutional protection. Wakeman's imprecise identification of criminally prosecutable obscenity as "filth" was comparable to Justice Potter Stewart's intuitive definition of "hard core pornography" in *Jacobellis v. Ohio* (1964) as "I know it when I see it."[37]

In his narrow focus on dismantling the Comstock Law, Wakeman was inadvertently opening a Pandora's box of community censorship. Despite the sophistication of his legal analysis for its time, he failed to anticipate Justice William O. Douglas's dissent in the Roth case. "If the First Amendment guarantee of freedom of speech and press is to mean anything in this field," Douglas stated, "it must allow protection even against the moral code that the standard of the day sets for the community." One cannot, however, be smug about the limitations of the Victorian perspective. Douglas's stand for the primacy of the First Amendment remains a minority opinion, while the entire issue of obscenity is still a legal bugbear.[38]

In addition, Wakeman and most other leaders of the league did not embrace the individualist anarchism of some of its members with its supralegal emphasis. Josephine S. Tilton, for example, opposed any governmental regulation of personal morality. She declared, "I will be mistress of my person and therein lies the right to private judgment in morals." Heywood's advocacy of free love was a secularized form of Protestant antinomianism. His rejection of civil authority for a higher standard of ethical conduct was in the tradition of William Lloyd Garrison's burning of the U.S. Constitution and Heywood's own pacifism during the Civil War. For Heywood, individualist anarchism imposed rigorous internal constraints in place of external governmental regulation. In his words, "Relieving one from outer restraint does not lessen but increases this Personal Accountability; for by making him FREE, we devolve on him the necessity of self-government; and he must respect the rights of others, or suffer the consequences of being an invader." For Wakeman, Wright, and Parton, individualist anarchists had every right to express their ideas about what Heywood called "the Natural Right and Necessity of Sexual Self-Government." They believed, however, as Wakeman said, "It is clearly the first duty of a Liberal to stand by the Constitution and its Bill of Rights as the foundation of our liberties." After all, Wakeman was an attorney, not an antinomian.[39]

The league was never able to reach a satisfactory resolution on the difficult issue of obscenity and censorship. The question was too divisive and factionalized the membership. Comstock himself identified two types of liberals: The Abbot faction included "the strong, pure, and clean men," and their opponents were "the howling, ranting, blaspheming mob of repealers." After three frustrating years as president of the league, Wakeman himself urged a return to first principles—"The Nine Demands of Liberalism"—and the creation of a united front. The delegates at the eighth convention of the league in 1884 dissolved the old organization in favor of a new society, The American Secular Union. In the spirit of reconciliation, they elected Ingersoll president.[40]

As Samuel P. Putnam, two-term president of the American Secular Union, frankly summed it up, "Freethought organization is difficult." Despite its brief existence, the National Liberal League represented the coming of age of religious infidelity in America. Liberals differed on what individualism meant, but they agreed that the collusion between church and state must end. Like slavery, they stigmatized Christianity as an unsavory relic of the benighted past, a medieval bondage of the mind unbefitting the scientific age. In the spirit of nineteenth-century liberalism, they also believed that the government that governed least—or, in the case of the individualist anarchists, not at all—was best because it allowed the widest possible latitude for individual freedom.[41]

In contrast, the vice crusaders sought to counteract the secular challenge to Christianity through legal coercion, such as the Comstock Law, which imposed an authoritarian value system. The government censored individual thought even to the extent of imprisoning religious infidels such as Heywood and Bennett for what amounted to blasphemy. Whereas liberals stressed personal freedom and the primacy of the First Amendment, Comstockians demanded social order through governmental supervision of morality. The contention over obscenity represented the breakdown of societal consensus for judging acceptable thought and behavior, a barometer of the social flux of the late nineteenth century. The controversial issue of obscenity (much as

Can a Woman Be an Individual?
The Discourse of Self-Reliance

Linda K. Kerber

S PEAKING in the midst of a major crisis of public confidence during the early years of the Massachusetts Bay Colony, Governor John Winthrop observed:

> [Civil or federal] liberty is maintained and exercised in a way of subjection to authority; it is of the same kind of liberty wherewith Christ hath made us free. The woman's own choice makes such a man her husband; yet being so chosen, he is her lord, and she is to be subject to him, yet in a way of liberty, not of bondage; and a true wife accounts her subjection her honor and freedom . . . Even so, brethren, it will be between you and your magistrates. [1]

Winthrop was struggling with the paradox that would occupy Rousseau a century later in *The Social Contract;* he needed a poetic image by which liberty on one hand and submission to authority on the other hand might comfortably be resolved. It seemed so obvious to Winthrop that wives embodied the paradox of authenticity and submission (as it later would to Rousseau—it was perhaps the only thing the two men had in common) that he felt no need to elaborate. Long after they had ceased to share Winthrop's assumptions about the proper relationship of church and state, Americans considered his notions about the relationship of men and women to be the common sense of the matter.

Winthrop's formulation of liberty contrasts with one embedded in Elizabeth Cady Stanton's greatest speech, written when she was seventy-seven. The title of the speech is "The Solitude of Self."

The point I wish plainly to bring before you on this occasion is the individuality of each human soul—our Protestant idea, the right of individual conscience and judgment—our republican idea, individual citizenship. In discussing the rights of woman, we are to consider, first, what belongs to her as an individual, in a world of her own, the arbiter of her own destiny, an imaginary Robinson Crusoe with her woman Friday on a solitary island. . . . The isolation of every human soul and the necessity of self dependence must give each individual the right to choose his own surroundings. The strongest reason for giving woman all the opportunities . . . for the full development of her faculties, her forces of mind and body . . . is the solitude and personal responsibility of her own individual life . . . as an individual she must rely on her self.[2]

Many years before, in the Seneca Falls Declaration of Sentiments of 1848, Stanton had attempted to cast the republican rhetoric of the American Revolution into terms congruent with women's experience. Now at the end of her life she was similarly recasting the individualist rhetoric of public discourse into terms congruent with women's experience. Both of her efforts may be understood as conservative efforts to link women to main themes in American political culture. Both were perceived by contemporaries as radical.

The concept of individualism has been linked to gender in ways that have generally eluded analysis. From John Winthrop through Tocqueville, and from Emerson to the team of sociologists headed by Robert Bellah, who recently published *Habits of the Heart,* most formulations of individualism in America have made the implicit assumption that the "individual" was male. Even when a vaguely generic language was adopted to make it seem that women were included, a careful reading reveals that virtually all commentators—except explicitly feminist ones like Stanton—contemplated the self-actualization of men. As R. W. B. Lewis named the individual seeking autonomy in the American landscape, we habitually discuss "the American Adam." The basic formula for American fiction has been the hero, "homeless, timeless, and alone," thrust into adventure. The "authentic" American narrative has been taken to be "the individual going forth toward experience, the inventor of his own character and creator of his personal history, the self-moving individual who is made to confront the world." The classic American setting is the untamed forest (Cooper), the wild ocean (Melville), the broad Mississippi (Twain).[3]

Some twenty years ago, in "American Women and the National Character," David Potter laid down a classic challenge—that historians test every familiar generalization about the American past and ask whether it applied equally well, and with similar nuance, to women. I shall argue here that what we have identified as the classic statements of American individualism are best understood as guides to masculine identity; if we seek to understand a female quest for self-actualization, we must turn to an alternate, competitive literature that is no less "American."

William Hesseltine once remarked that writing intellectual history is like pinning jelly against a wall, and individualism is as slippery a concept as any. One is tempted to go off chasing something that one can put in a computer. However, as we are reminded at least every two years and certainly every four, during congressional and presidential elections, the rhetoric of individualism is deeply embedded in the language by which Americans explain themselves to each other; it is embedded in our national discourse. And if, indeed, this discourse is gender specific, it is time that we looked at it again.[4]

Let us begin with Winthrop. Ostensibly he was describing the relationship of the individual to society. But he also had a practical agenda: to quell restiveness among the freemen of Massachusetts Bay. His speech has made its way into standard documentary compilations as an attempt to connect political and religious issues and as an expression of ideas that seemed to be the common sense of the matter to articulate Puritans. Winthrop's contractualism rested on the unexamined assumption that the submissive woman was in fact free. This paradox was so much a part of the lives of his male audience that Winthrop expected that they, in turn, would find it logical to place themselves in a similarly ambivalent and paradoxical relationship to the state: "A true wife accounts her subjection her honor and freedom." On this base the political edifice that would reconcile choice and necessity rested. What the relationship might be of women to the state went unremarked.

At least Winthrop had a certain degree of consistency. He demanded of men of the middling ranks of society no more than the same degree of submissiveness that they were already demanding—and presumably receiving—from their wives. But although Winthrop's speech had a degree of rhetorical brilliance—it was, Perry Miller observed, the culminating expression of the Puritan ideal in New England—it did not have the effect Winthrop sought. It could call for but not create a constituency of submissive men who would defer to their social betters. Men understood the role Winthrop asked for as effeminate—the word also had pejorative connotations then—and refused to play it.

In fact, the first generation of Puritan settlers had brought with them sharply conflicting notions of the proper place of women in the community. On the one hand, they believed that each Christian woman was responsible for placing herself in the path of salvation and the knowledge of grace, just as each man was. This involved enough education to read the Bible for herself and to take substantial responsibility for the religious education of her children. This strain of Puritan influence would support relatively high levels of female literacy in New England as compared, for example, to the South, a disparity which persisted into the nineteenth century.[5]

On the other hand, the example of Eve implied that women were particularly likely to sin; after all, Eve had taken the initiative. Her sins—of pride and of disobedience—were understood to be characteristic women's sins. Women could easily be construed to be weak, vulnerable, in need of guidance for their own good. Although women, like men, sought to realize themselves through Christ, still the *self* they were to realize was to be characteristically submissive. "Godly men," Carol Karlsen has observed, "needed helpmeets, not hindrances; companions, not competitors; alter egos, not autonomous mates. They needed wives who were faithful and loyal; who assisted them in their piety, in their vocations . . . who revered them . . . ."[6]

Both themes would persist throughout the colonial period, but one would be strengthened at the expense of the other. Within less than two decades after settlement, Anne Hutchinson and other heretics were squelched and, as Mary Maples Dunn has shown, even believing women were silenced. Puritan women were automatically transferred from one church to another when their husbands moved, and older women ceased to have a voice in the disciplining of church members.[7] When the male church had been insecure and marginal, it treated women as valued allies. When it became more secure politically, it left women to their husbands and fathers. As we read Puritan sermon literature, for example, we do not find in it the assumption that the women to whom the minister is speaking are engaged in an intense search for their own individual religious voices or their own idiosyncratic conversion experience. The Christian virtues of patience and faith were invariably linked with the general female virtues of submissiveness and docility. Even tracts stressing the reciprocal duties of husband and wife, like William Secker's widely read *A Wedding Ring Fit for the Finger,* grounded this reciprocity on initial female submission. Man and wife were, Secker writes, "like the sun and the moon: when the greater light goes down, the lesser light gets up. . . . The wife may be a sovereign in her husband's absence, but she must be a subject in her husband's presence." A man is encouraged to choose a woman who will be "subject to [his] dominion."[8] Jonathan Edwards's account of Sarah Pierrepont's conversion experience is the unusual case.[9]

The great texts of the Enlightenment—notably those of Rousseau (especially the *Confessions* and his fiction) and of Montesquieu (especially *The Persian Letters*)—addressed directly and with great subtlety the problem of how to invent a state that has the power to preserve order yet in which it is also possible for individuals to preserve their own integrity and authenticity.[10] To be authentic, Montesquieu concluded, freedom in the public world had to be echoed by freedom within the private family; the individual is not free in the state unless also free at home. This was a formulation largely overlooked in America, where republicans used the more abstract formulations of *The Spirit of the Laws* in their argumentation. When, for example, Abigail Adams argued in her famous letter of May 1776, "Put it out of the power of husbands to abuse us with impunity; remember all men would be tyrants if they could," John Adams coolly misread it as simply a plea for the vote.

It is possible to interpret the movement of resistance to England as energized in part by the urgency of a generation of middle-class men seeking careers by which to define themselves, who, finding their way blocked by England and English patronage appointees, turned in resentment to clear the way for self-fulfillment.[11] Even when one hastens to grant that this is only one among many reasons for resentment of England, the urgent demand for what the French, in their own Revolution, were soon to call "a career open to talents" was obvious.

The war and ensuing social change did indeed open up new choices for men—in the law, in politics, in trade, and in commerce. The language of the Declaration of Independence gave voice to an enlightened understanding that the nation existed for every man and not the reverse. But the Revolution offered women little except the chance to live vulnerable lives in a household from which men had gone to fight for one side or the other, to live in fear or in wonder, or to traipse after the troops, hanging on as one of the "women of the army" in a Brechtian world of cooks and laundresses.[12]

When women were actually "invited to war" as the title of one anonymous pamphlet put it, the war was not the war of the Revolution at all, but the great religious revival that began to build with the growth of Methodism in the 1780s and swelled into the Second Great Awakening of the first decades of the nineteenth century.[13] The women who followed Mother Ann Lee or Jemima Wilkinson, or the Methodists and Baptists, found a mode of personal choice and individual authenticity that was inconceivable for women in secular language. Methodism had a particular appear to women in the congruence of its rhetoric of method and system with the practical needs of housekeepers, and also in the honored figure of John Wesley's mother, Susannah. Susannah Wesley is a distinctive figure in that she was well read, admired for her judgment, and not afraid to speak in public. Indeed, during her husband's lengthy absences, she held worship services in her home, attended at their height by two hundred people, and successfully fended off complaints that they were an "illegal conventicle."[14]

It might be said that in the evangelical churches of the early Republic we find a revitalized tension between the individual and the community, which had leached out as the older churches became the province of women whose religious roles and social roles were comfortably congruent. The Second Great Awakening—whatever the denomination it affected—was characterized by what once would have been called the Arminian heresy: the assumption that one could affect the terms of one's own salvation. For women, heightened religiosity and a new community of believers could provide paths for self-fulfillment and an expression of personal independence possible in virtually no other sector of society.

Heightened religiosity could lead to mysticism, as it did in the case of Ralph Waldo Emerson's much-misunderstood aunt, Mary Moody Emerson. Though it risked leading one into eccentricity, mysticism also enabled one to carve out a private space that could command respect. If Mary Moody Emerson is remembered at all, it is as a rigid moralist and a religious eccentric who made a shroud for herself and wore it around the house in order, she said, to get accustomed to it. But in her voluminous diaries and letters we find an improvisation on Virginia Woolf's famous question about Shakespeare's sister. Ralph Waldo Emerson's aunt had great intelligence, a taste for writing, and absolutely no institutional context in which to exercise either. There was no Harvard College for her. As an adult woman without her own household to manage, she was vulnerable to the reproaches of her family, who expected her to define her life in terms of service to them. Ralph Waldo Emerson's widowed mother, Ruth, makes a unilateral decision to take in boarders, and then announces that of course her sister-in-law, Mary Moody Emerson, will come to assist with the work, and complains when she does not appear on the scene as soon as called. "I can not find time in your absence to do even the necessary sewing of the family with my other cares and have not 4 or 5 shirts for the children which they need, waiting to be made."[15]

Caught in the inexorable cycle of the natural and domestic world, Mary Moody Emerson made the best of it by turning to contemplation and private piety: "Piety can supply to the feeble what the strong possess by nature." Her musings often approached the hypnotic: "The hill on which we rambled [October 1795] is become barren the sun has since cut short his journey, and the skies begin to frown. But, tho the face of nature is constantly changing and now threatens a dismal appearance; the subjects on which we dwell are ever the same, always interesting and sublime." But private, contemplative piety had no exterior consequence; if anything, it reinforced the old separation between the affective worlds of women and men.[16] In 1817, Mary Moody Emerson wrote, "Alass, with low timid females or vulgar domestics how apt is this [moral grandeur] to lose its power when the nerves are weak. . . . But give me that oh God—it is holy independence—it is honor & immortality—dearer than friends wealth & influence. . . . I bless thee for giving me to see the advantage of loneliness."[17]

The journals of twenty-four-year old Eleanor Read, also a New Englander, reveal the ways in which religious conversion could provide psychological and intellectual options and the way that women might use the new evangelicalism for self-actualizing purposes.[18] She attended revival meetings in the fall of 1802, becoming increasingly interested; finally, she discovered that she was free of her jealousy of others who had found salvation. She gave way to "transports of joy" and saw everyone with "new eyes," in the traditional language of the evangelical conversion experience. In this spirit, she ventured to her baptism, no longer hesitating lest it imply reproach of her parents for the way they raised her, pleased that among the thirty with whom she was baptized were "young and old, illiterate and learned, rich and poor, and . . . a young mulatto man who had previously excited my indignation by mixing with others at conferences and other meetings." Now, shocking even herself, she looked on him as her "brother in Christ."[19]

After her conversion, Eleanor Read ceased to dwell on her human limitations; instead, she pressed at the boundaries of the possible. She stopped describing herself as anxious and indecisive. Her relationship with her mother now changed; instead of writing deferential letters, she wrote in a style verging on the impudent: "I have given myself away to God in a most solemn covenant. The child, whom you have so tenderly nursed, has sworn an eternal allegiance against you, unless you will serve my Lord and my God." She brought her religion into her classroom, overcoming her fear "that praying in my school would be deemed ridiculous enthusiasm." She decided that the injunction to women not to speak in church did not mean they could not pray in school. It was not usual (except among Quakers) for women to lead public prayer among their students, but Eleanor Read overcame her scruples and her fear of looking odd. (It clearly never occurred to her that she should keep her religious beliefs out of the classroom.)[20]

She traveled far from home, founding other schools in other communities, ultimately reaching Salem, Massachusetts, where she met the man she would marry. She argued with ministers—including her future husband—who thought women ought to confine their reading to religious tracts or who expected submissiveness in women.

Let the man of real piety carefully examine the origin of that detested sentiment which leads him to consider learning and mental improvement as undesirable in a female. Upon a thorough investigation of this important subject, will not the honest Christian blush before his God for the unchristian and cruel degradation of the female mind? If the discerning and virtuous part of men would teach us to expect their esteem, only when our accuracy of thought and amiableness of conduct give us the appearance of rational beings, what a surprising reformation might be expected in the female world.[21]

We have reason to regret Eleanor Read Emerson's early death. Her journals provide evidence of the style with which at least one young woman bent religious revivalism in the direction of independence and her own search for authenticity. Eleanor Read's story can stand as an emblem for the thousands of white and black women who would follow her, discovering that the rhetoric of religion provided justification for behavior that a secular society would otherwise not countenance.

A third route to authenticity for women was articulated during and soon after the American Revolution by Judith Sargeant Murray and others, male and female, who thought that the new Republic required a new woman as well as a new man. This set of ideas, the ideology of republican motherhood, called upon the women of the Republic to be forthright and practical, impervious to fashion and frivolity. They were to be prepared for a world that might literally turn upside down; a world in which violent changes, of the sort which the revolutionary generation had experienced, would be the rule rather than the exception. The rhetoric of republican virtue and independence provided the language for an insistence that women avoid subservience and docility, and, above all, be self-respecting. Women were called upon to assume an obligation to themselves and to the political society in which they lived, to educate themselves for economic competence and intellectual growth. For the first time in the history of the West, members of Murray's generation acknowledged and even welcomed female ambition— but only if ambition were developed in a context that also involved a companionable relationship with husbands and a pedagogical relationship with children. In the intensity of her insistence that a woman be trained to respect herself, to take pride in her own competence and to be prepared to support herself, Murray went far toward articulating a new model of female authenticity. But the model republican woman was still justified less on her own terms than by her service to her family and her children. The promise of service camouflaged and indeed undermined the independence and individualism that was also part of the concept. The promise of continued submission and deference made the republican woman politically palatable.[22]

These forms of individualism are by way of prehistory. The word "individualism" was not used until the 1820s, and then in France. It appears first in English in Alexis de Tocqueville's *Democracy in America*, published in 1832. Tocqueville used *individualisme* to describe a celebration of the claims of the individual that he took to be distinctive to American society and that he thought had its own dangers.[23]

> Individualism is a mature and calm feeling, which disposes each member of the community to sever himself from the mass of his fellows and to draw apart with his family and his friends; so that after he has thus formed a little circle of his own, he willingly leaves society at large to itself.

As social conditions become more equal, the number of persons increases who, although they are neither rich enough nor powerful enough to exercise any great influence over their fellows, have nevertheless acquired or retained sufficient education and fortune to satisfy their own wants. They owe nothing to any man, they expect nothing from any man; the acquire the habit of always considering themselves as standing alone, and they are apt to imagine that their whole destiny is in their own hands.

Thus not only does democracy make every man forget his ancestors, but it hides his descendants, and separates his contemporaries from him; it throws him back for ever upon himself alone, and threatens in the end to confine him entirely within the solitude of his own heart.[24]

As he so often did, Tocqueville provided a name for what many agreed was a distinctive quality of postrevolutionary American society. The American was Crèvecoeur's "new man," who tilled his own soil, grew his own food, built his own home. The democratic hero was paradoxically not the person embedded in the *demos* but the autonomous individual, the man who imagined that his whole destiny was "in his own hands." Throughout Jacksonian political culture—in political thought, in economic theory, in literature, in the popular notions of the self-made man, ran the trope of the individual posed *against* society. The concept, John William Ward observed, played the role of a "secular jeremiad, an exhortation to begin over again, sloughing off the complexities of society by returning to a natural state of grace."[25]

To Tocqueville's credit, he made it clear from the beginning (though many of his readers did not notice) that defining oneself as pure individual required a material base. The persons who may indulge in the notion "that their whole destiny is in their own hands" are those who have "sufficient education and fortune to satisfy their own wants." No economic independence, no individualism. Individualism in this sense is the psychological counterpart of liberalism and laissez-faire in the economic world; it is no accident that they appear in usage contemporaneously.[26]

What Tocqueville did not notice was that in a legal system molded by coverture, married women could not readily possess the material base that made individualism possible.[27] Mary Ryan's careful study of the changing political culture in Utica, New York, makes it clear that young men could take advantage of the opportunities of the new commercial world only if they were given the total resources of their families to draw on; in the end, mothers took in boarders and daughters aborted their educations in order that sons be kept in school longer and given a stake in society. "Self-made" men were launched into the world by other people's sacrifices—some voluntary, most involuntary—and they knew it, although their language carefully screened that reality from their consciousness.[28]

Kenneth Lynn has recently pointed to a nice irony in the life of Ralph Waldo Emerson, the man who, more than perhaps any other American, articulated the ideal of the independent individual. Emerson's period of betrothal to the frail Ellen Tucker was marred by his frequent raising of what she called "the ugly subject"—her will. By the time he married her, he was securely embedded in her will, despite the reservations of her uncle and guardian. After Ellen Tucker Emerson's death a few years later, when he used the money to support himself and his relatives, Ralph Waldo Emerson remarked that she continued to benefit him even in death. Emerson refrained from forcing his own dismissal from the Second Church of Boston until after her uncle's lawsuit contesting the will had been settled in Emerson's favor. When Emerson gave the "American Scholar" address, calling on his listeners to spurn materialism and dedicate themselves to the life of the mind, he did not mention that he could rely on a steady income from his brief marriage.[29]

David Leverenz has recently explored the explicitly male language that Emerson employed. "Give me initiative, spermatic, prophesying man-making words," he wrote in his journal in 1841.[30] Emerson begins his essay "Intellect" with a verse that analogizes intellect to the "sower" who "scatters broad his seed."[31]

The individual mythologized by antebellum writers was male; he *had* to be a Natty Bumppo, a Huck Finn, or an American Scholar with $1,200 a year. The myth of the lone individual is a trope, a rhetorical device. In real life no one is self-made; few are truly alone. Even those mythical lonely beings confronting the wilderness had companions to prepare their food and warn them of disaster. Trailing behind their real counterparts were wives, mothers, children, slaves, and servants to sustain the practical aspects of life. The myth of the wilderness either denied the reality of women (as in Moby Dick), trivialized them (as in Huck Finn), or, as Carroll Smith-Rosenberg has shown in a brilliant essay on Davy Crockett, indulged frankly in misogyny.

> [In the stories, Crockett is obsessed with a sexuality that is] oral, exhibitionistic, violent, and nonproductive. . . . What emerges from the Crockett myth as natural, timeless and inescapable is . . . young male violence . . . directed toward women [and] . . . toward the inhabitants of the wilderness—toward Indians, Mexicans, and escaped slaves. . . . [misogyny] and racism are central to the myth.[32]

The language of individualism as it developed in antebellum America was not a woman's language. How could it be? It was a trope whose major theme was the denial of dependence; it was a response to social changes that were making men increasingly aware of their dependence and vulnerability in a culture that had, only the generation before, reified the idea of personal independence in the private world and political independence in the public sector. Before the nineteenth century, landed wealth was a high proportion of the total wealth, even for the middling sort; no one could pretend that inherited land was their own creation. But when manufacturing and human capital, expressed in paper money, accounted for more and more wealth, it was possible to indulge in the fiction of the self-made man.[33]

Dependence remained the condition of most women's lives, whether they were black or white, rich or poor—although the pain of that dependence varied enormously with social status. Embedded in a legal system that endowed her husband with control of her property at marriage, embedded in an economy that offered white boys multiple career options, white girls only a handful, all of them marginal, and black women, even if free, virtually none, women first faced the intellectual and psychological task of *naming* their dependent condition. (The task of *rejecting* their dependent condition would not be faced until much later.)

In the early Republic, the woman who would, in Margaret Fuller's words, "beat my own self true to the heart of the world," had found that the most accessible path to female authenticity lay in heightened religiosity. In her own generation, Margaret Fuller attempted to move somewhat further in the direction of a secular definition of authenticity and independence for women, to connect women to Emersonian individualism, and to make the language of individualism congruent with the realities of women's lives. Her essays, which were printed in 1844 under the title *Woman in the Nineteenth Century,* had appeared first in *The Dial* under the impenetrable title "The Great Lawsuit: Man vs. Men, Woman vs. Women," by which she meant to contrast the ideal with the real. The essays combined the taste for the practical characteristic of Judith Sargent Murray with a mysticism close to that of Mary Moody Emerson—a mysticism that makes the essays occasionally impenetrable and accounts for their being honored but not widely read.

Fuller began by echoing Murray, offering as a model a fictional "Miranda" who was Fuller herself, only barely disguised; a girl raised by a father who respected even a girl child for possessing an "immortal intellect," who called upon her for "clear judgment, for courage, for honor and fidelity" and gave her, as all her portion, "a dignified sense of self-dependence," even though "self-dependence, which was honored in men, is deprecated as a fault in most women."[34] Like Murray, Fuller argued that a sure sense of self-worth would protect women against being seized by the current opinion that would try to sweep her "into the belief that she must marry, it if be only to find a protector."[35] Like Murray, she urged a richer education for women, a more serious cultivation of women's intellect; where she departed from Murray was that she was willing that women's education be *selfish.*

> Too much is said of women being better educated, that they may become better companions and mothers for MEN. . . . a being of infinite scope must not be treated with an exclusive view to any one relation. Give the soul free course, let the organization both of body and mind, be fully developed, and the being will be fit for any and every relation to which it may be called.[36]

Whether they knew Fuller's work or not, other women would articulate in the mid-century years the claim she made; slowly it became conceivable to claim self-fulfillment, independence, and individualism simply because a woman was entitled to it. "Our right to individuality is what I would most assert," wrote the journalist Elizabeth Oakes Smith in 1851. "Men seem resolved to have but one type in our sex. . . . The laws of stubborn utilitarianism must govern us, while they may be as fantastic as they please."[37]

The question is, did the "individuality" of which they spoke mean the same thing to women as it did when men used the term? When a woman imagined herself as escaping the laws of utilitarianism, did she imagine herself escaping to the same "fantastic" place, the same unmapped wilderness to which men fled? To ask the question is to answer it. The myth of the self-reliant man and the self-reliant woman were not synchronized. Young men received fictional images such as Tom Sawyer and Huck Finn—lively boys who run off on splendid adventures and prove themselves able to outwit the challenges of the adult world. It is an adult world in which, as Nina Baym long ago made clear, "the encroaching, constricting, destroying society is represented with particular urgency in the figure of one or more women"; women are not only the "other," they are the enemy.[38] The fictive female counterparts of Huck and Tom would be the March sisters of *Little Women,* who, as Susan Gubar and Sandra Gilbert suggested some years ago, sent a mixed message. The usual assumption of literary critics has been that *Little Women* is about women's free choices and about the achievement of autonomy. Jo, wrote Elizabeth Janeway, is "the one young woman in nineteenth-century fiction who maintains her individual independence, who gives up no part of her autonomy as payment for being born a woman, and who gets away with it."

Janeway seriously misreads the novel. Alcott is explicit. Independence and autonomy do come at a price; they are not, in fact, fully achieved. *Little Women* is shot through with ever-repeated images of restraint, resignation, endurance. Only Meg has a personality congruent with the demands of her community, and only to her is contentment possible because she does not need to push at the margins of what is permitted in order to devise her own life. Beth makes a death so beautiful that Gubar and Gilbert call it virtually a suicide; Amy whines, manipulates, and gets her way at others' expense, and Jo must settle for an ambivalent happiness accomplished by denying her own instincts. No wonder the figure of Jo Marsh has been a mystery that generations of girls have spend over a century trying to decipher. The most recent testimony comes from Cynthia Ozick, remembering her childhood: "I read *Little Women* a thousand times. Ten thousand. I am Jo in her 'vortex'; not Jo exactly, but some Jo of the future. I am under an enchantment; who I am must be deferred, waited for and waited for."[39]

Everyone remembers that Jo grows up to be a writer, but not everyone remembers that she also, with her husband, establishes a school. Sooner or later the search for female autonomy reverted to a dream of education. No sooner articulated, the rhetoric of female individualism quickly added the promise that it would not challenge men; that instead of lone individuals on unmapped frontiers, women would seek authenticity in schools and in communities of women.

Perhaps this was because for a long time the privately founded school, which might begin in one's own home or cheaply rented rooms, was the most accessible route for women to professional space and steady income. Perhaps it was because education was one of the few modes of work that offered gentility and protected at the same time against accusations of masculinity. Perhaps it was because to deflect restive women into educational institutions meant that they did not immediately threaten the hegemony of the male middle class, but were instead redefined as a group serving the male middle class. Perhaps it was because no dream dies harder than the one that promises that we will save the world if we can only square things for the next generation. And perhaps it was because, just as a cigar is sometimes just a cigar, women's education was clearly the next thing on most folks' agenda.

As early as 1776, Adam Smith had noted without criticizing the narrow practicality of women's education; "They are taught what their parents or guardians judge is necessary or useful for them to learn; and they are taught nothing else. Every part of their education tends . . . either to improve the natural attraction of their person, or to form their mind to reserve, to modesty, to chastity, and to economy; to render them both likely to become the mistresses of a family, and to behave properly when they have become such." There is, he concluded "nothing useless, absurd, or fantastical" in the education of women.[40] But for women like Elizabeth Smith, or Margaret Fuller, "the fantastical" was just the point.

And therefore throughout the nineteenth century, from Emma Willard opening an academy in her home in Middlebury, Vermont, at its beginning, to Annie Nathan Meyer raising money on Park Avenue for Barnard College at its end, independence for women was frequently defined in terms of schools, "Don't ever dare to take your college as a matter of course," wrote one women's college alumna in 1939, "because like freedom and democracy, many people you'll never know anything about have broken their hearts to get it for you."[41]

Women had to find room to develop their intellects without eliciting male hostility and contempt. It was assumed that the course of study for women required special justification; a standard question was: what studies are appropriate for the female mind? Adam Smith had said that what women needed was a continuation of what had been learned in the home and could be used directly and practically in adult life: "no absurdities." In the nineteenth century, the list of appropriate studies lengthened; it became respectable for women to contemplate a widening range of activities. But few would say with Margaret Fuller, "Let them be sea-captains if they will," and fewer would maintain that women might properly indulge in any form of study.[42]

To take the old language of individualism at face value could be dangerous. In the first third of the twentieth century, Rose Wilder Lane decided to assume that it was possible for a girl to link herself to the myth of the lone individual that she understood to be part of the American vision. Preparing herself by writing biographies of two exemplars of the self-made man, Jack London (whose *Call of the Wild* delineated a pure frontier for a new generation) and Herbert Hoover, Lane launched herself into the life of a free-lance journalist, arriving in Europe immediately after the war was over, reporting from devastated Eastern Europe, traveling with only one female companion to Albania, nearly as isolated from the West then as it was until 1989. Expecting to "make it" on her own, beholden to no one, she broke most friendships not long after they were made, proud of hanging on in a world of magazines that was feast or famine, briefly becoming one of the best paid popular feature writers for the *Saturday Evening Post,* but also suffering long stretches without pay.

During these stretches, she returned to her family home in the Ozarks, where her father and her mother, Laura Ingalls Wilder, hung on, leaning on her for support. In the years of the depression, Lane and her mother became increasingly embittered with a society in whose promises of success to the individual they had believed. Lane announced that she would no longer write so that she would not have to pay taxes to a New Deal government, but she did write fiction romanticizing the hardships of the homesteader on the late-nineteenth-century frontier, and she rewrote the rough drafts of her mother's memoirs, "passing them through my typewriter" and turning them into the *Little House* books in which the isolated family is pitted against the elements and makes it—or doesn't—with no help from the community. The self-reliance celebrated in the *Little House* books turns sour at their end, when Laura and Almanzo must face a reality unmediated by their parents. By the end of her life, untrammeled individualism had become for Lane a shrill anticommunism.[43]

In the years of the cold war, years which saw on American campuses the creation of programs in American Civilization (a shrill insistence that America *had* a civilization), the old image of the individual poised against society was moved into the core programs in liberal education. The theme of Columbia University's famous and widely imitated curriculum in contemporary civilization used the conflict between individual and society as its central theme: the American Civilization programs claimed Matthiessen's canonical American literature resting heavily on Emerson, Melville, and Twain. Offered to an undergraduate population that was half female, these selections made the easy assumption that the great work of the world had been done by men, and that the true American image was the lone male adventurer, pitting himself against the unknown, and that what he could expect from women was opposition, not camaraderie. We are beginning now to understand this canon as a cliché that served a wide range of only dimly acknowledged political purposes and political needs.[44]

This was not simply the antebellum trope revisited; rather, I think, it was a continuation of an ideology that had made World War II endurable by posing individual freedoms against Fascist states that offered no breathing space outside of group solidarity. The concept of individualism, as a mark of the limits of society's claims, which promised options outside the tyranny of the group, resonates through David Riesman's *The Lonely Crowd*. Riesman reinterpreted the old ideology of the self-made into the "inner-directed" individual; his extraordinarily popular book offered a sympathetic reading of the anxieties of modernism. But even Riesman wrote from inside the paradigm, still assuming that it is men who make the choices that define the individual and only occasionally considering whether his generalizations held up when applied to women.[45] The image of the male adventurer pitting himself, like Natty Bumppo, against the unknown was not a very practical image for young men whose career options lay in insurance or advertising; it was almost valueless for the young woman who knew that whatever she tried to do professionally she would need to be a support to a young man. Thus Adlai Stevenson, speaking at a Smith College commencement in 1956:

> You may be hitched to one of these creatures we call "Western man" and I think part of your job is to keep him Western, to keep him truly purposeful, to keep him whole. In short—while I have had very little experience as a wife or mother—I think one of the biggest jobs for many of you will be to frustrate the crushing and corrupting effects of specialization, to integrate means and

ends. . . . This assignment for you, as wives and mothers, has great advantages. In the first place, it is home work—you can do it in the living room with a baby in your lap . . .

"The language of individualism," wrote Robert Bellah and his colleagues recently in *Habits of the Heart,* "is the primary American language of self-understanding." That language is inadequate, Bellah argues, because it "limits the way people think." It permits a deracinated selfishness that makes the self-interest of the observer into the measure of value and shields people from confronting great social and moral issues.[46]

But that language is also inadequate, also limits the ways in which people think, because it has not been acknowledged that the language of individualism has been a male-centered discourse, that its imagery has traditionally served the self-interest of men, whatever their class. In the context of a bourgeois social order, an order of sexual politics that assumed continued deference from women toward their men and continued interruption of women's most private, imaginative lives so that domestic tasks could be done, the paradoxes of republican motherhood and the contradictions inherent in achieving female authenticity could not be resolved—not by the antebellum generation, not by the Progressive generation, not by any of the subsequent generations of the twentieth century, not even our own.

Years ago Antonio Gramsci put his mind to the problem of how ruling groups maintain consent to their power and argued that they do not do it by force alone. Rather, they use a language that limits the way other groups can *think* about their place in society. If the language is not available it becomes difficult to locate the source of unease. Unable to conceptualize a challenge to hegemonic language, women seem to have played the role of a "historical bloc" in Gramsci's sense—a group not completely distracted by the prevailing cultural hegemony and permanently in the process of groping for a language to describe its own perception of reality. I would say that in the long sweep of women's history there have been times—ours is one of them—when women have been particularly aggressive and imaginative in seizing their culture's tools of expression. And I would also say in the long sweep of American cultural history, the language of individualism helped them very little.

Individualism and National Identity

Yehoshua Arieli

"T HERE are," remarked James Bryce in *The American Commonwealth*, "certain dogmas or maxims which are in so far fundamental that they have told widely on political thought, and that one usually strikes upon them when sinking a shaft, so to speak, into an American mind."[1] Among these, Bryce thought, were the notions about man's inalienable rights, popular sovereignty, the distrust of centralized political power, and the conviction that the functions of the government must be kept at a minimum if the community and the individual were to prosper.[2] "Everything tended to make the United States in this respect more English than England, for the circumstances of colonial life, the process of settling the western wilderness, the feelings evoked by the struggle against George III, all went to intensify individualism, the love of enterprise, the pride in personal freedom. And from that day to this, individualism, the love of enterprise, and the pride in personal freedom, have been deemed by Americans not only their choicest, but their peculiar and exclusive possessions."[3]

This was, indeed, a far cry from Tocqueville's statement some forty years earlier that the Americans, by the use of liberty, fought and conquered the individualism that equality generated.

This striking discrepancy in the evaluation of the relationship of individualism to American life can be explained neither by a difference in the point of observation nor by a change in the scene observed. What had changed in the period that had elapsed between Tocqueville and Bryce was that Americans had transformed the concept of individualism from a term of abuse to one of approval, from a remote sociological notion to one which more than any other defined Americanism.

Bryce described what Americans considered in the 1880s as their basic attitude toward society and government on one hand and as the traditional ideal of their personal behavior and value pattern on the other hand. The first aspect was summed up in his statement that "the nation is nothing but so many individuals. The government is nothing but certain representatives and officials, agents who are here to-day and gone to-morrow."[4] This atomistic view of the social and political body was strengthened by a "common-sense notion that everybody knows his own business best, that individual enterprise has 'made America,' and will 'run America' better than the best government could do."[5] In its other aspect, individualism meant self-reliance, the love of enterprise, and fierce pride in personal independence. "So far as there can be said to be any theory on the subject," Bryce concluded, "*laissez aller* is the orthodox and accepted doctrine in the sphere both of the Federal and of State legislation."[6]

Bryce maintained these evaluations in spite of apparently contrary trends toward the growing demand for state interference into ever-widening fields.[7] He emphasized the paradox that the demand for state interference was strongest in the West, though that section prided itself as being preeminently the land of freedom, enterprise, and self-help, where the sentiment of individualism was strongest.[8] The apparent contradiction between the observed clamor for state interference and the no-less-obvious adherence to "individualism" did not, in Bryce's opinion, invalidate his observation. State interference was usually appealed to in order to protect the majority against the power of the few. Individualism as a behavior pattern was so deeply entrenched in the American that the paternalism of France and Germany was "repellent to him."[9]

Bryce's interpretation of the American concept of individualism revealed his close contacts with the New England and New York liberals, who in the late nineteenth century were America's intellectual leaders, the transatlantic counterpart of the progressive wing of British liberalism.[10] This group had elaborated the theory of individualism in the second half of the nineteenth century and applied it to the American scene. The group included practically all those who united in 1872 to found the Liberal Republican party, who supported Tilden and Cleveland, created the mugwump movement, and advocated civil service and free trade. The Free Religious Association (founded in 1867), the Boston Radical Club, and the American Social Science Association expressed the aims of this liberalism in the field of philosophy, ethics and social sciences.[11] Their organs, the *Nation, Harper's Weekly,* the *Springfield Republican,* and the *New York Evening Post* enjoyed a high prestige among educated Americans. Although they wielded little organized political power, they spoke with intellectual authority. Charles Francis Adams, Jr., Henry Adams, William Cullen Bryant, Charles A. Dana, Horace Greeley,

George W. Curtis, Charles Sumner, Carl Schurz, and Lyman Trumbull were all saturated with New England ideals. Their connection with the *Nation,* with the Free Religious Association, and with the Boston Radical Club showed the continuous development of a pre–Civil War New England humanism into the liberalism of the later period.

For this group, the Civil War was a victory for universal freedom and social equality. The promise of America had come true and a new nation had been conceived in freedom and in the service of man's rights. It was the sole duty of the democratic state to provide the framework within which to work out these aims. Further progress would not be achieved by political means but by moral, economic, and social forces that would by voluntary association and competition, and by the spread of enlightenment, realize the highest aims to which society could aspire. The platform of the Free Religious Association, as suggested by the Unitarian philosopher Francis Ellingwood Abbot, stated: "*Whereas,* the grand end of human society is the freest, fullest, and the highest development of the individual. . . . *Whereas,* the grand end of the individual soul is the realization, in itself and in the world, of the highest Ideal of Humanity, and is thus identical with the great cause of universal human progress;—*Article I* Therefore, we hereby associate ourselves into a Free Brotherhood, for the purpose of helping each other and our fellow-men in the endeavour after the perfect Spirit, Life and Truth."[12]

"For the first time in history personality is the sum of all purposes," wrote one member of this group.[13] C. C. Schackford defined the principle of the new civilization as "Manhood."[14] The Civil War and Reconstruction were the last acts of liberation in which the gospel of humanity achieved its final victory. It prepared the road on which mankind would "rush forth on the 'mighty winds' of Science, Trade, and Freedom that make one country of the world."[15] To William B. Scott, the great vehicle of progress was free cooperation and competition that, "unfettered by monopolies and subsidies, always elevates the superior over the inferior, and urges on genuine improvement and progress by the most efficient means."[16] "What we want," Scott continued, "is freedom and justice,—that is, freedom to do all that we will, provided that we . . . [do not] trespass . . . upon the freedom of any other person."[17]

The characterization of laissez-faire that James Bryce gave to the liberal version of individualism was accurate, in its nineteenth-century connotation. It stood for adherence to the theories of the classical political economy, utilitarian morality, and progress. The synthesis of liberty and social justice achieved in Whitman's concept of individualism, which was based on a humanistic interpretation of the natural-rights theory, was not maintained. The Protestant ethic prevailed over the eighteenth-century elements of the Enlightenment that were inherent in the Jeffersonian concept of society.

John W. Draper defined individualism as the principle that maintains "that man shall be his own master, that he shall have liberty to form his opinions, freedom to carry into effect his resolves. He is, therefore, ever brought into competition with his fellow men. His life is a display of energy."[18] Self-reliance and enlightened self-interest, competition and association, were the conditions of liberty and progress, to be preserved even though equality of conditions should perish.

Most post–Civil War liberals still maintained that individual liberty and social justice, meaning equality of economic opportunities, would inevitably result from a rigid application of laissez-faire individualism. Yet the more serious and sincere among them conceded the tension and contradictions between these concepts and were ready to affirm the priority of individual liberty over any other claim.

Post–Civil War liberalism, however, was haunted by the fear that American democracy would repeat the historic pattern of deterioration and end in class war, anarchy, and Caesarism. Macaulay's prophecy that "either some Caesar or Napoleon will seize the reins of government with a strong hand, or your Republic will be as fearfully plundered . . . in the twentieth century as the Roman Empire was in the fifth" seemed not unfounded.[19] These were the years of the Reconstruction, of the Tilden elections, of the regime of spoilsmen and politicos, of the impeachment trial of President Andrew Johnson, of growing labor unrest, and of the revolt of the farmers.

The liberal answer to Macaulay's dictum that "institutions purely democratic must, sooner or later, destroy liberty or civilization or both," was that American democracy was more than a political regime, that it was a new social system of which individualism was the outstanding characteristic and thus exempt from the dangers of decline.[20] The classical expression of this sobered liberalism was given by William Graham Sumner, professor of political and social science at Yale.[21] "The modern jural state, at least of the Anglo-American type, by its hostility to privileges and servitudes, aims to realize . . . liberty. . . . If all privileges and all servitudes are abolished, the individual finds that there are no prescriptions left either to lift him up or to hold him down. He simply has all his chances left open that he may make out of himself all there is in him. This is individualism and atomism. There is absolutely no escape from it except back into a system of privileges and servitudes."[22] Sumner emphasized the natural antagonism between liberty and democracy. Only in modern times were they "closely allied with each other, and democracy as a political form has helped and been helped by liberty in the social order. The product of liberty and democracy is individualism. Under it men have been emancipated from tradition, authority, caste, superstition . . . if we could maintain liberty and democracy long enough, we might perhaps produce individualistic results so great that men would be emancipated from delusions and from phrases."[23]

Edwin L. Godkin, editor of the *Nation* and the *New York Evening Post,* and one of the most influential writers of his generation, defined democracy as a sociopolitical system in which all relations were regulated by contract and not by status.[24] Social justice consisted in the creation of such conditions that each member entered into contractual relations as a perfectly free agent, with full knowledge of their nature and under no compulsion either to accept or to refuse them. Equality in education, land reform, restriction of monopolies, absolute free trade, and the right of collective bargaining were necessary conditions of contractual equality and the legitimate sphere of political action.[25]

This, then, was the mission of individualism: to liberate men from all compulsion and to make them perfectly free agents. The uniqueness of American democracy lay in the fact that individualism had become not only characteristic of the social and political organization but the source of the individual's behavior pattern and of the nation's value system.[26] "The cardinal idea of the American system . . . is . . . the development of the individual man; and that the individual man is best developed by being supplied with the means of education, and secured in the enjoyment of the fruits of his industry, and then let alone."[27]

The philosophy of laissez-faire individualism was upheld on two grounds. Laissez-faire was the social framework of individual liberty and at the same time the principle of social justice and progress. This twofold aspect of competitive individualism—as a system of liberty and as a principle of justice—explained the popularity, the academic dominance, and the persuasiveness of its influence in shaping public opinion and action. For whenever the validity of one aspect of this creed was questioned, the other was invoked as sufficient ground for the maintenance of the whole. Whenever purely economic theories, as, for example, the Malthusian law of population, the wage-fund theory, or that of prices, were challenged on philosophical grounds, it was pointed out that unless the laws of the market or of the accumulation of property were left to themselves, liberty would be destroyed by governmental despotism, and vice versa.

Yet individualism was not only the ideology of the intellectual elite of the country but a living faith of most Americans. One of the indications of the pervasiveness of this attitude is the incredible popularity and influence of the theories of Herbert Spencer in America during the last three decades of the nineteenth century. This influence affected all strata of American society. Businessmen, Protestant ministers, politicians, farmers, and workers resorted to his ideas and slogans no less than university teachers, writers, lawyers, and judges. Spencer's vogue was that of the philosopher of individualism par excellence, who seemed to have proved the harmony of the cosmic purposes with those of the American nation.[28] William James, who, though very critical of the merits of Spencer's *Synthetic Philosophy,* still admitted that "his politico-ethical activity in general breathes the purest

English spirit of liberty, and his attacks on over-administration and criticisms on the inferiority of great centralized systems are worthy to be textbooks of individualists the world over."[29]

Emile de Laveleye wrote concerning Spencer's *Man versus the State:* "The individualist theory was, I think, never expounded better or with stronger arguments based on first principles, or supported by so great a number of clearly analyzed and admirably grouped facts."[30] The same reason accounted for the attraction that Spencer held in a popularized version for the common people of the United States.[31] The social scientist John R. Commons recounted from his boyhood: "Every one of them in that Eastern section of Indiana was a Republican . . . and every one was a follower of Herbert Spencer who was then the shining light of evolution and individualism . . . I was brought up on Hoosierism, Republicanism, Presbyterianism, and Spencerism."[32]

This statement reveals the most peculiar aspect of Spencer's vogue in America, namely, his conquest of the Protestant church.[33] The initial distrust of Protestant ministers toward the philosophy of natural evolution began to wane in the 1870s. Henry Ward Beecher, the most popular of preachers, was already an admirer of Spencer in the 1860s and declared himself openly for evolution. The weekly *Independent* tried to prove the compatibility of Christianity and evolutionary natural selection and the survival of the fittest. Lyman Abbott, successor to Henry Ward Beecher at the Plymouth Church, New York, led the *Outlook* in a battle for a Christianized version of evolutionism. By 1885, when Josiah Strong published *Our Country* for the Home Missionary Society, the concept of evolution had already colored the viewpoint of many prominent Protestant ministers.

Spencer's impact was felt in legislation as well as in the decisions of the courts. The well-known dissenting opinion of Justice Holmes in the case of *Lochner v. New York* protested against decisions based on premises taken from the theory of laissez-faire while denying to the majority the right to embody its opinions in law. Speaking on the peculiar interpretation of the Fourteenth Amendment had received through lawyers and judges, Holmes declared: "The Fourteenth Amendment does not enact Mr. Herbert Spencer's *Social Statics,*" and "a constitution is not intended to embody a particular economic theory, whether of paternalism and the organic relation of the citizen to the state or of *laissez faire*."[34]

The combined action of legislators and ministers inspired by the Spencerian version of individualism was revealed in the famous Dawes Act of 1887, which formulated the federal policy toward most Indians for the next four decades. That act attempted to civilize the Indian, teach him agriculture, and merge him with the body politic of the nation. It provided for the dissolution of all but a few of the tribes as legal entities and the division of the tribal lands among the individual members.[35] In the formulation of that policy, humanitarian and landed interests worked together. Especially influential were Lyman Abbott; the Episcopal bishops Huntington, Hare, and Whipple; the Reverend Phillips Brooks of Boston; and Merrill E. Gates, president of Rutgers College, working through the Indian Rights Annexation and the annual Lake Mohonk Conference of the Friends of the Indians as well as through the United States Board of Indian Commissioners.[36]

As early as 1879, Lyman Abbott had advocated the destruction of the tribal system and the Indians' acculturation to Western civilization through the introduction of private property: "In this country we have tried . . . to fence around the Indian civilization (which is barbarism). . . . But God's way of making men and women is through suffering and by struggle, and there is no other way."[37] Abbott's interpretation of the ways of God and the growth of civilization was inspired less by the New Testament than by Spencer's gospel of progress through fierce competitive struggle for survival. This was also Gate's view. The Indians had to become individual citizens and be prepared for this by hard work, the acquisition of property, individual responsibility, and family life: "There is no other 'manifest destiny' for any man . . . to this we stand committed, by all the logic of two thousand years of Teutonic and Anglo-Saxon history, since Arminius . . . made a stand for liberty against the legions of Rome."[38]

The first step was the breakup of tribal organization, for community of lands and goods "cuts the nerve of all that manful effort which political economy teaches us proceeds from the desire for wealth."[39] "Individualism, the key-note of our socio-political ideas in this century, makes itself felt by sympathetic vibrations."[40] Like Abbott, Gates believed that the submission of the Indians to the discipline of competitive economy would do more good than missionary work. "It cultivates the habit of *looking to the future* and of seeking to modify the future for one's self by one's own efforts. And this habit persevered in develops . . . that power which is the highest prerogative of man . . . *will power,* intelligently and voluntarily exercised in subjection to law!"[41]

John T. Oberly, superintendent of Indian schools of the Department of Interior, declared to great applause at the third annual meeting of the Lake Mohonk Conference, that both Senator Dawes and Lyman Abbott were in agreement "that the first essential thing in the attempt to solve the Indian problem is agreement, that the Indian is a man and that he should have individualism."[42] The American doctrine of natural right to self-determination had given vitality to the political doctrine of individualism, and this was the answer to the agelong search for a just basis of politics. "When America said to the world, 'The answer to the great political power comes primarily from the individual,' a new truth was asserted."[43]

Senator Dawes agreed that the tribal community system was at the root of the Indians' backwardness: "It is Henry George's system, and under that there is no enterprise . . . there is no selfishness, which is at the bottom of civilization." He agreed with the view of Gates that "the desire for the acquisition of property is . . . on the whole the mainspring that daily keeps in motion the mechanism of the world's daily routine."[44] Here was a perfect example of that confluence of "Hoosierism, Republicanism, Presbyterianism, and Spencerism" into a working model of action.

The extraordinary influence of Spencer over the American mind has been explained by the fact that he supplied the new elite of industrial capitalism with a rationale appropriate to the necessities of adjustment to political democracy.[45] Spencer, by fusing Malthusianism with the laissez-faire ideology of the Manchester school, had created a formula of individualism that legitimized American capitalism.[46] Yet such an explanation does not account for Spencer's hold over the minds of intellectuals of radical democratic leanings, over single taxers, anarchists, and such acid critics of the Gilded Age as Hamlin Garland, Jack London, and Theodore Dreiser. The fact is that he appealed to divergent groups and interests—to the conservative liberalism of free traders and anti-imperialists such as William Graham Sumner and Grover Cleveland, to the preachers of the "gospel of wealth" and the "cult of success," to the conservative ideology of the courts, to the radical movement of farmers and workers, and to those who carried on the intellectual tradition of the New England Enlightenment.

The common ground of Spencer's appeal can be summed up under five headings: his concept of individuality as the end of cosmic and social evolution, his ethic of competitive individualism, his unswerving suspicion of the state, his almost anarchistic doctrine of the self-sufficiency of economic society, and his belief in laissez-faire policy, all four of which led to the fifth—an optimistic theory of cosmic progress culminating in a perfect adjustment between the individual and society. These doctrines were identical with those elaborated by American individualism before the arrival of Spencer's gospel in America. His success rested, to quote Henry George, on his capacity to give "coherence and scientific formula to opinions which already prevailed. Its wonderful spread . . . has not been so much a conquest as an assimilation."[47]

Henry George has given in *Progress and Poverty* a résumé of the popular version of Spencer's philosophy in America: The present civilization was the product of the law of evolution that ruled supreme in all realms of nature and in the social sciences. The law stated that the steady progress of differentiation and growing complexity was achieved in the social as in the biological realm through the struggle for existence and survival in the course of which the fittest individuals and species survive. The efforts, inventions, and habits created in this struggle were perpetuated and transmitted biologically as well as culturally to posterity.

> War, slavery, tyranny, . . . famine, . . . want and misery, which fester in modern civilization, are the impelling causes which drive man on, by eliminating poorer types and extending the higher. . . . Thus, while this theory is, as Herbert Spencer says, "radical to a degree beyond anything which current radicalism conceives," inasmuch as it looks for changes in the very nature of man; it is at the same time, "conservative to a degree beyond anything conceived by current conservatism," inasmuch as it holds that no change can avail save these slow changes in man's nature.

The law of evolution drove civilization inexorably, if slowly, to higher and higher levels of achievement and forms of social life.[48] Henry George here described that "hopeful fatalism" that justified ruthless competition and social exploitation through the vision of a final happy end and consoled itself with Andrew Carnegie's maxim, "All is well since all grows better."

Yet there existed in Spencer's philosophy facets that had appealed to Henry George no less than to other radicals, among them Spencer's prediction that society would develop higher and higher forms of social adjustment between the individual and the community until an equilibrium of highest individualization and highest cooperation should result. At that stage, the need for coercion and for the state would disappear, and each individual would spontaneously cooperate with the community.[49]

This ideal underlay Spencer's formulation of the law of evolution. "There is another form under which civilization can be generalized . . . a progress towards that constitution of man and society required for the complete manifestation of every one's individuality."[50] Spencer repeated here, only in different words, the "ideal union in actual individualism" of Emerson and the transcendentalists. Like them, he derived the rights of property from the concept of individuality.[51]

The contribution of Spencer to American thought consisted of the integration of economic, political, ethical, and philosophical individualism into an apparently consistent scientific theory of irresistible progress. At the core of his voluminous writing lay the will to prove the compatibility of absolute individual liberty with social cooperation and progress. His sociology was a deliberate attempt to demonstrate that the "tacit assumption that Individualism means the solitary life of the individual is an entire misapprehension. It may and does go along with an elaborate form of mutual dependence."[52] These were basic convictions of the Jeffersonian tradition and of the Enlightenment.

An analysis of Spencer's appeal to different segments of public opinion in America thus shows both the broad basis of common agreement and the sharp differences in the interpretation of the American concept of individualism. The radical wing of American democracy, the individualistic anarchists, Henry George and his followers, the radical transcendentalists, and labor leaders such as Samuel Gompers were all indebted to the author of *Social Statics*. They acclaimed the earlier writings of Spencer no less than the later writings of John Stuart Mill. Yet the same qualities that made Spencer attractive to the radicals made him suspect to the conservatives before the Civil War. The evaluation changed because the concept of individualism in Spencer's later writings was suited to the temper and aspirations of American democracy yet responded easily to the needs and interest of the new industrial and financial elite on the one hand and the fears of liberals on the other. By substituting nature and history for the organized will of the community as the instrument of progress and social well-being, Spencer fulfilled a popular demand in America. His theories could be utilized by all those who feared that the political revolution of the Civil War and Reconstruction period might develop into a social revolution. His "incongruous mixture of Natural Rights and physiological metaphor" and his theory of ruthless competition as the motive force of progress simultaneously supplied the new economic elite with a rationale and a vocabulary that they were reluctant to abandon.[53]

Competitive economic activity was, in Spencer's opinion, not only the way to progress but the principle of natural justice. The ambiguous expression, the "survival of the fittest," which seemed to make survival the criterion of fitness and therefore of value, became more definite through Spencer's statement that throughout life "each adult gets benefits in proportion to merit, reward in proportion to desert, merit and desert being understood as ability to fulfill all the requirements of life."[54]

In adapting this theory to the needs of American democracy through the gospel of wealth and the cult of success, an ideology was created that fulfilled the complex requirements of satisfying different strata of the American nation at the same time. Its main elements were the assertion that American democracy meant the equality of chances for success, the mobility of social classes, the beneficial effects of the private accumulation of wealth on the material well-being of the whole nation, and the correspondence between success and merit.[55] Moreover, to many who, like Andrew Carnegie, attempted to reconcile their positions with the rules of Christian morality and democratic principles, it provided an almost religious comfort.[56] The glorification of individual success gave democracy a new meaning by transforming equality of rights into an equality of opportunity. The popularity of the appeal was basically derived from the pioneer tradition of the moving frontier. It translated the character ideal of an earlier period, with its belief in self-reliance and faith in the identity of private and public interest, into a goal of the industrial urban world.[57] "Not simply do we see," wrote Spencer, "that in the competition among individuals of the same kind, survival of the fittest has from the beginning furthered production of a higher type; but we feel that the increasing warfare between Species is mainly due both to growth and organization. Without universal conflict there would have been no development of the active powers."[58]

A typical example of the identification of the interests of private industrial enterprise with that of the nation through the Spencerian concept of individualism was the address of Senator Chauncey M. Depew given at Vanderbilt University: "The American Commonwealth is built upon the individual. It recognizes neither classes nor masses . . . We have thus become a nation of self-made men. We live under just and equal laws and all avenues for a career are open . . . freedom of opportunity and preservation of the results of forecast, industry, thrift and honesty have made the United States the most prosperous and wealthy country in the world. Commodore Vanderbilt is a conspicuous example of the product and possibilities of our free and elastic conditions . . . he neither asked nor gave quarter. The same open avenues, the same opportunities which he had before him are equally before every other man."[59]

Andrew Carnegie, the only sincere disciple of Spencer among the giants of American industry, was less inclined to flatter the democratic sentiment by illusions.

> To those who propose to substitute Communism for this intense Individualism, the answer therefore is: The race has tried that. All progress from that barbarous day to the present time has resulted from its displacement. Not evil, but good, has come to the race from the accumulation of wealth by those who have had the ability and energy to produce it. But even if we admit for a moment that it might be better . . . a sufficient answer is, This is not evolution, but revolution. It necessitates the changing of human nature itself—a work of eons. . . . We might as well urge the destruction of the highest existing type of man because he failed to reach our ideal as to favor the destruction of Individualism, Private Property, the Law of Accumulation of Wealth, and the Law of Competition.[60]

The fusion of this business ideology with the laissez-faire philosophy of liberals and conservatives created a theory of individualism that remained a legitimate and popular formulation of the American way of life. The identification of this theory of individualism with American nationality was consistent after the last third of the nineteenth century.[61] Henry Clews, author of *The Wall Street Point of View,* made this identification blandly in an address delivered in 1907: "I stand firmly in favour of the principle of competition, and that system of Individualism which guards, protects and encourages competition. . . . Take away the spirit of Individualism from the people, and you at once eliminate the American Spirit—the love of free-dom,—of free industry,—free and unfettered opportunity,—you take away freedom itself."[62] The same message was repeated again in 1946, in the statement of the principles of the National Association of Manufacturers, *The American Individual Enterprise System:*

> Nearly every page of this book drives home the fundamental feature of our tra-ditional enterprise system, namely its individualism. At the threshold of our na-tional existence we solemnly asserted "the unalienable right to life, liberty, and the pursuit of happiness"; we fought the Revolutionary War for that right, and adopted a Constitution to guarantee and propagate it. We became a nation of free men not serving political masters but ourselves, free to pursue our happiness without interference from the state, with the greatest liberty of individual ac-tion ever known to man. Individuals, conscious of unbounded opportunity, in-flamed by the love of achievement, inspired by the hope of profit, ambitious of the comfort, power and influence that wealth brings, turned with . . . vigor to producing and offering goods and services in freely competitive markets. The individual wanted little from the government beyond police protection while he confidently worked out his own destiny. . . . Our "private enterprise system and our American form of government are inseparable and there can be no compro-mise between a free economy and a governmentally dictated economy without endangering our political as well as our economic freedom."[63]

This ideology of individualism as purposely propagated in the face of a reality that more and more contradicted the gospel of wealth and the cult of success in order to identify the masses with industrial and cooperative capitalism.[64] The fear of a movement toward socialism, of the revolutionary organization of the industrial masses, and of the growing demand for state intervention, regulation, and protection for the benefit of the laborers and middle class had been steadily growing since the 1870s. It pervaded the minds of business leaders and Republicans, especially in the first two de-cades of the twentieth century. The Progressive movement was largely com-mitted to an attack on the distortion of democracy and national unity by the ideology of laissez-faire individualism. The Progressives were conscious of the rapid transformation of the nation by the industrial and urban revolu-tions as well as by the growing immigration of non-Protestant ethnic groups from central, southern, and eastern Europe. Some turned to an organic and even racist nationalism, others to a neo-Jeffersonian democracy, and still others to a pragmatic espousal of measures that would lead to a welfare state. But all agreed on the dangers of a laissez-faire concept of the state and of an individualistic philosophy of the relation between the individual and society.

Frederick Jackson Turner had shown how the earlier experience of American life had fostered both equalitarian democracy and unrestrained individualism through the conditions of life on the moving frontier and through the free lands of the virgin West.[65] He had also shown how the ideal of the self-made man was translated from the agricultural to the industrial frontier.[66] This historical analysis of the simultaneous origins of American individualism and equalitarianism disclosed the reasons why equalitarian democracy and unrestrained individualism were incompatible. Democracy had begun with competitive individualism as well as with the belief in equality. But the farmers "gradually leaned that unrestrained competition and combination meant the triumph of the strongest, the seizure in the interest of a dominant class of the strategic points of the nation's life. They learned that between the ideal of individualism, unrestrained by society, and the ideal of democracy, was an innate conflict; that their very ambitions and forcefulness had endangered their democracy."[67] The question was whether a new concept of democracy could save the abiding values of individualism and yet create a "just social order that shall sustain the free, progressive, individual in a real democracy."[68] That became the central problem of the Progressive movement.

The American Economic Association, founded in 1885, had even earlier made a critical examination of the laissez-faire theory. Strongly influenced by the German historical school of economics, by the founders of the *Verein für Sozialpolitik,* and by the "socialism of the chair," Richard T. Ely, Henry C. Adams, Edmund James, Simon M. Patten, John B. Clark, E. R. A. Seligman, and Richard M. Smith criticized American ideological fundamentalism. The platform for the American Economic Association, as proposed by Ely, declared:

1. We regard the state as an educational and ethical agency whose positive aid is an indispensable condition of human progress. While we recognize the necessity of individual initiative in industrial life, we hold that the doctrine of *laissez-faire* is unsafe in politics and unsound in morals; and that it suggests an inadequate explanation of the relations between the state and the citizens.

2. We do not accept the final statements which characterized the political economy of the past generation.

3. We hold that the conflict of labor and capital has brought to the front a vast number of social problems whose solution is impossible without the united efforts of Church, state, and science.[69]

This platform, which was actually a very conservative adaptation of the principles that Simon Patten and Edmund James had suggested, clearly showed the impact of German thought, and especially of the ideas of Adolf Wagner that demonstrated that the ever-increasing participation of the state in social and economic life was the law of evolution.[70] Thoughtful Americans who confronted the chaotic consequences of the Industrial Revolution found in these theories a welcome antidote both to the individualism of Spencer and to the democratic radicalism of the masses.[71] The Historical school, wrote Ely, has "placed man as man, and not wealth in the foreground, and subordinated everything to his true welfare . . . in opposition to individualism, they emphasize Aristotle's maxim . . . or, as Blackstone has it, man was formed for society."[72]

Yet most of the members of the convention opposed the socialist glorification of the state with its purely historical approach toward the ideal of individualism. William G. Sumner, F. Lawrence Laughlin, Frank W. Taussig, and A. T. Hadley refused to accept even the compromise program of the Association. Others, like Henry C. Adams, E. R. A. Seligman, John B. Clark, and E. J. James, insisted on the differentiation between a laissez-faire individualism that could not be maintained and the general philosophy of individualism that in their opinion was the backbone of modern civilization. "We ought to be careful," asserted Professor Alexander Johnston of Princeton, "while fighting the illegitimate application of the doctrine [of laissez-faire] to matters properly within the domain of morals or the state, not to seem to ask the total abolition of the legitimate principles, the secret of individualism, the basis of modern society."[73]

Dealing with "The Relation of the State to Industrial Action," Adams insisted that, although laissez-faire had proved untenable, no other theory could "take the place of the principle of individualism which has been forced to abdicate its seat of authority."[74] He maintained that all progress was made by "the growth of individualism and the decay of communalism; and no one who fully appreciates the opportunities thus offered . . . can seriously advocate a return to the conditions of the past."[75] Laissez-faire was not intrinsic to the development of individualism but rather tended under certain conditions to destroy it. A theory of social direction must be worked out to preserve the basic achievements of individualism. "It is an intellectual blunder to say that all extensions of the functions of government are in the direction of socialism," Adams declared.[76] "The American people are obliged to choose between the principle of individualism and the principle of socialism." His own conclusions, he said, were "motivated by the theory of individualism, and not by the theory of socialism."[77]

The same, to a large extent, was true of the Social Gospel movement which, by 1912, was the dominant creed of Protestantism in America. As in other countries, industrialization, urbanization, and the creation of a rootless working class compelled the churches to ponder upon the social implications of Christianity. The threatening chaos and the disintegration of the Protestant pattern of American civilization, as well as the challenge of socialism, necessitated an ideological reorientation involving a criticism of the individualistic philosophy. The Social Gospel was the reaction of Protestantism to the ethics and practice of capitalism "markedly stimulated by socialism."[78]

The Protestant ministry was therefore preoccupied with the merits of the alternative systems of socialism and individualism. The claim that socialism realized the true intent of Christianity, although departing from its religious premises, presented a serious challenge.[79] "We wrestle with the problem of socialism and individualism," declared Phillips Brooks, "and we wonder which of the two must be sacrificed to the other."[80]

The strength of the Social Gospel movement lay in the fact that it incorporated the economic and historical views of those who had founded the American Economic Association. This enabled these Protestants not only to formulate a plan of social action but also to separate the ethical and religious values of individualism, which they wished to maintain, from its economic and social theories, which they wished to discard. The difficulty of such a separation was testified to by the Congregationalist minister Washington Gladden. "Absurd and unscientific" as was the inevitable alliance of individual freedom and laissez-faire economics, it had nevertheless "been dinned into the ears of the multitude so consistently for the last century that it is hard to get them to take any other view of social relations. Economic science is rapidly clearing itself of these errors, but the philosophy of the street . . . is still rank individualism."[81]

Yet most of the Social Gospelers, although they condemned the ruthless competitive capitalism of their times, ascribed to individualism an important historical role in the progress of humanity and maintained that it had abiding value as a regulative ideal of society and morality. John Rae, author of the immensely popular *Contemporary Socialism,* defined the attitude of progressive Americans toward the spheres of private and public action: "While opposed to the State doing anything either moral or material for individuals, which individuals could do better, or with better results, for themselves, they [English economists, philosophers, and statesmen] agreed in requiring the State, first, to undertake any individual work it had superior natural advantages for conducting successfully; and second, to protect the weaker classes effectively in the essentials of all rational and humane living . . . not only against the ravages of violence or fear or insecurity, but against those of ignorance, disease and want."[82]

It was, then, under the threefold assault of progressivism, radical democracy, and socialism that the Spencerian version of individualism combined with the gospel of wealth, and the cult of success was formulated and propagated.[83] There was a conscious effort to create through individualism an ideological identification between the nation, democracy, and industrial enterprise. Individualism made competitive private enterprise and American identity parts of one pattern, through which the new elite hoped to stabilize its own position inside the framework of democracy. This group considered individualism not only an ideology that gave wider significance to its activities, but also a system of values that expressed the aspirations and the sense of identity of the American nation as a whole. This accounts for the fact that not only the Republican party but also the Democrats under Bryan and Wilson, the Rooseveltian Progressives, and even the Populists, single taxers, and labor leaders were committed to the concept of individualism as a national ideal.

The Republican party consistently held to this ideology. The Great Depression dramatized Herbert Hoover's famous speech on the "American System of Rugged Individualism," setting his high confidence in the unique success of the American system in the ironic context of the collapse of the economy. But Hoover's faith in individualism as the American system was typical of the middle-of-the-road liberals of the early twentieth century.[84] It was under the leadership of Theodore Roosevelt that the GOP declared the "Republican Party stands for a wise and regulated individualism."[85] Roosevelt himself, in spite of his organic concept of nationhood and state, considered individualism "the fibre of our whole citizenship."[86] His progressivism came "not to destroy but to save individualism" from socialism and plutocracy.[87]

By the beginning of the twentieth century, members of each party, except for Herbert Croly's *New Republic* circle and the Socialists, felt obliged to invoke this idea in order to appear as the national standard-bearers. The Republican platform of 1912 abandoned even the mild qualifications it had made in 1908 and defined its concept of individualism in terms of strict constitutionalism and laissez-faire policy.[88] Elihu Root, the intellectual power behind the scenes at the convention of 1912, defended the Republican synthesis that welded laissez-faire philosophy to the gospel of wealth and to Spencerian evolution, as the only system that could maintain the "individualism which underlies the social system of Western civilization."[89]

Yet, William Jennings Bryan, the "Tribune of the People," also justified his radical attack on the corporate structure as necessary to preserve the American system of individualism.[90] The issue between the Republican and the Democratic concepts was accurately assessed by Thomas R. Marshall, governor of Indiana and Democratic candidate for the vice-presidency in 1912. Affirming that Wilson's New Freedom was an adaptation of the Jeffersonian ideal of social justice to changed conditions, he declared: "An individualism which teaches the right to success without emphasizing the duty of not depriving any other man of his opportunity, is as much an evil as the system which exalts our common right by depriving us of our personal rights." Rejecting the Republican version of individualism, he concluded: "Our birthright in America is the right to success, but it not success unless thereby men attain unto collective opportunity. . . . Unless the individualism of America rests upon fraternity and faith, it will crumble."[91]

The most revealing evidence for the identification of Americanism with the concept of individualism is afforded by the fact that the radical social criticism leveled against industrial capitalism by single taxers and Populists was also made in the name of individualism. After the Civil War, all radical democratic movements defined their aims in terms of Jeffersonian philosophy. The guiding principles of the "producers' philosophy" were like those of American anarchism, a radical extension of the natural-rights philosophy. Labor was the only title to property and the measure of value; free competition, in the absolute absence of privileges and monopolies, was the ideal regulator of the production and distribution of wealth; natural wealth belonged to the community and could not be privately owned; public services and utilities should, therefore, be under public control; and, finally, a producers' society was capable of directing its affairs by voluntary action, so the functions of the state were to be limited to purely administrative concerns or to measures safeguarding the existence of the natural order to society. These were the axiomatic beliefs of the leaders of radical democracy, of individualist-anarchists, of the followers of George Henry Evans, Edward Kellogg, and Henry George.[92]

State socialism, with its doctrine of class war and with its immense enlargement of the authority of the state, was rejected as inimical to the spirit of American democracy and as destructive to freedom and progress. Even the socialist wing of the indigenous American Labor movements—the International Working Men's Association and the IWW—were anarchistic in their ideals and rejected state socialism.[93]

The natural-rights philosophy persisted among left-wing radicals because it represented the national tradition and offered an alternative to socialism. It contained all the messianic elements of socialism, its promise of social justice, of ultimate harmony between individual and collective needs, and the perspective of material and spiritual progress. Yet, unlike socialism, these doctrines were capable of realization within American democracy, through the enlargement of the areas of liberty and equality. They were socially inclusive and affirmative of the nation, of democracy, and of the present pattern of life. They required for the fulfillment of their aims no eschatological revolutionary unheaval.[94]

The adherents of the producers' philosophy had, however, to reinterpret the term "individualism," which had already been preempted by defenders of the economic status quo. The process of adaptation was revealed in the writings of Henry George and his followers.

George himself never accepted unqualifiedly the term "individualism," unless it could be made to coincide with the ideal of a free society and the Jeffersonian concept of natural rights.[95] But Hamlin Garland's "New

Declaration of Rights'' on behalf of the Single-Tax League was less cautious and identified individualism with the cause of populism. "We are individualists mainly,'' he wrote in 1891, and he continued:

> We stand unalterably opposed to the paternal idea in government. We believe in fewer laws and juster interpretation thereof. We believe in less interference with individual liberty, less protection of the rapacious demands of the few, and more freedom of action on the part of the many. . . . *All men are born free and equal in opportunity, to live, to labor . . . and to enjoy the fruits of their own industry.* This is the reading which we, as single tax men put . . . upon that immortal and hollow sounding instrument. . . . We mean *all* men.[96]
>
> The past is not individualistic, but socialistic. The Age of Socialism is not coming on, but departing. . . . What the Nationalists anathematize as "individualism,'' we, as individualists, are as ready to condemn as they, because it is not individualism at all, but the surviving and slow retreating effect of socialism, paternalism and special privilege.[97]

The attachment to the term, revealed in that reinterpretation, showed the extent to which individualism at the end of the nineteenth century had become firmly embedded in the concept of national identity.

It has been the purpose of this inquiry to study the American quest for national identity through a description and analysis of the concepts of a natural social order, "free society,'' and "individualism.'' There was a striking degree of continuity in the formation and crystallization of these concepts throughout the nineteenth century. Not all aspects of American political and social thought fitted this pattern of ideas and values, but the conclusions here reached were not the products of arbitrary selection. Though no attempt has been made to present a comprehensive history of American thought, there has been an effort to examine those ideas concerned with the meaning of American nationhood and of national identification. Assuming that the basic trend of American history was toward growth in the quality and breadth of democracy and an ever-greater national integration, this survey has sought to analyze the relation between the democratic aspiration of the American people and the contents of their national consciousness.

This analysis revealed that American democracy has meant more and less than equality of political rights and the sovereignty of the people. Both were, rather, corollaries of the concept of the rights of men that sought to express itself in the establishment of a natural social order of men as a "free society.'' This concept explained the peculiarity of American democracy, its distrust of state interference and the political regimentation of society. Because of it, the idea of individualism became the symbol and ideal of its national identity.

The relationship between individualism and national identity raised the question: How could concepts, ideas, and values, universally valid, which were inimical to the idea of the sovereignty of the state, became the basis of national identification? Part of the answer lay in the English heritage— Puritanism and the Whig tradition—which, in the environment of an absolutely new beginning, constantly repeating itself through immigration and western migration, created the new contents of the national consciousness. These factors provided decisive, formative elements but were not conclusive. What was usually overlooked was the peculiar dynamic force by which American society constituted itself a nation. The revolutionary severance from the mother country that created the American nation compelled it to adopt the universal values and norms of the rights of man and of natural law, not only as the basis of independent statehood but as the definition of its own identity. Political emancipation involved a radical break with the past that made it imperative to define the character of the new nation. Universal and rational modes of thought, which had served Americans in their struggle against England, enabled them to interpret their own pattern of life, institutions, and traditions. Though neither deliberate nor conscious of its own direction, this revolutionary élan, which had broken historical continuity, established in America a new pattern of social life explainable by the natural-rights theory. The pattern of disrupting historical continuities inherent in colonization and legitimized by the Revolution was repeated with every new wave of immigrants and with the westward movement of settlement. Successive groups of new arrivals sought national and social equality by formulating their identity in terms of the universal norms of a moral and social order that gave them equality of status, liberty of expression, and the right to consider themselves citizens.

The revolutionary heritage was therefore permanently attached to the Jeffersonian tradition, which had identified American nationality with the ideals of a natural equalitarian order. With the spread of political democracy, the concept of the American society as a system of liberty and equality became the dominant concept of national identity. The growth of nationalism and the great crisis of the Civil War made it more necessary than ever to find terms to describe adequately this national consciousness and to serve as symbols of identification. These functions were fulfilled by the concept of individualism, which attempted to define the ideals of the American way of life in a generic way.

Individualism supplied the nation with a rationalization of its characteristic attitudes, behavior patterns, and aspirations. It endowed the past, the present, and the future with the perspective of unity and progress. It explained the peculiar social and political organization of the nation—unity in spite of heterogeneity—and it pointed toward an ideal of social organization in harmony with American experience. Above all, individualism expressed the universalism and idealism most characteristic of the national consciousness. This concept evolved in contradistinction to socialism, the universal and messianic character of which it shared. Both claimed to create systems of social justice and to show a way toward the perfection of the human race. This twofold aspect—universalism and the capacity to describe values peculiar to American society—made individualism a term synonymous with Americanism.

These developments help explain to some degree several phenomena peculiar to American history—the weakness of the socialist movement, the fixation of social ideologies through identification with national values, and, in recent years, the willingness to consider the United States the appointed leader of the West against world communism. The identification of Americanism with the ideals of a free society and individualism, occurring relatively early, made the socialist formulas seem not only impractical but "un-American," inimical to the traditions of democracy and the system of individual behavior in the United States. Socialism was incompatible with American nationalism because the latter was already committed to a rival ideology.

For this very reason, Americans considered themselves natural leaders of the "free world" and of "Western civilization." The concept of the "free world" had the same significance and the same emotional implications as the concept of a "free society" had had during the great controversy with the slaveholding South. The struggle for freedom had only moved from the national to the international sphere. The earlier struggle had created the identification of American nationalism with free society and individualism. The later one involved the application of terms that would reflect the existence of a supernational unity of values and of international solidarity.

Those who have attempted to disentangle the concept of American national identity from those of individualism and of a natural order of freedom have usually followed Tocqueville in maintaining that democracy in the United States was a social rather than a political system. In the late nineteenth and early twentieth centuries, the Progressive movement attempted to postulate an American ideal of democracy that would satisfy the needs of the people, without having recourse to the ideology of individualism. To do so it was necessary to find an alternative basis of identification and loyalty. Any redefinition of the nature of American nationality could be successful only if it preserved the peculiar pattern that distinguished the United States from other nations—its claim to represent a social order in which equality, liberty, and social justice were reconciled in the framework of a political structure.

The Progressive movement endeavored to keep within this formal structure of American national consciousness. Visualizing an immense enlargement of the functions of government in the service of social democracy, it hoped to create a new center of loyalty and identification in the state.

An alternative was to base national identification on ethnic loyalties, traditions, and common memories. Individualism, like democracy, could then be considered as embodying national, historical, or racial characteristics that could be subordinated to the higher unity of the nation as embodied in the state. This position was adopted with differing nuances and emphases by the followers of Theodore Roosevelt's organic and integral New Nationalism.

Both of these tendencies emanating from the Progressive movement had a permanent effect upon American national consciousness. The deliberate blocking of further mass immigration in the 1920s, the growth of the federal welfare state in the following decades, and the sheer accumulation of common historical experiences created a community of national identification that became increasingly independent of the ideological structure we have studied. Yet the repeated attempts to reformulate the basis of national identification in terms of purely historic, ethnic, religious, or racial loyalties have been halfhearted and, though powerful, have been unable to achieve their purpose. Only a concept that interpreted Americanism in terms of a social order aimed at the realization of universally valid ideals of humanity could serve as a basis of national identification.

A Confusion of Voices:
The Crisis of Individualism
in Twentieth-Century America

Lawrence B. Goodheart
and Richard O. Curry

RECALLING his triumphant solo flight across the Atlantic in the spring of 1927, Charles Lindbergh observed:

> What advantages there are to flying alone! I know now what my father meant when he warned me, years ago of depending too heavily on others. . . . By flying alone I've gained in range, in time, in flexibility; and above all, I've gained in freedom. . . . According to that saying of my father's—I'm a full boy—indepen-dent—alone.[1]

The cultural significance of the dramatic flight was, as historian John William Ward has pointed out, ambivalent for Americans of the time. On the one hand, Lindbergh, "the lone eagle," embodied American individual-ism, especially the potential for self-reliance and self-sufficiency. The young man was living proof that the solitary virtues of the legendary frontiersman were still the stuff of personal success in a mass society. On the other hand, the flight represented the interdependent achievements of an advanced indus-trial age. Indeed, the whole aeronautical adventure was a corporate promo-tion, a point not lost on Calvin Coolidge. "I am told," the president commented, "that more than 100 separate companies furnished materials, parts, or service in its construction."[2] In sum, the epic 1927 flight reflected the widening gulf separating traditional values and new realities caused by social change. As Ward put it, "We cherish the individualism of the Amer-

Goodheart wrote most of this chapter. Curry authored the concluding section that deals with the complexities and contradictions of the Reagan-Bush era.

ican creed at the same time that we worship the machine which increasingly enforces collectivized behavior. Whether we can have both, the freedom of the individual and the power of an organized society is a question that still haunts our minds."[3]

The problem posed by Ward has evoked numerous and diverse responses throughout the twentieth century. One major response might well be termed "denial," "avoidance," or "obliviousness"—the assertion by some writers, ministers, businessmen, and politicians that traditional individualist assumptions retained their validity despite the growth of corporate power and the concentration of wealth, persistent poverty, agrarian unrest, heightening of ethnic and racial antagonism, the specter of class conflict, and the use of political repression against groups such as anarchists, socialists, labor unions, and opponents of American entry into the First World War.

For example, Henry Clews, a champion of laissez-faire economics, declared in *Individualism versus Socialism* (1907), "Take away the spirit of Individualism from the people, and you at once eliminate the American spirit—the love of freedom—of free industry—free and unfettered opportunity—you take away freedom itself."[4] Russell H. Conwell, the Baptist minister, preached a similar message in his popular lecture "Acres of Diamonds," which he estimated that he delivered six thousand times to enthusiastic audiences totalling thirteen million people. "There is not a poor person in the United States." Conwell declared, "who was not made poor by his own shortcomings."[5] Moreover, South Side Chicago bartender Mr. Dooley, a character created by journalist Peter Finley Dunne, instructed an Irish Catholic compatriot, "A poor man is a man that rayfuses to cash in."[6] Even Booker T. Washington expressed the view that "The individual who can do something that the world wants done will, in the end, make his way regardless of his race."[7] And in 1922, future president Herbert Hoover asserted the validity of traditional values in his book *American Individualism*. Having witnessed the devastation of war-torn Europe as a relief official, he proclaimed, "And from it all I emerge an individualist . . . an American individualist." Unlike the "frozen strata" of European society, Hoover's "progressive individualism" stressed "the firm and fixed ideal" of equality of opportunity. The government's role, he declared, was to act as an umpire, to preserve "the fair chance of Abraham Lincoln" for individuals to sort themselves out in the race of life according to their abilities and willpower.[8]

There can be little doubt that traditional individualistic values appealed to large numbers of Americans, especially members of the middle and upper-middle class. Nevertheless, a number of thoughtful critics and social reformers began to challenge the accuracy of conventional wisdom during the late nineteenth and early twentieth centuries. Between 1890 and 1920, a series of diverse, though sometimes allied, reform movements, collectively known as Progressivism, arose in an effort to restore a sense of fair play to American society. Although engaged in a variety of projects, Progressives shared a central concern that unbridled individualism was a major source of the malaise ailing the nation. They wished to enhance personal freedom, but they also appreciated to a degree not previously recognized in mainstream American thought that institutions had the power to affect the individual's well-being. The problems caused by industrialization and urbanization could, they believed, best be solved through the principles of social science, efficiency, and limited government planning. In such a way they hoped to create a cooperative democracy in which a harmonious balance would be struck between equality of opportunity, capitalist prerogatives, and limited governmental regulation.

For Henry D. Lloyd, one of the earliest Muckrakers, the glorification of the individual pursuit of wealth was at the source of the nation's problems. In *Wealth against Commonwealth* (1894), he refuted as a "fallacy" Adam Smith's axiom that "the self-interest of the individual was a sufficient guide to the welfare of the individual and society." Laissez-faire economics, he concluded, had allowed plutocrats to run society for their own benefit. Instead, Lloyd urged that "the true law of business is that all must pursue the interest of all"—the substitution of the Golden Rule for economic individualism. Until that transformation occurred, he argued that the pursuit of private "wealth" would undermine the "commonwealth."[9]

Other Progressive intellectuals shared the perspective that social reform necessitated the containment of some individualistic prerogatives. Randolph S. Bourne, an essayist, ridiculed the traditional idea that "social ills may be cured by personal virtue."[10] The homilies of Benjamin Franklin and Horatio Alger that equated individual morality with worldly success appeared ill-suited to a new generation confronting the challenges of urban disorder, business monopolies, and political corruption. For Walter Rauschenbusch, a pioneer in the Social Gospel movement, "Sin is essentially selfishness." Individual transgression against the general welfare constituted Christian wrongdoing. Because the good of the whole was a primary value above the putative rights of personal profit making, he preached, "God is against capitalism, its methods, spirit, and results."[11] In his influential *The Promise of American Life* (1909), Herbert Croly, a founder of *The New Republic*, maintained that the Jeffersonian tradition of weak government, whose goal was to protect individual opportunities and rights, had degenerated to the point where "the 'Boss'" and "the tainted millionaire took advantage of this situation to secure for themselves an unusually large amount of political and economic power." His recommendation was a democratized Hamiltonianism, "a vigorous and conscious assertion of the public as opposed to private and special interests" by the federal government.[12]

The Progressive effort to redefine individualism is illustrated in the policies of Theodore Roosevelt and Woodrow Wilson. "A simple and poor society can exist," Roosevelt postulated, "as a democracy on the basis of sheer individualism. But a rich and complex society cannot so exist."[13] Inspired by Croly's vision, the former president called for a New Nationalism in 1910. "The essence of the struggle," he told a group of Civil War veterans, "is to equalize opportunity, destroy privilege, and give to the life and citizenship of every individual the highest possible value both to himself and to the commonwealth." In sum, the purpose of the New Nationalism was to put "the national need before sectional or personal advantage."[14]

Much of the appeal of Wilson's rival "New Freedom" was in the goal, derived from the ideas of the Progressive lawyer Louis Brandeis, to restore individualistic competition to the marketplace through governmental break-up of monopolies. Despite differences in their programs, Roosevelt and Wilson shared a deep commitment to individual freedom and equality of opportunity, which they believed only national leadership could ensure. It is the positive, regulatory role (limited though it was) that Progressives assigned to the federal government in the economic sphere that significantly distinguishes them from earlier attacks on special privilege, notably that of the Jacksonian Democrats.

Historian Frank Tariello, Jr., argues that Progressive social thought marked a turning point in the definition of American individualism. "The new individualism," he wrote, "played up the cooperative links among men and called for an overall increase in the power of the state for the attainment of social ends. Individuality consisted in the participation of the individual in socially valuable activities, not in a hypothetical freedom from society or in the cultivation of such anarchic traits as self-reliance and independent thinking."[15] But Progressives had not in fact abandoned traditional conceptions of individualism. Their recourse to state action was restricted "by the requirements," Otis L. Graham, Jr., observes, "that the right man be entrusted with power, that reformers display the right spirit of deliberation and caution, that they move according to a clear plan." Progressives were, he adds, "individualists at heart—the word 'individualism' appears hundreds of times in their literature—and they typically practiced an individualistic politics."[16]

If the Progressives reflected a somewhat limited departure from traditional individualist assumptions, their criticism of American society did little to change the harsh social and economic realities that faced most Americans during the early twentieth century. A study by the Brookings

Institution, for example, indicated that an annual income of two thousand dollars was needed for a typical family to buy basic necessities in 1929. An astounding 60 percent of all American families fell beneath that poverty line. Income distribution was increasingly concentrated during the 1920s into fewer hands. In 1919, the richest 5 percent controlled 30 percent of total family income, while the poorest 40 percent received a disproportionate 12.5 percent. Furthermore, Hoover appointed six millionaires to his cabinet, including the fabulously wealthy Andrew Mellon as secretary of treasury. Not surprisingly, Mellon oversaw tax cuts for the very rich that dropped their rates from 73 percent in 1921 to 24 percent in 1929. Although manufacturing output expanded 29 percent from 1923 to 1929, average weekly wages for manufacturing employees rose a scant 5 percent. Union membership declined 28 percent during the decade, and at least one-third of the nation's farmers were financially vulnerable tenants on the land that they worked. In sum, Progressive individualism provided the moral legitimacy for 1 percent of the population to control 59 percent of the nation's wealth, while 87 percent of the people owned only 10 percent. Discrimination based on gender, race, religion, and ethnicity presented further obstacles that blocked the achievement of the traditional ideals of self-improvement.[17]

It was the New Deal's response to the unprecedented economic collapse of the Great Depression that marks the shift not only away from the rugged individualism of the 1920s but also toward a more socialized interpretation of individualism, one that most (but not all) surviving Progressives were unwilling to endorse. For liberal intellectuals, "the Depression itself," historian Richard H. Pells explains, "encouraged the conviction that human problems could never be solved by the individual alone—indeed that an emphasis on personal liberation and self-expression might be positively harmful in the context of a national disaster."[18] Competing with newly fashionable Marxists such as V. F. Calverton, who accused liberals of overemphasizing "the importance of autonomy of the individual," philosopher John Dewey, sociologist Robert Lynd, and historian Charles Beard fashioned a new collectivism within which individualism of an entirely new sort might survive and even flourish. "The cold truth is," Beard observed in 1931, "that the individualist creed of everybody for himself and the devil take the hindmost is principally responsible for the distress Western civilization finds itself in."[19]

Writing in the wake of the stock market crash, Dewey's *Individualism Old and New* (1930) indicted the "perversion of the whole ideal of individualism to conform to the practices of a pecuniary culture. It has become the source and justification of inequalities and oppressions." Through social planning he hoped to move beyond the old economic individualism to a new humanitarian individualism that would extend "equality of opportunity and free association and intercommunication."[20] Robert Lynd was more attuned to traditional social concerns than Dewey. In Pell's words, "He shared the decade's characteristic fear of disorder and disunity" but also condemned what he called "the disjunction and contradictions within institutions" that blighted people's lives. As much as people needed protection from economic forces over which they had no control, he believed that "the human personality also craves a sense of freedom and diversity."[21] In short, he sought a happy balance between the individual and society.

Dewey's prediction that "the problem of social control of industry and the use of governmental agencies for constructive social ends will become the avowed center of political struggle" was fulfilled in the instrumental policies of the New Deal.[22] In his inaugural address on March 4, 1933, Franklin D. Roosevelt spoke of the nation's "interdependence" and the need for "broad Executive power to wage war" against economic collapse.[23] "We have suffered in the past," he warned, "from individualism run wild."[24] Rexford Tugwell, often considered the architect of the first New Deal, spoke of the need to abandon the laissez-faire assumptions characteristic of the previous Republican administrations. "We are turning away," he noted, "from the entrusting of crucial decisions, and the operation of institutions whose social consequences are their most characteristic feature, to individuals who are motivated by private interests." But he very accurately cautioned, "It will take a long time to learn how this may be done effectively."[25]

Despite Tugwell's advocacy of nationalized planning, the New Deal failed to implement a coherent policy of economic reform. President Roosevelt was not a sophisticated economist, but he was politically shrewd enough to back away from Tugwell's iconoclastic goal of restructuring the free market. Roosevelt's tentative economic policies never resolved the problem of underconsumption or ended high unemployment (which as late as 1938 stood at a dismal 19 percent) until the necessity of military Keynesianism during World War II put almost everyone back to work. Twenty years of Democratic rule by presidents Roosevelt and Truman heralded a dramatic expansion in presidential power and laid the institutional foundation for the welfare and warfare state, an unprecedented increase in the role of the federal government at home and abroad. Life was indeed better and more secure for millions of Americans—especially an expanded, white middle class—thanks to the welfare policies of the New Deal Democrats, which remain today the central feature of federal domestic policy.

Nevertheless, large corporations retained and expanded their economic hegemony, private property was safely intact, African-Americans remained largely mired in poverty, and wealth continued concentrated in relatively few hands. In 1941, the richest 5 percent of all families still controlled a hefty 24 percent of total family income. As historian Thomas C. Cochran put it, "The concept of the society as an interrelated whole, too complex to rely on 'the free market' for goods and service as its guide, was the most fundamental challenge to American values concerning individual responsibility and the virtues of competition."[26] But the New Deal's basic commitment to the individualistic values of liberal capitalism, as Cochran suggests, frustrated systematic national planning, stifled efforts to check the power of the big corporations, and glossed over the chronic problem of a maldistribution of wealth.

Since World War II, social commentators have taken a variety of positions regarding the status of individualism in American culture. Their assessment is often but not always colored by ideology. The Left is generally more likely than the Right to fault economic individualism and call for greater governmental regulation of the marketplace. On matters of personal morality, on expanding civil rights legislation for minorities, women, and homosexuals, and on First Amendment freedoms, conservatives tend to be more restrictive and less tolerant than liberals. Ideological labels, however useful in explaining perception, do not encompass all evaluations of individualism since 1945. Critics have also complained that Americans are too conformist or, conversely, too narcissistic. Some damn traditional individualist values; others praise them.

Several competing and contradictory schools of thought or major themes have appeared since the late 1940s regarding the value of individualism in modern American society. First, there was the continuation of the "New Deal Legacy," culminating in President Johnson's Great Society programs, which posited the existence of harmonious relationship between the welfare state and the protection of personal freedom. Second, there was a group of intellectual and popular writers such as David Riesman and William H. Whyte, Jr., who during the 1950s rejected the optimism of liberal reformers and argued that collective pressures had overwhelmed the individual, leading to "The Decline of Individualism." The third section discusses the implications of "Romantic Individualism," a series of intellectual constructs and social formulas produced by devotees of a neo-Emersonian cultivation of the self. The fourth theme, "Narcissism and Its Critics," discusses the views of writers, especially Christopher Lasch and Robert Bellah, who in best-selling books damned what they saw as the sin of self-indulgence in American society. Nevertheless, Bellah and Lasch have their own critics, most notably Herbert Gans, who argues that jeremiads against self-indulgence are not only misleading but irrelevant in attempting to create a viable social democracy.

In section five, we discuss "The Rehabilitation and Triumph of Economic Individualism," which gained intellectual respectability during the

1970s and emerged politically triumphant with the election of Ronald Reagan to the presidency in 1980. If Reagan's use of the traditional language of economic individualism ("getting government off our backs") struck a responsive chord, the effects of tax cuts, deregulation, and restrictions on social programs combined with a massive military buildup that served to enrich the wealthy and expand the power of the military-industrial complex. But one of the great ironies of the Reagan era was that Reagan's commitment to his version of economic individualism was accompanied in the name of "national security" by a sustained attack on civil liberties. In the last section, "Individualism Attacked: The Reagan Administration's Assault on the Bill of Rights," we analyze the implications of these repressive policies, which bode ill for enlightened aspects of our heritage of individualism such as the rights of free speech, privacy, and freedom from unreasonable searches and seizures (which have been seriously compromised during the cold war and accelerated during the Reagan-Bush era).

The New Deal Legacy

Advocates of the New Deal welfare state believed that an expanded federal government was not antithetical to personal freedom but even essential to the extension of equality of opportunity. Historian Arthur Schlesinger, Jr., a celebrant of the New Deal, announced that postwar politics had moved to "the vital center," a consensus between liberal Democrats and moderate Republicans that the state was actively responsible for social well-being.[27] Indeed, the Eisenhower administration's creation of the Department of Health, Education, and Welfare in 1954 reflected Republican recognition of the welfare state. "Freedom also seemed to be surviving," economist John Kenneth Galbraith, another New Deal partisan, declared in *The Affluent Society* (1958). "Perhaps it was realized that all organized activity requires concessions by the individual to the group."[28]

The culmination of postwar New Deal programs occurred, however, during the presidency of Lyndon Johnson, who, like Roosevelt, knew how to manipulate people and power for political ends. Johnson's goal was no less than a Great Society, the New Deal writ large. "The proper function of a government of the people, by the people, and for the people is," Johnson declared, "to make it possible for all citizens to experience a better, more secure, and more rewarding life."[29] Prodded by insistent African-American agitation, Johnson achieved more for black rights than any president since Lincoln. The Civil Rights Act of 1964, the Voting Rights Act of 1965, and the Housing Act of 1968 allowed the federal government to outlaw racial, religious, and gender discrimination in a variety of forms. The civil rights and black power movements spurred feminists, native Americans, and gays to demand their individual rights. In addition, Johnson's ambitious War on Poverty doubled federal spending on social programs that cut in half the number of poor people in the United States. A disastrously flawed foreign policy in Vietnam, however, subverted Johnson's short-lived domestic effort to extend equality of opportunity to more Americans.

Nevertheless, the liberal ascendancy continued in the Supreme Court, notably during the chief justiceship of Earl Warren (1953–69). The judicial activism of the Warren Court directly affected people's lives in very personal ways and extended constitutional rights in a variety of areas. As legal scholar Bernard Schwartz phrased it, "In expanding civil liberties, broadening political freedom, extending the franchise, reinforcing freedoms of speech, assembly, and religion, limiting the power of the politicians in smoke-filled rooms, [and] defining the limits of police power, the Warren Court had no equal in American history."[30] Even its successor, the more conservative Court headed by Warren Burger, made some important liberal decisions. In *Roe v. Wade* (1973), for example, the Court ruled that the fundamental "right of privacy" allowed women an unrestricted option to abortion during the first trimester of pregnancy, a decision that has provoked heated controversy.

The Decline of Individualism

During the 1950s, a number of social commentators declared that the sway of big government, big business, and big labor threatened the possibility for self-reliance, independence, and personal initiative. Author Vance Packard indicted Americans as a nation of status seekers who were concerned with conforming to public pressures.[31] Mass consumption of material goods—"keeping-up with the Joneses"—and a bipartisan cold war mentality—the fear of a monolithic communist conspiracy—characterized much of the Truman and Eisenhower years. No less a figure than Hubert Humphrey, the quintessential liberal Democrat, was chief sponsor of the repressive Communist Control Act, which passed both houses of Congress in 1954 with a total of only two dissenting votes. "From almost any angle of vision or historical perspective," historian Arthur A. Ekirch, Jr., bemoaned in 1958, "it is difficult to anticipate that the second half of the twentieth century will reverse the long-standing movement toward collectivism and away from individualism."[32]

The most authoritative announcement that mass society had submerged the individual was David Riesman's landmark study of national character, *The Lonely Crowd* (1954). With his collaborators, Reuel Denny and Nathan

Glazer, Riesman described two ideal types of personalities, the "inner-directed" and the "other-directed." While the inner-directed internalized cultural imperatives and was typical of the self-reliant individual of the nineteenth century, the other-directed took his cues from peers and was a product of twentieth-century mass society. Although an ideology of "free enterprise, individualism and all the rest" persisted, the authors argued that the modern character had evolved with changing times to the other-directed type. "The peer-group becomes the measure of all things," they wrote. "The individual has no defenses the group cannot batter down." Nevertheless, Riesman foresaw the possibility of a "saving remnant," a self-conscious personality type who could "tolerate freedom, even thrive on it," despite the pressure for conformity. These "autonomous" individuals would transcend the inner-directed and other-directed types who were "guided by voices other than their own."[33]

William H. Whyte, Jr.'s *The Organization Man* (1956) applied many of Riesman's assumptions to his popular study of conformity in large institutions. He was, however, more optimistic than Riesman about the viability of individualism in mass society. "Individualism is," he reassured, "as possible in our times as in others." The real problem was, this editor of *Fortune* believed, not the "evils of organization life" but the seductive "beneficence" of corporate paternalism. The solution was not to restructure business, because for Whyte corporate capitalism was efficient and productive. Instead, he instructed that each individual should strive to understand the constraints under which he worked and create a sphere of personal freedom within the institution, an "individualism within organization life."[34]

Romantic Individualism

Romantic individualism has taken various, sometimes exclusive, forms. Regardless of their compatibility, they share a basic concern with self-expression and inner feelings. Cultural radicals during the 1950s rebelled in their literary works against what they saw as the claustrophobia of the cold war consensus and the middle-class conformity of the Eisenhower years. For some white writers, the supposedly uninhibited life of the Negro jazz musician was the beau ideal. In his essay "The White Negro" (1959), novelist Norman Mailer idolized the anarchic individualism of the "hipster," who sought "the liberation of the self from the Super-Ego of society."[35] Allen Ginsberg, Jack Kerouac, Gregory Corso, and other "beatniks" celebrated a Dionysian excess of sex, drugs, and freedom. Even the occasional academic could sound like Emerson at his most transcendent. Classics scholar Norman O. Brown, author of the iconoclastic *Life against Death*

(1959), told Columbia University students in a 1961 address to discover the "God in us," to celebrate the mystery and holy madness of the unfettered mind.[36]

Whatever the direct relationship, the beatniks were at least a foreshadowing of a youthful counterculture that emerged during the 1960s in rebellion against the restraints of middle-class life. The phenomenon, epitomized by the hippies, celebrated a latter-day version of Emersonian transcendence and Whitmanesque diversity in their opposition to the Vietnam War and in their pantheistic embrace of human oneness, enhanced through psychedelic drugs and the pulsating rhythms of rock music. "Do your own thing," a defiant slogan coined in the black ghettos, was taken up by dissident youth as their individualistic motto.

The political radicalism during the 1960s also had a strong individualist quality. The diverse elements that comprised the New Left could agree on little except their general opposition to racism and the Vietnam War. Paul Goodman, the prominent anarchist and intellectual godfather of many radicals, advocated the autonomous individual as a necessity for a more humane society. "Forceful, graceful, and intelligent behavior occurs only when there is an uncoerced and direct response to the physical and social environment," Goodman postulated in 1965. "In most human affairs more harm than good results from compulsion, top-down direction, bureaucratic planning, [and] pre-ordained curricula."[37] Political theorist Herbert Marcuse hailed students and blacks as the revolutionary vanguard in America. In *An Essay on Liberation* (1969), he affirmed the supreme need of the individual to "satisfy his needs without hurting himself, without reproducing through his aspirations and satisfactions his dependence on an exploitive apparatus which, in satisfying his needs, perpetuates his servitude." Yet, Marcuse had also announced in *A Critique of Pure Tolerance* (1965) that "toleration of movements from the Left" required "intolerance against movements from the Right," an ominous warning that freedom did not apply to the opposition.[38]

The most important manifesto of the New Left was the Port Huron statement (1962) of the Students for a Democratic Society. It defined human beings as "infinitely precious and possessed of unfulfilled capacities for reason, freedom, and love. . . . Men have unrealized potential for self-cultivation, self-direction, self-understanding and creativity."[39] But this quest for a meaningful individualism degenerated by the end of the decade into the left-wing authoritarianism that Marcuse advocated—the nihilistic fury of the Weathermen and the rigid doctrines of the Progressive Labor party.

The search for an alternative form of individualism was thoughtfully explored by Philip Slater in his *The Pursuit of Loneliness* (1970). He indicted "the absurd assumption that the individual can be considered separately from the environment of which he or she is a part." He criticized David Riesman, "the most sophisticated apologist for individualism," for failing to recognize that "the universe does not consist of a lot of unrelated particles but is an interconnected whole." Instead of "unrealistic fantasies of self-sufficiency," Slater argued that the values of community, engagement, and dependency must be nurtured in modern American society. Echoing Marx's formulation in *The German Ideology,* a popular tract among New Left intellectuals, Slater concluded that true individuality is facilitated in the interdependent, cooperative society where people are free to act more spontaneously in their social relations. "The only obstacle to utopia," he prophesied, was "our invidious dreams of personal glory." Two decades later, Slater's work appears romantic, but it remains an eloquent statement of the utopian faith of an earlier era.[40]

Narcissism and Its Critics

Whether or not Americans became more selfish in the aftermath of the Vietnam War and the Watergate scandal is a debatable issue. Nevertheless, there were well-publicized signs that some Americans had turned away from the frustration of public affairs, which were so heightened during the civil rights and antiwar movements, and focused instead on self-improvement and career success. The popular prophet of "new age consciousness," Charles Reich asked, "What is the central idea of America, unless each man's ability to create his own life?" But instead of what Reich predicted would be "the greening of America," self-concern degenerated (so it seemed) into what became widely known as the "me decade," a descriptive phrase coined by author Tom Wolfe in a 1976 essay.[41]

Indeed, former Black Panther Eldridge Cleaver (in addition to becoming a pants designer who reintroduced the codpiece to men's fashion) joined seventy million other Americans as a born-again Christian. Jerry Rubin moved from confrontation to Wall Street, completing what the mass media glibly termed the transformation from "yippie" to "yuppie." Hollywood produced *The Big Chill* (1983), a movie that suggested that young idealists of the 1960s were aging (albeit with angst) into complacent bourgeoisie. Even the former editors of *Ramparts* abandoned the barricades and joined the conservative forces.

Traditional self-help nostrums certainly continued their appeal, though with a distinctly modish style. Self-help books vied for readership with alluring titles such as *You!, Looking Out for Number One, The Woman's*

Dress for Success Book, Thin Thighs in 30 Days, and *Eat to Win.* An amazing assortment of gurus, savants, clairvoyants, and psychotherapists promised their disciples "to get in touch with their feelings" and "to center themselves" through transcendental meditation, astral projection, rolfing, primal screaming, and biofeedback. Not only was the human potential movement a growth industry, but so was the physical-fitness cult, complete with Spandex outfits, workout videos, tanning salons, and diet regimes. Actress Jane Fonda and muscleman Arnold Schwarzenegger successfully marketed their sculpted torsos to a nation of underexercised, overfed Americans.

Historian Christopher Lasch has long been critical of an individualism gone awry. Unlike some academics who adopted a fashionable radical chic during the 1960s, he faulted the New Left for romantic individualism. "Acting out of an ideal of personal heroism rather than from an analysis of the sources of tension in American society and the possibilities for change," he chided, "the New Left vacillates between existential despair and absurdly inflated estimates of its own potential." A proponent of a rational program of social democracy for the United States, he also warned in the late 1960s that "the liberal values of self-reliance, sexual self-disipline, ambition, acquisition, and accomplishment, while often admirable in themselves, have come to be embodied in a social order resting on imperialism, elitism, racism, and inhuman acts of technological destruction" (the latter a reference to the Vietnam War).[42]

A decade later, he concluded gloomily that individualism had metastasized into a psychosocial cancer. "Americans have not really become more sociable and cooperative, as the theorists of other-direction and conformity would like us to believe," he explained, alluding to David Riesman's work. "They have merely become more adept at exploiting the conventions of inter-personal relations for their own benefit." His description of "a culture of narcissism" intermixed a clinical diagnosis with a jeremiad against self-indulgence. He indicted "a way of life that is dying—the culture of competitive individualism which in its decadence has carried the logic of individualism to the extreme of a war of all against all, the pursuit of happiness to the dead end of a narcissistic preoccupation with the self." Indeed, President Jimmy Carter in his well-known "crisis of the American spirit" speech in 1979 sounded very Laschian in what amounted to a national sermon against selfishness. Curiously, Lasch's antidote for a morbid individualism appeared nostalgically conservative—a return to the more stable values of the patriarchal family and preindustrial society.[43]

Complementing Lasch's attack on American narcissism was the best-selling *Habits of the Heart* (1985), a team project headed by sociologist Robert Bellah. Borrowing the title from a phrase in Tocqueville's classic study of American character, *Habits* was the equivalent for the 1980s of what Riesman's *Lonely Crowd* was for the 1950s. "Individualism lies at the very core of American culture," Bellah observed. It has over time, he concluded, eroded its own social foundations to the point that Tocqueville's fear that egoism would overwhelm enlightened self-interest has come true.[44]

Whereas Riesman in 1954 declared that Americans were obsessive conformists, Bellah found that an "expressive" (or "lifestyle") individualism had superseded a utilitarian (or economic) individualism, which for so long had been the dominant national trait. Numerous interviews and four detailed case studies, narrowly limited to the white middle and professional classes, led Bellah to conclude that the search for private satisfaction—often narrowed to career, family, or an idealized vision of the small town—occurred at the expense of public committment. Bellah suggested that the unbridled pursuit of self-interest in the marketplace no longer provided the core of emotional identity in a society dominated by huge impersonal institutions. He concluded that Americans might somehow draw upon the shared values of religion and republicanism in which, unlike classical liberalism, untrammeled individualism was not entirely condoned. Yet, a return to eighteenth-century ideals of Christian republicanism, which Bellah appears to advocate, ignores the inherent intolerance of the former church-dominated era.

An effective corrective to the moralism of the Lasch and Bellah studies is Herbert J. Gans's *Middle American Individualism: The Future of Liberal Democracy* (1988) the most thoughtful recent book on the subject. Gans, a former president of the American Sociological Association, criticizes the utopian qualities in Lasch's and Bellah's works and calls for a pragmatic program of social democracy that recognizes the importance of individualistic values to middle Americans, the broad base of the population. "Sermons against selfishness and attacks on self-development, or merely on the desire for more comfort, are not likely to be effective," Gans reminds the self-righteous. "Pragmatic ways of reducing poverty and inequality must be sought, but these cannot be practical unless they respect the middle American commitment to individualism," which includes home ownership, privacy, freedom of action, and self-expression. The organizational avoidance of middle Americans (unlike the professional classes) is a realistic response, Gans asserted, to their distrust of big government and big business as well as the decentralized living patterns of suburbanization, which render formal organizations more distant and less meaningful.[45]

Gans is not, however, an unabashed apologist for individualism. Indeed, he is a firm critic of what he calls "capitalist individualism," and he recognizes the ways that self-centered thought undermines the possibility for a just society. Gans suspects hedonism is no greater now than in the past, except that intellectuals snobbishly tend to fault the lower orders for their "bad" taste in the pursuit of private pleasures that greater affluence has given them. Instead of damning hedonism, the liberal agenda should be to create a more representative and responsive welfare state that can provide people with greater economic security. Jobs, affordable housing, education, and health care legislation are at the heart of Gan's liberal democracy. Upper-middle-class liberals have to understand that middle Americans have less economic security, less opportunity to manipulate the system for their benefit, and less control over their lives. Middle Americans, therefore, "choose self-reliance with all its faults." Unlike the moralistic chest beating of Lasch and Bellah, Gans presents a pragmatic program "centered around middle American individualism" but balanced with "an acceptable egalitarian welfare state that can promise the economic security people want while also minimizing the bureaucracy and taxes they do not want."[46]

The Rehabilitation and Triumph of Economic Individualism

The most politically successful appeals to individualistic values have in recent years come from a resurgent conservative movement that has rehabilitated the ideal of economic individualism. The effort to gain intellectual respectability after the debacle of the Great Depression and the institution of the welfare state was a long process. In novels and essays since the 1930s, Ayn Rand developed "objectivism," a system of thought based on what she regarded as the demonstrable moral virtues of a largely unrestricted capitalism. Capitalism, she wrote in *Atlas Shrugged* (1957), was the "only system that stood for man's right to his own mind, to his work, to his life, to his happiness, to himself."[47] Over the last three decades William F. Buckley, Jr., has also been a preeminent critic of New Deal liberalism. Author, columnist, and talk-show host, the sharp-tongued Buckley used the pages of his own magazine, *The National Review*, and the mass media to restore preeminence to the model of free-market individualism.

Complementing Buckley's conservative agenda, Nobel Prize–winning economist Milton Friedman also attacked the regulatory programs of the New Deal, most widely on his televised series "Free to Choose." "We have the opportunity," the former University of Chicago scholar told viewers in 1980, "to nudge the change in opinion toward greater reliance on individual initiative and voluntary cooperation, rather than toward the other extreme of total collectivism." In the tradition of the Austrian economists Ludwig von Mises and Friedrich A. Hayek, outspoken critics of socialism, he equated political freedom with capitalism and warned that greater governmental power over the economy paved the "road to [Communist] serfdom."[48] Similarly, former secretary of the treasury and self-made millionaire William E. Simon wrote, "There is only one social system that reflects this sovereignty of the individual: the free-market, or capitalist, system."[49]

The rise of libertarianism during the 1970s carried support for the free market in some cases to the extreme of antistatism. According to theorist Murray Rothbard, individual liberty was the product of the Industrial Revolution and of laissez-faire capitalism. Only free enterprise, he maintained, was "harmonious, peaceful, and mutually beneficial for all"; the twentieth-century welfare state was therefore an aberration from the course of human progress. The wealth created by capitalism during the nineteenth century had been, he argued, dissipated by the social spending of governments during the next century.[50] Some libertarians aim ultimately toward what Stephen L. Newman calls "anarcho-capitalism," in which society will be "nothing more than a loose collection of autonomous individuals."[51] The anarchy implicit in this vision is not a problem for libertarians because they see state power rather than economic inequality as the essence of social evil. As philosopher Robert Nozick explained in *Anarchy, State, and Utopia* (1974), only the minimal state can be morally justified because "it treats us as persons having individual rights with the dignity this constitutes."[52]

The political resurgence of conservatism, with its emphasis on traditional individualistic values such as the free market, found its embodiment, at least on the rhetorical level, in the contradictory pronouncements and programs of President Ronald Reagan. Reagan, a former spokesman for General Electric and popular critic of the welfare state, struck a responsive chord by promising to cut taxes, eliminate waste and inefficiency in government, bring escalating costs for social services under control, restore free enterprise to the marketplace through deregulation, close alleged "windows of vulnerability" in national security, and, at the same time, eliminate deficits and balance the federal budget. In sum, President Reagan was enormously successful in exploiting cold war anxieties and in utilizing the traditional language of individualism. In his second inaugural address, Reagan pledged to "tear down economic barriers and liberate the spirit of enterprise" by dismantling the New Deal regulatory programs that upset the smooth functioning of the free market. Three years later, in another typical pronouncement, he argued that "limited government" was "the best way of ensuring personal liberty and empowering the individual."[53]

According to critic Garry Wills, Reagan believed the "individualist myths" that helped him play his communal role. "He is the sincerest claimant," Wills wrote, "to a heritage that never existed, a perfect blend of an authentic America he grew up in and of that America's fables about its past.''[54] If, for the sake of argument, we accept President Reagan's sincerity in promoting his particular brand of individualism, contradictions in his program were recognized early on by foe and friend alike. Former director of the Office of Management and Budget, David Stockman, admitted that "Reaganomics" benefitted the wealthy, and former political rival George Bush declared that Reagan's agenda was based on "voodoo economics."

During the Reagan era, taxes and social services were cut. Yet massive military spending resulted in an alarming $2.8 trillion federal deficit—a deficit that continues to escalate under President Bush. This buildup, a type of military Keynesianism unprecedented in America during peacetime, demonstrated that it was not "big government" per se that the administration objected to, but the objectives that governmental power was designed to achieve. By combining individualistic rhetoric with grave pronouncements about the "evil empire," Reagan was able to justify tax cuts for the wealthy, including large corporations for whom regulatory standards were also relaxed. At the same time, the influence of the military-industrial complex, against which President Eisenhower had warned in his farewell address in 1961, increased unabated.

Reagan achieved some of his objectives by persuading a Democratic-controlled Congress to increase military spending and cut taxes and others by issuing Executive Order 12291 and 12498, which made the Office of Management and Budget the most powerful government agency in American history. OMB's power extended not only to budgetary issues but included the authority to prevent other regulatory agencies from implementing new policies without the consent of OMB's Office of Information and Regulatory Affairs. Thus Reagan's antistatist rhetoric ("getting government of our backs") had limited applicability at best.

Furthermore, Reagan's domestic policies, based on what was termed "supply-side" economics, accentuated extant class, gender, and racial divisions in American society. His administration cut back social spending by some $27 billion per year in 1982, while it reduced the nominal tax rate for the highest income bracket from 70 percent to 28 percent in 1986. By 1989, the highest rate was increased from 28 percent to 33 percent for married couples filing jointly, but only on that portion of adjusted gross income that exceeded seventy-five thousand dollars. These policies, combined with a decline in American industrial productivity, a leveling off of corporate investment in basic research and development, and the erosion of educational skills, contributed to the number of people living in poverty. By 1983 the percentage of poor in the total population had climbed to 15 percent (more than 30 million people). This included one-sixth of all people over age 65, one-third of all African-Americans, one-half of all black children, and one-half of all female-headed households.

By 1987, the total number of people living in poverty stood at 32.5 million. Of this number, the largest single group was children under the age of six, about 5 million in all. Another 2.7 million children in that age group lived so close to the poverty line that their lifestyles were virtually indistinguishable from those living in families with incomes below the official poverty line of $9,890 for a family of three and $12,675 for a family of four. The majority of poor children had at least one parent in the work force. Only 28 percent relied entirely on public assistance, whereas 37 percent lived in families whose incomes came entirely from employment. The 1987 figures were derived from a study completed by the National Center for Children in Poverty at Columbia University in 1989, which challenged the "monolithic view that says people are poor because they won't work." The percentage of children under age six living in poverty averaged 17 percent between 1968 and 1979, but rose to 25 percent in 1983 as a result of the Reagan administration's cutbacks in social programs. The largest number of poor children were white, but the highest percentages came from minority groups.

If the Reagan administration's hostility to the "welfare state" has had disastrous effects on the lives of the poor, the middle class also lost ground. Middle-class income, when adjusted for inflation, began to decline in the late 1960s, but the process accelerated during the Reagan era, and by 1988, 80 percent of all American families had suffered a loss in real income. The only beneficiaries of Reaganomics are the very rich who now control a greater percentage of national wealth than ever before in this century, even surpassing the previous high in the fateful year of 1929. According to *Forbes Magazine,* the four hundred wealthiest people in the United States enjoyed a 41 percent increase in income during 1987 alone, and the number of billionaires doubled in that year from twenty-five to forty-nine.[55]

Concentrated economic power, as every informed person knows, leads inevitably to concentrated political power; and Reagan-style individualism, which effectively utilized the rhetoric of liberty, equal opportunity, and the free market, proved to be little more than a cruel hoax for the vast majority of Americans. The social and economic realities of Reaganism threatens to erode further an already fragmented sense of community among the less fortunate; and the ideals of personal freedom and equal justice under the law are essential ingredients of the American heritage that the Reagan agenda deliberately and callously chose to ignore. His use of individualistic rhetoric played well politically not only in Peoria but throughout the nation. Thus the full price of Reagan's legacy remains to be paid. And a major part of that legacy, of which most Americans, unfortunately, appear to be unaware, involves questions of not only economic and social justice but political freedom as well.

Individualism Attacked: The Reagan Administration's
Assault on the Bill of Rights

One of the great ironies of the Reagan era is that his invocation of the language of freedom to protect the "free world" from the menace of international communism led in the name of "national security" to a massive assault on civil liberties that, arguably, was unparalleled in its scope and intensity. In one sense, there is nothing remarkable about President Reagan's use of conspiracy rhetoric to justify a repressive national security program. At various times, Roman Catholics, Jews, anarchists, international bankers, labor organizers, Japanese-Americans, Communists, and others have served as convenient scapegoats for those groups and individuals who are unwilling or unable to understand the realities of a fragmented and complex world. In part, therefore, the Reaganite belief that "individual liberties are secondary to the requirements of national security" is part of a continuum that needs to be placed in historical perspective. For example, the Reagan administration's utilization of the McCarran-Walter Act to deny entry visas to foreigners was hardly a new phenomenon.

McCarran-Walter, passed over President Truman's veto in 1952, contained two political sections. One permitted exclusion of aliens who are "members of the Communist party" or who advocated "the economic, international and government doctrines of world communism." The other was far more insidious. It permitted the Immigration and Naturalization Service to exclude aliens whose views were considered a danger to the "welfare, safety, or security of the United States" or whose ideas were deemed "prejudicial to the public interest."

Although every presidential administration since Eisenhower's has used McCarran-Walter to deny entry visas to "undesirable aliens," the Reagan administration concentrated its efforts primarily, though not exclusively, against opponents of its Central American policies. In 1983, for example, Nicaraguan Interior Minister Tomás Borge, who was scheduled to make a speaking tour in the United States, was denied entry. In 1985 *contra* defector Efraín Mondragon was not permitted to travel to Washington to testify about *contra* connections to the CIA. Moreover, Hortensia Allende, the widow of former Chilean president Salvador Allende, was denied permission to lecture at several American universities. Allende's denial occurred at a time when the Reagan administration was contemplating the resumption of arms sales to Chilean strongman, General Augusto Pinochet. In fact, the United States, the only western "democracy" to exclude foreigners for ideological reasons, has compiled the world's largest blacklist.[56] The State Department's Automated Visa Lookout System (AVLOS), a worldwide computer network, increased to nearly a million people during the Reagan era—including several Nobel laureates.[57]

Another repressive policy, whose origins antedated the Reagan era, has been the development of "balancing tests" by the Supreme Court, whereby the Court purports to balance the security of the state against the First Amendment Rights of individuals. In *Snepp v. United States* (1980), for example, the Court ruled that Snepp's publication of *Decent Interval,* a book exposing the dishonesty, malfeasance, and corruption he had witnessed in Vietnam as a CIA agent, constituted a violation of a pre-publication censorship agreement he had signed despite the fact that the book contained no classified information. Snepp, therefore, was barred from speaking or writing about CIA for the rest of his life without that agency's permission.

The Court, however, not only ignored First Amendment issues by viewing the case in contractual terms, but bought the prosecution's argument that Snepp's book had caused the government "irreparable harm and loss." The fact that the CIA had not attempted to enforce similar agreements against other government officials, such as Henry Kissinger, who had published secret information without permission, "strongly suggests that the real motive underlying the Snepp prosecution was the CIA's desire to silence arbitrarily a hostile critic."[58]

Other examples that reflect continuity in American policy since the 1950s include the use of disinformation and psycholinguistic devices in an effort to sway public opinion on domestic and foreign policy issues. In addition, attacks on the media, whether in the form of White House criticism, diatribes by right-wing organizations such as Accuracy in Media, or libel cases brought during the 1980s by Generals Sharon and Westmoreland have been familiar features in the political landscape for decades. The new wave of conspiracy trials that occurred during the 1980s were reminiscent of the conspiracy prosecutions during the Vietnam War. The Reagan administration, however, added several new twists: the use of preventive detention, anonymous juries, the "armed courtroom," and the elimination of justification defenses, which often led to acquittals in the late 1960s and early 1970s. (A justification defense is testimony that allows defendants to discuss their motives in taking a particular course of action.) Conspiracy trials reflect both continuity with and a radical departure from the history of the recent past—a radical departure because of the new tactics that were employed.

The same held true for the resumption of open-ended domestic-security investigations of opponents of Reagan's foreign policy, especially in Central America, by the FBI. Operation CONINTELPRO, a secret and illegal operation that was not authorized by Congress or any president, was carried

out between 1957 and 1973 by FBI Director J. Edgar Hoover. Secret files
were kept on nearly 500,000 Americans that Hoover and other FBI officials
considered to be subversives or potentially dangerous national security risks.
Among the illegal FBI policies were: break-ins, the use of warrantless wire-
taps, the use of paid informants, mail tampering, and character defamation.

As a result of these abuses, Attorney General Edward Levi in April 1976
promulgated for the first time a set of guidelines governing the initiation and
scope of FBI domestic-security investigations. The Levi guidelines, by establishing a criminal standard for investigations, eliminated FBI surveillance
of dissident political groups. The Levi guidelines had a dramatic impact. In
March 1976, the FBI was conducting 4,868 domestic security investigations. By December 1981, the number had dropped to only twenty-six, and
the organizations being investigated, such as the Jewish Defense League,
the Communist Workers Party, and the Arizona chapter of the Ku Klux
Klan, were clearly involved in violent criminal activity.

The Reagan administration eliminated, however, the safeguards against
FBI abuse that the Levi guidelines were designed to prevent. This was done
by promulgating two interrelated executive-branch initiatives: Executive Order 12333, which was issued in 1981; and Attorney General William French
Smith's guidelines, which replaced Levi's in 1983.

The central point is that the Reagan administration legitimized and institutionalized techniques and practices that were used illegally by J. Edgar
Hoover and banned by the Levi guidelines. For the first time in its existence,
the CIA was authorized to engage in surveillance of the lawful political
activities of American citizens so long as they coordinated these activities
with the FBI. The CIA's charter in 1947 specifically prohibited such action.
The requirement that the CIA coordinate its operations with the FBI was
nothing more than a subterfuge that permits the CIA to observe the letter if
not the spirit of its charter.

The FBI is now legally entitled in its counterintelligence operations and
domestic-security investigations to use intrusive techniques such as mail and
physical surveillance, theft, unconsented physical searches, and the use of
infiltrators. Executive Order 12333 also permits the use of warrantless wire-
taps against American citizens if the attorney general *"has determined in
each case that there is probable cause to believe that the technique is directed against a foreign power or an agent of a foreign power"* (emphasis
added).[59]

According to congressional sources, the FBI in 1985 alone conducted
ninety-six investigations of groups and individuals opposed to the Reagan
administration's Central American policies. Then, in late January 1988, the
Center for Constitutional Rights in New York released information obtained
from the FBI under the Freedom of Information Act that the FBI had tar-

geted such groups as the Committee in Solidarity with the People of El Salvador, the Sanctuary movement, Quest for Peace, antinuclear groups, the Southern Leadership Conference, the Maryknoll Sisters in Chicago, the American Federation of Teachers, and the United Auto Workers in Cleveland. All fifty-nine regional FBI offices were involved in open-ended domestic-security investigations.

Equally important, the Reagan administration's secrecy and censorship policies were the most sweeping in American history. The most highly publicized measure, National Security Decision Directive 84 (NSDD 84), required at least 290,000 government employees and contractors with access to classified information to sign nondisclosure agreements as a condition of employment. Although Reagan agreed to suspend, not rescind, this provision because of opposition in Congress, his pledge was a subterfuge. The administration continued to require government employees to sign lifetime nondisclosure agreements under the terms of an earlier 1981 mandate (Form 4193).

Even more astonishing was the administration's efforts to classify research by American professors based on unclassified information, and its decision to reclassify documents made available by previous administrations. In 1986, administration officials came up with their most amazing innovation, Standard Forms 189 and 189a, which declared that all government employees and contractors with security clearances were required to withhold information that was "nonclassified but classifiable." A government official explained: "A party to SF 189 would violate its nondisclosure provisions only if he or she disclosed without authorization classified information *or information that he or she knew, or reasonably could have known, was classified, although it not yet included required classified markings"* (emphasis added).[60] This new category, "nonclassified but classifiable," may have been as absurd as Catch-22, but employees accused of violating its murky provisions could be fired and prosecuted. Nearly two million federal employees signed the form "knowingly or blindly." Only twenty-four people refused to do so on First Amendment grounds; but this action led two government employee unions to file suit in federal district court in 1987, challenging its constitutionality. The outcome has yet to be decided. In short, the Reagan administration's "information policies," which also included attempts to destroy the effectiveness of the Freedom of Information Act and the Fulbright program, were based on exaggerated fears of Soviet capabilities and a demonstrated hostility to the concept of an open society.

No discussion of the administration's obsession with secrecy and censorship would be complete, however, without analyzing the implications of the Samuel Loring Morison case. For providing a British magazine with three classified photographs of an uncompleted Soviet aircraft carrier, Morison became the first person ever convicted of espionage for leaking information to the press. Morison's conviction was upheld by the United States Court of Appeals for the Fourth Circuit, and the Supreme Court, by refusing to hear his appeal, let his conviction stand.

Technically, the Supreme Court's inaction meant that the Morison case did not create a national precedent. In fact, however, it has had a "chilling effect." In the future, it is not only "leakers" who must beware but journalists, broadcasters, authors, and publishers who receive such information and dare to use it. Thus the Reagan administration achieved by judicial fiat an American equivalent of the British Official Secrets Act—an act that Congress had consistently refused to enact in the past. As one commentator phrased it, the Reagan administration's information policies not only focused attention on security but equated "security with secrecy" and treated "information as if it were a potentially contagious disease that must be controlled, quarantined, and ultimately cured."[61]

Finally, the Reagan administration's hostility to political individualism and to other constituent ideas inherent in the concept—such as a right to privacy—were reflected by Reagan's appointments to the federal judiciary. By the end of his second term, Reagan appointed approximately half of the nation's 744 federal judges. He gladly appointed qualified ideologues when they were available, but as the number of nominations mounted, the quality of judges selected declined. Ideological purity, not competence, was the primary criterion in Reagan's efforts to promote his constitutional agenda. What then was the Reagan constitutional agenda (which may prove to be the most enduring part of his legacy precisely because federal judges are appointed for life)? Among other things, the Reagan administration wanted to eliminate procedural protections for criminal defendants, reverse *Roe v. Wade,* abolish affirmative action, and adopt "a more relaxed standard" involving the separation of church and state.

In addition, Attorney General Meese attacked the "doctrine of incorporation," whereby the Supreme Court since the 1920s has applied the Bill of Rights to the states as well as the federal government. Furthermore, Meese called for the exercise of "judicial restraint" by federal judges—a demand that judges base their opinions on the "original intentions" of the Founding Fathers rather than their own subjective value judgments. "Judicial activism," however, is a double-edged sword. It can be used to promote conservative causes rather than the liberal causes to which Meese objected. In fact, it is clear that the doctrine of judicial restraint has already been downgraded or ignored by some of Reagan's appointees. If a degree of flexibility existed in the administration's judicial philosophy, it was surely one of means, not ends.

George Bush succeeded Reagan in the Oval Office in 1989, but this provides little reason to believe that the basic objectives of the Bush administration differ in substance from those of his predecessor. It cannot be too strongly emphasized that many of the objectives of the "Reagan Revolution" had already been achieved by the time Bush was given the president's mantle. For example, Reagan's executive orders and National Security Decision Directives affecting such things as secrecy and censorship policies and permissive standards for conducting open-ended FBI domestic-security investigations not only have the force of law during his term in office but remain in force until action is taken to modify or rescind them by his successors. Thus Executive Order 12333 (which determines the permissible activities of the FBI, CIA, and other intelligence agencies) is still in force, as is National Security Decision Directive 84. Bush has yet to modify or rescind any major policy initiative instituted by Reagan. Nor is he likely to do so.

Mr. Bush's rhetorical style has been based primarily on sound and fury rather than substance both as a presidential candidate and as the occupant of the Oval Office. In one of his campaign debates with Governor Michael Dukakis, Mr. Bush not only accused the Massachusetts governor of being a "card-carrying" member of the American Civil Liberties Union, but falsely charged the ACLU with condoning child pornography. Bush also maximized the use of his misleading and unprincipled campaign commercial on Willie Horton, blamed Dukakis for the pollution of Boston Harbor, asked people to "read my lips: no new taxes," and pledged to expand the war on drugs. This is not to say that drug use is not a major social problem. It is to say, rather, that random drug testing and the unreliability of current drug testing procedures eliminates a probable-cause standard and thus constitutes an unwarranted invasion of privacy, a violation of the rights of individuals to due process of law and protection from unreasonable searches and seizures. By placing the blame for drug abuse squarely upon the shoulders of drug dealers and users and by refusing to authorize adequate funding either for enforcement or rehabilitation, the current policy deliberately obscures some of the underlying causes of drug addiction—the poverty and hopelessness in American society that stems not only from the character flaws of pushers and addicts, but from the inequities in contemporary social, economic, and military priorities that fueled the Reagan Revolution.

Add to this President Bush's advocacy of a constitutional amendment against flag burning, his veto of the Civil Rights Act of 1990 because of its emphasis on affirmative action, the administration's attack on the use of federal funds to finance college scholarships for minority students, and the conservative motives that led Mr. Bush to appoint Judge David Souter to the

Notes

Individualism in Trans-National Context
Richard O. Curry and Lawrence B. Goodheart

1. James Bryce, *The American Commonwealth* (London: 1888), 2:406–7.
2. Steven Lukes, "Types of Individualism," in *The Dictionary of the History of Ideas,* ed. Philip P. Weiner, 4 vols. (New York: Charles Scribner's Sons, 1973), 2:597.
3. Ibid.
4. Ibid., 598.
5. Ibid.
6. Ibid.
7. Ibid.
8. Henry David Thoreau, "Civil Disobedience," in *Walden and Other Writings of Henry David Thoreau,* ed. Brooks Atkinson (New York: Modern Library, 1950), 645.
9. Lukes, "Types of Individualism," 599.
10. Ibid.
11. Ibid.
12. Ibid., 600.
13. Ibid., 601.
14. Ibid., 603.
15. Ibid., 600.
16. Ibid.
17. Ibid.
18. Ibid.
19. Ibid.
20. Ibid.
21. Ibid.
22. Ibid., 601.
23. Ibid.
24. Ibid., 600.

25. Ibid., 602.

26. Ibid.

27. Ibid., 602–3.

28. Bronson Alcott quoted in Lewis Perry, "Versions of Anarchism in the Antislavery Movement," *American Quarterly* 20 (Winter 1968): 771.

29. Lukes, "Types of Individualism," 603.

30. Elie Kedourie, *Nationalism* (London: Hutchinson Univ. Library, 1966).

31. Ibid., 22.

32. Ibid., 23.

33. Ibid.

34. Ibid., 24, 26.

35. Ibid., 26.

36. See Henry A. Pochman, *German Culture in America: Philosophical and Literary Influences* (Madison: Univ. of Wisconsin Press, 1957); René Wellek, "Emerson and German Philosophy," *New England Quarterly* 16 (March 1943): 16–62.

37. Lukes, "Types of Individualism," 603.

38. Auguste Comte quoted in Robert A. Nisbet, *The Sociological Tradition* (New York: Basic Books, 1966), 273.

39. Joseph de Maistre quoted in Steven Lukes, *Individualism* (New York: Harper and Row, 1973), 4.

40. Steven Lukes, "The Meanings of Individualism," *Journal of the History of Ideas* 32 (1971): 47.

41. Ibid., 48. See also Edmund Wilson, *To the Finland Station* (Garden City, N.Y.: Doubleday, 1940), 79–85; George Lichtheim, *The Origin of Socialism* (New York: Praeger, 1969), 50–51; G. D. H. Cole, *A History of Socialist Thought* (London: Macmillan, 1953–60), vols. 1, 2; Leszek Kolakowski, *Main Currents of Marxism* (New York: Oxford Univ. Press, 1978), vol. 1.

42. Lukes, "The Meanings of Individualism," 47–48, 52.

43. Alexis de Tocqueville, *Democracy in America*, ed. J. P. Mayer (Garden City, N.Y.: Doubleday, 1969), 507–8.

44. Lukes, "The Meanings of Individualism," 54–58.

45. Ibid.

46. Ibid., 55.

47. Ibid.

48. Robert W. Lougee, "German Romanticism and Political Thought," *The Review of Politics* 21 (October 1959): 638.

49. Ibid., 638.

50. Ibid., 640.

51. Franklin L. Baumer, *Modern European Thought: Continuity and Change in Ideas* (New York: Macmillan, 1979), 295.

52. Koppel S. Pinson, *Pietism as a Factor in the Rise of German Nationalism* (New York: Columbia Univ. Press, 1934) on individualism and German pietism.

53. Johann Gottlieb Fichte, *Reden an die Deutsche Nation*, 13th Address, in *The Political Thought of the German Romantics, 1793–1815*, ed. H. S. Reiss (Oxford: Basil Blackwell, 1955), 108.

54. Georg G. Iggers, *The German Conception of History: The National Tradition of Historical Thought from Herder to the Present* (Middletown, Conn.: Wesleyan Univ. Press, 1968), 7.

55. Ibid.

56. Ibid., 3–28.

57. Alan Macfarlane suggestively argues that individualism in social and economic life in

England extended well into the Middle Ages, a phenomenon exceptional to that country. "This means," he writes, "that it is no longer possible to 'explain' the origins of English individualism in terms of either Protestantism, population change, the development of a market economy at the end of the Middle Ages, or the other factors. . . . Individualism, however defined, predates sixteenth-century changes and can be said to shape them all. The explanation must lie elsewhere, but will remain obscure until we trace the origins even further than has been attempted in this work." *The Origins of English Individualism: The Family, Property, and Social Transition* (New York: Cambridge Univ. Press, 1978), 196–97.

58. Thomas Hobbes, *Leviathan* (1651; reprint, London: J. M. Dent and Sons, 1940), 64–65.

59. John Locke, *Two Treatises of Government*, ed. Peter Laslett (1690; reprint, Cambridge: Cambridge Univ. Press, 1960), 2:95.

60. C. B. MacPherson, *The Political Theory of Possessive Individualism: Hobbes to Locke* (Oxford: Oxford Univ. Press, 1962), 3, 263–64.

61. Adam Smith, *An Inquiry into the Nature and Causes of the Wealth of Nations* (1776; reprint, Oxford: Oxford Univ. Press, 1976), 56.

62. John Stuart Mill, *On Liberty*, ed. David Spitz (1859; reprint, New York: W. W. Norton, 1975), 11.

63. Marshall Cohen, ed., *The Philosophy of John Stuart Mill* (New York: Random House, 1961), 183.

The Emergence of an Individualistic Ethos in American Society
Richard O. Curry and Karl E. Valois

1. Quoted in C. B. MacPherson, *The Political Theory of Possessive Individualism: Hobbes to Locke* (New York: Oxford Univ. Press, 1964), 198–99.

2. Ibid., 198, 215.

3. Ibid., 262.

4. Bernard Bailyn, "Political Experience and Enlightenment Ideas in Eighteenth-Century America," *American Historical Review* 67 (1961–62): 339–51; Bernard Bailyn, *The Ideological Origins of the American Revolution* (Cambridge: Harvard Univ. Press, 1967), vi–vii.

5. Gordon S. Wood, *The Creation of the American Republic* (New York: W. W. Norton, 1969), 593–615.

6. Ibid., 602.

7. Thomas Jefferson to Peter Carr, August 10, 1787, *The Portable Jefferson*, ed. Merrill Peterson (New York: Penguin Books, 1975), 424.

8. Quoted in Eric Foner, *Tom Paine and Revolutionary America* (New York: Oxford Univ. Press, 1976), 89.

9. Quoted in Wood, *The Creation of the American Republic*, 577.

10. James Madison, "The Federalist No. 10," in *The Federalist Papers*, ed. Clinton Rossiter (New York: New American Library, 1961), 79.

11. Ibid., 83.

12. Wood, *The Creation of the American Republic*, 612.

13. Quoted in Yehoshua Arieli, *Individualism and Nationalism in American Ideology* (Cambridge: Harvard Univ. Press, 1964), 247.

14. Richard Hofstadter, *The Idea of a Party System: The Rise of Legitimate Opposition in the United States, 1780–1840* (Berkeley: Univ. of California Press, 1970), 10–11, 64–65.

15. A number of historians have objected to the use of the term "party" to describe the political rivalry between the Federalists and the Jeffersonian Republicans. In general, they believe that the political organizations of the 1790s lacked "modern" structures and machinery,

and were mostly temporary, partisan alliances of individuals and groups. See, for example, Roy F. Nichols, *The Invention of American Political Parties* (New York: Macmillan, 1967); Paul Goodman, "The First American Party System," in *The American Party Systems*, ed. W. N. Chambers and W. D. Burnham (New York: Oxford Univ. Press, 1967), 56–89; Ronald P. Formisano, "Deferential-Participant Politics: The Early Republic's Political Culture, 1789–1840," *American Political Science Review* 68 (June 1974): 473–87; Ronald P. Formisano, *The Transformation of Political Culture: Massachusetts Politics, 1790s–1840s* (New York: Oxford Univ. Press, 1984). Recent examples of "revisionist" literature include several works by Joyce Appleby: "Commercial Farming and the 'Agrarian Myth' in the Early Republic," *Journal of American History* 67 (March 1982): 833–49; and *Capitalism and a New Social Order: The Republican Vision of the 1790s* (New York: New York Univ. Press, 1984). Also consult John R. Nelson, Jr., *Liberty and Property: Political Economy and Policymaking in the New Nation, 1789–1812* (Baltimore: Johns Hopkins Univ. Press, 1987).

16. An impressive body of scholarship has been amassed on the Federalists and their era. Among the most important works are John C. Miller, *The Federalist Era, 1789–1801* (New York: Harper and Row, 1960); James M. Banner, Jr., *To the Hartford Convention: The Federalists and the Origins of Party Politics in Massachusetts, 1789–1815* (New York: Knopf, 1970); David H. Fischer, *The Revolution of American Conservatism: The Federalist Party in the Era of Jeffersonian Democracy* (New York: Harper and Row, 1965); Shaw Livermore, Jr., *The Twilight of Federalism: The Disintegration of the Federalist Party, 1815–1830* (Princeton: Princeton Univ. Press, 1962); Linda Kerber, *Federalists in Dissent: Imagery and Ideology in Jeffersonian America* (Ithaca: Cornell Univ. Press, 1970); James Broussard, *The Southern Federalists, 1800–1816* (Baton Rouge: Louisiana State Univ. Press, 1978); and Richard Buel, Jr., *Securing the Revolution: Ideology in American Politics, 1789–1815* (Ithaca: Cornell Univ. Press, 1972).

17. The Jeffersonian Republicans have received no less attention. In addition to the books by Buel and Miller cited above, see Lance Banning, *The Jeffersonian Persuasion: Evolution of a Party Ideology* (Ithaca: Cornell Univ. Press, 1978); Drew McCoy, *The Elusive Republic: Political Economy in Jeffersonian America* (Chapel Hill: Univ. of North Carolina Press, 1980); Joyce Appleby, *Capitalism and a New Social Order;* Marshall Smelser, *The Democratic Republic, 1801–1815* (New York: Harper and Row, 1968); Noble E. Cunningham, Jr., *The Jeffersonian Republicans: The Formation of Party Organization, 1789–1801* (Chapel Hill: Univ. of North Carolina Press, 1957) and *The Jeffersonian Republicans in Power: Party Operations, 1801–1809* (Chapel Hill: Univ. of North Carolina Press, 1963); Paul Goodman, *The Democratic-Republicans of Massachusetts: Politics in a Young Republic* (Cambridge: Harvard Univ. Press, 1964); and Alfred F. Young, *The Democratic-Republicans of New York: The Origins, 1763–1797* (Chapel Hill: Univ. of North Carolina Press, 1967).

18. An overview of the fear of conspiracy in American history can be found in Richard O. Curry and Thomas M. Brown, eds., *Conspiracy: The Fear of Subversion in American History* (New York: Holt, Rinehart, and Winston, 1972). Also consult Curry's introductory essay in Richard O. Curry, ed., *Freedom at Risk: Secrecy, Censorship, and Repression in the 1980s* (Philadelphia: Temple Univ. Press, 1988); and David Brion Davis, ed., *The Fear of Conspiracy: Images of Un-American Subversion from the Revolution to the Present* (Ithaca: Cornell Univ. Press, 1971).

19. Arieli, *Individualism and Nationalism*, 249.

20. On disestablishment, see William G. McLoughlin, *New England Dissent, 1630–1833: The Baptists and the Separation of Church and State*, 2 vols. (Cambridge: Harvard Univ. Press, 1971); and Elwyn A. Smith, *Religious Liberty in the United States: The Development of Church-State Thought Since the Revolutionary Era* (Philadelphia: Fortress Press, 1972). On the application of conspiracy theory by Evangelicals to the Unitarians, see Lawrence B. Goodheart

and Richard O. Curry, eds., "The Trinitarian Indictment of Unitarianism: The Letters of Elizur Wright, Jr., 1826–1827," *Journal of the Early Republic* 3 (Fall 1983): 281–96.

21. Caroline Robbins, *The Eighteenth-Century Commonwealthmen: Studies in the Transmission, Development, and Circumstances of English Liberal Thought from the Restoration of Charles II until the War with the Thirteen Colonies* (Cambridge: Harvard Univ. Press, 1959); Bernard Bailyn, *The Ideological Origins of the American Revolution;* Wood, *The Creation of the American Republic;* J. G. A. Pocock, *The Machiavellian Moment: Florentine Political Thought and the Atlantic Republican Tradition* (Princeton: Princeton Univ. Press, 1975); Banning, *The Jeffersonian Persuasion.* Historical work on republicanism has been enormous. See the special issue of *American Quarterly* on the subject and two historiographical essays by Robert E. Shalhope: "Toward a Republican Synthesis: The Emergence of an Understanding of Republicanism in American Historiography," *William and Mary Quarterly* 29 (January 1972): 49–80; and "Republicanism and Early American Historiography," ibid. 39 (April 1982): 334–56. Robert Kelley, meanwhile, has discerned four varieties of republicanism in "Ideology and Political Culture from Jefferson to Nixon," *American Historical Review* 82 (March 1977): 531–62; and *The Cultural Pattern in American Politics: The First Century* (New York: Knopf, 1979).

22. In addition to the works by Appleby listed above, see her "Republicanism in Old and New Contexts," *William and Mary Quarterly* 43 (January 1986): 20–34; "The Social Origins of American Revolutionary Ideology," *Journal of American History* 64 (March 1978): 939–58; and "Liberalism and the American Revolution," *New England Quarterly* 49 (March 1976): 3–26. Also consult Isaac Kramnick, "Republican Revisionism Revisited," *American Historical Review* 87 (June 1982): 629–64; John P. Diggins, *The Lost Soul of American Politics: Virtue, Self-Interest, and the Foundations of Liberalism* (New York: Basic Books, 1984); and "Comrades and Citizens: New Mythologies in American Historiography," *American Historical Review* 90 (June 1985): 614–38.

23. Lance Banning, "QUID TRANSIT? Paradigms and Process in the Transformation of Republican Ideas," *Reviews in American History* 17 (June 1989): 199–204. See also his "Jeffersonian Ideology Revisited: Liberal and Classical Ideas in the New American Republic," *William and Mary Quarterly* 43 (January 1986): 3–19; and "Some Second Thoughts on Virtue and the Course of Revolutionary Thinking," in *Conceptual Change and the Constitution,* ed. Terrence Ball and J. G. A. Pocock (Topeka: Univ. Press of Kansas, 1988), 194–212. James T. Kloppenberg attempts a synthesis in "The Virtues of Liberalism: Christianity, Republicanism, and Ethics in Early American Political Discourse," *Journal of American History* 74 (June 1987): 9–33.

24. John Murrin, "Self-Interest Conquers Patriotism: Republicans, Liberals, and Indians Reshape the Nation," in *The American Revolution: Its Character and Limits,* ed. Jack P. Greene (New York: New York Univ. Press, 1987), 225.

25. Gordon S. Wood, "The Significance of the Early Republic," *Journal of the Early Republic* 8 (Spring 1988): 1–20. Stephen Watts has argued that liberalism triumphed between the early 1790s and 1815 in *The Republic Reborn: War and the Making of Liberal America, 1790–1820* (Baltimore: Johns Hopkins Univ. Press, 1987). Michael Lienesch, meanwhile, claims that the classical thinking of the Founding Fathers had been transformed by 1800, but that a mixture of republican and liberal ideas has predominated ever since. Consult his *New Order of the Ages: Time, the Constitution, and the Making of Modern American Political Thought* (Princeton: Princeton Univ. Press, 1988).

26. Chilton Williamson, *American Suffrage: From Property to Democracy, 1760–1860* (Princeton: Princeton Univ. Press, 1960); J. R. Pole, "Historians and the Problem of Early American Democracy," *American Historical Review* 67 (April 1962): 626–46.

27. Richard P. McCormick, *The Presidential Game: The Origins of American Presidential*

Politics (New York: Oxford Univ. Press, 1982) and *The Second American Party System: Party Formation in the Jacksonian Era* (Chapel Hill: Univ. of North Carolina Press, 1966).

28. Two works by Edward Pessen are *Riches, Class, and Power Before the Civil War* (Lexington, Mass.: D. C. Heath & Co., 1973) and *Jacksonian America: Society, Personality, and Politics* (Homewood, Ill.: The Dorsey Press, 1978). See also his "The Egalitarian Myth and the American Social Reality: Wealth, Mobility, and Equality in the 'Era of the Common Man,' " *American Historical Review* 76 (October 1971): 989–1034. Consult, too, Douglas T. Miller, *Jacksonian Aristocracy: Class and Democracy in New York, 1830–1860* (New York: Oxford Univ. Press, 1967).

29. Almost all of the works cited in note 16 are useful here. In particular, see Fischer, especially chapter 8.

30. On deference, see John B. Kirby, "Early American Politics—The Search for Ideology: An Historiographical Critique of the Concept of 'Deference'," *Journal of Politics* 32 (November 1970): 808–38. Richard D. Brown has discussed the subject in three works: "Modernization and the Modern Personality in Early America, 1680–1865: A Sketch of a Synthesis," *Journal of Interdisciplinary History* 2 (Winter 1972): 214–20; "Why Great Men No Longer Run for President," *American Heritage* 35 (February–March 1984): 12–19; and *Modernization: The Transformation of American Life, 1600–1865* (New York: Hill and Wang, 1976), 108–10. J. R. Pole discovered persistent levels of deference in "Representation and Authority in Virginia from the Revolution to Reform," *Journal of Southern History* 24 (February 1958): 16–50. See also Formisano, "Deferential-Participant Politics."

31. Quoted in M. J. Heale, *The Making of American Politics, 1750–1850* (New York: Longman, 1977), 130.

32. William L. Barney, *The Passage of the Republic: An Interdisciplinary History of Nineteenth-Century America* (Lexington, Mass.: D. C. Heath & Co., 1987), 20.

33. On social and economic change in the late eighteenth century and early decades of the nineteenth century see Brown, "Modernization"; James Henretta, *The Evolution of American Society: An Interdisciplinary Analysis, 1700–1815* (Lexington, Mass.: D. C. Heath & Co., 1973); M. J. Rohrbaugh, *The Trans-Appalachian Frontier: People, Societies, and Institutions, 1775–1850* (New York: Oxford Univ. Press, 1978); Peter D. McClelland and Richard J. Zeckhauser, *Demographic Dimensions of the New Republic: American Interregional Migration, Vital Statistics and Manumissions, 1800–1860* (Cambridge: Harvard Univ. Press, 1982); George Rogers Taylor, *The Transportation Revolution, 1815–1860* (New York: Rinehart, 1951); W. E. Brownlee, *Dynamics of Ascent: A History of the American Economy* (New York: Knopf, 1974); Douglas C. North, *The Economic Growth of the United States, 1790–1860* (Englewood Cliffs, N.J.: Prentice-Hall, 1961); Stuart Bruchey, *Growth of the Modern American Economy* (New York: Dodd, Mead, & Co. 1975); Robert L. Heilbroner, *The Economic Transformation of America* (New York: Harcourt Brace Jovanovich, 1984); Thomas C. Cochran, *Frontiers of Change: Early Industrialism in America* (New York: Oxford Univ. Press, 1981); Nathan Rosenburg, *Technology and American Economic Growth* (White Plains, N.Y.: M. E. Sharpe, 1972); and Howard Chudacoff, *The Evolution of American Urban Society* (Englewood Cliffs, N.J.: Prentice-Hall, 1988). For references to other important works see the excellent bibliography in Barney, *Passage of the Republic*.

34. Sean Wilentz, *Chants Democratic: New York City and the Rise of the American Working Class* (New York: Oxford Univ. Press, 1986), 101–2.

35. See Barney, *Passage of the Republic*, especially chapters 2 and 3.

36. Alexis de Tocqueville, *Democracy in America*, ed. J. P. Mayer (Garden City, N.Y.: Doubleday, Anchor Books, 1969). See especially vol. 2, pt. 2, 503–61.

37. Barney, *Passage of the Republic*, 56–57. On attitudes toward women see Carl N. Deglar, *At Odds: Women and the Family in America from the Revolution* (New York: Oxford

Univ. Press, 1980); Catherine Clinton, *The Other Civil War: American Women in the Nineteenth Century* (New York: Hill and Wang, 1984); Linda K. Kerber, *Women of the Republic* (Chapel Hill: Univ. of North Carolina Press, 1980); Nancy F. Cott, *The Bonds of Womanhood: Woman's Sphere in New England, 1780-1835* (New Haven: Yale Univ. Press, 1977); and Mary Beth Norton, *Liberty's Daughters* (Boston: Little, Brown & Co., 1980). On the black experience see especially Ira Berlin, *Slaves Without Masters: The Free Negro in the Antebellum South* (New York: Pantheon, 1974); Leon Litwack, *North of Slavery* (Chicago: Univ. of Chicago Press, 1961); William Stanton, *The Leopard's Spots: Scientific Attitudes Toward Race in America, 1815-1859* (Chicago: Univ. of Chicago Press, 1960); P. J. Staudenraus, *The African Colonization Movement, 1816-1865* (New York: Columbia Univ. Press, 1961); Leonard P. Curry, *The Free Black in Urban America, 1800-1850* (Chicago: Univ. of Chicago Press, 1981); George M. Fredrickson, *The Black Image in the White Mind* (Middletown, Conn.: Wesleyan Univ. Press, 1971); Leonard I. Sweet, *Black Images of America, 1784-1870* (New York: W. W. Norton, 1976); and Reginald Horsman, *Race and Manifest Destiny* (Cambridge: Harvard Univ. Press, 1981). On American Indians see Robert Berkhofer, *The White Man's Indian* (New York: Knopf, 1978); Richard Drinnon, *Facing West: The Metaphysics of Indian Hating and Empire Building* (Minneapolis: Univ. of Minnesota Press, 1980); Roy Harvey Pearce, *The Savages of America* (Baltimore: Johns Hopkins Univ. Press, 1965); Richard Slotkin, *Regeneration Through Violence* (Middletown, Conn.: Wesleyan Univ. Press, 1973); Roderick Nash, *Wilderness in the American Mind* (New Haven: Yale Univ. Press, 1967); and Bernard Sheehan, *Seeds of Extinction: Jeffersonian Philanthropy and the Indian* (Chapel Hill: Univ. of North Carolina Press, 1973).

38. Phillip Schaff, *America: A Sketch of Its Political, Social, and Religious Character*, ed. Perry Miller (Cambridge: Harvard Univ. Press, 1961), 101.

39. On religion, especially evangelical revivalism, millennialism, and social reform, see Whitney R. Cross, *The Burned-Over District: The Social and Intellectual History of Enthusiastic Religion in Western New York, 1800-1850* (Ithaca: Cornell Univ. Press, 1950); Paul Boyer, *Urban Masses and Moral Order, 1820-1920* (Cambridge: Harvard Univ. Press, 1978); William G. McLoughlin, *Modern Revivalism: Charles Grandison Finney to Billy Graham* (New York: Ronald Press Co., 1959); Donald G. Matthews, "The Second Great Awakening as an Organizing Process," *American Quarterly* 21 (Spring 1969): 23–43; John L. Thomas, "Romantic Reform in America, 1861-1865," ibid. 17 (Winter 1965): 656–81; Richard D. Birdsall, "The Second Great Awakening and the New England Social Order," *Church History* 39 (September 1970): 345–64; Sacvan Bercovitch, *The American Jeremiad* (Madison: Univ. of Wisconsin Press, 1978); Ernest L. Tuveson, *Redeemer Nation: The Idea of America's Millennial Role* (Chicago: Univ. of Chicago Press, 1968); William G. McLoughlin, *Revivals, Awakenings, and Reform: An Essay on Religion and Social Change in America, 1607-1977* (Chicago: Univ. of Chicago Press, 1978); James H. Moorhead, "Between Progress and Apocalypse: A Reassessment of Millennialism in American Religious Thought, 1800-1880," *Journal of American History* 81 (December 1984): 524–42; Timothy L. Smith, *Revivalism and Social Reform: American Protestantism on the Eve of the Civil War* (Baltimore: Johns Hopkins Univ. Press, 1980); Clifford S. Griffin, *Their Brothers' Keepers: Moral Stewardship in the United States, 1800-1860* (New Brunswick: Rutgers Univ. Press, 1960); John R. Bodo, *The Protestant Clergy and Public Issues* (Princeton: Princeton Univ. Press, 1954); Charles C. Cole, *The Social Ideas of the Northern Evangelists, 1826-1860* (New York: Columbia Univ. Press, 1954); Paul E. Johnson, *A Shopkeepers Millennium: Society and Revivals in Rochester, New York, 1815-1837* (New York: Hill and Wang, 1978); Charles I. Foster, *An Errand of Mercy: The Evangelical United Front, 1790-1837* (Chapel Hill: Univ. of North Carolina Press, 1960); Charles G. Finney, *Lectures on Revivals of Religion*, ed. William G. McLoughlin (1835; reprint, Cambridge: Harvard Univ. Press, 1960); Lyman Beecher, *The Autobiography of Lyman Beecher*, ed.

Barbara M. Cross, 2 vols. (Cambridge: Harvard Univ. Press, 1961); and Lois W. Banner, "Religious Benevolence as Social Control: A Critique of the Interpretation," *Journal of American History* 60 (June 1973): 23–41.

40. Quoted in Burton J. Bledstein, *The Culture of Professionalism: The Middle Class and the Development of Higher Education in America* (New York: W. W. Norton, 1976), 21.

41. Quoted in Robert H. Abzug, *Passionate Liberator: Theodore Dwight Weld and the Dilemma of Reform* (New York: Oxford Univ. Press, 1980), 92–93.

42. On the abolitionist schism see especially Richard O. Curry and Lawrence B. Goodheart, eds., "The Complexities of Factionalism: Letters of Elizur Wright, Jr., on the Abolitionist Schism, 1837–1840," *Civil War History* 29 (September 1983): 245–59; Aileen Kraditor, "An Interpretation of Factionalism in the Abolitionist Movement," in *The Abolitionists*, ed. Richard O. Curry, 2d ed. (Hinsdale, Ill.: Dryden, 1973), 76–83; Kraditor, *Means and Ends in American Abolitionism: Garrison and His Critics on Strategy and Tactics, 1834–1850* (New York: Pantheon, 1967); Bertram Wyatt-Brown, "William Lloyd Garrison and Antislavery Unity: A Reappraisal," *Civil War History* 13 (March 1967): 5–24; James B. Stewart, *Holy Warriors: The Abolitionists and American Slavery* (New York: Hill and Wang, 1976); Ronald G. Walters, *The Antislavery Appeal: American Abolitionism After 1830* (Baltimore: Johns Hopkins Univ. Press, 1976); Lewis Perry, *Radical Abolitionism: Anarchy and the Government of God in Antislavery Thought* (Ithaca: Cornell Univ. Press, 1973); Perry, *Childhood, Marriage and Reform: Henry Clarke Wright, 1797–1870* (Chicago: Univ. of Chicago Press, 1980); and Lawrence J. Friedman, *Gregarious Saints: Self and Community in American Abolitionism, 1830–1870* (New York: Cambridge Univ. Press, 1982).

43. Elizur Wright, Jr., to Amos A. Phelps, September 5, 1837, "Complexities of Factionalism," ed. Curry and Goodheart, 249.

44. Wright to William Lloyd Garrison, written in 1837 prior to September 16, ibid., 251.

45. Ibid.

46. Wright to Garrison, November 6, 1837, ibid., 253–55. See also Wright to Phelps, October 29, 1837, and July 11, 1838, ibid., 252–53, 255–56. Wright's letters, which are housed in the Library of Congress, clearly demonstrate that he sought to purge Garrison from the abolitionist movement for the heresy of nonresistance—a point well made by Aileen Kraditor about the anti-Garrisonian position in general in her *Means and Ends*. Wright has long needed a biographer. That need has now been met in admirable fashion by Lawrence B. Goodheart, *Abolitionist, Actuary, Atheist: Elizur Wright and the Reform Impulse* (Kent, Ohio: Kent State Univ. Press, 1990).

47. Perry, *Radical Abolitionism*, 78.

48. Richard O. Curry and Lawrence B. Goodheart, "Ambivalence, Ambiguity, and Contradiction: Garrisonian Abolitionists and Nonviolence," *Journal of Libertarian Studies* 6 (Summer–Fall 1982): 217–26. See also Robert H. Abzug, "The Influence of Garrisonian Abolitionists' Fears of Slave Violence on the Antislavery Argument, 1829–1840," *Journal of Negro History* 45 (January 1970): 15–28; John Demos, "The Antislavery Movement and the Problem of Violent Means," *New England Quarterly* 37 (December 1984): 501–26; Jane H. and William H. Pease, "Confrontation and Abolition in the 1850s," *Journal of American History* 58 (December 1972): 928–37; Benjamin Quarles, *Black Abolitionists* (New York: Oxford Univ. Press, 1969); and Perry's *Radical Abolitionism* and *Childhood, Marriage and Reform*.

49. Quoted in Lewis Perry, "Visions of Anarchy in the Antislavery Movement," *American Quarterly* 20 (Winter 1968): 771.

50. Peter F. Walker, *Moral Choices: Memory, Desire and Imagination in Nineteenth-Century American Abolition* (Baton Rouge: Louisiana State Univ. Press, 1978), 11.

51. Perry, *Radical Abolitionism*, 1–17.

52. For related discussions see Eric Foner, "Radical Individualism in America: Revolution to Civil War," *Literature on Liberty* 1 (July–September 1978): 5–29; and Wendy McElroy, "The Culture of Individualist Anarchism in Late Nineteenth-Century America," *Journal of Libertarian Studies* 5 (March 1981): 291–304.

53. David DeLeon, *The American as Anarchist: Reflections on Indigenous Radicalism* (Baltimore: Johns Hopkins Univ. Press, 1978).

54. Smith, *Revivalism and Social Reform*, 204–37; and Perry, *Radical Abolitionism*, 55–91.

55. Quotes in Arieli, *Individualism and Nationalism* (Cambridge: Harvard Univ. Press, 1964), 257.

56. Octavius Brooks Frothingham, *Transcendentalism in New England: A History* (1890; reprint, Gloucester, Mass.: Peter Smith, 1965), 110.

57. W. E. Channing, "On the Elevation of the Working Classes," quoted in Arieli, *Individualism and Nationalism*, 267.

58. Channing, "Remarks on Association," quoted in ibid., 267–68.

59. Channing, "Remarks on National Literature," quoted in ibid., 268. On Channing see also Arthur W. Brown, *William Ellery Channing* (New York: Twayne Publishers, 1962); Madeleine H. Rice, *Federal Street Pastor: The Life of William Ellery Channing* (New York: Bookman Associates, 1961); Jack Mendelsohn, *Channing: The Reluctant Radical* (Boston: Little, Brown & Co., 1971); Andrew DelBanco, *William Ellery Channing: An Essay on the Liberal Spirit in America* (Cambridge: Harvard Univ. Press, 1981); Daniel Walker Howe, *The Unitarian Conscience: Harvard Moral Philosophy, 1805–1861* (Cambridge: Harvard Univ. Press, 1970); and David Robinson, ed., *William Ellery Channing: Selected Writings* (Mahwah, N.J.: Paulist Press, 1985).

60. Quoted in Arieli, *Individualism and Nationalism*, 278.

61. Quoted in Amy Schrager Lang, *Prophetic Woman: Anne Hutchinson and the Problem of Dissent in the Literature of New England* (Berkeley: Univ. of California Press, 1987), 116.

62. Ibid.

63. Ibid., 117. Lang refers here to works by Roy Harvey Pearce, *The Continuity of American Poetry* (Princeton: Princeton Univ. Press, 1961), 189; Quentin Anderson, *The Imperial Self: An Essay in American Literary and Cultural History* (New York: Random House, 1971); Stephen Whicher, *Freedom and Fate* (Philadelphia: Univ. of Pennsylvania Press, 1971); Larzer Ziff, *Puritanism in America* (New York: Viking Press, 1972); and Joel Porte, *Representative Man: Ralph Waldo Emerson in His Time* (New York: Oxford Univ. Press, 1979).

64. Lang, *Prophetic Woman*, 117.

65. The quotations in this paragraph are found in ibid., 118, 125–26. Although my analysis of Emerson's thought draws heavily upon Lang's work, it must be pointed out that Lang's point of view is similar to the analysis of Lou Anne Lange, *The Riddle of Liberty: Emerson on Alienation, Freedom and Obedience* (Atlanta: Scholars, 1986).

66. Quotations in this paragraph are found in Lang, *Prophetic Woman*, 118–19.

67. Ibid., 121.

68. Ibid., 131–32.

69. Quoted in Arieli, *Individualism and Nationalism*, 286.

70. Ibid., 268.

71. Henry David Thoreau, *Walden and Other Writings of Henry David Thoreau*, ed. Brooks Atkinson (New York: Modern Library, 1950), 7.

72. Ibid.

73. Ibid., 635.

74. Ibid., 290.

75. Herman Melville, *Moby Dick* (1851; reprint, New York: Holt, Rinehart, and Winston, 1957), 564.

76. Ibid., 165.

77. Quoted in Irving H. Bartlett, *The American Mind in the Mid-Nineteenth Century* (New York: Thomas Y. Crowell Co., 1967), 111.

78. Ibid.

79. Ibid.

80. Ibid., 113.

81. Ibid., 112.

82. Ibid.

83. Ibid., 107.

84. Ibid., 108.

85. Quoted in Edwin Rozwenc and Thomas Bender, *The Making of American Society* (New York: Knopf, 1978), 1, 461.

86. Sam B. Girgus, *Law of the Heart: Individualism and the Modern Self in American Literature* (Austin: Univ. of Texas Press, 1979), 17.

87. Ibid. This quote was taken from Géorg Lukács, "The Ideology of Modernism," in his *Realism in Our Time* (1958; reprint, New York: Harper and Row, Torchbook, 1971), 20.

88. Girgus, *Law of the Heart*, 16. See D. H. Lawrence, *Studies in Classic American Literature* (1923; reprint, Garden City, N.Y.: Doubleday, Anchor Books, 1951), 59–73.

89. Quoted in Bartlett, *The American Mind*, 101–2.

90. For a brilliant discussion of these issues and transformation see Arieli, *Individualism and Nationalism*, 297–322.

Religion and Individualism in Early America
Robert M. Calhoon

The author acknowledges financial support from the Research Council of the University of North Carolina at Greensboro and the American Council of Learned Societies and thanks David Huff, Jerald McArthur, Donald G. Mathews, Lawrence B. Goodheart, and Richard O. Curry for their criticisms of drafts of this paper.

A portion of this essay is adapted from Robert M. Calhoon, *Evangelicals and Conservatives in the Early South, 1740–1861* with permission of the University of South Carolina Press.

1. Allan Bloom, *The Closing of the American Mind* (New York: Simon and Schuster, 1987), 82–91, 178–79; Gordon S. Wood, "The Fundamentalists and the Constitution," *New York Review of Books*, February 18, 1988, 33–40.

2. Daniel J. Boorstin, *The Americans: The Colonial Experience* (New York: Random, 1958) and *The Americans: The National Experience* (New York: Random, 1965). See also John P. Diggins, "Consciousness and Ideology in American History: The Burden of Daniel J. Boorstin," *American Historical Review* 76 (February 1971): 99–101.

3. J. E. Crowley, *This Sheba, Self: The Conceptualization of Economic Life in Eighteenth-Century America* (Baltimore: Johns Hopkins Univ. Press, 1974), 2–3. Emphasis added.

4. Jack P. Greene, "Search for Identity: An Interpretation of the Meaning of Selected Patterns of Social Response in Eighteenth-Century America," *Journal of Social History* 3 (Spring 1970): 190–91.

5. W. M. Spellman, *John Locke and the Problem of Depravity* (Oxford: Oxford Univ. Press, 1988), 15–38, 209–14.

6. David D. Hall, ed., *The Antinomian Controversy, 1636–1638: A Documentary History* (Middletown, Conn.: Wesleyan Univ. Press, 1968), 312, 337.

7. Ibid., 336.

8. Ibid., 11–20; Carol F. Karlsen, *The Devil in the Shape of a Woman: Witchcraft in Colonial New England* (New York: W. W. Norton, 1987), 18.

9. Charles E. Hambrick-Stowe, *The Practice of Piety: Puritan Devotional Disciplines in Seventeenth-Century New England* (Chapel Hill: Univ. of North Carolina Press, 1982), 166.

10. Philip F. Gura, *A Glimpse of Sion's Glory: Puritan Radicalism in New England, 1620–1660* (Middletown, Conn.: Wesleyan Univ. Press, 1984), 291–92.

11. Sacvan Bercovitch, *The Puritan Origins of the American Self* (New Haven: Yale Univ. Press, 1975), 60.

12. Mitchell Robert Breitwieser, *Cotton Mather and Benjamin Franklin: The Price of Representative Personality* (Cambridge: Cambridge Univ. Press, 1984), 150.

13. Ibid., 2.

14. James Hoopes, "Jonathan Edwards's Religious Psychology," *Journal of American History* 69 (March 1983): 859.

15. Henry F. May, "Jonathan Edwards and America" and James Hoopes, "Calvinism and Consciousness from Edwards to Beecher," in *Jonathan Edwards and the American Experience,* ed. Nathan O. Hatch and Harry S. Stout (New York: Oxford Univ. Press, 1988), 26–27, 205–14.

16. Jonathan Edwards, "A Divine and Supernatural Light," in *Jonathan Edwards: Representative Selections,* ed. C. H. Faust and Thomas H. Johnson (New York: American Book Co., 1925), 103, 107.

17. Hoopes, "Edwards's Religious Psychology," 856; Mechal Sobel, *The World They Made Together: Black and White Values in Eighteenth-Century Virginia* (Princeton: Princeton Univ. Press, 1988).

18. Edmund S. Morgan, *American Slavery/American Freedom: The Ordeal of Colonial Virginia* (New York: W. W. Norton, 1975), 248.

19. David Curtis Skaggs, "Thomas Cradock and the Chesapeake Golden Age," *William and Mary Quarterly* 30 (1973): 101.

20. Jack P. Greene, review of *Advice to a Son* and *The Complete Gentleman, William and Mary Quarterly* 21 (January 1964): 134. Enumeration added.

21. Richard Beale Davis, ed., *William Fitzhugh and his Chesapeake World, 1676–1701* (Chapel Hill: Univ. of North Carolina Press, 1963), 46–48.

22. Rhys Isaac, *The Transformation of Virginia, 1740–1790* (Chapel Hill: Univ. of North Carolina Press, 1982), 131–32.

23. "Extract of a Letter from the Rev. Mr. *Davies* at *Hanover* in *Virginia* to the Rev. Mr. F[awcett], Feb. 7, 1757," *Letters from the Rev. Samuel Davies &c. Shewing the State of Religion in Virginia, particularly among the Negroes* (London, 1757), 27–31.

24. Sobel, *The World They Made Together,* 19, 76, 98, 171–72, 176, 182–89, 194–97, 214, 216–17, 221, 222, 223–24, 235.

25. Harvey H. Jackson, "Hugh Bryan and the Evangelical Movement in Colonial South Carolina," *William and Mary Quarterly* 43 (October 1986): 601–14; Robert M. Calhoon, *Evangelicals and Conservatives in the Early South, 1740–1861* (Columbia: Univ. of South Carolina Press, 1988), 25–29.

26. Gordon S. Wood, "Conspiracy and the Paranoid Style: Causality and Deceit in the Eighteenth Century," *William and Mary Quarterly* 39 (July 1982): 417–18.

27. Davies to Fawcett, February 7, 1757, Letters, 27.

28. Samuel Davies, *The Duty of Christians to Propagate their Religion among the Heathens, Earnestly Recommended to the Masters of Negro Slaves in Virginia: A Sermon Preached in Hanover, January 8, 1757* (London, 1758), 38–39.

29. James D. Essig, *The Bonds of Wickedness: American Evangelicals against Slavery, 1770–1808* (Philadelphia: Temple Univ. Press, 1982), 13.

30. *Virginia Evangelical and Literary Magazine* 4 (October 1821): 552.

31. George Whitefield, *Three Letters from the Reverend Mr. G. Whitefield . . .* (Philadelphia, 1751), 13.

32. Essig, *Bonds of Wickedness*, 10.

33. Alexander Garden, *Six Letters to the Rev. George Whitefield . . .* (Boston, 1740), 54.

34. Richard J. Hooker, ed., *The Carolina Backcountry on the Eve of the Revolution: The Journal and Other Writings of Charles Woodmason, Anglican Itinerant* (Chapel Hill: Univ. of North Carolina Press, 1953), 102–3.

35. "Biography of Rev. Dr. Richard Furman," Richard Furman Papers, Furman University Library, Greenville, S.C.

36. Josiah Smith, *The Character, Preaching, &c. of the Reverend Mr. George Whitefield . . .* (Charlestown, 1765), 9.

37. *Benjamin Franklin's Autobiography*, ed. J. A. Leo Lemay and P. M. Zall (New York, 1986), 88–89.

38. Paul W. Connor, *Poor Richard's Politics: Benjamin Franklin and His New American Order* (New York: Oxford Univ. Press, 1965), 153.

39. Ronald A. Bosco, " 'He That Best Understands the World, Least Likes It': The Dark Side of Benjamin Franklin," *Pennsylvania Magazine of History and Biography* 111 (October 1987): 525–54.

40. Elizabeth E. Dunn, "From a Bold Youth to a Reflective Sage; A Reevaluation of Benjamin Franklin's Religion," ibid., 518.

41. Ibid., 509–10.

42. Ibid., 512.

43. Norman S. Fiering, "Benjamin Franklin and the Way to Virtue," *American Quarterly* 30 (Summer 1978): 212–15.

44. *Franklin's Autobiography*, ed. Lemay and Zall, 67–68.

45. Lance Banning, "Jeffersonian Ideology Revisited: Liberal and Classical Ideas in the New American Republic," and Isaac Kramnick, "The 'Great National Discussion': The Discourse of Politics in 1878," *William and Mary Quarterly* 43 (January 1986): 3–19, 45; (January 1988): 3–32.

46. Rush to Elhanan Winchester, November 12, 1791, *Letters of Benjamin Rush*, ed. L. H. Butterfield (Princeton: Princeton Univ. Press, 1951), 611–12.

47. Ibid., 512.

48. Nathan O. Hatch, *The Democratization of American Christianity* (New Haven: Yale Univ. Press, 1989), 173–74.

49. Rush to Jefferson, August 22, 1800, and Jefferson to Rush, September 23, 1800, *Jefferson's Extracts from the Gospels: "The Philosophy of Jesus" and "The Life and Morals of Jesus,"* ed. Dickinson W. Adams (Princeton: Princeton Univ. Press, 1983), 317–20.

50. Merrill D. Peterson, *The Jeffersonian Image in the American Mind* (New York: Oxford Univ. Press, 1960), 302–4.

51. Eugene R. Sheridan, "Introduction," in *Jefferson's Extracts*, ed. Adams, 3.

52. Ibid., 334. I have reversed the sequence of these two statements.

53. Steven Watts, *The Republic Reborn: War and the Making of Liberal America* (Baltimore: Johns Hopkins Univ. Press, 1987), 113.

54. Mark A. Noll, "The Irony of the Enlightenment for Presbyterians in the Early Republic," *Journal of the Early Republic* 5 (Summer 1985): 161–65.

55. Patricia U. Bonomi, *Under the Cope of Heaven: Religion, Society, and Politics in Colonial America* (New York: Oxford Univ. Press, 1986), chap. 8.

Individualism in the Early Republic
Robert E. Shalhope

This essay reorganizes disparate portions of my book *The Roots of Democracy: American Thought and Culture, 1760–1800* into a coherent whole.

1. For an outstanding analysis of the tension between these world views, see Kenneth Lockridge, *Settlement and Unsettlement: The Crisis of Political Legitimacy before the Revolution* (New York: Oxford Univ. Press, 1981).

2. The following works provide excellent insight into the diverse manifestations of the conflict between advocates of hierarchy and the advocates of localism: James Whittenburg, "Planters, Merchants and Lawyers: Social Change and the Origins of the North Carolina Regulators," *William and Mary Quarterly* 3d ser. 34 (1977): 215–38; Robert E. Shalhope, "South Carolina in the Founding Era: A Localist Perspective," *South Carolina Historical Magazine* 89 (1988): 102–13; Gary Nash, *The Urban Crucible: Social Change, Political Consciousness, and the Origins of the American Revolution* (Cambridge: Harvard Univ. Press, 1979); Rhys Isaac, "Evangelical Revolt: The Nature of the Baptists' Challenge to the Traditional Order in Virginia, 1765–1775," *William and Mary Quarterly,* 3d ser., 31 (1974): 345–68; William G. McLoughlin, *New England Dissent, 1630–1833,* 2 vols., (Cambridge: Harvard Univ. Press, 1971); Edward Countryman, " 'Out of the Bounds of the Law': Northern Land Rioters in the Eighteenth Century," in *The American Revolution: Explorations in the History of American Radicalism,* ed. Alfred Young (DeKalb, Ill.: Northern Illinois Univ. Press, 1976), 39–69; Jackson Turner Main, *Political Parties before the Constitution* (Chapel Hill: Univ. of North Carolina Press, 1973); Gordon S. Wood, *The Creation of the American Republic, 1776–1787* (Chapel Hill: Univ. of North Carolina Press, 1969); David Szatmary, *Shays' Rebellion: The Making of an Agrarian Insurrection* (Amherst: Univ. of Massachusetts Press, 1980); and Thomas P. Slaughter, *The Whiskey Rebellion: Frontier Epilogue to the American Revolution* (New York: Oxford Univ. Press, 1986).

3. Robert E. Shalhope explores the impact of republicanism within American society in two essays: "Toward a Republican Synthesis: The Emergence of an Understanding of Republicanism in American Historiography," *William and Mary Quarterly* 3d ser., 29 (1972): 49–80 and "Republicanism and Early American Historiography," ibid., 39 (1982): 334–56. Throughout this essay, "republicanism" refers to the political philosophy adhered to by the vast majority of Americans, whereas "Republican" represents the political movement that emerged in opposition to the Federalists in the 1790s.

4. For my understanding of Federalism, I draw upon the work of David H. Fischer, *The Revolution of American Conservatism: The Federalist Party in the Era of Jeffersonian Democracy* (New York: Harper and Row, 1965); James M. Banner, Jr., *To the Hartford Convention: The Federalists and the Origins of Party Politics in Massachusetts, 1789–1815* (New York: Knopf, 1970); and Linda Kerber, *Federalists in Dissent: Imagery and Ideology in Jeffersonian America* (Ithaca: Cornell Univ. Press, 1970).

5. Quoted in Fischer, *Revolution,* 3–5.

6. Quoted in ibid., 5.

7. Jonathan Jackson, *Thoughts upon the Political Situation* (Worcester, Mass.: Thomas, 1788), 27, 58.

8. Nathaniel Chipman, *Sketches of the Principles of Government* (Rutland, Vt.: Haswell, 1793), 42.

9. Quoted in Fischer, *Revolution,* 17.

10. Quoted in Banner, *To the Hartford Convention,* 77.

11. Quoted in ibid., 77.

12. Quoted in Kerber, *Federalists in Dissent*, 21.

13. Quoted in Banner, *To the Hartford Convention*, 78.

14. John R. Howe discusses Adams's thought in his *The Changing Political Thought of John Adams* (Princeton: Princeton Univ. Press, 1966). See particularly 133–55.

15. Jackson, *Thoughts*, 164–65.

16. Quoted in John Zvesper, *Political Philosophy and Rhetoric: A Study of the Origins of American Party Politics* (New York: Cambridge Univ. Press, 1977), 49.

17. Quoted in ibid., 49–50.

18. For an excellent analysis of these writers as well as the liberal perspective that pervaded their work, see Isaac Kramnick, "Republican Revisionism Revisited," *American Historical Review* 87 (1982): 629–64.

19. John Cartwright, *Take Your Choice! Representation and Respect: Imposition and Contempt* (London: J. Almon, 1776), 21; James Burgh, *Political Disquisitions*, 2 vols. (London: E. and C. Dilly, 1774), 2:89–90.

20. George Logan, *Letters Addressed to the Yeomanry of the United States* (Philadelphia: Oswald, 1791), 32, 11.

21. John Taylor, *An Enquiry into the Principles and Tendency of Certain Public Measures* (Philadelphia: Dobson, 1794), 7.

22. "Franklin" essays, *National Gazette*, March 2, 1793.

23. Taylor, *Enquiry*, 56.

24. John Taylor, *Definition of Parties, or the Political Effects of the Paper System Considered* (Philadelphia: Bailey, 1794), 10.

25. William Findley, *A Review of the Revenue System adopted by the First Congress under the Federal Constitution* (Philadelphia: Dobson, 1794), 52, 48, 43, 114, 127.

26. Quoted in Aleine Austin, *Matthew Lyon: "New Man" of the Democratic Revolution, 1749–1822* (University Park: Pennsylvania State Univ. Press, 1981), 80.

27. *Scourge of Aristocracy*, 1 (1798): 21; 2 (1798): 46–47.

28. George Warner, *Means for the Preservation of Public Liberty* (New York: Greenleaf and Judah, 1797), 13–14.

29. Quoted in Alfred Young, "The Mechanics and the Jeffersonians: New York, 1789–1801," *Labor History* 5 (1964): 274.

30. Benjamin Austin, *Constitutional Republicanism in Opposition to Fallacious Federalism* (Boston: Adams and Rhodes, 1803), 3, 16, 33.

31. The following quotations appear in Donald H. Stewart, *The Opposition Press of the Federalist Period* (Albany: State Univ. of New York Press, 1969), 103, 389, 390.

32. This essay, which was sent to the *Independent Chronicle* in Boston, was never published by that paper. It is printed in its entirety in Samuel Eliot Morison, "William Manning's The Key to Liberty," *William and Mary Quarterly*, 3d ser., 13 (1956): 202–54. The quotations appear on 211, 217, 220.

33. James Kloppenberg presents a brilliant analysis of the affective nature of individualism in the thought of Locke and Adam Smith in "The Virtues of Liberalism: Christianity, Republicanism, and Ethics in Early American Political Discourse," *Journal of American History* 74 (1987): 9–33. My view of Republicanism profits greatly from Kloppenberg's work.

34. My discussion of Adam Smith rests principally upon Joseph Cropsey, *Polity and Economy: An Interpretation of the Principles of Adam Smith* (The Hague: Nijhoff, 1957) and Robert Kelley, *The Transatlantic Persuasion: The Liberal-Democratic Mind in the Age of Gladstone* (New York: Knopf, 1969).

35. Lockridge suggests this in *Settlement and Unsettlement*.

36. My analysis of Republicanism integrates the work of a number of historians. Most prominent among these are Kloppenberg, "The Virtues of Liberalism"; Joyce Appleby, *Capi-*

talism and a New Social Order: The Republican Vision of the 1790s (New York: New York Univ. Press, 1984); Lance Banning, *The Jeffersonian Persuasion: Evolution of a Party Ideology* (Ithaca: Cornell Univ. Press, 1978); Drew McCoy, *The Elusive Republic: Political Economy in Jeffersonian America* (Chapel Hill: Univ. of North Carolina Press, 1980); and Zvesper, *Political Philosophy and Rhetoric.*

37. Joyce Appleby draws a clear link between liberal economic and political values within the Republican movement in her essays "Commercial Farming and the 'Agrarian Myth' in the Early Republic," *Journal of American History* 68 (1982): 833–49 and "What is Still American in the Political Philosophy of Thomas Jefferson?" *William and Mary Quarterly,* 3d ser., 39 (1982): 287–309. My analysis gains considerably from Appleby's provocative insights.

38. The above quotations appear in Philip S. Foner, ed., *The Democratic-Republican Societies, 1790–1800* (Westport, Conn.: Greenwood Press, 1976), 3, 7, 8, 11, 26.

39. The following discussion of the struggle between Federalists and Republicans over the Alien and Sedition Laws draws upon Gordon S. Wood, "The Democratization of Mind in the American Revolution," in *Leadership in the American Revolution* (Washington, D.C.: Library of Congress, 1974), 63–88.

40. Quoted in ibid., 81.

41. *The Kentucky-Virginia Resolutions and Mr. Madison's Report of 1799* (Richmond: Virginia Commission on Constitutional Government, 1960), 63.

42. Steven Watts offers provocative insights into the dynamic nature of American republican thought in the late eighteenth and early nineteenth centuries. My understanding of the Republican movement profits greatly from his *The Republic Reborn: War and the Making of Liberal America, 1790–1820* (Baltimore: Johns Hopkins Univ. Press, 1987).

43. Rowland Berthoff offers an outstanding analysis of this phenomenon in his "Independence and Attachment, Virtue and Interest: From Republican Citizen to Free Enterpriser, 1787–1837," in Richard Bushman et al., *Uprooted Americans: Essays to Honor Oscar Handlin* (Boston: Little, Brown & Co., 1979), 99–124.

44. Quoted in Gordon S. Wood, "Interests and Disinterestedness in the Making of the Constitution," in Richard Beeman et al., *Beyond Confederation: Origins of the Constitution and American National Identity* (Chapel Hill: Univ. of North Carolina Press, 1987), 69–109. The quotation appears on 102.

45. This is Kloppenberg's term for describing the state of American culture at the turn of the eighteenth century.

The Slow Triumph of Liberal Individualism
James A. Henretta

The author gratefully acknowledges the assistance provided by a Liberal Arts Fellowship at the Harvard Law School, a sabbatical from Boston University, and research grants from the American Council of Learned Societies, the National Endowment for the Humanities through the American Antiquarian Society, and the American Philosophical Society.

1. Louis Hartz, *The Liberal Tradition in America: An Interpretation of American Political Thought Since the Revolution* (New York: Harcourt Brace, 1955), 78, 60.

2. Stanley Elkins, *Slavery: A Study in American Institutional and Intellectual Life* (Chicago: Univ. of Chicago Press, 1959), 50, 43, 49, 82. For a more sophisticated version of this interpretation, see Carl N. Degler, *Neither Black Nor White: Slavery and Race Relations in Brazil and the United States* (New York: Macmillan, 1971), 261–64. Recent research has demonstrated the existence of purposeful slaves, coherent black families, and a partially autonomous African-American culture. See, for example, Philip D. Morgan, "Work and Culture: The

Task System and the World of Lowcountry Blacks, 1700 to 1880," *William and Mary Quarterly*, 3d ser., 39 (1982): 563–99; Herbert G. Gutman, *The Black Family in Slavery and Freedom, 1750–1925* (New York: Pantheon, 1976); and Eugene Genovese, *Roll, Jordon, Roll: The World the Slaves Made* (New York: Pantheon, 1974).

3. Hartz, *Liberal Tradition*, 35, 64–66, 14, 60, 5, 46n.

4. See, for example, David Grayson Allen, *In English Ways: The Transfer of English Local Law and Custom to Massachusetts Bay in the Seventeenth Century* (Chapel Hill: Univ. of North Carolina Press, 1981); Edmund S. Morgan, *American Slavery, American Freedom: The Ordeal of Colonial Virginia* (New York: W. W. Norton, 1975); and Jack P. Greene and J. R. Pole, eds., *Colonial British America: Essays in the New History of the Early Modern Era* (Baltimore: John Hopkins Univ. Press, 1984).

5. Donald Sutherland, *France 1789–1815: Revolution and Counter Revolution* (New York: Oxford Univ. Press, 1986) is a fine synthesis of recent research. On the transition from feudalism to capitalism in England, see T. H. Aston and C. H. E. Philpin, eds., *The Brenner Debate: Agrarian Class Structure and Economic Development in Pre-industrial Europe* (New York: Cambridge Univ. Press, 1985). Bernard Bailyn, *Voyagers To The West: A Passage In The Peopling of America On The Eye Of The Revolution* (New York: Knopf, 1986) offers a panoramic view of this migratory process.

6. Rhys Isaac, *The Transformation of Virginia, 1740–1790* (Chapel Hill: Univ. of North Carolina Press, 1982); John M. Murrin and Rowland Berthoff, "Feudalism, Communalism, and the Yeoman Freeholder: The American Revolution Considered as a Social Accident," in *Essays on the American Revolution*, eds., Stephen G. Kurtz and James H. Hutson (Chapel Hill: Univ. of North Carolina Press, 1973); Sung Bok Kim, *Landlord and Tenant in Colonial New York: Manorial Society, 1667–1775* (Chapel Hill: Univ. of North Carolina Press, 1978); Patricia U. Bonomi, *A Factious People: Politics and Society in Colonial New York* (New York: Columbia Univ. Press, 1971).

7. Eric Foner, "Radical Individualism in America: Revolution to Civil War," *Literature of Liberty: A Review of Contemporary Liberal Thought* 1 (July–September 1978): 6–13; Joyce Appleby, *Capitalism and a New Social Order: The Republican Vision of the 1790s* (New York: New York Univ. Press, 1984), 17; Paul A. Rahe, "The Primacy of Politics in Classical Greece," *American Historical Review* 89 (April 1984): 271.

8. Hartz, *Liberal Tradition*, 108, 94–95.

9. Appleby, *Capitalism and a New Social Order*, 16–20; Rahe, "Primacy of Politics," 277, emphasizes politics as an end in itself but incorrectly excludes the American patriot statesmen from this tradition.

10. James T. Kloppenberg, "The Virtues of Liberalism," *Journal of American History* 74 (1987): 14.

11. Appleby, *Capitalism and a New Social Order*, 82, 67.

12. Lance Banning, "Jefferson Ideology Revisited: Liberal and Classical Ideas in the New American Republic," and Joyce Appleby, "Republicanism in Old and New Contexts," *William and Mary Quarterly*, 3d ser., 43 (1986): 3–34; Kloppenberg, "Virtues of Liberalism," 16, 18, 23.

13. Appleby, *Capitalism and a New Social Order*, 52–53.

14. Hartz, *Liberal Tradition*, 5, 95, 108, 110.

15. Norma Basch, *In the Eyes of the Law: Women, Marriage, and Property in Nineteenth-Century New York* (Ithaca: Cornell Univ. Press, 1982), 47–57.

16. Marylynn Salmon, *Women and the Law of Property in Early America* (Chapel Hill: Univ. of North Carolina Press, 1986), chap. 2.

17. Quoted in Salmon, *Women and Property*, 146.

18. Salmon, *Women and Property*, chap. 7, esp. 160–68.

19. Palmer v. Horton, 1 Johnson 28 (1799); Salmon, *Women and Property*, ch. 2; Appleby, *Capitalism and a New Social Order*, 44; James W. Ely, Jr., "Law in a Republican Society: Continuity and Change in the Legal System of Postrevolutionary America," in *Perspectives on Evolution and Revolution*, ed. Richard A. Preston, (Durham: Duke Univ. Press, 1979), 51. Dower remained part of the statute law of Massachusetts until 1958.

20. Basch, *In the Eyes of the Law*, 71–78. Quoted in Ely, "Law in a Republican Society," 51.

21. Morton J. Horwitz, *The Transformation of American Law, 1780–1860* (Cambridge: Harvard Univ. Press, 1977), chap. 6; William E. Nelson, *The Americanization of the Common Law: The Impact of Legal Change on Massachusetts Society, 1760–1830* (Cambridge: Harvard Univ. Press, 1975), 54–63, 136–58. Recent research suggests that this transition from public control to private bargains began in the 1720s. See Bruce H. Mann, *Neighbors and Strangers: Law and Community in Early Connecticut* (Chapel Hill: Univ. of North Carolina Press, 1987).

22. Basch, *In the Eyes of the Law*, 75–77.

23. Horwitz, *Transformation of American Law*, 179; Jamil Zainaldin, *Law in Antebellum Society: Legal Change and Economic Expansion* (New York: Knopf, 1983), 56–57.

24. Basch, *In the Eyes of the Law*, 153–59.

25. Elizabeth Blackmar, "The Distress of Property Law: Landlord-Tenant Relations in Antebellum New York," in *The Law in America, 1607–1861*, eds. William Pencak and Wythe Holt (New York: New-York Historical Society, 1989). William G. Bishop and William H. Attree, *Report on the Debates and Proceedings of the Convention for the Revision of the Constitution of New York, 1846* (Albany: Albany Evening Journal, 1846), 240ff. As late as 1844, the judiciary committee of the New York Assembly upheld the legal legitimacy of the leasehold system.

26. Quoted in Stephen Skowronek, *Building a New American State: The Expansion of National Administrative Capacities, 1877–1920* (Cambridge: Cambridge Univ. Press, 1982), 6.

27. Hegel quoted in Skowronek, *New American State*, 7.

28. Ibid., 7–8.

29. Bishop and Attree, *Report*, 334.

30. Convention report quoted in Skowronek, *New American State*, 30, and see 22–29.

31. Hendrik Hartog, *Public Property and Private Power: The Corporation of the City of New York in American Law, 1730–1870* (Chapel Hill: Univ. of North Carolina Press, 1983), 9, 80, 127–32, 142.

32. Hartog, *Public Property and Private Power*, 168–69.

33. Hendrik Hartog, "Losing the World of the Massachusetts Whig" and "Distancing Oneself from the Eighteenth Century: A Commentary on Changing Pictures of American Legal History," in *Law in the American Revolution and the Revolution in the Law*, ed. Hartog (New York: New York Univ. Press, 1981), 143–66, 229–57.

34. See John Philip Reid, *In a Defiant Stance: The Conditions of Law in Massachusetts Bay, the Irish Comparison, and the Coming of the American Revolution* (University Park: Pennsylvania State Univ. Press, 1977).

35. Quoted in Edward Countryman, *A People in Revolution: The American Revolution and Political Society in New York, 1760–1790* (Baltimore: Johns Hopkins Univ. Press, 1964), 166.

36. Bishop and Attree, *Report*, 347.

37. Quoted in Lee Benson, *The Concept of Jacksonian Democracy: New York as a Test Case* (Princeton: Princeton Univ. Press, 1981), 10, 24, 48–49.

38. Nathaniel Carter and William Stone, eds., *Reports of the Proceedings and Debates of the Convention of 1821* (Albany: Evening Argus, 1821), 53, 93; James A. Henretta, "The Transformation of Constitution-Making in New York, 1777–1846," paper presented at the New York Historical Society, May 1985.

39. Benson, *The Concept of Jacksonian Democracy,* 20–24.

40. Bishop and Attree, *Report,* 58; see also L. Ray Gunn, "The Crisis of Distributive Politics: The Debate over State Debts and Development Policy in New York, 1837–1842," in *New York and the Rise of American Capitalism: Economic Development and the Social and Political History of an American State, 1780–1870,* ed. William Pencak and Conrad Edick Wright (New York: New-York Historical Society, 1989), 168–202.

41. Quoted in Robert W. Gordon, "Lawyers as an American Aristocracy," paper presented at Johns Hopkins University, October 1985, 10.

42. Quoted in ibid., 18–19.

43. Alexis de Tocqueville, *Democracy in America,* ed. Phillips Bradley (1845, 1850; reprint, New York: Vintage Books, 1945), 2:104, 130; Richard Herr, *Tocqueville and the Old Regime* (Princeton: Princeton Univ. Press, 1962), 131.

The Right to Self-Government
Richard O. Curry

1. My jointly authored essay in this collection, "The Emergence of an Individualistic Ethos in American Society," contains numerous references to social, political, economic, and religious developments during the early decades of the nineteenth century. Thus, it would be redundant to include these citations here.

2. Quoted in Robert H. Abzug, *Passionate Liberator: Theodore Dwight Weld and the Dilemma of Reform* (New York: Oxford Univ. Press, 1980), 92–93.

3. See, especially, Richard O. Curry and Lawrence B. Goodheart, "Ambivalence, Ambiguity, and Contradiction: Garrisonian Abolitionists and Nonviolence," *Journal of Libertarian Studies* 6 (Summer–Fall 1982): 217–26. The notes in this essay contain complete bibliographical information on numerous other important works.

4. Lewis Perry, *Radical Abolitionism: Anarchy and the Kingdom of God in Antislavery Thought* (Ithaca: Cornell Univ. Press, 1973), x–xi.

5. Ibid., 57.

6. Ibid., 45–46.

7. Lewis Perry, *Childhood, Marriage, and Reform: Henry Clarke Wright, 1797–1870* (Chicago: Univ. of Chicago Press, 1980), 39, 86–87.

8. Perry, *Radical Abolitionism,* 232.

9. Ibid., 76, 78.

10. Ibid., 78–80, 70.

11. For a perspective discussion of the stimulus-response thesis, see John Demos, "The Antislavery Movement and the Problem of Violent Means," *New England Quarterly* 37 (December 1964): 501–26. For a theoretical discussion on how violence becomes socially and psychologically sanctioned, see Herbert C. Kelman, "Violence Without Restraint: Reflections on the Dehumanization of Victims and Victimizers," in *Varieties of Psychohistory,* ed. George M. Kren and Leon D. Rappaport (New York: Springer, 1976), 282–314.

12. Quoted in Peter Brock, *Pacifism in the United States from the Colonial Era to the First World War* (Princeton: Princeton Univ. Press, 1968), 671.

13. Quoted in Jane H. and William H. Pease, "Confrontation and Abolition in the 1850s," *Journal of American History* 58 (December 1972): 928–29. Douglass had observed earlier: "I was non-resistant 'til I got to fighting with a mob in Pendleton, Indiana. . . . I fell, never to rise again, and yet I cannot feel I did wrong." Quoted in Leslie F. Goldstein, "Violence as an Instrument for Social Change: The Views of Frederick Douglass, 1819–1895," *Journal of Negro History* 41 (January 1976): 64. See also Benjamin Quarles, *Black Abolitionists* (New York:

Oxford Univ. Press, 1969); and Jane H. and William H. Pease, *They Who Would Be Free: Blacks Search for Freedom, 1831–1861* (New York: Atheneum, 1974).

14. Quoted in Demos, "Antislavery Movement," 522–23.

15. Quoted in Lawrence J. Friedman, *Gregarious Saints: Self and Community in American Abolitionism, 1830–1870* (New York: Cambridge Univ. Press, 1982), 216.

16. Ibid., 217.

17. Quoted in Demos, "Antislavery Movement," 523–24.

18. Quoted in Lewis Perry, "Visions of Anarchy in the Antislavery Movement," *American Quarterly* 20 (Winter 1968): 771.

19. Quoted in Ronald G. Walters, *The Antislavery Appeal: American Abolitionism After 1830* (Baltimore: Johns Hopkins Univ. Press, 1976), 30.

20. Quoted in Brock, *Pacifism*, 699.

21. Friedman, *Gregarious Saints*, 216.

22. Ibid.

23. Quoted in Brock, *Pacifism*, 697.

24. Ibid., 678. For a similar development in the expression of militant nationalism, see James H. Moorhead, *American Apocalypse: Yankee Protestants and the Civil War, 1860–1869* (New Haven: Yale Univ. Press, 1978).

25. Quoted in Carleton Mabee, *Black Freedom: The Nonviolent Abolitionists from 1830 Through the Civil War* (London: Macmillan, 1970), 365. See also Sheldon Richman, "The Anti-War Abolitionists: The Peace Movement's Split Over the Civil War," *Journal of Libertarian Studies* 5 (Fall 1981): 327–40. Lysander Spooner, a leading libertarian anarchist, presented another perspective on the use of violence versus nonviolence. He contrasted the personal right to employ violence to combat slavery through voluntary action such as John Brown's raid with the Civil War, which represented coercive state-sponsored violence. See John A. Alexander, "The Ideas of Lysander Spooner," *New England Quarterly* 23 (September 1950): 212–13; and Perry, *Radical Abolitionism*, 205–8.

26. Quoted in Mabee, *Black Freedom*, 346.

27. Curry and Goodheart, "Ambivalence, Ambiguity, and Contradiction," 223.

28. Quoted in Peter F. Walker, *Moral Choices: Memory, Desire, and Imagination in Nineteenth-Century American Abolitionism* (Baton Rouge: Louisiana State Univ. Press, 1978), 16.

29. Ibid., 3.

30. Ibid., 11.

31. Perry, *Radical Abolitionism*, 1–17. For the survival of more secularized versions of individualist anarchism, see Wendy McElroy, "The Culture of Individualist Anarchism in Late Nineteenth-Century America," *Journal of Libertarian Studies* 5 (Fall 1981): 291–304.

32. George M. Fredrickson, *The Inner Civil War: Northern Intellectuals and the Crisis of the Union* (New York: Harper and Row, 1968), 192–93. This criticism also applies to Harold M. Hyman's conclusion that Darwinism helped undermine "the white man's concern for the Negro" during Reconstruction. See Hyman, ed., *The Radical Republican and Reconstruction, 1861–1870* (Indianapolis: Bobbs-Merrill, 1967), xxvi–xxix. For an analysis of abolitionist historiography during the postwar period, see Richard O. Curry, "The Abolitionists and Reconstruction: A Reappraisal," *The Journal of Southern History* 34 (November 1968): 527–45.

33. James M. McPherson, *The Struggle for Equality: Abolitionists and the Negro in the Civil War and Reconstruction* (Princeton: Princeton Univ. Press, 1964); and John G. Sproat, "Blueprint for Radical Reconstruction," *Journal of Southern History* 23 (February 1957): 25–44. The quotation is taken from Sproat, "Blueprint," 41–42.

34. Curry, "Abolitionists and Reconstruction," 538–44.

35. Willie Lee Rose, *Rehearsal for Reconstruction: The Port Royal Experiment* (Indianapolis: Bobbs-Merrill, 1964); and Rose, " 'Iconaclasm Has Had Its Day': Abolitionists and the Freedmen in South Carolina," in *The Antislavery Vanguard: New Essays on the Abolitionists,* ed. Martin Duberman (Princeton: Princeton Univ. Press, 1965). The quotation is found in Curry, "Abolitionists and Reconstruction," 541.

36. Ibid.

37. Quoted in John L. Thomas, *The Liberator, William Lloyd Garrison: A Biography* (Boston: Little, Brown & Co., 1963), 326–27.

38. Quoted in Curry, "Abolitionists and Reconstruction," 538.

39. Quoted in ibid.

40. Quoted in ibid.

41. Quoted in ibid., 538–39.

42. Quoted in ibid., 539.

43. Thomas, *The Liberator,* 326–27.

44. See, for example, James M. McPherson, *The Abolitionist Legacy: From Reconstruction to the NAACP* (Princeton: Princeton Univ. Press, 1975); Lawrence B. Goodheart, *Abolitionist, Actuary, Atheist: Elizur Wright and the Reform Impulse* (Kent, Ohio: Kent State Univ. Press, 1990); and James B. Stewart, *Wendall Phillips: Liberty's Hero* (Baton Rouge: Louisiana State Univ. Press, 1986).

45. Glickstein's essay is published in Lewis Perry and Michael Fellman, eds., *Antislavery Reconsidered: New Perspectives on the Abolitionists* (Baton Rouge: Louisiana State Univ. Press, 1979), 195–218.

46. Ibid., 197, 204.

47. See Herbert G. Gutman's essay, "Protestantism and the American Labor Movement: The Christian Spirit in the Golden Age," in Gutman, *Work, Culture and Society in Industrializing America* (New York: Vintage Books, 1977), 79–113.

48. Quoted in James Brewer Stewart, "Wendell Phillips: From Slave Power to Money Power, 1837–1870," paper presented at the meeting of the American Historical Association, San Francisco, December 28, 1983. See also Stewart, *Wendell Phillips.*

49. Boyer, *Urban Masses and Moral Order, 1820–1920* (Cambridge: Harvard Univ. Press, 1978); and Dawley, *Class and Community: The Industrial Revolution in Lynn* (Cambridge: Harvard Univ. Press, 1976).

50. Gutman, "Protestantism and the American Labor Movement," 79–113.

51. Briggs, review of Edward P. Thompson, *The Making of the English Working Class,* quoted in ibid., 85.

52. Ibid., 85–86.

53. Louis S. Gerteis's *Morality and Utility in American Antislavery Reform* (Chapel Hill: Univ. of North Carolina Press, 1987) takes a different and fundamentally incompatible approach to abolitionism than that contained in this essay. If Gerteis does not deny the importance of "post-millennialist and perfectionist doctrines of the Second Great Awakening" in shaping abolitionist ideology, neither does he analyze its significance. For example, the terminology Gerteis uses in his brief discussion of religious influences is misleading. The "reforming impulse first emerged," he states, from a strong "Calvinist tradition," and abolitionist appeals to the "memory of the Puritan 'fathers' as well as the Founding Fathers" suggest that reformers felt the need to enlist "Puritanism as well as republicanism" in the "struggle against slavery and other barriers to human progress." Religious declension, as it progressed from the 1620s to the 1820s, makes the use of terms such as "Puritanism" and "Calvinism" misleading and inappropriate in attempting to characterize the religious views of abolitionists. Such views cannot be approached, must less understood, without using the work of scholars such a Gilbert

H. Barnes, Whitney R. Cross, John L. Thomas, Timothy L. Smith, Aileen Kraditor, and Lewis Perry, among others—references to which are conspicuously absent either in Gerteis's text or footnotes.

In short, Gerteis's analysis is concerned almost exclusively with the influence of utilitarianism—that is, "the doctrines of political economy and the related ethical theories directly associated with [John Stuart] Mill and his mentor Jeremy Bentham." Utilitarianism, Gerteis states, including its American applications, stressed the belief "that men act and interact in society to maximize their individual pleasures and that the greatest happiness of the greatest number will be achieved in the pursuit of individual self-interest." By the 1860s, Gerteis argues, "utilitarianism subsumed older and narrower laissez-faire doctrines and became incorporated into the optimistic language of political liberalism, which invoked state powers to promote individual autonomy and the liberty to pursue material gain."

Gerteis's interpretation is problematic in part because he fails to demonstrate precisely how evangelical abolitionist ideas and utilitarianism are interconnected. Moreover, it is not entirely clear whether his use of the terms "antislavery reformer" and "abolitionist" are interchangeable or whether Gerteis intends them to be. Even so, Gerteis asserts that "morality and utility" merged to become "a single course of human endeavour." This is not to say that American abolitionists did not have secular values or concerns. Of course they did. It is to say that, in my view, Gerteis understates the importance of the religious origins and implications of abolitionism and overstates the importance of utilitarianism.

Precisely what Gerteis has in mind when he concludes that antislavery reformers "invoked state powers to promote individual autonomy" is not clear. While it is true that most abolitionists approved or acquiesced in the use of force to destroy the institution of slavery, this by no means indicates that they supported the use of state power to promote other types of social change. In addition, Gerteis does not appear to be aware that not only are the ideas of Bentham and Mill not identical but the utilitarian idea that emphasized "the greatest good of the greatest number" was a modified version of utilitarianism put forth by early twentieth-century utilitarian theorists Hastings Randall and G. E. Moore. Thus, the issue is not only whether utilitarian doctrines influenced the abolitionists but whether Gerteis fully understands the complexities, modifications, confusions, and conundrums inherent in utilitarian theories. See especially D. H. Monro, "Utilitarianism," in *Dictionary of the History of Ideas: Studies of Selected Pivotal Ideas* (New York: Charles Scribner's Sons, 1973), 4:444–49; and Nicholas Georgescu-Roegon, "Utility and Value in Economic Thought," ibid., 450–58.

From Assertiveness to Individualism
Loren Schweninger

1. David Imes to Frederick Douglass, March 29, 1869, Frederick Douglass Papers, reel 2, Library of Congress.

2. See Larry Gara, *The Liberty Line: The Legend of the Underground Railroad* (Lexington: Univ. of Kentucky Press, 1961); Wilbur H. Siebert, *The Underground Railroad: From Slavery to Freedom* (New York: Macmillan, 1898); Juliet E. K. Walker, "Racism, Slavery, and Free Enterprise: Black Entrepreneurship in the United States before the Civil War," *Business History Review* 60 (Autumn 1986): 343–82; Edmund S. Morgan, "Slavery and Freedom: The American Paradox," *Journal of American History* 59 (June 1972): 5–29.

3. Nathan I. Huggins, *Black Odyssey: The Afro-American Ordeal in Slavery* (New York: Oxford Univ. Press, 1977), 5; John Mbiti, *African Religions and Philosophy* (1969; reprint,

New York: Doubleday, 1970), 32; Olaudah Equiano, *Equiano's Travels: The Interesting Narrative of the Life of Olaudah Equiano or Gustavus Vassa the African* (1789; reprint, New York: Praeger, 1967), 7–8, 25; Philip Curtin et al., *African History* (Boston: Little, Brown & Co., 1978), 79–81.

4. Although recent studies have not focused on individualism, they do show the processes of cultural change. See Ira Berlin, "Time, Space, and the Evolution of Afro-American Society on British Mainland North America," *The American Historical Review* 85 (February 1980): 44–78; Daniel C. Littlefield, *Rice and Slaves: Ethnicity and the Slave Trade in Colonial South Carolina* (Baton Rouge: Louisiana State Univ. Press, 1981), 74–114; Russell R. Menard, *Economy and Society in Early Colonial Maryland* (New York: Garland Publishing, 1985), chap. 7; Allan Kulikoff, *Tobacco and Slaves: The Development of Southern Cultures in the Chesapeake, 1680–1800* (Chapel Hill: Univ. of North Carolina Press, 1986); Philip D. Morgan, "Black Life in Eighteenth-Century Charleston," *Perspectives in American History*, new ser., 1 (1984): 187–232; and "Work and Culture: The Task System and the World of Lowcountry Blacks, 1700–1880," *William and Mary Quarterly* 3d ser., 35 (October 1982): 563–99.

5. Sidney W. Mintz, *Caribbean Transformations* (Chicago: Aldine Publishing Co., 1974), 155. See also Ciro Flamarion S. Cardoso, "The Peasant Breach in the Slave System: New Developments in Brazil," *Luso-Brazilian Review* 25 (Summer 1988): 49–57; Stuart B. Schwartz, "Resistance and Accommodation in Eighteenth-Century Brazil: The Slaves' View of Slavery," *Hispanic American Historical Review* 57 (February 1977): 69–81.

6. Berlin, "Time, Space," 54; Peter H. Wood, " 'More like a Negro Country': Demographic Patterns in Colonial South Carolina, 1670–1740," in *Race and Slavery in the Western Hemisphere: Quantitative Studies,* ed. Stanley Engerman and Eugene Genovese (Princeton: Princeton Univ. Press, 1975), 134; Converse D. Clowse, *Economic Beginnings of Colonial South Carolina, 1670–1730* (Columbia: Univ. of South Carolina Press, 1971), 61; and *Measuring Charleston's Overseas Commerce, 1717–1767: Statistics from the Port's Naval Lists* (Washington, D.C.: Univ. Press of America, 1981), 30–33.

7. Gerald W. Mullin, *Flight and Rebellion: Slave Resistance in Eighteenth-Century Virginia* (New York: Oxford Univ. Press, 1972), chap. 3; Winthrop D. Jordan, *White Over Black: American Attitudes Toward the Negro, 1550–1812* (Chapel Hill: Univ. of North Carolina Press, 1968), 212–15.

8. Andrew Bryan to John Rippon, December 23, 1800, *The Baptist Annual Register for 1797–1801,* 3:366–67; John W. Davis, "George Liele and Andrew Bryan: Pioneer Negro Preachers," *Journal of Negro History* 3 (April 1918): 119–27; Records of the County Probate Court, Chatham Co., Ga., Deeds, September 4, 1793, 77–78, copy in Vertical File, Georgia Historical Society, Savannah, Georgia. I am very grateful to Professor Robert Calhoon for bringing Bryan's letter to my attention, for his critique of this essay, and for his suggestion of the title.

9. Peter Kolchin, "Reevaluating the Antebellum Slave Community: A Comparative Perspective," *Journal of American History* 70 (December 1983): 587; Peter J. Parish, *Slavery: History and Historians* (New York: Harper and Row, 1989), 2–5; Carl Degler, "The Irony of American Negro Slavery," in *Perspectives and Irony in American Slavery,* ed. Harry P. Owens (Jackson: Univ. Press of Mississippi, 1976), 3–5.

10. John Blassingame, *The Slave Community: Plantation Life in the Antebellum South,* rev. ed. (New York: Oxford Univ. Press, 1979), 105. See Eugene Genovese, *Roll, Jordan, Roll: The World the Slaves Made* (New York: Pantheon, 1974); Herbert Gutman, *The Black Family in Slavery and Freedom, 1750–1925* (New York: Pantheon, 1976); Lawrence W. Levine, *Black Culture and Black Consciousness: Afro-American Folk Thought from Slavery to Freedom* (New York: Oxford Univ. Press, 1977); Leslie Howard Owens, *This Species of Property: Slave Life and Culture in the Old South* (New York: W. W. Norton, 1976); Thomas L. Webber, *Deep Like*

the Rivers: Education in the Slave Quarter Community, 1831–1865 (New York: W. W. Norton, 1978); George P. Rawick, *From Sundown to Sunup: The Making of the Black Community* (Westport, Conn.: Greenwood Press, 1972); Charles Joyner, *Down by the Riverside: A South Carolina Slave Community* (Urbana: Univ. of Illinois Press, 1984); Paul D. Escott, *Slavery Remembered: A Record of Twentieth-Century Slave Narratives* (Chapel Hill: Univ. of North Carolina Press, 1979).

11. Jordan, *White over Black*, 318–20; Philip D. Morgan, "The Ownership of Property by Slaves in the Mid-Nineteenth–Century Low Country," *Journal of Southern History* 49 (August 1983): 399–420; Joyner, *Down by the Riverside*, chap. 1.

12. Eugene D. Genovese, *From Rebellion to Revolution: Afro-American Slave Revolts in the Making of the Modern World* (Baton Rouge: Louisiana State Univ. Press, 1979), chap. 1; *Nashville Whig*, August 26, 1840; Loren Schweninger, ed., *From Tennessee Slave to St. Louis Entrepreneur: The Autobiography of James Thomas* (Columbia: Univ. of Missouri Press, 1984), 59.

13. Mullin, *Flight and Rebellion*, 106–7; *Federal Gazette and Baltimore Daily Advertiser*, April 11, 1805.

14. Clement Eaton, "Slave-Hiring in the Upper South: A Step toward Freedom," *Mississippi Valley Historical Review* 46 (March 1960): 663–78; Richard B. Morris, "The Measure of Bondage in the Slave States," ibid. 41 (September 1954): 219–40; John Hope Franklin, "Slaves Virtually Free in Ante-Bellum North Carolina," *Journal of Negro History* 28 (July 1943): 284–310; Loren Schweninger, "The Free-Slave Phenomenon: James P. Thomas and the Black Community in Ante-Bellum Nashville," *Civil War History* 22 (December 1976): 293–307.

15. *Southern Watchman*, April 28, 1859, quoted in E. Merton Coulter, "Slavery and Freedom in Athens, Georgia, 1860–1866," *Georgia Historical Quarterly* 49 (September 1965): 265; Samuel Rhea to Ralph R. Gurley, May 24, 1833, Records of the American Colonization Society, reel 20, Library of Congress. See General Assembly, Session Records, Petition of John Bryan et al. to the North Carolina General Assembly, October 10, 1833, North Carolina State Archives; Charles C. Jones, Jr. to Charles C. Jones, October 1, 1856, *The Children of Pride: A True Story of Georgia and the Civil War*, ed. Robert Myers (New Haven: Yale Univ. Press, 1972), 240; Charles Syndor, "The Free Negro in Mississippi Before the Civil War," *American Historical Review* 33 (July 1927): 776.

16. Samuel Anderson to Benjamin W. Womack, February 3, 1848, Carter Woodson Collection, container 15, Library of Congress; Petition of the Citizens of Hamilton County to the Tennessee General Assembly, October 1845, Tennessee State Library and Archives, Nashville, Tennessee.

17. Carter Woodson, "The Negroes of Cincinnati Prior to the Civil War," *Journal of Negro History* 1 (January 1916): 21; C. W. Dudley to Commissioner of Claims, June 3, 1874, Records of the Claims Commission, Records of the Treasury Department, Record Group 56, reel 4, National Archives; General Assembly, Session Records, Petition and Memorial of the Incorporated Mechanical Society of Wilmington to the North Carolina General Assembly, November 29, 1802, North Carolina State Archives, Raleigh, North Carolina.

18. Benjamin S. Turner to Claims Commission, April 21, 1871, Deposition, Case 285, Records of the Claims Commission, National Archives.

19. Rosser H. Taylor, "Free Negro in North Carolina," in *The James Sprunt Historical Publications*, ed. J. G. de Roulhac Hamilton (Chapel Hill: Univ. of North Carolina Press, 1920), vol. 17, no. 1, 11–13; Herbert Sterkx, *The Free Negro in Ante-Bellum Louisiana* (Rutherford, N.J.: Fairleigh Dickinson Univ. Press, 1972), 121; *Acts of the State of Tennessee Passed at the First Session of the Twenty-ninth General Assembly* (Nashville: McKennie, 1852), 571.

20. John W. Blassingame, ed., *Slave Testimony: Two Centuries of Letters, Speeches, Interviews, and Autobiographies* (Baton Rouge: Louisiana State Univ. Press, 1977), 82–86; W. B. Cooper to Mary Carrol, January 7, 1860, Carter Woodson Collection, Library of Congress; Helen T. Catterall, ed., *Judicial Cases Concerning American Slavery and the Negro* (Washington, D.C.: W. F. Roberts Co., 1932), 1:157.

21. Frederick Bancroft, *Slave Trading in the Old South* (Baltimore: J. H. Furst Co., 1931), 341; Claudia Goldin, *Urban Slavery in the American South, 1820–1860* (Chicago: Univ. of Chicago Press, 1976), 72–73; James McDowell to Ralph R. Gurley, October 25, 1831, Records of the American Colonization Society, reel 12, Library of Congress.

22. Ohio Anti-Slavery Society, *Memorial of the Ohio Anti-Slavery Society to the General Assembly of the State of Ohio* (Cincinnati: Pugh and Dodd, 1838), 20, 23; Records of the County Probate Court, Elizabeth City County, Vir., Deed of Emancipation, January 10, 1849, Carter Woodson Collection, Library of Congress; John W. Cromwell, "Education, Suffrage, Progress," speech given January 1, 1901, in ibid.

23. Ohio Anti-Slavery Society, *Condition of the People of Color in the State of Ohio with Interesting Anecdotes* (Boston: Isaac Knapp, 1839), 23; Society for Promoting the Abolition of Slavery, *A Statistical Inquiry into the Condition of the People of Colour of the City and Districts of Philadelphia* (Philadelphia: Kite and Walton, 1849), 12; Lorenzo Greene, "Self-Purchase by Negroes in Cole County, Missouri," *Midwest Journal* 1 (Winter 1948): 83–85; Luther Porter Jackson, "Manumission in Certain Virginia Cities," *Journal of Negro History* 15 (July 1930): 284–85.

24. James Thomas to John Rapier, January 8, 1859, *From Tennessee Slave to St. Louis Entrepreneur*, ed. Schweninger, 212. Although Thomas misspelled his name (Nelville), he was probably thinking about Melville's fictional character Bartleby, whose spiritual birth occurs during the solitary, cocoonlike passage of the soul toward physical death. See William B. Dillingham, *Melville's Short Fiction, 1853–1856* (Athens, Ga.: Univ. of Georgia Press, 1977), 46–55; Hershel Parker, "The 'Sequel' in 'Bartleby,' " in *Bartleby the Inscrutable: A Collection of Commentary on Herman Melville's Tale "Bartleby the Scrivener,"* ed. M. Thomas Inge (Hamden, Conn.: Archon Books, 1979), 159–61.

25. Leon F. Litwack, *Been in the Storm So Long: The Aftermath of Slavery* (New York: Vintage Books, 1979), 252–53, chap. 6.

26. George Rawick, ed., *The American Slave: A Composite Autobiography* (Westport, Conn.: Greenwood Press, 1972), vol. 4, pt. 2, 251–52. See Whitelaw Reid, *After the War: A Tour of the Southern States, 1865–66*, ed. by C. Vann Woodward (New York: Harper, Torchbooks, 1965), 564; Roger L. Ransom and Richard Sutch, *One Kind of Freedom: The Economic Consequences of Emancipation* (London: Cambridge Univ. Press, 1977), 81–87.

27. W. E. B. Du Bois, "The Negro Farmer," in *Special Reports: Supplementary Analysis and Derivative Tables [of the] Twelfth Census of the United States* (Washington, D.C.: Government Printing Office [hereafter GPO], 1906), 523.

28. U.S. Dept. of Interior, *Report on Farms and Homes: Proprietorship and Indebtedness in the United States* (Washington, D.C.: GPO, 1896), 566–70; *Negro Population 1790–1915* (Washington, D.C.: GPO, 1918), 607, 625–26; Loren Schweninger, *Black Property Owners in the South, 1790–1915* (Urbana: Univ. of Illinois Press, 1990), 164, 174; James M. McPherson, *Ordeal by Fire: The Civil War and Reconstruction* (New York: Knopf, 1982), 579–80.

29. Waldo E. Martin, Jr., *The Mind of Frederick Douglass* (Chapel Hill: Univ. of North Carolina Press, 1984), 256–58, 281; Frederick Douglass, *Life and Times of Frederick Douglass, Written by Himself* (1881; facsimile edition, Secaucus, N.J.: Citadel Press, 1983), 487–88; Raymond Gavins, "The Meaning of Freedom: Black North Carolina in the Nadir, 1880–1900," in *Race, Class, and Politics in Southern History: Essays in Honor of Robert F. Durden*, ed. Jeffrey J. Crow, Paul D. Escott, and Charles L. Flynn, Jr. (Baton Rouge: Louisiana

State Univ. Press, 1989), 175; Michael Meyer, ed., *Frederick Douglass: The Narrative and Selected Writings* (New York: Modern Library, 1984), 139; Richard O. Curry, "The Abolitionists and Reconstruction: A Critical Appraisal," *Journal of Southern History* 34 (November 1968): 538–39.

30. Louis R. Harlan, ed., *The Booker T. Washington Papers* (Urbana: Univ. of Illinois Press, 1972–1989), 3:583–87 and *Booker T. Washington: The Making of a Black Leader, 1856–1901* (New York: Oxford Univ. Press, 1972), 288; August Meier, *Negro Thought in America, 1880–1915: Racial Ideologies in the Age of Booker T. Washington* (Ann Arbor: Univ. of Michigan Press, 1963), 98. See also Booker T. Washington, *Frederick Douglass* (Philadelphia: George W. Jacobs and Co., 1906).

31. Emma Lou Thornbrough, ed., *Booker T. Washington* (Englewood Cliffs, N.J.: Prentice-Hall, 1969), 48.

The Ambiguity of Individualism
Lawrence B. Goodheart

1. "A Convention for a Free People to Make a Free Land!" (Aug. 11, 1879), box 22, vol. 2, Elizur Wright Papers, Library of Congress; and Thomas Jefferson to Nehemiah Dodge and Others, Jan. 1, 1802, *The Portable Thomas Jefferson*, ed. Merrill D. Peterson (New York: Viking, 1975), 303.

2. Henry Adams, *The Education of Henry Adams: An Autobiography* (Boston: Houghton Mifflin, 1961), 499–500. The best study of religious skepticism is James Turner, *Without God, Without Creed: The Origins of Unbelief in America* (Baltimore: Johns Hopkins Univ. Press, 1985).

3. Abbot is quoted in Turner, *Without God*, 191. Except for two dissertations, Abbot has not been the subject of a biography. See Sydney Ahlstrom, "Francis Ellingwood Abbot: His Education and Active Career" (Ph.D. diss., Harvard Univ., 1952); and Fred M. Rivers, "Francis Ellingwood Abbot: Free Religionist and Cosmic Philosopher" (Ph.D. diss., Univ. of Maryland, 1970).

For the Free Religious Association and related developments, see Sidney Warren, *American Freethought, 1860–1914* (New York: Columbia Univ. Press, 1943), 96–116; Stow Persons, *Free Religion: An American Faith* (New Haven: Yale Univ. Press, 1947), 42–55; and Ralph H. Gabriel, *The Course of American Democratic Thought* (New York: Ronald Press, 1956), 183–96. The quotation from the constitution of the Free Religious Association is from Yehoshua Arieli, *Individualism and Nationalism in American Ideology* (Cambridge: Harvard Univ. Press, 1964), 325.

4. The Christian amendment is quoted in *The Centennial Congress of Liberals* (Philadelphia: National Library League, 1876), 7–8. Background on the Christian amendment is in Person, *Free Religion*, 114–15; and Warren, *Freethought*, 176–77.

5. "The Nine Demands of Liberalism" were first published in *The Index*, April 6, 1872.

6. *Congressional Record*, 43d Cong., 1st sess., 1874, 432; "Religious Freedom Amendment," *The Index*, January 1, 1874; and *Centennial Congress of Liberals*, 14.

7. *Centennial Congress of Liberals*, 7–8; and Samuel P. Putnam, *Four Hundred Years of Freethought* (New York: Truth Seeker Co., 1894).

8. *Centennial Congress of Liberals*, 114–18, 169, 175; *Patriotic Address to the People of the U.S. Adopted at Philadelphia on the Fourth of July, 1876 by the National Liberal League* (Boston: National Liberal League, 1879), 9–13, 15–16; and *The Index*, July 13, 1876. An overview of the National Liberal League is in Persons, *Free Religion*, 114–25; Warren, *Freethought*, 162–67; and Hal D. Sears, *Free Love in High Victorian America* (Lawrence: Regents Press of Kansas, 1977), 34–41.

9. Felix Adler is quoted in "Church Life in the City," *New York Times,* October 16, 1882; and Elizur Wright, "Clippings," Elizur Wright Papers, case 3, Baker Library, Harvard University.

10. Eric Foner, "Radical Individualism in America: Revolution to Civil War," *Literature of Liberty: A Review of Contemporary Liberal Thought* (July–September 1978), 26. William James Potter is quoted in Persons, *Free Religion,* 42; Francis E. Abbot is quoted in Rivers, "Abbot," 74; and Robert G. Ingersoll is quoted in Putnam, *Four Hundred Years,* 829.

11. Lucy Colman, *Reminiscences* (Buffalo: H. L. Green, 1891), 8.

12. *Congressional Globe,* 42d Cong., 3d sess., 1873, vol. 46, pts. 2, 3:1525, 1571; and *U.S. Statutes* 17 (1871–73), 598–600.

13. *Congressional Globe,* 42d Cong., 3d sess., 1873, vol. 46, pt. 2, 3, 1240, 1436–37, 1525–26, 1571, 2004–5, and appendix, vol. 46, pt. 3: 297; and *U.S. Statutes* 19 (1875–77), 90; A useful sketch of Comstock is in Robert Bremner, ed., *Traps for the Young* (Cambridge: Harvard Univ. Press, 1967), vii–xxxi.

14. Congressional Globe, 42d Cong., 3d sess., 1873, vol. 46, pt. 2, 3:1525.

15. Anthony Comstock, *Frauds Exposed: Or, How the People Are Deceived and Youth Corrupted* (New York: J. H. Brown, 1880), 526–39; and James C. N. Paul and Murray L. Schwartz, *Federal Censorship: Obscenity in the Mail* (New York: Free Press of Glencoe, 1961), 18–29.

16. Comstock, *Frauds,* 390; and Comstock, *Traps for the Young* (New York: Funk and Wagnalls, 1883), 240. See the New York Society for the Suppression of Vice Papers, "Arrests, 1872–84," July 14, 1878, 120, Manuscript Room, Library of Congress.

17. See Theodore W. Adorno et al., *The Authoritarian Personality* (New York: Harper, 1950). Comstock, *Frauds,* 186, 433, 443; and Comstock, *Morals Versus Art* (New York: Ogilvie, 1887), 5.

18. "Suppression of Vice," *New York Times,* January 1, 1876; *Congressional Globe,* 42d Cong., 3d sess., 1873, appendix, 168; Richard Hofstadter, *Social Darwinism in American Thought* (New York: George Braziller, 1955), 31–50; and Paul Boyer, *Purity in Print: The Vice-Society Movement and Book Censorship in America* (New York: Charles Scribner's Sons, 1968), 5–10. The social control thesis of the vice societies is developed in David J. Pivar, *Purity Crusade, Sexual Morality and Social Control, 1868–1900* (Westport, Conn.: Greenwood Press, 1973); and in Paul Boyer, *Urban Masses and Moral Order in America, 1820–1920* (Cambridge: Harvard Univ. Press, 1978), 123–90.

19. Rev. J. M. Buckley, "The Suppression of Vice," *North American Review* 135 (1882): 496; Harriet Beecher Stowe, *My Wife and I: Or Harry Henderson's History* (New York: J. S. Ford, 1871), 41; Comstock, *Frauds,* 440; and Comstock, "Vampire Literature," *North American Review* 153 (1891): 162.

20. Comstock, *Traps for the Young,* 186. On the religious ferment of the age, see Paul Carter, *The Spiritual Crisis of the Gilded Age* (Dekalb: Northern Illinois Univ. Press, 1971).

21. Buckley, "The Suppression of Vice," 496; John B. Ellis, *Free Love and Its Votaries: Or American Socialism Unmasked* (New York: United States Publishing Co., 1870), 10; and Clinton L. Merriam is quoted in the *Congressional Globe,* 42d Cong., 3d sess., 1873, appendix, 168. See Emanie Sachs, *"The Terrible Siren": Victoria Woodhull, 1838–1927* (New York: Harper, 1928); and Altina L. Waller, *Rev. Beecher and Mrs. Tilton: Sex and Class in Victorian America* (Amherst: Univ. of Massachusetts Press, 1982).

22. Comstock, "Vampire Literature," 160–71; and Comstock, *Frauds,* 556.

23. *Centennial Congress of Liberals,* 157–62, 170. See Madeleine B. Stern, *The Pantarch: A Biography of Stephen Pearl Andrews* (Austin: Univ. of Texas Press, 1968).

24. Ezra D. Heywood, *Cupid's Yokes: Or the Binding Forces of Conjugal Life* (Princeton, Mass.: Co-operative Publishing Co., 1876), 24. See Lewis Perry, *Radical Abolitionism: Anar-*

chy and the Government of God in Anti-Slavery Thought (Ithaca: Cornell Univ. Press, 1973), 286–90; and Martin H. Blatt, *Free Love and Anarchism: The Biography of Ezra Heywood* (Urbana: Univ. of Illinois Press, 1989).

25. Heywood, *Cupid's Yokes*, 5, 9n, 19, 22–23.

26. Ezra Heywood, *Free Speech* (Princeton, Mass.: Co-operative Publishing Co., 1885), 51; New York Society for the Suppression of Vice Papers, "Arrests 1872–1884," 103–6, Manuscript Room, Library of Congress; D. M. Bennett, *Anthony Comstock: His Career of Cruelty and Crime* (New York: Liberal and Scientific Publishing Co., 1878), 1060–64; Heywood Broun and Margaret Leech, *Anthony Comstock: Roundsman of the Lord* (New York: Albert and Charles Boni, 1927), 173–74, 179; and Sears, *The Sex Radicals*, 153–62.

27. NYSSV is quoted in Putnam, *Four Hundred Years*, 537; National Defense Association, *Words of Warning to Those Who Aid and Abet in the Suppression of Free Speech and Free Press* (New York: National Defense Association, 1879), back cover; and Sears, *Sex Radicals*, 200–201.

28. *The Index*, November 7, 1878.

29. Ibid.; "The Liberty of Printing," *Truth Seeker Tracts*, no. 150, which is reprinted in Thaddeus B. Wakeman, *Liberty and Purity* (New York: Liberal Publishing Co., 1881), 17–18.

30. C. P. Farrell, ed., *The Works of Robert G. Ingersoll* (New York: Ingersoll Publishers, 1900), 12:216. Orvin Larson, *American Infidel: Robert G. Ingersoll* (Secaucus, N.J.: Ingersoll Publishers, 1900), 150; Ahlstrom, "Abbot," 219–28; and Rivers, "Abbot," 105–8.

31. Farrell, ed., *Ingersoll*, 12:226; Larson, *Ingersoll*, 152; and Wakeman, *Liberty and Purity*, 32–34.

32. Thaddeus B. Wakeman, *The Comstock Laws Considered as to Their Constitutionality* (New York: D. M. Bennett, 1880), 45; Wakeman, *Liberty and Purity*, 44, 49, 62–63; and Lindsay Rodgers, *The Postal Powers of Congress: A Study in Constitutional Expansion* (Baltimore: Johns Hopkins Univ. Press, 1916), 51n, 52. Contrary to Wakeman, Lindsay argued that Congress had the constitutional right to deny access to the mails, a position sustained by the Supreme Court in *Ex Parte Jackson* (1877) and subsequent decisions.

33. Wakeman, *Liberty and Purity*, 49–52.

34. Ibid., 69–70; Wakeman, *The Comstock Laws Considered*, 16–19, 37–38; Paul and Schwartz, *Federal Censorship*, 15–16, 26–27, 31–33, 145; Theodore Schroeder, ed., *Free Press Anthology* (New York: Free Speech League and Truth Seeker, 1909), 221; Harry M. Clor, *Obscenity and Public Morality in a Liberal Society* (Chicago: Univ. of Chicago Press, 1969), 14–15; Nat Hentoff, *The First Freedom: The Tumultuous History of Free Speech in America* (New York: Delacorte, 1980), 283–85; and Joel Feinberg, "Pornography and the Criminal Law," in *Pornography and Censorship*, ed. David Copp and Susan Wendell (New York: Prometheus, 1983), 116–20.

35. Wakeman, *Liberty and Purity*, 51, 91; Wakeman, *The Comstock Law Considered*, 41–43; and Wakeman to Elizur Wright, April 11, 1879, Elizur Wright Papers, Library of Congress.

36. In Miller v. California (1973), the Court stated that community standards should be applied to two other tests for determining legally prosecutable obscenity as set forth in that ruling. Namely that depictions or descriptions of sexual conduct may be banned as obscene in "works which, taken as a whole, appeal to the prurient interest in sex, which portray sexual conduct in a patently offensive way, and which, taken as a whole, do not have serious literary, artistic, political or scientific value," the so-called LAPS test. A refinement of the Miller decision occurred in *Pope v. Illinois* (1987). In that 5-to-4 ruling the Court substituted the viewpoint of a "reasonable person" rather than the community standard for determining legal obscenity. Similar problems persist, however, in defining obscenity, despite the recognition in Pope that community standards will vary significantly and thereby subvert the universality of the First Amendment. Not only does the question of who is a "reasonable person" produce a

muddle, but "reasonable people" can be expected to disagree about whether a book, play, or movie is criminally obscene. See *Miller v. California*, U.S. Supreme Court Reports, vol. 413 (Washington, D.C.: U.S. Government Printing Office, 1974), 15–48; "High Court Refines Standard on Obscenity Cases," *New York Times*, May 5, 1987, B5; "Leave Sexually Oriented Art Alone," *New York Times*, May 22, 1987, A31; "Injustice in an 'Obscenity' Case," *New York Times*, February 18, 1988, A27; Hentoff, *The First Freedom*, 290–92; Feinberg, "Pornography and the Criminal Law," 129–30.

37. Wakeman, *Liberty and Purity*, 40–41; Wakeman to Elizur Wright, April 11, 1879, Elizur Wright Papers, Library of Congress; Paul and Schwartz, *Federal Censorship*, 146; Hentoff, *The First Freedom*, 284–85; and Feinberg, "Pornography and the Criminal Law," 117–20.

38. Hentoff, *The First Freedom*, 293.

39. Josephine S. Tilton to Elizur Wright, September 12, 1879, Elizur Wright Papers, Library of Congress; Heywood, *Cupid's Yokes*, 4; Wakeman, *Liberty and Purity*, 4; and Wakeman, *The Comstock Law Considered*, 41.

40. Comstock, *Frauds*, 392–93.

41. Putnam, *Four Hundred Years*, 519.

42. See, for example, *Take Back the Night: Women on Pornography*, ed. Laura Lederer (New York: Morrow, 1980).

Can a Woman Be an Individual?
Linda K. Kerber

An earlier version of this essay was published under the title, "Women and Individualism in American History" in *The Massachusetts Review* (Winter 1989), 589–609.

1. John Winthrop's Journal, "History of New England," 1630–1649, ed. James Kendall Hosmer (New York: Scribner's, 1908), 2:239.

2. The speech was given February 20, 1892. Elizabeth Cady Stanton, "The Solitude of Self," in *The History of Woman Suffrage*, ed. Susan B. Anthony and Ida Husted Harper (Rochester, N.Y., 1902), 4:189–90.

3. Myra Jehlen, *American Incarnation: The Individual, the Nation, and the Continent* (Cambridge: Harvard Univ. Press, 1986). Jehlen links the themes; as she puts it, "Incarnation—the idea that the methods of liberal individualism inheres in the American continent . . ." The writers she discusses are a triad—Emerson, Hawthorne, Melville; the similarities between Emerson and Thoreau "are characteristic of American thought" (11). Jehlen sees the identification of the individual with the wide expanse of land as "the great American tautology" (235). Annette Kolodny has written thoughtfully about the implications of this way of thinking about the American landscape. See Annette Kolodny, *The Lay of the Land: Metaphor as Experience and History in American Life and Letters* (Chapel Hill: Univ. of North Carolina Press, 1975) and *The Land Before Her: Fantasy and Experience of the American Frontiers, 1630–1860* (Chapel Hill: Univ. of North Carolina Press, 1984).

4. As John William Ward wrote some years ago when he wrestled with the same subject, the concept of individualism has had "massive emotional associations. . . . American culture has a deep affective stake in the historical connotations of the concept of individualism and will not lightly surrender it on the grounds of being responsible to some intellectual demand for historical accuracy and logical consistency." "The Ideal of Individualism and the Reality of Organization," in *Red, White, and Blue: Men, Books and Ideas in American Culture* (New York: Oxford Univ. Press, 1969), 260.

5. Gerald Moran and Maris Vinovskis, "The Puritan Family and Religion: A Critical Reappraisal," *William and Mary Quarterly* 3d ser., 39 (1982): 42–49. See also William J. Gilmore, "Elementary Literacy on the Eve of the Industrial Revolution: Trends in Rural New

England, 1760–1830," *Proceedings of the American Antiquarian Society* vol. 92, pt. 1 (1982): 87–171; and David D. Hall, *Worlds of Wonder, Days of Judgment: Popular Religious Belief in Early New England* (New York: Knopf, 1989), 32–34.

6. Carol Karlsen, *The Devil in the Shape of a Woman: Witchcraft in Colonial New England* (New York: W. W. Norton, 1987), 165.

7. Mary Maples Dunn, "Saints and Sisters: Congregational and Quaker Women in the Early Colonial Period," in *Women in American Religion*, ed. Janet Wilson James (Philadelphia: Univ. of Pennsylvania Press, 1980), 30–35.

8. William Secker, *A Wedding Ring, Fit for the Finger; or the Salve of Divinity on the Sore of Humanity, With Directions to Those Men that Want Wives, How to Choose Them, and to Those Women that Have Husbands, How to Use Them* 10th ed. (Portland, Maine: John McKown, 1806), 12, 14, 15, 22. Although Secker had died in 1681, his popular sermon was still being reprinted. On the extent to which gendered assumptions are embedded in the very conceptualization of rhetoric itself, and on the "mutually reflective relation between particular tropes and the orders they exemplify," see Patricia Parker, *Literary Fat Ladies: Rhetoric, Gender, Property* (London: Methuen, 1987), ch. 6, "Motivated Rhetorics: Gender, Order, Rule."

9. Clarence Faust and Thomas H. Johnson, eds., *Jonathan Edwards: Representative Selections* (New York: Hill and Wang, 1962), 56. Lacking as we do a large body of Puritan women's introspective literature, it is impossible to say how widely shared was the experience of "civil wars within," which Sacvan Bercovitch has so persuasively identified as the center of the Puritan man's religiosity. *The Puritan Origins of the American Self* (New Haven: Yale Univ. Press, 1975). In *Worlds of Wonder, Days of Judgment: Popular Religious Belief in Early New England* (New York: Knopf, 1989), David D. Hall offers a fresh and important interpretation of the mental world of Puritans that stresses the shared beliefs of women and men. But see Ivy Schweitzer, *The Work of Self-Representation: Lyric Poetry in Colonial New England* (Chapel Hill: Univ. of North Carolina Press, forthcoming 1991), for a brilliant interpretation of Puritan thought which examines "the discursive deployment of the metaphor of woman," and argues "that the sexes experienced the Puritan regimentation of selfhood differently: while women were subordinated, men were coerced."

10. See Marshall Berman, *The Politics of Authenticity: Radical Individualism and the Emergence of Modern Society* (New York: Atheneum, 1970).

11. For a subtle handling of this psychological pattern, see Peter Shaw, *American Patriots and the Rituals of Revolution,* (Cambridge: Harvard Univ. Press, 1981).

12. See Holly A. Mayer, "Belonging to the Army: Camp Followers and the Military Community During the American Revolution," Ph.D. diss., College of William and Mary, 1990. I have discussed this phenomenon in *Women of the Republic: Intellect and Ideology in Revolutionary America,* (Chapel Hill: Univ. of North Carolina Press, 1980), ch. 2, and " 'History Will Do It No Justice': Women and the Reinterpretation of the American Revolution," in *Women in the Age of the American Revolution*, ed., Ronald Hoffman (Charlottesville: Univ. of Virginia Press, 1989), 3–42.

13. *Women Invited to War. Or a Friendly Address to the Honourable Women of the United States. By a Daughter of America* (Boston, 1787). In her essay on Mary Moody Emerson, cited below, Phyllis Cole discusses Emerson's concern "with eternity [rather] than time . . . this unworldly consciousness in itself one expression of time and place, of a woman's opportunities and exclusions in the years of the early Republic" (5).

14. See Stephen A. Marini, *Radical Sects of Revolutionary New England* (Cambridge: Harvard Univ. Press, 1982); and Deborah Valenze, *Prophetic Sons and Daughters: Female Preaching and Popular Religion in Industrial England* (Princeton: Princeton Univ. Press, 1985).

15. Ruth Haskins Emerson to Mary Moody Emerson, July 20, 1813, Emerson Family Papers, Houghton Library, Harvard University. Cited by permission of the Ralph Waldo Emerson

Memorial Association and the Houghton Library. See also Phyllis Cole, "The Advantage of Loneliness: Mary Moody Emerson's Almanacks, 1802–1855," in *Emerson: Retrospect and Prospect*, ed. Joel Porte (Cambridge: Harvard Univ. Press, 1983), 1–32.

16. Mary Moody Emerson Journals, Emerson Family Papers, Houghton Library, Harvard University. Cole begins "The Advantage of Loneliness" by quoting Mary Moody Emerson's journal, 1804: "Were the genius of the Xian religion painted, her form would be full of majesty, her mien solemn, her aspect benign . . . " Cole adds her own gloss: "A single female form, unaccompanied by parents or husband or children, friends or congregation—raises its eyes directly to Heaven, without the intercession of priest or even redeeming Christ. In fact she hopes herself to intercede for others. . . . She seems a New England Rachel or Virgin Mary, but also a Jeremiah: an explicitly female figure, she nonetheless goes beyond the conventional piety of New England women in her separation from the domestic sphere and her unfeminine prophetic power. Such an idealization of the solitary self was radical for both its gender and its time: indeed a significant anticipation of the self-reliance that Mary's nephew Ralph Waldo Emerson would articulate as the primarily masculine romantic vision of the next generation." Cole discusses Emerson's "holy individualism" (6n. 9).

Mary Moody Emerson understood herself to be a "daughter of the revolution"; her father had been chaplain to the Concord minutemen, and he died en route home from Ticonderoga in 1777. She was raised as the ward of an impoverished aunt. Phyllis Cole writes: "William anticipated the Revolution as millennial glory: his daughter inherited the Revolution as social chaos, deprivation, orphanhood." On the fiftieth anniversary of the American Revolution, she writes, "Hail happy day—tho the revolution gave me to slavery of poverty & ignorance & long orphanship,—yet it gave my fellow men liberty" (7).

17. Quoted in Cole, "The Advantage of Loneliness," 10. See also Evelyn Barish, "Emerson and the Angel of Midnight: The Legacy of Mary Moody Emerson," in *Mothering the Mind: Twelve Studies of Writers and their Silent Partners*, eds. Ruth Perry and Martine Watson Brownley (New York: Holmes and Meier, 1984), 218–35.

18. Eleanor Read wrote in the long evangelical tradition of biography and autobiography that recounted an individual's struggle against sin. As David Hall has recently observed, this dramatization of the lives of ordinary men and women served some of the same functions that novels did in the imaginative lives of their readers. "Ordinary people thus learned that, whatever their worldly circumstances, they were actors in the greatest drama of them all. In this light we grasp why Bunyan wrote his masterpiece and why dozens of lay men and women in New England spoke and wrote so fluently about spiritual experience. Steady sellers—and remember, these were books presented to their readers as the truth—succeeded in the book trade because of their essential plot of sinners vitalized to overcome the Devil and gain saving grace." Hall, *Worlds of Wonder*, 57.

19. Samuel Worcester, *The Christian Mourning with Hope: A Sermon . . . on the Occasion of the Death of Mrs. Eleanor [Read] Emerson . . . To Which Are Annexed Writings of Mrs. Emerson* (Boston: Lincoln & Edmonds, 1809), 31–37, 55.

20. Ibid., 58–59, 39.

21. Ibid., 72. See also Joanna Bowen Gillespie, " 'The Clear Leadings of Providence': Pious Memoirs and the Problems of Self-Realization for Women in the Early Nineteenth Century," *Journal of the Early Republic* 5 (1985): 197–222.

22. See Linda K. Kerber, "Separate Spheres, Female Worlds, Woman's Place: The Rhetoric of Women's History," *Journal of American History* 75 (June 1988): 9–39.

23. See James T. Schleifer, *The Making of Tocqueville's Democracy in America* (Chapel Hill: Univ. of North Carolina Press, 1980), 245–59. Steven Lukes emphasizes that the French continue to stress "the opposition . . . between *individualisme* (implying anarchy and social atomization) and *individualité* (implying personal liberty and self-development). In French thought *individualisme* has almost always pointed to the sources of social dissolution. . . . "

"Types of Individualism," in *Dictionary of the History of Ideas*, ed. Philip Wiener (New York: Charles Scribner's Sons, 1973), 2:594.

24. Alexis de Tocqueville, *Democracy in America* (1832; reprint, New York: Knopf, 1945), vol. 2, bk. 2, chap. 2.

25. Ward, "The Ideal of Individualism," 237–38. But the meaning of individualism shifts; one must watch each author carefully for what they intend: In "Individualism Reconsidered," in *Individualism Reconsidered and Other Essays* (1951; reprint, Glencoe, N.Y.: Free Press, 1954). David Riesman opens by setting himself apart from "ruthless individualism" and, like David Potter, understands individualism to involve the freedom to develop one's private self and "escape from any particular group." Reisman wrote as social psychologist; concerned with the development of a "character-type," he set individualism off against the traditional town, with its "web of gossip and surveillance . . . " (35).

26. The link of individualism to the capitalist transformation has long been discussed; see C. B. MacPherson, *The Political Theory of Possessive Individualism* (Oxford: Clarendon Press, 1962); J. G. A. Pocock, *Virtue, Commerce and History* (Cambridge: Cambridge Univ. Press, 1985); and, most recently, Stephen Watts, *The Republic Reborn: War and the Making of Liberal America 1790–1820* (Baltimore: Johns Hopkins Univ. Press, 1987).

27. I have discussed the erosion of older systems of property relations by capitalism in "Separate Spheres, Female Worlds, Woman's Place: The Rhetoric of Women's History," *Journal of American History* 75 (June 1988): 21–23.

28. Mary P. Ryan, *Cradle of the Middle Class: The Family in Oneida County, New York 1790–1865* (New York: Cambridge Univ. Press, 1981). See also Richard Hofstadter, *The American Political Tradition and the Men Who Made It* (New York: Knopf, 1948) and John William Ward, *Andrew Jackson: Symbol for an Age* (New York: Oxford Univ. Press, 1955).

29. Kenneth S. Lynn, *The Air-Line to Seattle: Studies in Literary and Historical Writing About America* (Chicago: Univ. of Chicago Press, 1983), chap. 3, 27–32. See also Richard A. Grusin, " 'Put God in Your Debt': Emerson's Economy of Expenditure," *PMLA* 103 (1988): 35–44.

30. David Leverenz, "The Politics of Emerson's Man-Making Words," *PMLA* 101 (1986): 39. Leverenz is quoting a journal entry November–December 1841, in Joel Porte, ed., *Emerson in his Journals* (Cambridge: Harvard Univ. Press, 1982), 271.

31. "Essays: First Series," in *The Collected Works of Ralph Waldo Emerson* (Cambridge: Harvard Univ. Press, 1979), 191.

32. Carroll Smith-Rosenberg, *Disorderly Conduct: Visions of Gender in Victorian America* (New York: Knopf, 1985), 105, 108.

33. See Carole Shammas, Marylynn Salmon, and Michel Dahlin, *Inheritance in America* (New Brunswick: Rutgers Univ. Press, 1987), which, by emphasizing how extensive inheritance as a source of wealth (about 80 percent) is and has been, undermines even further the language of the self-made.

34. Margaret Fuller, *Woman in the Nineteenth Century* (New York: W. W. Norton, 1971) 38–40.

35. Ibid., 71.

36. Ibid., 95.

37. Quoted in Susan Phinney Conrad, *Perish the Thought: Intellectual Women in Romantic America 1830–1860* (New York: Oxford Univ. Press, 1976), 123.

38. Nina Baym, "Melodramas of Beset Manhood: How Theories of American Fiction Exclude Women Authors," *American Quarterly* 33 (1981): 132–33. "Both . . . the entrammelling society and the promising landscape . . . are depicted in unmistakably feminine terms, and this gives a sexual character to the protagonist's story which does, indeed, limit its applicability to women. And this sexual definition has melodramatic, misogynist implication . . . the encroaching, constricting, destroying society is represented with particular urgency in the figure of one or more women.

39. Elizabeth Janeway in *New York Times Book Review*, September 29, 1968; Sandra M. Gilbert and Susan Gubar, *The Madwoman in the Attic: The Woman Writer and the Nineteenth-Century Imagination* (New Haven: Yale Univ. Press, 1979), 483; Cynthia Ozick in *New York Times Book Review*, January 31, 1982.

40. Adam Smith, *An Inquiry into the Nature and Causes of the Wealth of Nations*, ed. Edwin Canaan (New York: Modern Library, Random House, 1937), bk. 5, 734.

41. Alice Duer Miller, quoted in Virginia Crocheron Gildersleeve, *Many a Good Crusade* (New York: Macmillan, 1954), 227–80.

42. Both colleges and political organizations could provide space that empowered women to make these claims. See, for example, Antoinette Brown's address at the Oberlin Ladies Department graduation, "Original Investigation Necessary to the Right Development of Mind," *Oberlin Evangelist*, September 29, 1847. Cited in Carol Lasser and Marlene Deahl Merrill, eds., *Friends and Sisters: Letters between Lucy Tone and Antoinette Brown Blackwell, 1846–93* (Urbana: Univ. of Illinois Press, 1987), 11. Planning a women's rights meeting in Worcester, Massachusetts, Lucy Stone wrote to Antoinette Brown: "The Anti-Slavery women I think are more intelligent than most women, at any rate they have *thought* more, and they talk good sense. Still many of them, are not accustomed to take comprehensive views, as men are. How long it will be before Women will even *begin*, to be what they ought to be. Still a great change is working, and the right *will come uppermost*. I dont now, ever wish that I was a man." Stone to Brown, June 9, 1850, Ibid., 73.

43. Linda K. Kerber, "Laura Ingalls Wilder," in *Notable American Women: The Modern Period*, ed. Barbara Sicherman and Carol Hurd Green (Cambridge: Harvard Univ. Press, 1980), 732–34. Rose Wilder Lane's papers are at the Herbert Hoover Presidential Library, West Branch, Iowa. For her influence on Laura Ingalls Wilder's work, see especially Box 12.

44. See, for example, Richard Pells, *The Liberal Mind in a Conservative Age* (New York: Harper and Row, 1985), 117–18. I have discussed this issue in "Diversity and the Transformation of American Studies," *American Quarterly* 41 (1989): 415–31.

45. When Riesman was invited to address women directly, however, as he did in a graduation address at a women's college, he would urge the students to make their own claims to an education that would "put pressure on life," open up new worlds of learning, encourage new ambitions, and make room for the problematic. See "Continuities and Discontinuities in Women's Education," Paper presented at commencement, Bennington College, 1956.

46. Robert Bellah et al., *Habits of the Heart: Individualism and Commitment in American Life* (Berkeley: Univ. of California Press, 1985). Although quotations from women are scattered throughout the book, only one of the main subjects of the interviews was a woman, and the descriptions of work that are central to the argument invariably refer to the significance of paid professional work to men. Thus Bellah can come to the easy conclusion that "a less frantic concern for advancement and a reduction of working hours for both men and women would make it easier for women to be full participants in the workplace without abandoning family life—and men would be freed to take on an equal role at home and in child care." His conclusion makes the assumption that there is a consensus that the methods of work *ought* to be made less brutally competitive or that men in large numbers will agree to do what women do.

Individualism and National Identity
Yehoshua Arieli

Reprinted by permission of the publishers from Yehoshua Arieli, *Individualism and Nationalism in American Ideology*, Cambridge, Mass.: Harvard Univ. Press, Copyright © 1964 by the President and Fellows of Harvard College.

1. James Bryce, *The American Commonwealth* (London: Macmillan, 1888), 2:404.

2. Ibid., 404–5.

3. Ibid., 406–7.

4. Ibid., 405.

5. Ibid., 406.

6. Ibid., 408.

7. Ibid., 407.

8. Ibid., 409.

9. Ibid., 409–10. See also his chapter "Kearneyism in California," ibid., 2:391.

10. See the list of names to which Bryce makes acknowledgment in his *American Commonwealth*. On Bryce's friendship with E. L. Godkin, see Herbert A. L. Fisher, *James Bryce* (London: Macmillan, 1927), 1:135–36; *Life and Letters of Edwin Lawrence Godkin*, ed. Rollo Ogden (New York: Macmilllan, 1907); also Robert H. Murray, *Studies in the English Social and Political Thinkers of the Nineteenth Century* (Cambridge: W. Heffer and Sons, 1929), 2:328–29.

11. Among others, see Allan Nevins, *Grover Cleveland: A Study in Courage* (New York: Dodd, Mead, & Co., 1948), 156ff; Matthew Josephson, *The Politicos, 1865–1896* (New York: Harcourt and Brace, 1938), 158–66; Van Wyck Brooks, *New England Indian Summer, 1865–1915* (New York: E. P. Dutton, 1940), 115–19; Ralph H. Gabriel, *The Course of American Democratic Thought: An Intellectual History Since 1815* (New York: Ronald Press, 1940), 178; Stow Persons, *Free Religion in American Faith* (New Haven: Yale Univ. Press, 1947), chaps. 2, 3, 4; F. B. Sanborn, "Social Science in Theory and Practice," *Journal of Social Science,* 9 (January 1878): 5–10.

12. Francis E. Abbott, "Organization," *The Radical* 2 (December 1866): 224.

13. Samuel Johnson, "The Spiritual Promise of America," *The Radical* 2 (April 1867): 453.

14. C. C. Shackford, "The Modern Problem Social, Not Political," *The Radical* 6 (December 1869): 441–54.

15. Johnson, "The Spiritual Promise of America," *The Radical* 2 (April 1867): 463.

16. William B. Scott, "Does Social Advancement Depend upon Political Organizations?" *The Radical* 6 (September 1869): 242.

17. Ibid., 244.

18. John W. Draper, *History of the Conflict Between Religion and Science* (New York: D. Appleton, 1876), 295.

19. Harry H. Clark, "The Vogue of Macaulay in America," *Wisconsin Academy of Sciences, Arts and Letters* (1941): 256. A full reprint of Macaulay's letters to H. S. Randall is given in "What Did Macaulay Say About America?" *Bulletin of the New York Public Library* 29 (July 1915): 463–73.

20. Clark, "The Vogue of Macaulay," 256.

21. For instances of the preoccupation of American liberals with Macaulay's prediction, see "The Communistic Movement," *Nation* 26 (May 9, 1878): 302–3; "The Dangers of Playing Tricks with the Labor Question," *Nation* 15 (September 5, 1872): 148; William G. Sumner, "Separation of State and Market," in *Earth, Hunger and Other Essays,* ed. Albert G. Keller (New Haven: Yale Univ. Press, 1913), 306–7; and Henry George, *Progress and Poverty* (New York: Robert Schalkonbach Foundation, 1880), 320–21, 506–20. See also "German Socialism in America," *North American Review* 127 (1879): 482–83.

22. William G. Sumner, "What Is Civil Liberty?" in *Earth, Hunger,* 127–28.

23. Sumner, "Separation of State and Market," in ibid., 308; Sumner, "State Interference," in *War and Other Essays,* ed. Albert G. Keller (New Haven: Yale Univ. Press, 1911), 219.

24. See William James on Godkin in Ogden, *Life and Letters of Edwin Lawrence Godkin*, 1:221; W. G. Bleyer, *Main Currents in the History of American Journalism* (Boston: Houghton Mifflin, 1927, 270–90. See also Edwin L. Godkin, "Aristocratic Opinions of Democracy," in his *Problems of Modern Democracy* (New York: Charles Scribner's Sons, 1896), 55–56; and "The Labor Crisis," *North American Review* 105 (July 1867): 183.

25. Godkin, "The Labor Crisis," 181, 186–90, 199–202.

26. Godkin, "Aristocratic Opinions," 55–64; Godkin, "The Duty of the Educated Man," in *Problems of Modern Democracy*, 216–17.

27. Godkin, "The Labor Crisis," 212–13.

28. Herbert Spencer designated his theories as philosophy of individualism for the first time in the Introduction to the American edition of *Social Statics; or, the Conditions Essential to Human Happiness Specified, and the First of Them Developed* (New York: D. Appleton, 1865), x. For the early recognition of Spencer as philosopher of individualism: Henry C. Carey, *Memoir of Stephen Colwell* (Philadelphia: H. C. Beard, 1871), 17–24; George F. Holmes, "Theory of Political Individualism," *DeBow's Review* 22 (February 1857): 133–49; Émile de Laveleye, "The State Versus the Man: A Criticism of Mr. Herbert Spencer," *Popular Science Monthly* 27 (1885): 165–87; Henry George, *A Perplexed Philosopher* (New York: C. L. Webster, 1892), 87; Arthur T. Hadley, "Individualism," in *New Encyclopedia of Social Reform*, ed. W. D. P. Bliss (New York: Funk and Wagnalls, 1908).

29. William James, "Herbert Spencer's Autobiography," in *Memories and Studies* (New York: Longmens Green, 1912), 140–41.

30. Laveleye, "The State Versus the Man." See also Ludwig Gumplowicz, *Grundriss der Sociologie* (Vienna: Wienman, 1885), 10–13.

31. For a general treatment of Spencer's influence in America see Richard Hofstadter, *Social Darwinism in American Thought* (Boston: George Braziller, 1955); Vernon L. Parrington, *Main Currents in American Thought* (New York: Harcourt Brace, 1927), 3:197–211; Bert J. Loewenberg, "Darwinism Comes to America, 1859–1908," *The Mississippi Valley Historical Review* 28 (December 1941): 352–56; Gabriel, *The Course of American Democratic Thought*, 154; Brooks, *New England Indian Summer*, 107–11, 262–63.

32. Quoted in Hofstadter, *Social Darwinism*, 21.

33. See Henry F. May, *Protestant Church and Industrial America* (New York: Harper, 1949), 142–47. Bert J. Loewenberg, "Controversy over Darwinism in New England, 1859–1873," *New England Quarterly* 8 (1935): 232–57.

34. See Lochner v. New York, 198 U.S. 45, in *Documents of American History*, ed. Henry S. Commager (New York: Appleton-Century Crofts, 1948), 2:221.

35. Samuel E. Morison and Henry S. Commager, *The Growth of the American Republic* (New York: Oxford, 1942), 2:86.

36. See Ida M. Tarbell, *Nationalizing of Business, 1878–1898* (New York: Macmillan, 1936), vol. 9 of *History of American Life* series, 30–31; Nevins, *Grover Cleveland*, 357–59; Arthur M. Schlesinger, *The Rise of the City, 1878–1898* (New York: Macmillan, 1933), vol. 10 of *History of American Life* series, 368–72; Ira V. Brown, *Lyman Abbott, Christian Evolutionist* (Cambridge: Harvard Univ. Press, 1953), 89–95; and Board of Indian Commissioners, *Seventeenth Annual Report for the Year 1885* (Washington, D.C., 1886), 73.

37. Lyman Abbott, *The Rights of Man: A Study in Twentieth Century Problems* (New York: Houghton Mifflin, 1901), 219–22.

38. See M. E. Gates, "Land and Law as Agents in Educating Indians," *Journal of Social Science* 21 (September 1886): 119. The article is identical with the report of Gates in Board of Indian Commissioners, *Seventeenth Annual Report*.

39. Gates, "Land and Law," *Journal of Social Science* 21 (1886): 134.

40. Ibid., 132.

41. Ibid., 134–35.

42. Board of Indian Commissioners, *Seventeenth Annual Report*, 96–97.

43. Ibid., 98.

44. Ibid., 90, 28.

45. See Hofstadter, *Social Darwinism*, 31; Hofstadter, *The American Political Tradition*, chap. 4; Charles E. Merriam, *American Political Ideas: Studies in the Development of American Political Thought* (New York: Macmillan, 1920), 324–25.

46. Charles A. Beard, "The Myth of Rugged American Individualism," *Harper's Magazine* 164 (December 1931): 20–21.

47. Henry George, *Progress and Poverty* (New York: Modern Library, 1938), 479.

48. Ibid., 478–81.

49. Spencer, *Social Statics*, 481–83.

50. Ibid., 474–77.

51. Ibid., 477–81.

52. Herbert Spencer to Horace Seal, quoted in David Duncan, *The Life and Letters of Herbert Spencer* (London: Williams and Norgate, 1908), 353. See also Murray, *Studies*, 2:25–26.

53. Ernest Barker, *Political Thought in England, 1848 to 1914* (London: Butterworth, 1930), 85. See Thomas C. Cochran and William Miller, *The Age of Enterprise, A Social History of Industrial America* (New York: Macmillan, 1942), 120.

54. Herbert Spencer, *The Man vs. the State: A Collection of Essays* (New York: Appleton, 1884), 65, 67; Spencer to J. A. Cairnes in Duncan, *Life and Letters*, 161, 300; see also Herbert Spencer, *Principles of Sociology* (London: Appleton, 1897), 3:563–64, 570ff; Herbert Spencer, *The Principles of Ethics* (New York: Appleton, 1892), 148–49.

55. The influence of Spencer's theory on the elaboration of a private-enterprise ideology has been repeatedly studied, and the literature on it is abundant. Among others, see Sigmund O. Diamond, *The Reputation of the American Businessman* (Cambridge: Harvard Univ. Press, 1955), chap. iii; Alfred W. Griswold, "The American Cult of Success," (Ph.D. diss., Yale Univ. 1933); Sidney Fine, "Laissez Faire and the General-Welfare State in American Thought" (Ph.D. diss., Univ. of Michigan, 1948); Hofstadter, *The American Political Tradition*, 166–85; John W. Hollenbach, "A Study of Economic Individualism in the American Novel from 1865 to 1888" (Ph.D. diss., Univ. of Wisconsin, 1941).

56. See Andrew Carnegie, *Autobiography* (New York: Houghton Mifflin, 1920), 327; and Carnegie, *The Gospel of Wealth, and Other Timely Essays* (New York: Century, 1900), 6, 7, 13.

57. See Herbert D. Croly, *Marcus Alonzo Hanna: His Life and Work* (New York: Macmillan, 1912), 464ff; see Andrew Carnegie, *The Empire of Business* (New York: Doubleday, Page, 1902); Carnegie, "The Road to Business Success," 18; and Carnegie, "How to Win a Fortune," 103–23.

58. Herbert Spencer, *Principles of Sociology* (New York: Williams and Norgate, 1877), 2:210–11.

59. Diamond, *Reputation of the American Businessman*, 53. See also Fine, "Laissez Faire and the General-Welfare State," 145–88; Josephson, *The Politicos*, 443–45.

60. Carnegie, *The Gospel of Wealth*, 5–6.

61. See, apart from Carnegie's work, Robert Shackleton, *Acres of Diamonds by Russell H. Conwell. His Life and Achievements* (New York: Harper, 1915), 18, 20; see also May, *Protestant Church and Industrial America*, 199–200; Henry F. Pringle, *Theodore Roosevelt: A Biography* (New York: Harcourt Brace, 1931), 26ff; Gustavus Myers, *History of the Great American Fortunes* (New York: Modern Library, 1936), 366–67, n. 17; Charles M. Schwab, *Succeeding With What You Have* (New York: Century, 1917), 63; Henry Wood, *Natural Law in the Business World* (Boston: Lee and Shephard, 1887), 220; Samuel C. T. Dodd, *Combinations: Their*

Uses and Abuses, with a History of the Standard Oil Trust (New York: G. F. Nesbett, 1888), 24; Cochran and Miller, *Age of Enterprise*, 331–32. See also the series of pamphlets published by the NAM in the first decade of the twentieth century; for instance, Pamphlet No. 1, "Class Distinction and Americanism," NAM (May 19, 1909) and Pamphlet No. 4, "The Next Step in Education," 9–18.

62. Henry Clews, *Individualism versus Socialism* (New York: N.p., 1907), 1–3.

63. *The American Individual Enterprise System: Its Nature, Evolution, and Future*, Economic Principles Commission of the N.M.A. (New York: McGraw-Hill, 1946), 2:1018–21. For an identical formulation, see *Facing the Future's Risk: Studies Toward Predicting the Unforeseen*, ed. Lyman Bryson (New York: Harper, 1953), 248–73; see also "Individualism Comes of Age," *Fortune* 43 (February 1951): 113–15.

64. See especially Diamond, *Reputation of the American Businessman*.

65. Frederick J. Turner, "The Significance of the Frontier in American History," in *The Frontier in American History* (New York: Holt, 1920), 29–32; Turner, "The Problems of the West," ibid., 205–6; Turner, "The Mississippi Valley," ibid., 203.

66. Turner, "Pioneer Ideal and the State University," ibid., 271–72, 279–80; "The Contribution of the West to American Democracy," ibid., 258; and "The Significance of the Frontier," ibid., 30–35.

67. Turner, "The Mississippi Valley," ibid., 203.

68. Ibid., 204.

69. R. T. Ely, "Report of the Organization of the American Economic Association," in *Publications of the American Economic Association* (1886), 1:6–7.

70. See Fine, "Laissez Faire and the General-Welfare State," 325–28.

71. Richard T. Ely, *The Past and Present of Political Economy* (Baltimore: Johns Hopkins Univ. Press, 1884), vol. 3; Ely, *Recent American Socialism* (Baltimore: Johns Hopkins Univ. Press, 1885), vol. 4; see also Ely's opening address at the founding convention of the AEA in *Publications of the AEA* 1 (1886): 15–16.

72. Ely, *Past and Present of Political Economy*, 48.

73. "Report," *Publications of the AEA* 1 (1886): 22ff.

74. Henry C. Adams, "Relation of the State to Industrial Action," *Publications of the AEA*, 1 (1887); 490 n. 2, and 479, 477, 482–83.

75. Ibid., 499–500.

76. Ibid., 546.

77. Ibid., 542–44. See the change of opinions in Clark concerning individualism by comparing "The Nature and Progress of True Socialism," *The New Englander* 38 (July 1879): 566, 571 with John B. Clark, *The Philosophy of Wealth* (Boston: Ginn, 1886), 176, 201, 207; Woodrow Wilson, *The State* (Boston: Heath, 1889), 620–38. On the influence of Clark on Wilson see William Diamond, *The Economic Thought of Woodrow Wilson* (Baltimore: AMS, 1943), 37.

78. Charles H. Hopkins, *The Rise of the Social Gospel in American Protestantism, 1865–1915* (New Haven: Yale Univ. Press, 1940), 319.

79. See R. H. Newton, "Communism," *Unitarian Review* 16 (December 1881): 485ff; Roswell D. Hitchcock, *Socialism* (New York: A. D. F. Randolph, 1879); Joseph Cook, *Socialism* (Boston: Houghton Mifflin, 1880); John B. Clark, "How to Deal with Communism," *New Englander* 37 (July 1878): 533ff; Adolphus J. F. Behrends, *Socialism and Christianity* (New York: Baker and Taylor, 1886); Washington Gladden, "The Strength and Weakness of Socialism," *Century Magazine* 31 (February 1886): 736–49; Gladden, "Socialism and Unsocialism," *Forum* 3 (April 1887): 122–30; Edward W. Bemis, "Socialism and the State Action," *Journal of Social Science* 21 (September 1886): 52–66; John Bascom, "The Gist of the Labor Question," *Forum* 4 (September 1887): 87–95; Frederic D. Huntington, "Causes of Social

Discontent," *Forum* 6 (September 1888): 2–9; Nicholas P. Gilman, *Socialism and the American Spirit* (New York: Houghton Mifflin, 1893); Franklin M. Sprague, *Socialism from Genesis to Revelation* (Boston: Zee and Shepard, 1893).

80. Quoted in May, *Protestant Church and Industrial America*, 65–66.

81. Gladden, "Socialism and Unsocialism," 129; see also F. D. Huntington, "Causes of Social Discontent," *Forum* 6 (1888): 2–3; Bascom, "The Gist of the Labor Question," *Forum* 4 (1887): 95; and Gladden, "Three Dangers," *Century Magazine* 28 (1884): 620ff.

82. John Rae, *Contemporary Socialism* (New York: Charles Scribner and Sons, 1891), 395.

83. See, among others, Sidney Ratner, *A Political and Social History of Federal Taxation* (New York: W. W. Norton, 1942), 177, 183, 186, 200; Chester McArthur Destler, "The Opposition of American Businessmen to Social Control during the 'Gilded age,' " *Mississippi Valley Historical Review* 39 (March 1953): 641–72; Benjamin R. Twiss, *Lawyers and the Constitution; How Laissez-faire Came to the Supreme Court* (Princeton: Princeton Univ. Press, 1942).

84. See Herbert Hoover's *American Individualism* (New York: Doubleday, 1922).

85. George D. Ellis, comp., *Platforms of the Two Great Political Parties—1856–1928* (Washington, D.C.: Government Printing Office [hereafter GPO], 1928), 165–66; see also correspondence between Taft and Roosevelt from 1907 to 1908 in Henry F. Pringle, *The Life and Times of William Howard Taft: A Biography* (New York: Farrar and Rinehart, 1939), 1:341–42, 347.

86. William Griffith, ed., *The Roosevelt Policy* (New York: Current Literature Publishing Co., 1919), 2:513.

87. Theodore Roosevelt, *Works* (New York: Charles Scribner's, 1926), 18:393; see also "Nationalism and Special Privilege," *Outlook* 97 (January 28, 1911): 145.

88. *Platforms of the Two Great Political Parties*, 181.

89. Elihu Root, *Essentials of the Constitution* (Washington: GPO, 1913), *Senate Document No. 168*, 63d Cong., 1st sess., 3; William Allen White, *Autobiography* (New York: Ayer, 1946), 469–71. On Root's role in the convention of 1912, see George E. Mowry, *Theodore Roosevelt and the Progressive Movement* (Madison: Univ. of Wisconsin Press, 1946), 462. For similar views of Root see "The Union League Club," Root, *Miscellaneous Addresses*, ed. Robert Bacon and James B. Scott (Cambridge: Harvard Univ. Press, 1917), 124–25; "The Preservation of American Ideals," ibid., 259–65; "Business and Politics," ibid., 249–57. See also "Socialism and Its Menace: Why Government Ownership Would Not Help the Wage Earners," the views of President Taft as reported by Charles Dewey Hilles in *Century Magazine* 84 (October 1912): 943–48. The classical document of this Republican outlook is given in the new edition of Herbert Spencer's *The Man vs. the State: A Collection of Essays*, ed. Truxton Beale (New York: Kennedy, 1916), in which Truxton Beale, Elihu Root, Henry Cabot Lodge, E. M. Gary, Nicholas M. Butler, David J. Hill, Harlan F. Stone, and Charles W. Eliot applied Spencer's view to the contemporary scene by critical and interpretative essays.

90. William J. Bryan, *Speeches of William J. Bryan* (New York: N.p., 1909), 2:88–89; William J. Bryan, "Individualism versus Socialism," *Century Magazine* 71 (1906): 856–57.

91. Thomas R. Marshall, "The Automatic Citizen," *Atlantic Monthly*, August 1912, 297, 300–330; Woodrow Wilson, *The New Freedom: A Call for the Emancipation of the Generous Energies of a People* (New York: Doubleday, 1919), 57.

92. Chester McArthur Destler, "The Influence of Edward Kellog upon American Radicalism," *Journal of Political Economy* 40 (1932): 345–63; James J. Martin, *Man against the State*, 109–10, 142–44, 202–3; John R. Commons et al., *History of Labor in the United States* (New York: Doubleday, 1918–35), 2:136–44, 337–400, 167–71, 244–48; Terence V. Powderly, *Thirty Years of Labor, 1859 to 1889* (Columbus: Excelsior, 1890), 234ff; Frederick E. Haynes,

Third Party Movements Since the Civil War, with Special Reference to Iowa (Iowa City: State Historical Society of Iowa, 1916), 93–96; John D. Hicks, *The Populist Revolt: A History of the Farmers' Alliance and the People's Party* (Minneapolis: Univ. of Minnesota Press, 1931, 427–30; see also *The Labor Movement: The Problem of Today,* ed. George E. MacNeill (Boston: A. M. Bridgman, 1887) with Terence Powderly, R. Heber Newton, Henry George, and others. In chapter iv., "The Labour Movement in America to 1861," MacNeill traces the aspirations of organized labor back to the founders of the Republic and the ideals of New England civilization. Josiah Warren's ideas are fully appreciated in their significance for the labor movement (ibid., 67–73).

93. John G. Brooks, *American Syndicalism: the I.W.W.* (New York: Ayer, 1913), 641; *Socialism and American Life,* ed. Donald D. Egbert and Stow Persons (Princeton: Princeton Univ. Press, 1952), 1:497.

94. See Daniel Bell, "The Background and Development of Marxian Socialism in the United States," in *Socialism and American Life,* ed. Egbert and Persons, 1:215–22; Sidney Hook, "The Philosophical Basis of Marxian Socialism in the United States," ibid., 450–51.

95. See Henry George's interpretation of the Jeffersonian philosophy and his confrontation with the concepts of socialism and individualism in *Progress and Poverty* (New York: Sterling, 1880), 316–21, 455–56; Louis F. Post and Fred C. Leubuscher, *An Account of the George-Hewitt Campaign in the New York Municipal Election of 1886* (New York: J. W. Lovell, 1887), 27–28, 53; Henry George, *Protection or Free Trade, in Complete Works,* 10 vols. (New York: Tribner, 1911), 304–6, 308–10; George's absolute rejection of socialism in his *The Science of Political Economy* (New York: Schalkenbach Foundation, 1898), 198.

96. Hamlin Garland, "A New Declaration of Rights," *Arena* 3 (January 1891): 159, 160.

97. Ibid., 167–68.

A Confusion of Voices
Lawrence B. Goodheart and Richard O. Curry

1. Charles A Lindbergh, *The Spirit of St. Louis* (New York: Charles Scribner's Sons, 1953), 191–92. See also Lindbergh, *Autobiography of Values* (New York: Harcourt Brace Jovanovich, 1976), 120.

2. Coolidge quoted in John Williams Ward, "The Meaning of Lindbergh's Flight," *American Quarterly* 10 (1958): 14.

3. Ward, "Lindbergh's Flight." See also Ward, "Tumult in the Clouds," *New York Review of Books,* June 23, 1977, 32–34.

4. Henry Clews quoted in Yehoshua Arieli, *Individualism and Nationalism* (Cambridge: Harvard Univ. Press, 1964), 336.

5. Russell H. Conwell, *Acres of Diamonds* (New York: Harper and Row, 1943), 21.

6. Finley Peter Dunne, *Dissertations by Mr. Dooley* (New York: Harper and Brothers, 1906), 37.

7. Booker T. Washington, *Up from Slavery* (New York: Doubleday, 1970), 108.

8. Herbert Hoover, *American Individualism* (New York: Doubleday, Page and Co., 1922), 7–10.

9. Henry D. Lloyd, *Wealth against Commonwealth* (New York: Harper and Brothers, 1894), 494–97.

10. Randolph S. Bourne, "This Older Generation," *The Atlantic Monthly,* September 1915, 387.

11. Walter Rauschenbusch, *A Theology for the Social Gospel* (New York: Macmillan, 1917), 147, 184.

12. Herbert Croly, *The Promise of American Life* (New York: Macmillan, 1909), 148–54.

13. Theodore Roosevelt quoted in Bernard Bailyn et al., *The Great Republic* (Boston: D. C. Heath, 1977), 927.

14. Theodore Roosevelt quoted in Richard N. Current, John A. Garraty, and Julia Weinberg, *Words That Made American History Since the Civil War*, 3d ed. (Boston: Little Brown, 1962), 303.

15. Frank Tariello, Jr., *The Reconstruction of American Political Ideology* (Charlottesville: Univ. of Virginia Press, 1982), 13.

16. Otis L. Graham, Jr., *An Encore for Reform: The Old Progressives and the New Deal* (New York: Oxford Univ. Press, 1967), 166–67, 175–76.

17. Daniel Lazare, "If the '80s Are like the '20s, Are These the Bad Old Days?" *In These Times*, November 12–18, 1986, 8, 10.

18. Richard H. Pells, *Radical Visions and American Dreams: Culture and Society in the Depression Years* (New York: Harper and Row, 1973), 114–15.

19. Ibid., 118–25; Charles A. Beard, "The Myth of Rugged American Individualism," *Harper's Magazine*, December 1931, 22.

20. John Dewey, *Individualism Old and New* (New York: Minton, Balch and Co., 1930), 30.

21. Pells, *Radical Visions*, 123.

22. Dewey, *Individualism*, 113.

23. Franklin Delano Roosevelt, "The Text of the Inaugural Address," *New York Times*, March 5, 1933, 3.

24. Samuel I. Rosenman, ed., *Public Papers and Addresses of Franklin Delano Roosevelt* (New York: Random House, 1938), 5:488.

25. Rexford G. Tugwell, *The Battle for Democracy* (New York: Greenwood Press, 1969), 95–96.

26. Thomas C. Cochran, *Challenges to American Values: Society, Business, Religion* (New York: Oxford Univ. Press, 1985), 29.

27. Arthur Schlesinger, Jr., *The Vital Center: The Politics of Freedom* (Boston: Houghton Mifflin, 1949).

28. John Kenneth Galbraith, *The Affluent Society* (Boston: Houghton Mifflin, 1958), 269.

29. Lyndon Baines Johnson, *The Vantage Point: Perspectives of the Presidency, 1963–1969* (New York: Holt, Rhinehart, and Winston, 1971), 345.

30. Bernard Schwartz, *The Unpublished Opinions of the Warren Court* (New York: Oxford Univ. Press, 1985), 17.

31. Vance Packard, *The Status Seekers* (New York: Pocket Books, 1959).

32. Arthur A. Ekirch, Jr., "Individuality in American History," in *Essays on Individuality*, ed. Felix Morley (Philadelphia: Univ. of Pennsylvania Press, 1958), 221.

33. David Riesman, Reuel Denny, and Nathan Glazer, *The Lonely Crowd: A Study of the Changing American Character* (New Haven: Yale Univ. Press, 1950), 83; Riesman, *Individualism Reconsidered and Other Essays* (Glencoe, N.Y.: Free Press, 1954), 99–100.

34. William H. Whyte, Jr., *The Organization Man* (Garden City, N.Y.: Doubleday, 1957), 11–13, 439, 448.

35. Norman Mailer, "The White Negro," in *The American Experience: Radical Reader*, ed. Harold Jaffe and John Tytell (New York: Harper and Row, 1970), 23.

36. Norman O. Brown, "Apocalypse: The Place of Mystery in the Life of the Mind," *Harper's Magazine*, May 1961, 47–49.

37. Paul Goodman, "The Empty Society," *Commentary* 42 (November 1965): 59.

38. Herbert Marcuse, *An Essay on Liberation* (Boston: Beacon Press, 1969), 4; Robert P. Wolff, Barrington Moore, Jr., and Herbert Marcuse, *A Critique of Pure Tolerance* (Boston: Beacon Press, 1965), 109.

39. The Port Huron Statement quoted in Loren Baritz, ed., *The American Left: Radical Political Thought in the Twentieth Century* (New York: Basic Books, 1971), 392–93.

40. Philip Slater, *The Pursuit of Loneliness: American Culture at the Breaking Point* (Boston: Beacon Press, 1976), 15–16, 33–37. His *The Glory of Hera: Greek Mythology and the Greek Family* (Boston: Beacon Press, 1968) concludes that a destructive narcissistic motivation was at the heart of ancient Greek culture as well as contemporary American society.

41. Charles A. Reich, *The Greening of America* (New York: Random House, 1970), 356.

42. Christopher Lasch, *The Agony of the American Left* (New York: Knopf, 1969), 182, 209.

43. Christopher Lasch, *The Culture of Narcissism: American Life in an Age of Diminishing Expectations* (New York: W. W. Norton, 1978), 66.

44. Robert N. Bellah et al., *Habits of the Heart: Individualism and Commitment in American Life* (Berkeley: Univ. of California Press, 1985), 142.

45. Herbert J. Gans, *Middle American Individualism: The Future of Liberal Democracy* (New York: Free Press, 1988), 103–4. Peter Clecak's *America's Quest for the Ideal Self: Dissent and Fulfillment in the 60s and 70s* (New York: Oxford Univ. Press, 1983) argues, contrary to Lasche and Bellah, that the search for "full personhood" was largely a beneficial phenomenon and that the alarm over rampant selfishness was overplayed.

46. Gans, *Middle American Individualism*, 155.

47. Ayn Rand, *Capitalism: The Unknown Ideal* (New York: New American Library, 1966), 192.

48. Milton and Rose Friedman, *Free to Choose: A Personal Statement* (New York: Harcourt Brace Jovanovich, 1980), 7.

49. William E. Simon, *A Time for Truth* (New York: McGraw-Hill, 1978), 221.

50. Murray Rothbard, *Power and Market: Government and the Economy* (Kansas City: Sheed Andrews and McMeel, 1970), vi.

51. Stephen L. Newman, *Liberalism at Wit's End: The Libertarian Revolt against the Modern State* (Ithaca: Cornell Univ. Press, 1984), 43.

52. Robert Nozick, *Anarchy, State and Utopia* (New York: Basic Books, 1974), 334.

53. Ronald Reagan "Second Inaugural Speech," *New York Times*, January 22, 1985, A17; "State of the Union," *New York Times*, January 26, 1988, A16.

54. Garry Wills, *Reagan's America: Innocents at Home* (New York: Doubleday, 1987), 94.

55. The data in the preceding paragraphs was found in: "Scandals at the Fed?" *Dollars and Sense* 125 (April 1987): 10–11, 22; "1990 and the Profits of Doom," *In These Times*, September 30–October 6, 1987, 19; "Forbes Ranks Richest People," *New York Times*, October 13, 1987, D2; "Tax Burden is Found to Rise for Poor in U.S.," *New York Times*, November 12, 1987, A26; "Rising Tide, Sinking Boats," *New York Times*, September 3, 1988, A2; "Children in Poverty," *Willimantic Chronicle*, April 16, 1990, 1, 7.

56. Richard O. Curry, "Keeping America Pure: the Surreal World of McCarran-Walter," *Curbstone Ink* (September 1989): 3–4; Mark Schapiro, "The Excludables," in *Freedom at Risk: Secrecy, Censorship, and Repression in the 1980s*, ed. Richard O. Curry (Philadelphia: Temple Univ. Press, 1988), 162–69.

57. "Reports of the McCarran Walter Act's death are greatly exaggerated," wrote Georgetown University law professor David Cole. "Its spirit lives on in the 1990 revisions." For example, immigrants can still be barred for mere membership in the Communist party; and it bars officials and representatives of the Palestine Liberation Organization. The law's language

defining terrorism is so sweeping, Cole continues, that "the government could deport every alien who collected donations for the African National Congress during Nelson Mandela's visit, and Mr. Mandela himself would be barred from entering." The law also permits the Secretary of State to exclude individuals whose presence involves "potentially serious foreign policy considerations" without revealing the reasons for or evidence upon which such exclusions are based. This authority, Senator Daniel Patrick Moynihan declared, "constitutes a deeply regrettable retreat from our efforts to expunge the cold war from our statutes." See David Cole, "McCarran-Walter Reborn?" *The Washington Post,* November 18, 1990 and the *Congressional Record–Senate,* 101st Congress, October 26, 1990, S 17114–16.

58. Judith Koffler, "The New Seditious Libel," in Curry, *Freedom at Risk,* 147–52.

59. Ibid., 21.

60. Ibid., 12–13.

61. Ibid., 15.

62. On President Bush's policy in appointing federal judges at all levels, see especially Linda Greenhouse, "Bush Travels Reagan's Course in Nominating Judges," *New York Times,* April 8, 1990.

63. Curry, *Freedom at Risk,* 3.

Suggested Reading

Individualism in Trans-National Context
Richard O. Curry and Lawrence B. Goodheart

Individualism is a major theme that runs throughout Western culture. It is discussed in passing in many works, but relatively few scholars have dealt with it in depth. The philosopher Steven Lukes provides an essential starting point with his precise definitions of the word. See his "The Meanings of 'Individualism,'" *Journal of the History of Ideas* 32 (1971): 45–66; and "Types of Individualism," *Dictionary of the History of Ideas,* 4 vols. (New York: Charles Scribner's Sons, 1973), 2:594–604.

A definitive history of the individualism in Western European thought remains to be written. Pertinent general works include: Steven Lukes, *Individualism* (New York: Harper and Row, 1973); Thomas C. Heller, Morton Sosna, and David E. Wellberg, eds., *Reconstructing Individualism: Autonomy, Individuality, and the Self in Western Thought* (Stanford: Stanford Univ. Press, 1986); Roger Chartier, ed., *A History of Private Life: Passions of the Renaissance* (Cambridge: Harvard Univ. Press, 1988); and Koenrad W. Swart, "Individualism in the Mid-Nineteenth Century (1826–1860)," *Journal of the History of Ideas* 23 (1962): 77–90.

On the national level, the following studies are instructive. On France, see Steven Lukes, *Individualism* (New York: Harper and Row, 1973); Marshall Berman, *The Politics of Authenticity: Radical Individualism and the Emergence of Modern Society* (New York: Atheneum, 1970); and James T. Schliefer, *The Making of Tocqueville's Democracy in America* (Chapel Hill: Univ. of North Carolina Press, 1980). On Germany, see Koppel S. Pinson, *German Pietism as a Factor in the Rise of German Nationalism* (New York: Columbia Univ. Press, 1934); Georg G. Iggers, *The German Conception of History: The National Tradition of Historical Thought from Herder to the Present* (Middletown, Conn.: Wesleyan Univ. Press, 1968); and Elie Kedourie, *Nationalism* (London: Hutchinson Univ. Library, 1966). On England, see C. B. MacPherson, *The Political Theory of Possessive Individualism: Hobbes to Locke* (Oxford: Oxford Univ. Press, 1962); and Alan Macfarlane, *The Origins of English Individualism: The Family, Property, and Social Transition* (New York: Cambridge Univ. Press, 1978). The outstanding work on the United States is Yehoshua Arieli, *Individualism and Nationalism in American*

Ideology (Cambridge: Harvard Univ. Press, 1964). See also J. R. Pole's Rhodes lecture, which is reprinted as *American Individualism and the Promise of Progress* (Oxford: Clarendon Press, 1980).

The Emergence of an Individualistic Ethos in American Society
Richard O. Curry and Karl E. Valois

This essay is a broad-based analysis of the emergence of an individualistic ethos in American society. The topic is far too complex to provide a useful short list, whereas a longer one would be redundant. The reader is referred to the notes at the end of this essay for suggested readings on specialized topics such as religion and reform, perfectionism, the emergence of a market economy, the transportation and industrial revolutions, politics and literature.

Religion and Individualism in Early America
Robert M. Calhoon

Much broader than its title suggests, J. E. Crowley, *This Sheba, Self: The Conceptualization of Economic Life in Eighteenth-Century America* (Baltimore: Johns Hopkins Univ. Press, 1974) looks closely at individuals trying to understand their relationship to society and values, often a religious struggle. Joyce Appleby, "Value and Society," in *Colonial British America: Essays in the New History of the Early Modern Era*, ed. Jack P. Greene and J. R. Pole (Baltimore: Johns Hopkins Univ. Press, 1984) is also an excellent introduction to colonial individualism. Though sharply torn between their senses of themselves as individual children of God and as members of the body of Christ, Puritans articulated this tension in sources quoted in David D. Hall, ed., *The Antinomian Movement: A Documentary History* (Middletown, Conn.: Wesleyan Univ. Press, 1968); Charles Hambrick-Stowe, *The Practice of Piety: Puritan Devotional Disciplines in Seventeenth-Century New England* (Chapel Hill: Univ. of North Carolina Press, 1984); and Philip F. Gura, *A Glimpse of Sion's Glory: Puritan Radicalism in New England, 1620–1660* (Middletown, Conn.: Wesleyan Univ. Press, 1984). Mitchell Robert Breitwieser, *Cotton Mather and Benjamin Franklin: The Price of Representative Personality* (Cambridge, Eng.: Cambridge Univ. Press, 1984) is a marvelous study of two colonial exponents of personal self-consciousness. Jonathan Edwards's contribution to individualism can be found conveniently in many of chapters of Nathan O. Hatch and Harry S. Stout, eds., *Jonathan Edwards and the American Experience* (New York: Oxford Univ. Press, 1988). Rhys Isaac, *The Transformation of Virginia, 1740–1790* (Chapel Hill: Univ. of North Carolina Press, 1982), Robert M. Calhoon, *Evangelicals and Conservatives in the Early South, 1740–1861* (Columbia: Univ. of South Carolina Press, 1988), Nathan O. Hatch, *The Democratization of American Christianity* (New Haven: Yale Univ. Press, 1989), and Jon Butler, *Awash in a Sea of Faith: Christianizing the American People* (Cambridge: Harvard Univ. Press, 1990) all explore the rise of an evangelical self-consciousness. Finally, Steven Watts, *The Republic Reborn: War and the Making of Liberal America* (Baltimore: Johns Hopkins Univ. Press, 1987) assesses the religious, political, and philosophical underpinnings of individualism in the new Republic.

Individualism in the Early Republic
Robert E. Shalhope

Those interested in the development of individualism in American culture in the late eighteenth and early nineteenth centuries must be aware of the fact that the word "individualism" did not come into common usage in America until the last two decades of the nineteenth century. Americans in the revolutionary and early national eras employed such terms as "self-reliance," "self-help," or "independence" to articulate their deep belief in the power of the individual or individuality. Therefore, students investigating the emergence of individualism in late eighteenth-century America should focus not upon the use of the term but upon the changing conditions present in the culture that enhanced the opportunity for the development of personal choices—that promoted the emergence of "masterless men."

For an excellent discussion of the term "individualism," see Koenrad W. Swart, "'Individualism' in the Mid-Nineteenth Century (1826–1860)," *The Journal of the History of Ideas* 23 (1962): 77–90. J. R. Pole offers an insightful analysis of both the use of the term and the emergence of conditions conducive to the rise of individualism in *American Individualism and the Promise of Progress* (Oxford: Clarendon Press, 1980). Yehoshua Arieli places the concept of individualism in an even broader context in his *Individualism and Nationalism in American Ideology* (Cambridge: Harvard Univ. Press, 1964).

The conflict between proponents and opponents of hierarchy in late eighteenth-century America contributed greatly to the creation of cultural conditions that promoted individual choices and opportunities. Kenneth Lockridge provides an excellent analysis of the struggle over hierarchy in his *Settlement and Unsettlement: The Crisis of Political Legitimacy before the Revolution* (New York: Cambridge Univ. Press, 1981). Jackson Turner Main presents a provocative analysis of the tension between localists and cosmopolitans in his *Political Parties before the Constitution* (Chapel Hill: Univ. of North Carolina Press, 1973). For insights into this strain in specific locales, see David Szatmary, *Shays' Rebellion: The Making of an Agrarian Insurrection* (Amherst: Univ. of Massachusetts Press, 1980); Thomas Slaughter, *The Whiskey Rebellion: Frontier Epilogue to the American Revolution* (New York: Oxford Univ. Press, 1986); James P. Whittenburg, "Planters, Merchants and Lawyers: Social Change and the Origins of North Carolina Regulators," *William and Mary Quarterly* 3d ser., 34 (1977): 215–38; and Robert E. Shalhope, "South Carolina in the Founding Era: A Localist Perspective," *South Carolina Historical Magazine* 89 (1988): 102–13.

Works that analyze the differences between Federalist and Jeffersonian perceptions of the individual and society include: John Zvesper, *Political Philosophy and Rhetoric: A Study of the Origins of American Party Politics* (New York: Cambridge Univ. Press, 1977); David H. Fischer, *The Revolution of American Conservatism: The Federalist Party in the Era of Jeffersonian Democracy* (New York: Harper and Row, 1965); James M. Banner, Jr., *To the Hartford Convention: The Federalists and the Origins of Party Politics in Massachusetts, 1789–1815* (New York: Knopf, 1970); Drew R. McCoy, *The Elusive Republic: Political Economy in Jeffersonian America* (Chapel Hill: Univ. of North Carolina Press, 1980); and Joyce Appleby, *Capitalism and a New Social Order: The Republican Vision of the 1790s* (New York: New York Univ. Press, 1984).

Recently, historians have begun to analyze the dialectical relationship between communal and individualistic attitudes so vital to understanding American culture in the early Republic. Scholars dealing with this phenomenon include: Rowland Berthoff, "Independence and Attachment, Virtue and Interests: From Republican Citizen to Free Enterpriser, 1787–1837," in *Uprooted Americans: Essays to Honor Oscar Handling*, ed. Richard Bushman et al. (Boston: Little, Brown & Co., 1979), 99–124; Steven Watts, *The Republic Reborn: War and the Making of Liberal America, 1790–1820* (Baltimore: Johns Hopkins Univ. Press, 1987); James Kloppenberg, "The Virtues of Liberalism: Christianity, Republicanism, and Ethics in Early American Political Discourse," *Journal of American History* 74 (1987): 9–33; and Robert E. Shalhope, *The Roots of Democracy: American Thought and Culture, 1760–1800* (Boston: Twayne Publishers, 1990).

The Slow Triumph of Liberal Individualism
James A. Henretta

Louis Hartz's *The Liberal Tradition in America* (New York: Harcourt Brace, 1955) remains the point of departure for an understanding of nineteenth-century liberalism in the United States. More recent studies of merit include: Joyce Appleby, *Capitalism and a New Social Order: The Republican Vision of the 1790s* (New York: New York Univ. Press, 1984) and John P. Diggins, *The Lost Soul of American Politics: Virtue, Self-Interest, and the Foundations of Liberalism* (New York: Basic Books, 1984).

The creation of a liberal, capitalist system of legal doctrine is described in the pathbreaking study by Morton J. Horwitz, *The Transformation of American Law, 1780–1860* (Cambridge: Harvard Univ. Press, 1977). More specialized studies that reveal the continuing importance of republican, patriarchal legal concepts are: Marylynn Salmon, *Women and the Law of Property in Early America* (Chapel Hill: Univ. of North Carolina Press, 1986); Norma Basch, *In the Eyes of the Law: Women, Marriage, and Property in Nineteenth-Century New York* (Ithaca: Cornell Univ. Press, 1982); and Michael Grossberg, *Governing the Hearth: Law and the Family in Nineteenth-Century America* (Chapel Hill: Univ. of North Carolina Press, 1985).

Few studies probe the relationship among individual rights, political parties, and state power during the early nineteenth century. Lee Benson, *The Concept of Jacksonian Democracy: New York as a Test Case* (Princeton: Princeton Univ. Press, 1964) opened up many avenues of scholarly research. More recent studies of significance are: Ronald P. Formisano, *The Transformation of Political Culture: Massachusetts Parties, 1790s–1840s* (New York: Oxford Univ. Press, 1983); Richard L. McCormick, *The Party Period and Public Policy: American Politics from the Age of Jackson to the Progressive Era* (New York: Oxford Univ. Press, 1986); and Michael E. McGerr, *The Decline of Popular Politics: The American North, 1865–1928* (New York: Oxford Univ. Press, 1986).

The Right to Self-Government
Richard O. Curry

The most comprehensive analysis of the individualistic and anti-institutional aspects of abolitionist thought during the antebellum years is contained in Lewis Perry's *Radical Abolitionism: Anarchy and the Kingdom of God in Abolitionist Thought* (Ithaca: Cornell Univ. Press, 1973) and his *Childhood, Marriage, and Reform: Henry Clarke Wright, 1787–1870* (Chicago: Univ. of Chicago Press, 1980). In addition, see Perry's "Visions of Anarchy in the Antislavery Movement," *American Quarterly* 20 (Winter 1968): 768–82; Richard O. Curry, "Romantic Radicalism in Antebellum America," *Reviews in American History* 1 (December 1973): 524–31; and Curry and Lawrence B. Goodheart, " 'Knives in Their Heads': Passionate Self-Analysis and the Search for Identity in American Abolitionism," *Canadian Review of American Studies* 14 (December 1983): 401–14.

On the issue of the use of violence versus nonviolence, which has implications for understanding the individualistic nature of abolitionist thought, see Curry and Goodheart, "Ambivalence, Ambiguity, and Contradiction: Garrisonian Abolitionists and Nonviolence," *Journal of Libertarian Studies* 6 (Summer–Fall 1982): 217–26. On the Civil War, see especially James H. Moorhead, *American Apocalypse: Yankee Protestants and the Civil War, 1860–1869* (New Haven: Yale Univ. Press, 1978); Sheldon Richman, "The Anti-War Abolitionists: The Peace Movement's Split Over the Civil War," *Journal of Libertarian Studies* 5 (Fall 1981): 327–40;

and Peter Walker, *Moral Choices: Memory, Desire, and Imagination in Nineteenth Century Abolitionism* (Baton Rouge: Louisiana State Univ. Press, 1978).

For the Reconstruction era, see especially Curry, "The Abolitionists and Reconstruction: A Critical Appraisal," *Journal of Southern History* 34 (November 1968): 527–45. This essay provides a critical analysis of works by historians such as George Fredrickson, John G. Sproat, John L. Thomas, Willie Lee Rose, and James M. McPherson. This essay needs to be supplemented by reading more recent works such as Robert H. Abzug, *Passionate Liberator: Theodore Dwight Weld and the Dilemma of Reform* (New York: Oxford Univ. Press, 1980); Paul S. Boyer, *Urban Masses and Moral Order, 1820–1920* (Cambridge: Harvard Univ. Press, 1978); James B. Stewart, *Wendell Phillips; Liberty's Hero* (Baton Rouge: Louisiana State Univ. Press, 1986); and Herbert G. Gutman, "Protestantism and the American Labor Movement: The Christian Spirit in the Golden Age," in his *Culture and Society in Industrializing America* (New York: Vintage Books, 1977), 79–113.

Important works that deal not only with abolitionism but with the post-Reconstruction careers of some abolitionists include Goodheart, *Abolitionist, Actuary, Atheist: Elizur Wright and the Reform Impulse* (Kent, Ohio: Kent State Univ. Press, 1990); and James M. McPherson, *The Abolitionist Legacy: From Reconstruction to the NAACP* (Princeton: Princeton Univ. Press, 1975). Other significant recent books dealing with various aspects of abolitionist history include Perry and Michael Fellman, eds., *Antislavery Reconsidered: New Perspectives on the Abolitionists* (Baton Rouge: Louisiana State Univ. Press, 1979); Lawrence J. Friedman, *Gregarious Saints: Self and Community in Abolitionism, 1830–1870* (New York: Cambridge Univ. Press, 1982); and Ronald G. Walters, *The Antislavery Appeal: American Abolitionism After 1830* (Baltimore: Johns Hopkins Univ. Press, 1976). Finally, the reader's attention is directed to Louis S. Gerteis, *Morality and Utility in American Antislavery Reform* (Chapel Hill: Univ. of North Carolina Press, 1987). Gerteis's study, which places overriding importance upon the concept of utilitarianism, is sui generis in the extant literature on abolitionism.

From Assertiveness to Individualism
Loren Schweninger

There is no study of nineteenth-century black individualism, but several works provide a good beginning for those interested in the subject. Gerald W. Mullin's *Flight and Rebellion: Slave Resistance in Eighteenth-Century Virginia* (New York: Oxford Univ. Press, 1972) still offers the best introduction to the period. The autobiographies of Frederick Douglass (updated and rewritten three times) are indispensable, as is Waldo E. Martin, Jr.'s intellectual biography *The Mind of Frederick Douglass* (Chapel Hill: Univ. of North Carolina Press, 1984). Several authors have focused at least tangentially on slave and free black individualism, including Philip D. Morgan, "The Ownership Property by Slaves in the Mid-Nineteenth-Century Low Country," *Journal of Southern History* 49 (August 1983): 399–420; John Hope Franklin, "Slaves Virtually Free in Ante-Bellum North Carolina," *Journal of Negro History* 28 (July 1943): 284–310; Loren Schweninger, "John Carruthers Stanly and the Anomaly of Black Slaveholding," *North Carolina Historical Review* 67 (April 1990): 159–192. For the transition period during the Civil War, Leon F. Litwack's Pulitzer Prize–winning *Been in the Storm So Long: The Aftermath of Slavery* (New York: Vintage Books, 1979) has a good deal of information on the subject. For the late nineteenth century, readers should consult Louis R. Harlan, *Booker T. Washington: The Wizard of Tuskegee, 1901–1915* (New York: Oxford Univ. Press, 1983), and August Meier, *Negro Thought in America, 1880–1915: Racial Ideologies in the Age of Booker T. Washington* (Ann Arbor: Univ. of Michigan Press, 1963).

The Ambiguity of Individualism
Lawrence B. Goodheart

The best general study of religious infidelism during the nineteenth century in the United States is James Turner, *Without God, Without Creed: The Origins of Unbelief in America* (Baltimore: Johns Hopkins Univ. Press, 1985). See Lawrence B. Goodheart, *Abolitionist, Acutary, Atheist: Elizur Wright and the Reform Impulse* (Kent, Ohio: Kent State Univ. Press, 1990) for a biography of a prominent religious dissenter who was influential in the National Liberal League. Two older works that still provide useful overviews are Sidney Warren, *American Freethought, 1860–1914* (New York: Columbia Univ. Press, 1943); and Stow Persons, *Free Religion: An American Faith* (New Haven: Yale Univ. Press, 1947).

Good studies of the vice societies are: Paul Boyer, *Purity in Print: The Vice-Society Movement and Book Censorship in America* (New York: Scribner's, 1968); Boyer, *Urban Masses and Moral Order in America, 1820–1920* (Cambridge: Harvard Univ. Press, 1978); and David J. Pivar, *Purity Crusade, Sexual Morality and Social Control, 1868–1900* (Westport, Conn.: Greenwood Press, 1973). In lieu of an existing modern biography of Anthony Comstock, see Robert Bremner, ed., *Traps for the Young* (Cambridge: Harvard Univ. Press. 1967), which contains an informative sketch of Comstock's activities. For an excellent case study, see Altina L. Waller, *Rev. Beecher and Mrs. Tilton: Sex and Class in Victorian America* (Amherst: Univ. of Massachusetts Press, 1982).

The issue of legal obscenity can be approached through: James C. N. Paul and Murray L. Schwartz, *Federal Censorship: Obscenity in the Mail* (Glencoe, N.Y.: Free Press, 1961); Harry M. Clor, *Obscenity and Public Morality in a Liberal Society* (Chicago: Univ. of Chicago Press, 1969); Nat Hentoff, *The First Freedom: The Tumultuous History of Free Speech in America* (New York: Delacorte, 1980); and David Copp and Susan Wendell, eds., *Pornography and Censorship* (New York: Prometheus, 1983).

Can a Woman Be an Individual?
Linda K. Kerber

For John Winthrop and his contemporaries, see Edmund S. Morgan, ed., *Puritan Political Ideals* (Indianapolis: Bobbs-Merrill, 1965); and Timothy H. Breen, *The Character of the Good Ruler* (New Haven: Yale Univ. Press, 1970).

On Elizabeth Cady Stanton, begin with Ellen Carol Dubois, ed., *Elizabeth Cady Stanton and Susan B. Anthony: Correspondence, Writings, Speeches* (New York: Schocken Books, 1981).

On literacy, see William J. Gilmore, *Reading Becomes a Necessity of Life: Material and Cultural Life in Rural New England 1780–1835* (Knoxville: Univ. of Tennessee Press, 1989); and Richard D. Brown, *Knowledge is Power: The Diffusion of Information in Early America 1700–1865* (New York: Oxford Univ. Press, 1989), especially chapter 7. On the role of books and reading in women's lives, see Cathy N. Davidson, *Revolution and the Word: The Rise of the Novel in America* (New York: Oxford Univ. Press, 1986); and Barbara Sicherman, "Sense and Sensibility: A Case Study of Women's Reading in Late-Victorian America," in *Reading in America: Literature and Social History* (Baltimore: Johns Hopkins Univ. Press, 1989).

On women's claims to intellectual authority, see Linda K. Kerber, *Women of the Republic: Intellect and Ideology in Revolutionary America* (Chapel Hill: Univ. of North Carolina Press, 1980); Mary Kelley, *Private Woman, Public Stage: Literary Domesticity in Nineteenth Century America* (New York: Oxford Univ. Press, 1984); Susan Phinney Conrad, *Perish the Thought: Intellectual Women in Romantic America 1830–1860* (New York: Oxford Univ. Press, 1976);

Barbara Miller Solomon, *In the Company of Educated Women: A History of Women and Higher Education in America* (New Haven: Yale Univ. Press, 1985).

Much has been written about individualism in American culture, but little deals distinctively with women; an exception is Elizabeth Fox-Genovese, *Feminism Without Illusions: A Critique of Individualism* (Chapel Hill: Univ. of North Carolina Press, 1990). See also Joyce Warren, *The American Narcissus: Individualism and Women in Nineteenth Century American Fiction* (New Brunswick, N.J.: Rutgers Univ. Press, 1984).

Individualism and National Identity
Yehoshua Arieli

Because of the broad and extensive coverage of this essay, the reader is referred to the endnotes, which are extremely comprehensive, especially in regard to primary sources. Some notable books, however, that deal with the issue of individualism in the broad sweep of United States history are: Thomas C. Cochran, *Challenges to American Values: Society, Business, Religion* (New York: Oxford Univ. Press, 1985); John P. Diggins, *The Lost Soul of American Politics: Virtue, Self-Interest, and the Foundations of Liberalism* (New York: Basic Books, 1984); Sam B. Girgus, *The American Self: Myth, Ideology and Popular Culture* (Albuquerque: Univ. of New Mexico Press, 1981); Myra Jehlen, *American Incarnation: The Individual, The Nation, and The Continent* (Cambridge: Harvard Univ. Press, 1986); C. B. MacPherson, *The Life and Times of Liberal Democracy* (New York: Oxford Univ. Press, 1977); Moses Rischin, *The American Gospel of Success: Individualism and Beyond* (Chicago: Quadrangle Books, 1965); and John W. Ward, *Red, White and Blue* (New York: Oxford Univ. Press, 1969).

A Confusion of Voices
Lawrence B. Goodheart and Richard O. Curry

Although a number of studies mention individualism in their discussion of twentieth-century American culture, relatively few deal with it systematically. A good place to begin is with John William Ward's "The Meaning of Lindbergh's Flight," *American Quarterly* 10 (1958): 3–16, which explores the tension between a nostalgia for individualistic virtues and the corporate reality of the urban, industrial age. Herbert Hoover's *American Individualism* (New York: Doubleday, Page, and Co., 1922) echoes Theodore Roosevelt's and Woodrow Wilson's concerns that the government must ensure equality of opportunity in the society so that individuals can compete fairly in the race of life. John Dewey, *Individualism Old and New* (New York: Minton, Balch, and Co., 1930), and Charles A. Beard, "The Myth of Rugged American Individualism," *Harper's Magazine*, (December 1931): 11–22, call for a fundamental reassessment of individualistic values at the onset of the Great Depression, including the need for government planning of the economy.

The perceived decline of individualistic values and the rise of the pressure of social conformity characterized most analysis during the 1950s. The pivotal study was David Riesman, Reuel Denny, and Nathan Glazer, *The Lonely Crowd: A Study of the Changing American Character* (New Haven: Yale Univ. Press, 1950). See also Riesman, *Individualism Reconsidered and Other Essays* (Glencoe, New York: Free Press, 1954). A useful set of essays, including Arthur A. Ekirch, Jr., "Individuality in American History," is in *Essays on Individuality*, ed. Felix Morley (Philadelphia: Univ. of Pennsylvania Press, 1958).

A virtual cottage industry on the malaise of individualistic values has appeared during the last two decades. Although his New Left agenda appears somewhat dated, Philip Slater, *The*

Pursuit of Loneliness: American Culture at the Breaking Point (Boston: Beacon Press, 1976) still makes some telling points about individualism in American culture. Christopher Lasch, *The Culture of Narcissism: American Life in an Age of Diminishing Expectations* (New York: W. W. Norton, 1978) gained national media attention with his diagnosis that individualism had degenerated into mere self-centeredness. Robert N. Bellah et al. in *Habits of the Heart: Individualism and Commitment in American Life* (Berkeley: Univ. of California Press, 1985) also made the best-seller list with their conclusion that individualism had collapsed into the cultivation of personal pursuits to the neglect of civic engagement. The best recent book, however, is Herbert J. Gans, *Middle American Individualism: The Future of Liberal Democracy* (Glencoe, New York: Free Press, 1988), which makes a thoughtful argument for the place of individualism in a social democracy.

Among the works that show the dark side of Ronald Reagan's rhetoric of individualism, see Garry Wills, *Reagan's America: Innocents at Home* (New York: Doubleday, 1987); and Richard O. Curry, ed., *Freedom at Risk: Secrecy, Censorship, and Repression in the 1980s* (Philadelphia: Temple Univ. Press, 1988).

Contributors

RICHARD O. CURRY received his Ph.D. in American History from the University of Pennsylvania. At present he is professor of history at the University of Connecticut. Curry is the author, coauthor, or editor of seven other books. These include *A House Divided* (1964), *The Abolitionists* (1965, 1973, 1985), *Radicalism, Racism and Party Realignment* (1969, 1973), *Conspiracy: The Fear of Subversion in American History* (1972), and *The Shaping of America* (1972). His most recent book, *Freedom at Risk: Secrecy, Censorship and Repression in the 1980s* (1988) received the 1989 H. L. Mencken Award from the Free Press Association and a 1989 Outstanding Book Award from the Gustavus Myers Center for the Study of Human Rights in the United States.

LAWRENCE B. GOODHEART received his Ph.D. from the University of Connecticut, where he now teaches at the Hartford campus. He is the author of *Abolitionist, Actuary, Atheist: Elizur Wright and the Reform Impulse* (1990) and coeditor of *Slavery in America* (1992). He and Richard O. Curry have collaborated on a number of essays, including "Encounters with Clio: The Evolution of Modern American Historical Writing," in the May 1984 *OAH Newsletter.* His most recent essay is "The Odyssey of Malcolm X," in the Fall 1990 issue of *The Historian.*

YEHOSHUA ARIELI is James G. Macdonald Professor of American History and Professor of Modern History at the Hebrew University, Jerusalem. He is the author of a number of books, including *Individualism and Nationalism in American Ideology* (1964), *The Conspiracy* (1965), *The Future-Directedness of the American Experience* (1966), *Political Thought in the United States* (1967–69), and, most recently, *History and Politics* (1990).

ROBERT M. CALHOON received his Ph.D. from Western Reserve University and is Professor of History at the University of North Carolina at Greensboro. He has published *The Loyalists in Revolutionary America, 1760–1781* (1973), *Revolutionary America: An Interpretative Overview* (1976), *Evangelicals and Conservatives in the Early South, 1740–1861* (1988), and *The Loyalist Perception and Other Essays* (1989).

JAMES A. HENRETTA received his Ph.D. from Harvard University and is Priscilla Alden Burke Professor of History at the University of Maryland. He is the author of various articles and books on early American history, including *"Salutary Neglect": Colonial Administration*

263

under the Duke of Newcastle (1972) and *Evolution and Revolution: American Society, 1600–1820* (1987) and coauthor of a survey test, *America's History.*

LINDA K. KERBER received her Ph.D. from Columbia University and is May Brodbeck Professor of History at the University of Iowa. She is author of *Federalists in Dissent: Imagery and Ideology in Jeffersonian America* (1970) and *Women of the Republic: Intellect and Ideology in Revolutionary America* (1980) and coeditor of *Women's America: Refocusing the Past* (1991).

LOREN SCHWENINGER is Professor of History at the University of North Carolina at Greensboro. He has written or edited *James T. Rapier and Reconstruction* (1978), *From Tennessee Slave to St. Louis Entrepreneur: The Autobiography of James Thomas* (1989), and *Black Property Owners in the South* (1990).

ROBERT E. SHALHOPE received his Ph.D. from the University of Missouri and is Professor of History at the University of Oklahoma. He has published *Sterling Price: Portrait of a Southerner* (1971), *John Taylor of Caroline: Pastoral Republican* (1980), and *The Roots of Democracy: American Culture and Thought, 1760–1800* (1990).

KARL E. VALOIS has served as Department Chairman of History at St. Joseph High School in Trumbull, Connecticut, since 1978. Over the last four years, he has also taught American and European history at the Torrington branch of the University of Connecticut. An author of five essays in the forthcoming *Encyclopedia of American Political Parties and Elections* and of over twenty popular history articles, Valois is a Ph.D. candidate in history at the University of Connecticut and is completing a dissertation on "To Revolutionize the World: The American Tract Society and the Regeneration of the Republic, 1825–1877."

Index

AMERICAN CHAMELEON

was composed in 10/12 Times Roman on a Xyvision system
with Linotron 202 output
by BookMasters, Inc.;
printed by sheet-fed offset on 50-pound, acid-free,
Glatfelter Natural stock,
Smyth sewn and bound over .088'' binders boards
in ICG Arrestox B cloth
and wrapped with dust jackets printed in two colors
on 100-pound enamel stock and film laminated,
also adhesive bound with paper covers printed in two colors
on 12-point coated-one-side stock and film laminated
by Thomson-Shore, Inc.;
designed by Diana Gordy;
and published by
THE KENT STATE UNIVERSITY PRESS
KENT, OHIO 44242